# Economics, Strategy and the Firm

# Economics, Strategy and the Firm

PAUL CASHIAN

palgrave
macmillan

First published 2007 by
PALGRAVE MACMILLAN

Palgrave Macmillan in the UK is an imprint of Macmillan Publishers Limited, registered in England, company number 785998, of Houndmills, Basingstoke, Hampshire RG21 6XS.

Palgrave Macmillan in the US is a division of St Martin's Press LLC, 175 Fifth Avenue, New York, NY 10010.

Palgrave Macmillan is the global academic imprint of the above companies and has companies and representatives throughout the world.

Palgrave® and Macmillan® are registered trademarks in the United States, the United Kingdom, Europe and other countries.

ISBN-13: 978–0–333–99297–5
ISBN-10: 0–333–99279–0

This book is printed on paper suitable for recycling and made from fully managed and sustained forest sources. Logging, pulping and manufacturing processes are expected to conform to the environmental regulations of the country of origin.

A catalogue record for this book is available from the British Library.


Printed and bound in Great Britain by
CPI Antony Rowe, Chippenham and Eastbourne

# Dedication

To the memory of my Dad, and his favourite place, Maine Road, Manchester 14.

# Contents

# Preface and Acknowledgements

This book has had a long gestation period and is largely based on material that has been developed and used to teach a module in the second year of the Economics programme at Coventry University. A short review of how this module has developed over the years perhaps helps place in context the material and approach to be found in the book. When I took over the module in 1991 it was entitled *Industrial Economics.* The content of the module I inherited, was heavily theoretical and focused mainly on the content of Chapter 2 (the neo-classical firm), parts of Chapter 3 (the managerial models of the firm) and Chapter 11 (the structure-conduct-performance model). To this core content, I initially added material on transaction costs and game theory i.e. much less well developed versions of Chapters 5 and 8. However, as my own career developed I began to drift away from my purely economists view of the world and became increasingly involved in the business disciplines, particularly business strategy. For anyone who comes from an economics background the first sight of the strategy subject area can be a bit bewildering with its array of sources, techniques, discreet theories and lack of any central unifying conceptual basis which neo-classical theory gives to economics (a theme developed in Chapter 1). However, what strategy seemed to provide for students was immediacy with the real world often lacking in economics – it used real-world companies as case studies and provided techniques and frameworks which were readily useable by student. What I also began to realise was that although there are important conceptual differences between economics and strategy there were also important linkages where the theoretical rigour of economics could be married with the more real-world focus of strategy. Over the years, the *Industrial Economics* module inherited in 1991 became the *Economics of Business* module of today and increasingly began to incorporate some of the ideas and concepts from the business strategy area, gradually changing the focus of the module from purely theoretical to, still a recognisably economics module, but with a much more applied real-world focus. However, what I have tried not to lose is a unifying conceptual basis to the model developed for analysing the firm and how it behaves in the real world.

My first debt of gratitude must be to the generations of economics students at Coventry who, unknowingly, have been the guinea pigs for much of the material presented in this book. I should also acknowledge many of my past and present colleagues from within the Business School at Coventry who, again often unknow-ingly, have helped to clarify and develop various parts of the framework presented in the book. Whether this book will be enough to convince some of them that economics is not an arcane pursuit, unconnected to the real world of business, remains to be seen. I would also like to acknowledge the help of my secretary, Kanta Mistry, in preparing the final manuscript. Finally however I must acknow-ledge, and apologise to, my long suffering wife Denise and children Sarah and Amy (who also helped provide some of the examples used in the book) for the lost weekends, evenings and time taken out of holidays during the writing of this book. Particular thanks go to Sarah for taking time out of her summer vacation from university to read through the final manuscript. That said however I take full responsibility for any remaining errors and omissions.

*March*
2007

# Introduction 1

## LEARNING OUTCOMES

On completion of this chapter the reader should be able to

- Explain the similarities and differences between the economists' and strategists' perspectives of the firm
- Assess how the differences in the development of the two subject areas have contributed to these similarities and, particularly, the differences
- Understand in broad terms the approach and structure of the rest of the book

## KEY NEW CONCEPTS

| | | |
|---|---|---|
| Profits | Management costs | Structural entry barriers |
| Value | Competitive costs | Strategic entry barriers |
| Value added | Competitive advantage | Resource entry barriers |
| Revenue | Transformation process | Utilitarianism |
| Costs | Rent | |

## KEY NEW MODELS

| | | |
|---|---|---|
| The neo-classical firm | SWOT | Structure–Conduct-Performance framework |
| Transaction cost economics | Resource-based model of the firm | Five forces framework |
| Game theory | Natural Monopolies | |

In the course of this book, we shall look at a wide range of firms in a wide range of contexts. We shall look at the layout of the Bear Factory shops, the contrasting structures of United Biscuits and Anthony Alan Foods, the development of Ryanair and Direct Line insurance, and so on. We shall look in detail at the supermarket and national daily newspaper industries and consider the competitive structure of the cinema industry and the horseracing industry, as well as look at how the fossil fuel, music and short-haul airline markets are changing. Many companies also feature in less detail – some well known, some not so well known – Marks and Spencer, Guident, David Lloyd Healthclubs, Telecity, British Gas, Mont Blanc and others. What all these firms have in common, whether they are a small producer of medical components (Guident) or a large multinational food manufacturer (United Biscuits), is that they undertake the basic economic function of transforming inputs into outputs.

On a broader social scale, it is difficult to over-estimate the central importance of firms. For individuals in the developed world, the 'firm' (or 'company', or 'business') dominates their everyday economic life. In addition to the specific firms referred to above, the word 'firm' is used to denote any institution that is engaged in productive economic activity. This covers manufacturing firms producing what are termed as 'goods' (for example, cars or pens), or firms providing services (for example, hairdressing or banking). It also covers both the private sector and the public sector (universities, for example). For the overwhelming majority of people, working for a firm generates their income upon which they depend for survival. Even those people who do not work (the retired or unemployed, for example) rely either upon income arising from the fact that they have worked in the past and have savings (for example, in the form of a pension) or upon other members of society working and generating income tax revenue to pay for state benefits. Outside of working for a firm, we spend a large part of our time engaged in consuming the output of firms. Travelling to work, eating and drinking, reading, watching TV, buying clothes, surfing the Internet, listening to music – all of these activities involve us in consuming the output of firms.

Therefore, given that firms play such a central role in our everyday lives, it is not surprising that they have been subjected to analysis and theorising by academics from a wide range of subject areas. You will find parts of economics, strategy, sociology, psychology, social and economic history, geography and other subject areas that deal with firms and their impact. This book is concerned with two of these areas – economics and strategy. The approach taken is essentially an economic analysis of the firm, but an analysis that is strengthened and complemented by the incorporation of models, ideas and concepts from the business strategy field. What the book is not is a technical explanation of the neo-classical firm.

Central to the book is the development of an analytical model of the firm that develops and expands upon the economists' traditional model of the firm, referred to throughout the book as the 'neo-classical firm', a summary of which is presented in Chapter 2. The book assumes a basic knowledge of microeconomic theory of a level typically found in level-1 business and economics undergraduate courses. No prior knowledge of business strategy is assumed. Minimal use is made of mathematics, but where maths is used a diagrammatic alternative is also presented. The central core of the book is, by necessity, theoretical, but throughout the book an attempt is made to use the theory to help explain, and analyse, what we see happening in the business world around us.

## 1.1 Economists, strategists and theory of the firm

The idea of 'the firm' is central to both microeconomics and business strategy (although the strategists may call it a 'company' or 'Single Business Unit' or some other name). There are indeed many similarities between the economists' and the strategists' view of the firm, particularly between the two traditional schools of thought found in the two subject areas (the economists' 'neo-classical' school and the strategists' 'classical' school as described below). Both approaches rely heavily on the rational and analytical approach to the development of theory and application of theory. Thus the neo-classical economists' approach to the firm focuses on developing a mathematical model of the firm that is used to explain how firms operate in changing markets and react to changes in markets.

The classical strategists' tradition has a similar analytical flavour to its development. Initially, strategy focused on the development of elaborate planning models that were aimed at enabling firms to organise and plan their internal structures to best effect to gain the most from the market. Later, the analysis turned to the external environment and the need for firms to analyse this environment and take rational decisions on how they should position themselves within their particular business environment. Both traditions make assumptions that the environment, and actors within the environment, act in a consistently rational manner. Decisions are rationally taken in a fairly static environment, and these decisions are the correct decisions. This idea of global rationality in an environment of full and certain information is discussed in more depth in Chapter 2.

Both traditions also start from a common viewpoint of what exactly a firm is – a firm is a transformer of inputs into outputs. Figure 1.1 summarises this shared view on the role of the firm.

The firm (as embodied in the firm's management) employs a work-force, buys raw materials from product markets and buys components from its suppliers. The firm (again its managers) then combines these inputs together to produce goods and services that (hopefully) its customers want to buy. Put another way, the firm is a transformer of inputs into outputs. Take, for example, the Bear Factory. This firm owns shops all over the UK into which are put staff of various kinds, plus

**Figure 1.1** The firm as a transformer of inputs into outputs

stock (half complete teddy bears, as we shall see), shop fittings and accessories of various sorts. The firm also has a website and will undertake a range of marketing activities; it will need to make use of a range of supporting functions such as banking and insurance as well. All of these inputs are organised by the Bear Factory's management and the end result is teddy bears bought by the firm's customers. Both economics and strategy traditions see as the ultimate raison d'etre behind the creation of firms, such as the Bear Factory, as being the creation of profits. Conceptually, however, economists and strategists think of 'profit' in different ways.

### 1.1.1 The economist and profits

To an economist, profit is simply a residual payment made to the entrepreneur. The residual comes about when the costs incurred in the creation of goods and services is less than the revenue gained through the sale of those goods and services in the marketplace (Figure 1.2).

How the firm tries to maximise profits is by minimising the payments made for inputs whilst maximising the amount received for outputs from their customers. The Bear Factory shops will try and sell as many teddy bears as possible, at as high a price as possible, whilst keeping the costs of the transformation process as low as possible. By minimising costs and maximising revenue, the firm aims to maximise profits.

### 1.1.2 The strategists and value added

The strategists tend to think in terms not of profit, but of value added – how much additional monetary value does a firm through its particular production process add. If the total value of the goods and services going out of the factory gates is greater than the cost of creating those goods and services then the firm is adding value. The aim of the firm though is to maximise the value added (Figure 1.3).

The whole production chain of transforming inputs into outputs adds value – the value at one end of the production chain is £X and the value at the other end is £X + Y. The objective of the firm is to ensure that it claims as much of the added value £Y for itself as possible. The way the firm does this is by minimising value loss to its suppliers, typically through negotiating as low a price for these supplies as possible and, conversely, maximising value gain by charging as high a price as possible for its outputs. In this way, it accrues as much of the added value

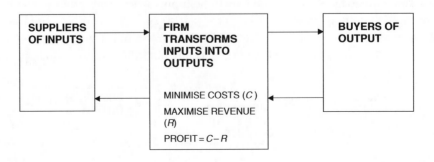

**Figure 1.2** The economists' perspective: maximise profits

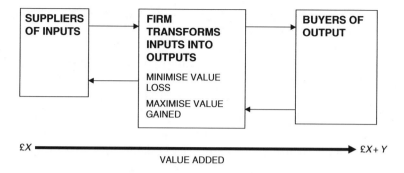

**Figure 1.3** The strategists' perspective: maximising value added

£Y created by the production chain to itself. However, there is a third element to maximising added value, which is absent from the economists' perspective, namely the firm must be organised and managed effectively to take as much valued added as possible.

The other key aspect to the strategists' view is the idea of competitive advantage. Competitive advantage is the source of a firm's added value – it is something the firm has which its rivals do not. This 'something' could be any one of a number of things, a unique product, a unique location, a distinctive brand – anything which is allowing the firm to outperform their rivals. Identifying the source of a firm's 'competitive advantage' is one of the key themes in this book – but will be presented more from the economists' perspective of trying to explain how firms create and sustain abnormal profits.

Let us use the Bear Factory shops again as an example. They are involved in a production chain the end result of which is the production of teddy bears worth, for the sake of argument, £50m (= £X + Y in Figure 1.3). If we assume the total initial cost is £20m (= X) then the objective of the Bear Factory is to take as much of the £30m (= Y) value added for themselves. Thus they will try to minimise both the amount of the £30m lost to their suppliers and to their customers – they negotiate the lowest possible prices for their inputs and charge as high a price as possible for their outputs.

Although given different names, the economists' 'profit' and the strategists' 'value added' are essentially very similar concepts. Both amount to the creation of a monetary residual that, in both traditions, belongs to the owner(s) of the firm and both assume that the firm is trying to maximise the size of this residual. However, the similarities between the two subject areas can be over-emphasised, as important differences exist in terms of both perspective and the development of theory and concepts.

### 1.1.3 The development of the economics perspective on the firm

Economics is the much older of the two subject areas. Modern microeconomic thought is usually traced back to Adam Smith and his book *The Wealth of Nations* published in 1776 (Smith, 1911). However, the beginnings of recognisable economic analysis of the rational analytical type briefly discussed above really begins with David Ricardo (1911), Jeremy Bentham and J.S. Mill (1911) all writing in the early to mid-nineteenth century.

Neo-classical economics has developed from these roots over the last two centuries and consists of an established core of concepts and theories that form the backbone of any level-1 university microeconomics course. However, despite the considerable development in both the range and content of microeconomics since Ricardo it still rests heavily on the positivist and utilitarian principles of Ricardo, Mill and, particularly, Bentham. The positivist approach to theory deals with theories explaining 'what is', whereas the alternative normative approach deals with questions of what 'ought to be'. Thus, theory of the firm says that if the price of labour increases then the costs of the firm also increase, which leads to a reduction in supply and hence an increase in the market price of the good being produced. Over the last 150 years, economists have developed mathematical models to show how and why this happens and the subsequent effects it has on the consumers who buy the product being produced. This is a positivists' approach – (a) leads to (b) which leads to (c); this is the logical sequence of events as predicted by the mathematical model.

The alternative approach would be a normative approach. This is a more questioning approach dealing not with the logical sequencing of events, but with whether this is the sequence that ought to happen. Should the firm increase its price after an increase in labour costs, or should it absorb the cost by lowering profit margins? As if to emphasise the positivist roots of modern microeconomics the leading UK level-1 text throughout the 1960s, 1970s and 1980s was Richard Lipseys' *An Introduction to Positive Economics* (Lipsey, 1989).

### 1.1.4 Utilitarianism

Utilitarianism describes a particular philosophical approach that emphasises the importance of the outcome of actions rather than the process by which a particular action is arrived at – 'the end justifies the means'. This is clearly reflected in the neo-classical theory of the firm. All the emphasis is on the end result of the firm's action – does the firm maximise profits? The firm is reduced to a mathematical model, which reacts to changes in its environment by constantly adjusting its level of output so as to always achieve its single objective of maximising profits. The end outcome is all that matters. The internal process of how the firm adjusts to change as it strives to achieve its single objective is incidental. The utilitarian roots also show in the economists' view of the profit outcome.

The purpose of neo-classical economics is to study the allocation of society's scarce resources to their best possible use. This relates back directly to the utilitarian principle of trying to achieve the greatest happiness for the greatest number as the underlying principle on which society should be based. In terms of the theory of the firm, this leads to the identification of long-run profits as being undesirable as they represent a misallocation of resources. As a result, society suffers a 'deadweight' efficiency loss (explored in more detail in Chapter 4) as the 'happiness' of some members of society is increased, but at the expense of a reduction in the overall 'happiness' level of society. This utilitarian view of profits is reflected in the term used by economists, who refer to long-run profits as being 'abnormal'.

### 1.1.5 The development of the strategists' perspective on the firm

In many ways, the differences in the strategists' perspective on the firm relate to the differing backgrounds of the principal writers and developers of the subject areas. The early economists tended to be social and political philosophers followed later in the nineteenth century and throughout the twentieth century by a series of academics, initially mathematicians then academically trained economists. Business strategy is a much newer subject area, most writers would date it back to the work of writers such as Ansoff (1965), Andrews (Learned, Christensen, Andrews and Guth, 1965) and Sloan (1963) in the late 1950s and early 1960s. One of the key, and unique, features in the development of the subject has been the diversity of backgrounds of its key writers. A number of well-known strategists do have backgrounds in economics (Porter and Kay, for example), and some also come from other established social science disciplines such as a sociology and psychology (for example, Mintzberg). However, of perhaps more significance, when compared to the development of economics, is the influence of practitioners and consultants. One of the earliest, and most famous, writers on strategy was Sloan (1963).

Sloan was not an academic; he was a practical businessman who had spent most of his working life with the General Motors motor company. Similarly, the multinational companies Shell and General Electric will also be found in most standard business strategy textbooks not as case studies but as contributors to theory (Shell with their approach to scenario planning and GE with their approach to portfolio management). Similarly, the management consultants Boston Consulting Group and McKinseys will also be in most strategy text as well, BCG, with their widely used growth-share portfolio grid, and McKinseys, with their 7s framework.

This diversity of contributors provides strategy with an array of perspectives on the firm, many of them developed through experiences of actually running or working with firms. This is a crucial difference when looking at the development of the strategy subject area in comparison with economics. Economic theory was developed by academics in universities. However, people working in, or advising, firms who needed practical solutions to specific problems have heavily influenced strategic theory. The need for practical relevance and the direct applicability of theories has meant that strategists have been more interested in the actual process of profit creation rather than the economists' concern with the consequences.

The early writing (Ansoff, Chandler, Sloan) focussed very much on how firms should organise and plan themselves to achieve efficiency and maximise value created. Since the 1970s, the emphasis has shifted in mainstream strategy to the importance of the creation of competitive advantage, being able to outperform your rivals, either through the relating of the environment to the choice of strategy (Porter, 1980, 1985) or through the recognition of internal strengths or competencies that can be exploited (Hamal and Prahalad, 1994; Barney, 1997). This central strand of strategy is best summed up by the idea of SWOT analysis, first developed back at the birth of strategy as an academic subject by Andrews at Harvard in the early 1960s. 'SW' represents 'strengths and weaknesses' and refers to the analysis of the internal workings of a firm to identify those things that a firm is good at and those at which it is not so good. 'OT' refers to the analysis of the external environment and the identification of opportunities for the firm and threats to the firm. In the classic definition of strategy, firms should be trying to match their internal strengths to the external opportunities, whilst being aware of their own internal weaknesses and external threats (Chapter 12 deals with SWOT and other frameworks of strategic analysis in a lot more depth).

Barney typifies the development of strategy as

an attempt to "fill in the blanks" created by the SWOT framework; i.e. to move beyond suggesting that strengths, weaknesses, opportunities, and threats are important for understanding competitive advantage to suggest models and frameworks that can be used to analyze and evaluate these phenomena. (Barney, 1995)

This line of development of strategic theory is sometimes referred to as the 'classical' school of strategy. However, this is not the only approach to strategy that has evolved since the 1960s. Other well-developed approaches to strategy have looked at the importance of organisation design and its relationship to strategy (Mintzberg, 1979; Chandler, 1977) or have adopted a more systems-orientated approach to strategy (Stacey, 2003).

However, the diversity of strategic theory is also its great weakness as an academic discipline. Unlike in economics, there is no coherent core of theory that underpins business strategy as a discipline. In many ways, the weakness of business strategy as an academic discipline is the exact opposite to that of economics, where, certainly at lower levels, economics is dominated by one prescriptive school of thought, the neo-classical school. Anybody coming to the subject area of business strategy from another discipline, be it economics or sociology or psychology, is immediately struck by the great diversity of approaches represented by the main texts for the area. For example, three of the most commonly used undergraduate texts in UK universities are Stacey (2003), Johnson, Scholes and Whittington (2005) (or Lynch, 2002) and Kay (1995), all of which take quite different approaches to the subject. Mintzberg, Ahlstrand and Lampel (1998) in their book *Strategy Safari* actually identify ten distinct schools of thought; all developed since the early 1960s. Whittington (2002) whittles this down to four.

However, the common feature that unites all these schools of strategy is that, in contrast to the positivist utilitarian economists' view of the firm, all are concerned with process – either the process of decision-making or the means by which profits are made and maintained. The other major difference of perspectives between economists and strategists is in relation to profit itself. As outlined above, the academic public-policy-orientated economist regards profits as representing a misallocation of resources. To the practitioner-firm-orientated strategists, however, the high levels of profit are an indication of a successful and efficient firm.

Thus, it can be seen that although microeconomics and business strategy both have the firm as their central focus, the lens through which the firm is seen and analysed creates some major differences in both the nature and the outcome of that analysis. As stated initially, this book is essentially an economics book, but will view the theory of the firm as a tool that is more directly relevant to the explanation of what we see happening in the real world around us. Why do some firms not only create profits, but also manage to maintain those profits over periods of time? How can we explain common features of competitive behaviour such as 'buy one get one free', 'money-back guarantees' and all the other manifestations of the massive amounts of money firms spend on marketing? Given the neo-classical emphasis on the efficiency of markets in allocating resources how can we explain the existence of firms in the first place? To analyse some of these issues we use concepts and theories taken from business strategy to supplement, enhance and expand upon the economists' neo-classical model of the firm. In essence, microeconomic theory provides the stable base for analysing the firm that is missing from business strategy, whereas business strategy can help in relating this to the real-world experience of watching firms compete and operate in markets.

## 1.2 The framework of the book

Figure 1.4 shows the model of the firm that is developed in the course of the book. The model forms the basis for the analysis of the behaviour of firms as observed in the real world.

The book is divided into four parts:

1. The firm
2. Managing the transformation process
3. Firms and market behaviour
4. The firm and its environmental context

The rest of this section provides an overview of the book and explains how the model in Figure 1.4 is to be developed and used.

### 1.2.1 The firm

As discussed in the previous section, both economics and mainstream strategy regard the firm as essentially performing a transformation function, the firm takes in inputs (the economists' factors of production: land, labour and capital) and turns them into outputs (goods and services). The motivation for the owners of the firm is to generate profits, or, in strategy terms, create added value (Figures 1.2 and 1.3). The central core of Figure 1.4 shows this transformation process undertaken by firms. Part I of the book reviews the economists' neo-classical model of the firm,

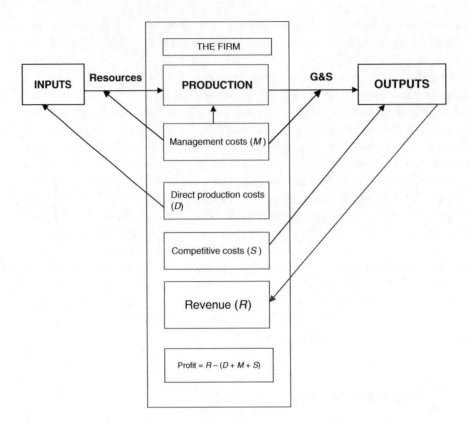

**Figure 1.4** The model of the firm

and suggests some of the ways in which this basic model will be expanded as we progress through the book.

Chapter 2 begins by presenting a concise summary of the model of the neo-classical firm, familiar to anybody who has done a basic course in microeconomics, which also forms the basis for the view of the firm developed through this book. However, towards the end of the chapter a new dimension is added to the usual representation of the model by making explicit some of the underlying assumptions on which the neo-classical model rests. Five assumptions are discussed, which are then contrasted with our real-world experiences:

1. Profit maximisation – firms always aim to maximise profits.
2. Holistic behaviour – firms automatically react to change in a manner defined by their production function and the need to maximise profits.
3. Full and certain information – firms operate in an environment where there is no hidden information, and all the information available is correct.
4. Global rationality – the firm is able to take in, and process, all the available information and will always make the correct decision.
5. Homogeneity – all units of a particular type of input are identical, as is each unit of output produced.

The following chapter considers some of the alternative models of the firm that have been developed to try and take into account the implications of one, or more, of the above assumptions being relaxed. A number of themes emerge during the chapter which are picked up later in the book. Are firms in the same industry always the same? Why do some firms succeed and others fail in the same industry? What are the consequences of the owners of a firm not actually managing the firm? How effectively do firms cope with a complex and uncertain world?

Chapter 4 continues with the review of the neo-classical firm and, in many ways, is the central chapter of the whole book. The key theme of the chapter is the generation and sustaining of profits. There are essentially two elements to the profit equation, costs and revenue. Firms should aim to minimise their costs, as these represent an outflow of money, and at the same time maximise their revenue, which represents an inflow of money. These two elements are examined separately. Revenue maximisation relates to the firm's ability to sell its output to customers. Microeconomic theory tells us that the firm's ability to sell output is constrained by a whole list of factors, referred to as the factors affecting demand. However, only some of these factors are available to a firm to use as tools in pursuit of the maximisation of revenue, principally price or output, marketing (and by inference possibly tastes and fashions) and research and development.

However, this provides us with a problem when looking at the costs of the firm. A marketing campaign costs money, as does research and development, and as does a whole host of actions taken by firms while competing in their output markets (loss leaders, loyalty cards, two for the price of one offers). These are costs that arise through the need for firms to compete with other firms in their output markets for revenue. In Figure 1.4, these types of costs are termed 'competitive costs' and are denoted by $S$ to reflect that they are, in effect, the costs of firms behaving strategically in their output markets.

Chapter 4 also notes another type of cost which, again, is not related directly to the production of output. All firms employ staff they term as 'managers' – these are the people who organise the transformation process but do not actually take part in it directly. Therefore, we have a third type of cost to consider, management cost, shown as $M$ in Figure 1.4. However, the splitting of costs into three distinct types does not change the basic requirement that firms need to minimise costs if they are to maximise profit.

The generation of profits by ensuring that revenue exceeds cost is only part of the story, however. Firms try to not only generate profits but also sustain these profits into the long run. Neo-classical theory provides two ways by which firms can achieve sustained long-run profits. First, by there being some restrictions on the market that prevent the entry of new firms, which allows the incumbent firm to sustain profits in the long run (usually referred to as monopoly rent). Secondly, in input markets where there is scarcity, an incumbent firm may have access to lower cost resources than a new firm entering the industry (usually referred to as Ricardian rent). Both of these cases relate to the existence of entry barriers – factors existing in the market which allow incumbent firms to prevent the entry of new firms into the market. The key to firms being able to sustain profits is, in fact, the ability of firms to create entry barriers.

Figure 1.4 suggests three means by which a firm could generate and sustain profits:

1. By achieving a lower level of direct production costs (*D*) than other firms.
2. By generating a higher level of revenue from its output markets than other firms (*R*).
3. By performing the transformation of inputs into outputs more efficiently than other firms (*M*).

The first of these includes the neo-classical idea of Ricardian rent. By achieving a lower level of direct production cost this creates what is referred to as a structural entry barrier into the industry. These types of entry barriers arise from firms pursuing production cost efficiency, and they are sometimes referred to as being 'innocent' in the sense that the firm is not deliberately trying to restrict entry to the market. This is in contrast to the means by which firms can try and sustain profits by extracting higher levels of revenue from their output markets. There are two elements. First, as before, entry barriers can be erected to prevent the entry of new firms. However, these types of entry barriers are strategic; they are deliberately put in place to restrict access to the market by potential new firms. Secondly, a firm can try to increase its market share through directly competing with other firms in the market. In terms of Figure 1.4, this source of sustained profits relates to the efficiency of the competitive cost *S*, the extra revenue gained from each pound spent on *S*. The final source of sustained profits is through the firm performing the transformation process more effectively than its rivals. This partly relates back to the efficiency with which a firm minimises its management cost *M*, and partly to how effectively it organises its internal and external relationships. However, as we shall see in Chapters 6 and 7 the internal structure and culture of the firm also have a role to play.

## 1.2.2 Managing the transformation process

The second part of the book looks in more detail at the cost referred to as 'management cost'. Chapter 5 deals with a fundamental paradox that lies at the heart of neo-classical economics. Why do we have firms? Microeconomic theory emphasises the importance of markets as being the most efficient means of allocating resources, and yet firms also appear to allocate resources and in effect replace markets. How can we explain this?

In response, the chapter presents the transaction cost approach to economics associated with Coase and Williamson, in an attempt to answer the question as to why firms exist. In relation to Figure 1.4, the transaction cost approach focuses on the nature of the relationship a firm has with the suppliers of its inputs and the consumers who purchase its outputs. Neo-classical theory assumes that these relationships are market relationships; firms obtain their inputs through a series of input markets and sell their outputs through another set of output markets. The transactions in these markets take place at a price that either relates to the productivity of the input, or the cost of producing the output.

The transaction cost approach examines these relationships but in a situation where neo-classical assumptions 2–5 above do not hold – the firm does not have full information, is not globally rational, has heterogeneous inputs and (possibly) outputs and can make incorrect decisions. In this situation, market transactions become less transparent, more risky and need to be managed by firms through the negotiating, implementing and monitoring of legal contracts. The argument put forward by Williamson and Coase is that when the cost to a firm of managing these market relationships becomes too great, then the firm will take the market inside the firm and allocate the resources itself. Firms exist as an alternative, more efficient means of allocating resources when the costs of using a market become too high.

The transaction cost approach to the explanation of the existence of firms also provides an explanation for another feature of real-world firms, namely the existence within the input 'labour' of people referred to as 'management'. This is the subject of Chapter 6. Managers do not contribute directly to the transformation of inputs into outputs. They have two roles: one is to manage the external relations of the firm in relation to the obtaining of inputs and the selling of output; the second is to allocate resources within the firm. In other words, 'management' actually take on the role of the market process when the market has been internalised. As already noted, this role of managing the firm's internal and external relationships adds another type of cost which the firm needs to try to minimise, shown in Figure 1.4 as management cost or $M$. It also means that if profits are to be made, then the revenue taken from output markets needs to be greater than not just the direct production cost of the output, but also the management cost of organising the firm both internally and externally (Profit $= R - (D + M)$).

Chapter 7 moves on to look at the resource-based view of the firm, a perspective that has been developed in recent years within the business strategy literature. From this perspective, the firm is viewed as a bundle of resources that are used within the firm to develop all the internal processes and routines required to undertake the transformation process. One possible source of profits for a firm is to have some unique resources, one part of their resource base that is not available for other firms. What is even better is for these unique resources to be difficult to copy by other firms or, as they are referred to, being non-imitable. If this is the case, then a firm has the potential to not only create profits, but to also sustain them. However, what is underlying all of this is the ability of the firm's management to acquire and organise their unique and, possibly, non-imitable resources. Thus the $M$ in Figure 1.4 refers not only to the ability of the firm to minimise its transaction costs, but also to its ability to acquire resources, organise those resources most effectively, and to ensure the effective distribution of output to its markets.

### 1.2.3 Firms and market behaviour

The third part of the book moves on to look more closely at how firms behave in their output markets. Chapter 8 introduces and develops the game theory approach to the analysis of firms' behaviour. Game theory provides a different emphasis in the analysis of markets. Central to the game theory approach is the idea of the proactive firm – firms that are interacting with their environments and trying to change and manipulate them for their own benefit. The key is to recognise the interdependence between firms – the decisions and resulting actions taken by one firm influence, and are influenced by, the actions of other firms. This interdependence of decision-making provides a much more realistic framework for explaining the actions of firms as observed in the real world, where markets tend to invariably be oligopolies. The game theory approach also throws up the possibility that firms may not always be competing with each other, sometimes they also cooperate – in fact some writers suggest that the cooperative urge amongst firms is actually greater than the competitive urge.

Having established the game theory framework, Chapters 9 and 10 move on to look at aspects of strategic behaviour by firms within their output markets – picking up the theme that firms sometimes compete and sometimes cooperate. Chapter 9 looks at the sources of the competitive cost element in Figure 1.4 and discusses a whole range of means by which firms try and maximise their revenue – product differentiation, reputation, pricing strategies and so on. Chapter 10 looks at the other side of the coin and examines some of the cooperative methods used by firms to try and coordinate their behaviour.

### 1.2.4 The firm within its broader environment

The final part of the book broadens the analysis out to look at the issues relating to the firm within its environmental context. Chapters 11 and 12 deal with the issue of environmental analysis, in particular the concept of efficiency – Chapter 11 from the economists' perspective and Chapter 12 from the strategists' perspective. The idea of 'efficiency' and 'value added' are looked at and contrasted, in particular the views they lead to about the desirability of abnormal profit. To the economist, abnormal profits are an indication that there may be inefficiencies in a market – to the strategist they are an indication that the firm has a competitive advantage and is successful in maximising its added value.

The chapters illustrate the differences and similarities between the two subject areas. This is highlighted by two of the common frameworks used to assess the environment – the Structure–Conduct–Performance (SCP) framework from economics, and the five forces framework from business strategy. Both methods share a common root and have at their heart the same transformation process discussed in Section 1.2. However, the manner in which the models have developed, and are used, illustrates the different perspectives taken by the two subject areas. The SCP framework has a strong public policy orientation trying to identify the structural characteristics of an industry that will lead to the most (economically) efficient outcome. Whereas, the five forces framework is meant to be used to assess the strengths of five types of influences (forces) on an industry that will impinge on a firm's ability to earn profits from the industry. As discussed in Section 1.2 this is the main area of divergence between the two subject areas.

The final chapters look at competition policy and bring together many of the different strands that have been developed in the rest of the book. Chapter 13 places the development of policy within the context of the analytical framework developed throughout the book. Competition policy has as its overriding aim the desire to improve the economic efficiency of markets. In pursuing this aim two strands within public policy can be identified. First, competition policy has tried to deal with the problems that are posed by monopolies, which includes the particular problems caused by natural monopolies (a natural monopoly occurs in an industry where the cost structure is such that the most efficient market structure is in fact a monopoly). Secondly, policy has been concerned with controlling aspects of strategic behaviour by firms that are limiting the competitiveness of the market. The final chapter considers a range of cases and shows how much of the material presented in the book can be used in practice.

## 1.3 | Review and further reading

As stated at the outset of this chapter, the aim of the book is to develop a model of the firm that has a strong economic base, but incorporates elements of strategy, which leads to an extended representation of the firm. Figure 1.4 encapsulates the model of the firm to be developed and provides an underlying unifying framework to the rest of the book.

There are many excellent books dealing with the development of economic thought; however, a good recent starting point is Backhouse (2002), Chapters 6 and 7 which cover some of the issues raised in this chapter. There are no corresponding books providing a comprehensive survey of the development of strategy as a subject area. However, a good (and very readable) introduction to the diversity of strategy as a subject area is provided by Mintzberg, Ahlstrand and Lampel (1998).

# The Firm

# The Economists' Firm

## LEARNING OUTCOMES

On completion of this chapter, the reader should be able to

- Outline the neo-classical model of the firm.
- Use the model to predict the effect of changes in market conditions.
- List and explain the underlying assumptions of the neo-classical model.

## KEY NEW CONCEPTS

| | | |
|---|---|---|
| The holistic firm | Profit maximisation | Entrepreneur |
| Full and certain information | Tangible and intangible goods | Physical and monetary flows |
| Bounded/global rationality | Uncertainty and complexity | Opportunity cost |
| Homogeneity/heterogeneity | Factors of production | Asymmetric and imperfect information |

## KEY NEW MODELS

Demand, supply and price determination

## MODELS AND CONCEPTS DEVELOPED FURTHER

| | | |
|---|---|---|
| The neo-classical firm | Direct production costs | Profit |
| Revenue | The transformation process | |

As discussed in Chapter 1, firms can be regarded as the transformers of inputs into outputs. During the chapter, the economists' neo-classical model of the firm was also introduced. The present chapter takes a closer look at this model and how it is incorporated into the economists' view of how markets work. The chapter then moves on to consider how the model of the firm can be used as a predictor of the reaction of firms to changes in market conditions. Finally, we shall look behind the neo-classical model to consider some of the underlying assumptions that are made about the model.

Let us begin by considering three issues that have come to the fore during the last couple of years:

1. The depletion of fossil fuels
2. Online music sales
3. Pollution caused by aeroplanes

*The depletion of fossil fuels.* The industrialised economies have for many years relied on cheap fossil fuels, initially coal, but more recently oil (and its by-product, petrol) and gas. These fuels have been used to power these economies' industries and transport systems, at the same time keeping their consumers warm. However, for a number of years, fuel industry analysts having been warning that the era of relatively cheap fossil fuel is drawing to a close. Some studies suggest that during the last couple of years, we have passed the crossover point where the known oil reserves left in the ground are now less than what has been extracted and used. As oil reserves start to run down, so does its complementary fuel of natural gas. An additional factor affecting the world's fuel reserves has been the massive growth in the fuel consumption of China and, increasingly, India, as these two economies undergo rapid industrialisation.

*Online music sales.* Until recently, if you wished to purchase pre-recorded music you had to go to a music shop (either physically or virtually) and buy the CD you required. More recently, however, an alternative means of buying music has developed that uses the Internet, whereby purchasers of music download their choices directly onto either blank CDs or portable MP3 music players. The added advantage of this method of purchasing music is that you can choose to purchase only those specific tracks you wish to buy, rather than having to buy an entire album. The increasing popularity of purchasing music in this way was illustrated by reports in February 2006 that downloads of new singles exceeded more traditional purchase methods for the first time. Further evidence emerged a few months later in April when a single by the singer Gnarles Barkley, which was available only as a download, topped the UK music charts.

*Pollution caused by air travel.* In 2005, the number of airline passengers reached two billion, with the industry contributing 8 per cent of the world's GDP. In the last ten years, the number of passengers travelling by air has been increasing at a rate of 6–7 per cent per annum. This growth is not expected to decline, with a further 20 per cent increase on current levels expected by 2010. However, for many people the downside of this growth is that aeroplane emissions contribute just over 2 per cent of the world's greenhouse gases, which, as the numbers flying continue to rise, is set to increase significantly over the next 20 years. In the UK, the industry operates in a largely tax-free market – there are no taxes on tickets, fuel emissions or even on kerosene, the fuel used for aircraft.

*The neo-classical model of the firm.* One of the key questions to be considered in relation to the above three cases is what has been the effect of the changes that are taking place on firms in the three industries? Over the last 130 years, economists have developed a sophisticated model of the firm that tries to explain, and predict, how the firms in the three industries will behave in response to the changes. This model is often referred to as the neo-classical model of the firm. The model rests on the assumption that firms are at the centre of, and their actions are governed by, two sets of markets. One set of markets relates to where the firm acquires its inputs – land, labour and capital – that allow it to produce goods and services. The second set of markets relates to where the firm sells the goods and services that have been produced – the firm's output markets. Take, for example, the traditional high-street shops selling music CDs. Their input markets would relate to things such as their sources of CDs, the hiring of staff, the acquisition of premises and the fitting-out of those premises. The music shops' output market relates to the customer coming into the shop and buying the CDs.

In the neo-classical model, the firm has little or no control over either its input or output markets, or if it does then there are assumed to be imperfections in the market system that need to be rectified. Traditionally, introductory microeconomics courses reflect this representation of the firm. To explain the input markets' effect on the firm, students are taught cost theory, on the output side they are taught consumer theory. The two are brought together in the familiar demand and supply diagrams that determine the price at which an exchange takes place. One final key aspect of the model is the assumption that the overriding motivational force behind the firm is the desire to maximise profits, and the way in which it does this is by minimising costs and maximising revenue.

The first part of this chapter summarises, and reviews, the implicit nature of the 'firm' as described in neo-classical microeconomic theory. The following section will then return to the three cases above and consider what this model of the firm predicts will be the effect on the markets of the changes discussed. These predictions are then considered in the light of what is actually happening in these industries. The chapter concludes by examining the underlying assumptions of the neo-classical model – the 'taken for granted' assumptions and their implications for the validity of the model as an explanation for the real-world behaviour of firms.

## 2.1 | The neo-classical firm

### 2.1.1 The production process

In neo-classical theory, the firm can be seen as a means of transforming inputs into outputs through a production process. The inputs into the production process are the three factors of production, namely raw material resources ('land'), human resources ('labour') and manufactured resources ('capital'). The actual production process is the means by which these inputs are combined and transformed into outputs, either goods (tangible output) or services (intangible output). The entrepreneur organises and oversees this transformation. The entrepreneur is motivated by the potential for profit being generated from the production process. They will acquire the inputs needed at a cost, but sell the output in exchange for revenue. The entrepreneur will seek to acquire the inputs at as low a cost as possible whilst selling the output at as high a price as possible. Any residual from the transformation process is profit, which belongs to the entrepreneur as their reward for organising the transformation process. The organisation created by the entrepreneur in order to undertake the transformation of inputs into outputs is what economists refer to as 'the firm'.

This basic transformation process can be looked at from two inter-related perspectives. There is a physical flow of resources being transformed, through the production process, into either goods or services. However, corresponding to this physical flow is a monetary flow, as money flows into the firm as revenue from the sale of output, and flows out of the firm in the form of costs incurred in the acquisition of inputs.

### 2.1.1.1 The physical flow

Figure 2.1 represents the transformation process as a physical flow. Let us take a fairly simple example of a production process by way of illustration. Consider the production process of cleaning windows. The inputs into this production process would constitute water ('land'), a ladder, chamois leather, bucket and window scraper (all 'capital') plus the window cleaner ('labour'). The production process involves the window cleaner organising himself, in combination with the water, bucket, scraper and leather, to produce the output of clean windows. The underlying basic transformation process involved in the production of clean windows is exactly the same for a large multinational company such as Ford Motors producing motor cars. The range of inputs are obviously much greater and more varied than for the window cleaner, but can still be classified as land (for example, oil, rubber), labour (for example, production workers, administration staff) or capital (for example, steel, glass, factories). These are organised and combined, not by one

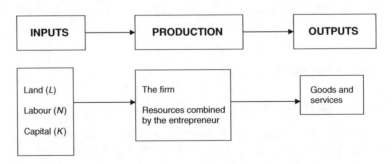

**Figure 2.1** The production process (physical flow)

person, but by a group of people referred to as 'management', to produce motor vehicles that constitute the output. Not all production processes, of course, require all three types of inputs. Banking, for instance, has no input we could class as 'land', but still follows the basic transformation process of input → production → output.

### 2.1.1.2 The monetary flow

Corresponding to this physical flow, we can also identify a monetary flow moving in the opposite direction as illustrated in Figure 2.2. The firm acquires its inputs from a series of factor markets. In the factor markets, the firm demands the inputs it requires for its production process; the owners of these factors supply them to the market, and a free market equilibrium price is obtained. The combination of these factor prices with the quantities of each input purchased by the firm represents a firm's total cost. Similarly, once the inputs have been transformed into goods and services through the production process, these outputs are sold onto a series of output markets. This time the firm is supplying the output, with the demand coming from the firm's customers. Output markets fall into two broad categories: intermediate output markets where the firm is the supplier of the factor of production 'capital', which becomes the input to another production process (the companies supplying Ford with steel, for example); or final output markets where the firm supplies the finished product to the end user. The output market determines the price for the output which, when multiplied by the amount sold by the firm, becomes the firm's revenue.

Figure 2.2 summarises the monetary flow for the firm. As can be seen, the money flows in the opposite direction to the physical flow, costs represent money flowing out of the firm whilst revenue is money flowing into the firm. Profit represents the difference between the money coming in and going out, that is, revenue minus cost. It is this potential difference that is the main motivating force behind the entrepreneur organising the firm to undertake the transformation process of turning inputs into outputs. The entrepreneur, as the organiser and owner of the firm, is entitled to the residual left once the cost of inputs has been deducted from the revenue obtained from selling the

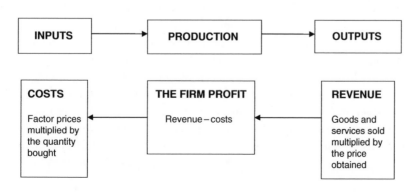

**Figure 2.2** The production process (monetary flow)

output. To maximise this residual, and therefore his potential income, the entrepreneur will seek to obtain his inputs as cheaply as possible whilst, at the same time, seeking to gain as much revenue as possible from his output. In other words, the firm will seek to maximise its profits by minimising costs and maximising revenue.

### 2.1.1.3  An illustrative example

To illustrate this, let us return to our window cleaner. He will probably acquire the capital inputs (buckets, leathers, window scraper, ladders) from a local DIY or hardware store which, in this case, represents his 'capital' market. The purchase of these capital items would represent the window cleaner's capital costs. As a one-man business, the labour costs would be what the window cleaner could be earning in his next best job, in other words his opportunity cost (the concept of opportunity cost is explained in more detail in Section 4.2.1). Unusually, his land costs would probably incur no cost to himself, water being obtained from the customer. These capital and land costs would therefore represent the window cleaner's direct costs of production, but not necessarily the total costs of the business. It may well be that in acquiring the business the window cleaner purchased an existing cleaning round. This would incur another type of capital cost for the firm, namely start-up cost, which may be in the form of a bank loan that needs to be paid back in fixed monthly instalments. This distinction between the ongoing costs of running a business and the initial start-up cost is important and will be returned to later in the book (Chapter 4).

The revenue the window cleaner receives depends upon two factors:

1. The number of house/shop windows cleaned (quantity or $q$)
2. The price charged to his customers ($p$)

The number of windows cleaned multiplied by the price charged gives the window cleaner his total revenue (TR = $pq$). The price charged will depend upon various factors such as the number of other window cleaners in the area, and the prices they charge, which may well have an important influence on the price our window cleaner negotiates with his customers. The motivation for the window cleaner is that the revenue he earns from his window round is greater than the cost of acquiring his equipment, how much he could be earning in his next best job and the monthly payment on his bank loan. If the revenue is greater, then the window cleaner is making a profit and he will carry on organising the production process. Again, Ford Motors goes through the same basic exchange process, acquiring inputs from all its relevant factor markets (labour markets, steel markets, etc.) and raising revenue from selling its motor vehicles. However, the price formation in these markets may be less market-driven – Ford, perhaps, has a greater say, given its size in both the input and output markets, than our window cleaner has in acquiring his inputs and negotiating a price for his output.

In essence, neo-classical theory represents the firm as a production process that transforms inputs into outputs organised for this purpose by a profit-seeking entrepreneur.

## 2.1.2  The mathematical model

The model presented in the previous section can be said to be a generic model of the firm, as it provides a general framework for helping to explain what a firm in neo-classical theory actually does. However, neo-classical theory has developed a more specific mathematical model, which allows not only a general overview of what a firm is about, but provides a powerful tool for predicting precisely how a firm behaves. Figure 2.3 is a translation of Figure 2.2 into a mathematical form.

The firm is represented by a production, or transformation, function. This is shown in the diagram in its general form as $Q = q(L, N, K)$ which merely states that output ($Q$) is produced by the combination of inputs – $L$ being 'land' or raw material resources, $N$ being 'labour' or human resources and $K$ being 'capital' or manufactured resources. For a particular production process, a more specific form of the production function could be shown which defines the ratio of inputs used in order to produce the specific output. For example, the production function for window cleaning would show a higher ratio of labour to capital than that for the more capital-intensive production process of motor car production. The cost of inputs is simply the sum of the price of each input ($P_L$, $P_N$, $P_K$) multiplied by the quantity in which they are purchased by the firm ($L$, $N$, $K$) – as shown in Figure 2.3.

In a more general functional form, the costs of a firm depend upon the price of each input ($C$) and the quantity of each input purchased, which in turn depends directly upon the amount of output produced ($Q$); the quantity of input required in the production process is determined by how much output is sold. The revenue flowing into a firm is simply the amount sold ($Q$) multiplied by the price per unit ($P$). The level of profit obtained by the firm ($\Pi$) remains, as before, the amount left once the costs incurred are taken away from the revenue obtained ($\Pi = R - C$).

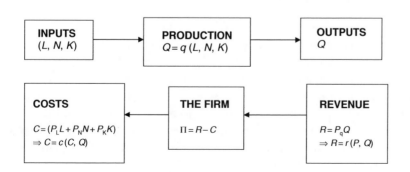

**Figure 2.3**  The production process (mathematical representation)

The assumption is that the firm's aim is to make the gap between costs and revenue as great as possible, in other words its objective is to maximise profits. In mathematical terms, the firm's objective function is to maximise the profit function:

$$\text{Max } \Pi = R - C \tag{2.1}$$

$$\text{Max } \Pi = r(P, Q) - c(C, Q) \tag{2.2}$$

However, this is a constrained optimisation, there are limits imposed on the firm in its pursuit of profit. First, there is a constraint on the input side. The manner in which the inputs are combined to produce the desired output is largely determined by the current state of technology. In some cases, the state of technology may remain fairly stable over a long period of time. For example, the technology involved in cleaning windows will have hardly changed since widow cleaning began. However, the technology involved in the building of motor cars, and also how firms organise themselves to carry out the production process, has changed radically in the last 100 years. The current state of technology is what defines the specific form that the production function will take. Technology influences the production function in two ways. First, by altering the ratio of capital to labour, usually in favour of capital; and secondly, by increasing the output gained for a constant level of input ('increasing returns to scale'). Thus, car producers at the beginning of the twenty-first century are a lot more capital intensive and more productive than their early twentieth century counterparts.

The second constraint relates to the output side. The amount of revenue that a firm can obtain from the output market depends upon the state of the market, in particular the demand curve of the consumers. The demand curve determines how much can be sold at each price, and hence the revenue that can be obtained. The firm must decide either how much to charge for its output or how much output to produce.

Equation 2.2 would seem to suggest that in order to achieve its objective of maximising profits the firm has four sets of decisions to make:

1. the price it will pay for inputs;
2. the amount of each input to purchase;
3. the price to charge for output;
4. the amount of output to produce.

However, in its purest form, neo-classical theory assumes that the input and output markets are perfectly competitive, therefore the firm has no decision to make with regard to either $C$ or $P$ as they are determined by their various markets. Also, given that the amount of inputs required relates directly to the amount of output sold, the firm only has one decision to make, which is how much output to produce. Equation 2.3 shows the firm's objective function, which is to maximise profits given the constraints discussed above. The firm needs to maximise the difference between revenue and costs – but can only do this by varying its output level ($Q$) as the price is fixed by the market.

$$\text{Max } \Pi = r(P, Q) - c(C, Q) \text{ w.r.t } Q \qquad (2.3)$$

From this, we thus arrive at the familiar profit maximisation condition that marginal revenue, the revenue from the last unit produced, should equal marginal cost, the cost incurred in producing the last unit.

$$\text{MAX} P = r(P, Q) - c(C, Q) \text{ w.r.t } Q \Rightarrow \qquad (2.4)$$

$$\Rightarrow \delta R/\delta Q - \delta C/\delta Q = 0$$

$$\Rightarrow \delta R/\delta Q = \delta C/\delta Q$$

$$\text{MR} = \text{MC}$$

In effect, all firms pick a level of output $Q$ that maximises Equation 2.4. This profit maximising condition can also be represented graphically as shown in Figure 2.4.

The explanation for the shape of the various curves forms the central part of any introductory microeconomics course on production theory, and readers are referred to any of the numerous texts for an explanation (for example, Sloman and Sutcliffe, 2003). The profit maximising output of $q*$ is shown as where the

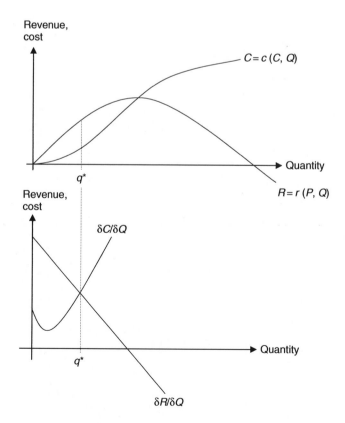

**Figure 2.4** The production process (graphical representation)

gap between the revenue function ($R$) and the cost function ($C$) is at its largest, or where MC equals MR ($\delta C/\delta q = \delta R/\delta q$).

## 2.2 | Using the neo-classical model of the firm

The purpose of creating models is twofold. First, they allow us to make sense of the real world that we experience in our everyday lives, and secondly they allow us to make predictions about what might happen in the future. The purpose of this section is to use the neo-classical model of the firm, developed above, to see whether we can predict what might happen to firms affected by the changes in the three industries discussed at the outset of this chapter.

### 2.2.1 Effects of the depletion of fossil fuels on a manufacturing firm

Figure 2.5 shows the initial effect on the market for fossil fuels of the depletion of supplies. $Q_0$ represents the current quantity of fossil fuel determined by the current supply curve (Supply 0). However, in the future the reduction in supplies will shift the supply curve to the left, resulting in a rise in price from the current $P_0$ to a new higher price in the future of $P_1$.

Figure 2.6 shows the possible effect of the rise in fossil fuel prices on a manufacturing firm. One of the major inputs into a manufacturing firm's production process is going to be the power to operate the machinery. Any rise in the costs of energy due to the rise in fossil fuel prices is going to have a significant effect on the costs of the firm. In Figure 2.6(a), we can see that the increase in energy costs causes the average cost curve of the firm to increase from $AC_0$ to $AC_1$ – the costs of producing each unit of output has increased. Figure 2.6(b) shows the firm's output market – the market which the firm is supplying with goods. At the original energy cost, the market price was $P$. At this price, the firm supplied $q$ to the output market (Figure 2.6(a)). However, after the increase in energy prices and shift in the firm's

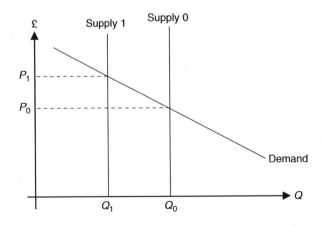

**Figure 2.5** The depletion of fossil fuel supplies

(a) Firm's costs

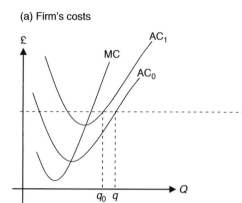

(b) Effect on firm's output market

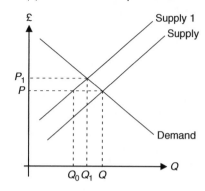

**Figure 2.6** Effects of rise in price of fossil fuels

average cost curve to $AC_1$, the firm would only supply $q_0$ at this market price. This decrease in supply would be replicated across the market, and the market supply curve in Figure 2.6(b) would shift to the left to supply 1, showing a reduction in supply at each and every price. The outcome is a rise in the market price to $P_1$.

Therefore, the neo-classical model of the firm predicts that the depletion of fossil fuels will lead to a rise in energy costs for manufacturing firms. The result of this will be an increase in the price of the output of manufacturing firms, and a resulting decrease in demand.

## 2.2.2 The effects of the growth of online music sales on CD shops

The evidence from the market suggests that the purchase of new music is moving away from buying CDs which have the music pre-recorded on them to consumers downloading the music directly from the Internet. For music shops, which rely on the sales of CDs for much of their revenue, this is bad news. Figure 2.7 shows the predicted effect of this switch on shops selling CDs.

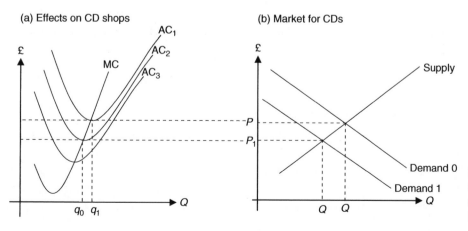

**Figure 2.7** Effect on CD shops of the switch to online music sales

Downloading music from the Internet represents a substitute good to the purchasing of music on CDs, therefore there will be a decrease in demand for CDs. This is shown as a leftward shift in the demand curve in Figure 2.7(b) from demand 0 to demand 1. Figure 2.7(a) shows the effect this may have on three shops selling CDs. The three shops each have different average cost curves – $AC_1$, $AC_2$ and $AC_3$ – reflecting differing levels of efficiency (the reasons why this may be are discussed at length in future chapters). At the original market price of $P$, all three shops were at least covering their costs of production. However, the fall in demand leads to a fall in price to $P_1$ and, as a result, this means that shop 1 (with the average cost curve $AC_1$) leaves the market. This is because at the new lower price, shop 1 can no longer cover its costs – in other words, it starts making losses. At this new lower price, shop 2 is now only just covering its costs ($AC_2$) whereas shop 3, although still making profits, has seen those profits fall substantially. Any further fall in demand, and hence price of CDs, will force shop 2 out of the market as well.

The model, therefore, predicts that the move away from CDs to a substitute good leads to a fall in price and a decline in the number of firms in the industry. So far, the model has proved correct as one national retailer of CDs, MVC, indeed left the market in early 2006.

### 2.2.3 The effects of an emissions tax to reduce airline pollution

As commented earlier, the tremendous growth in the number of people flying has led to increasing concerns about the effects this is having, and will have in the future, on the production of greenhouse gases and the subsequent effects on the environment. One way of trying to reduce this effect which is frequently advocated is to impose emissions taxes on the airlines. Figure 2.8 summarises the possible effects this may have on the market and the airline firms.

The effect of the tax on emissions is shown in Figure 2.8(a). The tax, in effect, reduces the amount of supply at each and every price as the airline firms try to pass onto the passengers the cost of the tax. The extent to which they can do this depends upon how elastic the demand curve is – the more inelastic the

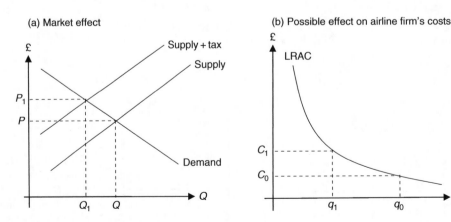

**Figure 2.8** The imposition of an emissions tax on airlines

demand curve the higher the proportion of the tax that is paid by the passengers. However, Figure 2.8(b) shows one possible secondary effect of the emissions tax. Figure 2.8(a) shows that the tax leads to a rise in price of fuel which, subsequently, leads to a reduction in demand. The airline industry is a fairly capital-intensive industry and has substantial economies of scale. If an airline firm is still only producing on the downward sloping part of their long-run average cost curve at $q$ (that is, they have not reached their minimum efficient size) then the decrease in demand to $q_1$ will increase costs from $C_0$ to $C_1$. The effects of this could be twofold. The supply to the market will decrease even further – as in the case of the rise in energy costs in Figure 2.6(a). Also the less efficient airlines may find they are not able to cover their costs and will be forced to leave the industry.

# 2.3 | A critique of the neo-classical model

The neo-classical model and its predictions about how markets and firms behave, as presented in the previous sections, rely on a set of fairly strong underlying assumptions. These assumptions relate not only to the nature of the firm, but also to the environment within which it is operating. Indeed, the assumptions do not just hold true for the theory of the firm, but also for neo-classical theory in general.

## 2.3.1 The neo-classical assumptions

The assumptions fall into five interrelated categories:

1. Maximising behaviour
2. The holistic nature of the firm
3. Full and certain information
4. Global rationality
5. Homogeneity.

### 2.3.1.1 Maximising behaviour

In each of the three examples used in the previous section, the implicit assumption was that the firms discussed were profit maximisers – their primary concern was the maximising of the gap between revenue and costs. For the vast majority of firms this assumption is probably true. Even outside of the private sector this is also still true – although the surplus they aim to generate is often not referred to as profits. Charities, for example, are often referred to as being in the 'not for profit' sector, as their principle concern is to raise money for the charity they represent. This, however, does not mean charities do not aim to minimise costs and maximise revenues – this is precisely what they do. What charities aim to maximise is the monies they can pass on to the worthy cause they are working for, but the way in which they do this is exactly the same as profit maximising firms, only the name of the resulting surplus is different.

Therefore, the assumption made by neo-classical theory that firms have only one objective, which is to maximise profits (or whatever the surplus is referred to as), is probably true. In the case of consumers, the purchasers of the firm's output, the sole constituent of that function is utility, which again they try to maximise. Therefore, in a neo-classical world, on one side of the market we have consumers with limited incomes, striving to achieve the highest level of satisfaction they can from the goods and services provided by firms. Whilst on the other side of the market we have firms run by risk-taking entrepreneurs, trying to maximise the profits from the production of goods and services.

The issue explored in more detail in this book is not the fact that firms are trying to maximise profits but, first, how do they know they are actually maximising profits and, a key theme throughout the book, if they are making profits how can they sustain them.

### 2.3.1.2 The holistic nature of the economic agents

In neo-classical theory, the firm is represented by a production function, and the consumer by a utility function. Both firms and consumers behave in a purely reactionary way to maintain their maximising positions as the variables in those functions change. As shown in Figure 2.3 the firm's production function relies upon the cost of inputs ($C$) and the quantity of output sold ($Q$). Any change in these variables results in the firm reacting automatically by simply adjusting the level of inputs used and/or the amount of output produced so as to maintain their profit maximising position.

The question has to be asked as to how closely this representation of the firm matches your own everyday experience of working in, and dealing with, firms? Are firms purely reacting to changes in their environment, or do they behave more proactively in seeking to change and affect their environments to their own benefits? Will the shops selling CDs simply sit back and wait for the market price to fall below their average costs, or will they actively seek ways to protect the business by, for example, becoming less reliant on CD sales, maybe selling DVDs or MP3 players. Similarly, will the airlines when faced with a possible emissions tax simply accept the tax and do nothing? Or will they try to reduce the effects of the tax by, perhaps, developing cleaner ways of operating?

This difference between the neo-classical firm as a reactive entity merely adjusting its position as the environment changes, as opposed to the real-world proactive firm anticipating and changing the environment to suit itself, is the central theme of Part III of this book.

### 2.3.1.3 Full and certain information

The assumption is made that the environment in the neo-classical world is known, both now and in the future. 'Full' information refers to the idea that no information is hidden from firms, or their suppliers of inputs or the purchasers of the firm's output. So, for example, all the prices on offer for a particular good or service are known to everybody involved in the market. In addition, all the firms in the market know the costs of all their rivals and of all their suppliers and consumers. On top of this, information is 'certain' in the sense that it is never incorrect.

In reality, of course, there are very few circumstances when we have full and certain information; the real world is simply too complex and unpredictable for this assumption to hold. In the example above concerning the depletion of fossil fuels, some experts deny that we have crossed over the peak of supplies and that there is still more in the ground than has been used. Also we do not know whether there may be significant new finds of fossil fuels in the future, as happened in the 1960s with the discovery of North Sea oil and gas, or whether a completely new and cheaper alternative source of energy will be discovered.

### 2.3.1.4 Global rationality

Rationality refers to the reasons behind a course of action that is taken. In relation to economic agents, this means the decisions are taken in relation to output levels (by firms) or goods and services purchased (by consumers). In other words, rationality is the base on which the decision-making processes of both firms and consumers lie.

Neo-classical theory assumes that the rationality of economic agents is global. What this means is that when a decision is made it is taken with all the possible information needed to make that decision, and the decisions taken are consistent with achieving the final objective of the economic agent. Thus, when consumers take decisions on which goods and services to buy they do so in the full knowledge of all the prices available (full and certain information) and they will always choose the combination of goods and services that maximises their utility function. Similarly, firms, when choosing a particular input, say widgets, for their production process, will know all the prices on offer and will always choose the lowest priced widget. Generally, firms will always aim to minimise their costs of production by using a least cost combination of inputs. Likewise, they will try to maximise revenue by supplying output at the correct quantity, given the price determined by the market. The objective that underlies these decisions is to maximise profits, thus firms will try to minimise costs and maximise revenue so as to maximise profits.

The assumption of global rationality is closely linked to the full and certain information assumption – the two taken together underpin the analytical basis of neo-classical theory. When the two are combined, the decisions taken by firms (and consumers) will always be correct, in the sense that they will always be the decisions that maximise their profits (or utility). Thus, when a particular firm fixes its output level so as to maximise profit, this decision is not only the correct decision but is taken on the basis that it has all the information on costs and prices and this information is also correct. Taken further, this assumes that all the firms in a particular market have access to exactly the same correct information and all share the same aim of maximising profits. The implication is that all the firms will, therefore, take the same decisions based on their identical production and revenue functions. Thus we arrive at the 'representative firm' approach encountered in all introductory microeconomic textbooks. By analysing one firm, and how they respond as the environment changes, you are in fact analysing how all the firms in a market will react.

As ever, however, the real world does not correspond with the transparent neo-classical world where firms take rationally consistent decisions based upon all the information required being available. The real world is complex where information is both uncertain and incomplete and decisions are not necessarily rational or consistent.

Informational problems in the real world arise from two sources:

- The nature of the environment
- The nature of people.

For firms in the real world the future is unknown. Ice cream firms, for example, when setting their production levels in April for the following quarter do not know with any certainty what the weather in the forthcoming summer is likely to be like. They can make guesstimates based on previous summers' levels of demand, but if the summer turns out to be unusually hot and sunny they may have problems meeting demand. Similarly, if the summer turns out to be cold and wet they may be left with excess stocks. If the firms were operating in a neo-classical world then they would know what the summer was to be like, and over- or under-stocking would not be an issue. Other less predictable variations in the environment can also add to problems for firms. For example, a number of producers of specialist food products and certain kitchen utensils have been caught completely unprepared for massive increases in demand due to recommenda-tions for their products by popular TV chefs. Other examples may be unforeseen delays in supply caused by, perhaps, a strike at a key supplier or, maybe, adverse weather conditions. In the real world, the future cannot be seen with complete certainty, firms do not have perfect foresight. Thus in the real world the future is uncertain.

The neo-classical model makes some fairly strong assumptions concerning the nature and motivations of people. In the neo-classical world people are open, honest and only interested in maximising their own utility and, if they are entrepreneurs, the profits of the firm that they own. The human input into a firm (labour) is one part of the production function and is treated no differently than the other inanimate inputs of capital and land. Neo-classical people therefore act in entirely rational and predictable ways, as determined by their utility, or their role as defined by the production function.

Unfortunately, in reality people are not like this, some (most) people are less than honest at least part of the time. Consumers may well be driven by the desire to maximise their utility function, but in a complex and uncertain environment, this may imply that people act dishonestly. People may well take advantage of mistakes made by firms, keeping a product for which they know they have been under-charged for example, or dodging fares on the London underground. In an environment where information may not be transparent, and some information may be hidden, then people may choose to manipulate and hide information to suit their own ends. When selling a house, for example, you may choose not to tell prospective buyers about the noisy neighbours, or the summer aroma from the nearby sewage farm. People can also act in an entirely irrational manner, whether through personal whim or deliberate action. For example, in 1999 when selling Virgin Radio, Richard Branson chose to sell to the lower of two bids, Chris Evan's Ginger Products rather than Capital Radio because 'the maverick in me prefers the idea of Chris Evans to Capital Radio' (*Management Today*, July, 1999, p. 52).

Therefore, the fact that the real world is one where the future is not entirely predictable and people may not always be honest or rational in their decisions leads to a world where information on which firms base decisions is both incomplete and uncertain. This uncertainty also impacts on the assumption of firms taking decisions with the benefit of global rationality. What is more likely is that decisions are taken by people within firms who have only, as described by Simon, 'bounded rationality' (Simon, 1955).

Generally speaking, bounded rationality refers to the fact that people take decisions on limited information. A world where both the environment and the behaviour of people within the environment are uncertain leads to a much more complex world. This complexity is added to, in many instances, by the amount of information that may be available. Thus, our ice cream producer not only has to contend with the uncertainties of the weather when determining production levels, but also the possible behaviour of competitors in the market, possible changes in the behaviour of consumers, and coping with a large number of retail outlets that sell his ice cream. He also will be faced with a mass of information relating to the factor markets from which he is acquiring his inputs. Is he actually getting the best deal available for his inputs? Are some of his suppliers hiding financial problems that may mean he might suddenly be left without a vital input? On top of this the firm has to be organised to turn inputs (including the unpredictable labour input) into outputs. Simon contends that one source of bounded rationality is the fact that humans have limited computational abilities; we are unable to take in and correctly interpret and act upon all the information that is available to us. Thus the ice cream producer may try to act in a rational way, as suggested by neo-classical theory, but may be unable to do so because of the uncertainty and complexity of the environment the firm faces.

This computational problem is the most common reason put forward for bounded rationality when discussed in economics/strategy textbooks. However, Simon also discussed another source of bounded rationality which, although beyond the scope of this book, is worth bearing in mind. Simon suggests that how humans communicate is also a barrier to achieving global rationality. Language is seen as an imprecise form of communication. The receiver can misinterpret even the simplest statements or requests. How we interpret language depends upon many factors such as our own frame of reference, or the context, or our perception of the person making the statement, or our interpretation of what the information provider actually means. For example, in the late 1990s the US space agency NASA lost a Mars space probe because one part of the project team had been working in imperial measurements, whilst another team had been working to metric measurements. There was obviously a fundamental breakdown in communication at an early stage of the production process! The use of language to communicate adds another dimension to the complexity and uncertainty faced by firms when taking and, more importantly, communicating decisions.

Thus we conclude that real-world firms face a very different world from that assumed by neo-classical theory. In the real world the information on which firms base their decisions is uncertain, imperfect and unevenly spread between economic agents. The world, and the people in it, is too complex for firms to know everything (imperfect information) and, by implication, each actor in the environment will have different pieces of information (asymmetric information) that they use to their own best advantage. The complexity also means that actors take decisions with only bounded rationality. This means that decisions can be wrong. Our ice cream producer, for example, can over-stock because he failed to foresee a poor summer, or can enter into a contract with a supplier who is not actually the lowest cost source. The other implication is that all the firms in a market are not going to be identical; they will have different pieces of information, which will be interpreted in different ways, and hence will reach different decisions. The representative firm approach no longer suffices as a means of analysing how firms behave.

Many of the themes discussed above will be explored in more depth in later chapters.

### 2.3.1.5 Homogeneity

In a neo-classical world, inputs and outputs in a particular transformation process are identical and perfectly divisible. Thus a firm when hiring a particular type of labour for its production process will be supplied with identical workers up to exactly the quantity required. In other words, firms can always purchase inputs of the same type in quantities which are exactly required to maintain minimum cost. Likewise, each unit of output produced is identical, both within the firm and across the market.

We have already relaxed this assumption in looking at some of the cases in the last section – we had three CD shops that were operating from different average cost functions in Figure 2.7(a). What typifies the real world is not homogeneity but heterogeneity – inputs, and to some extent outputs, differ. Again, later in the book (Part II) we shall look closely at some of the causes of differences between firms in the real world.

### 2.3.1.6 The representative firm

The five assumptions outlined above underpin the traditional neo-classical model of the firm presented in Section 2.1. Taken together, they lead to the common assumption that every firm in an industry must be identical. This arises from the fact that each firm is faced with input markets supplying homogenous resources at the same price. Likewise, each firm is also selling identical output at the same price, thus each firm engaged in a particular production process must face an identical production function. In addition, the assumptions of full information and global rationality mean that each firm is reacting correctly to changes in the environment in an identical manner which maintains them all in their (identical) profit maximising position. Therefore, the outcome is the approach commonly taken in microeconomics of concentrating analysis on one 'representative' firm (or consumer) as a proxy for the entire industry.

## 2.4 | Review and further reading

This chapter has presented a review of the neo-classical model of the firm – the model which forms the basis of the economists' view of a firm. We have also looked at how the model of the firm can be used to make predictions about how changes in a firm's environment will alter the equilibrium position of the firm. The chapter concluded with an overview and discussion of the underlying assumptions behind the economists' model of the firm. Table 2.1 summarises this discussion by comparing the neo-classical assumptions with what we tend to observe in the real world.

The rest of this book uses the basic model of the firm presented in this chapter – the firm as a transformer of inputs into outputs driven by the desire to minimise costs and maximise revenue – as the basis for our analysis of how firms behave in the real world. The neo-classical model is taken as the starting point on which to build. The rest of this part of the book expands and explores the neo-classical model further. Chapter 3 looks at a range of models that have been developed to deal with the differences highlighted in Table 2.1 between the neo-classical world

**Table 2.1** The neo-classical world versus the real world

| Neo-classical assumption | Real world |
| --- | --- |
| Firms maximise profits | Most private sector firms will *aim* to make profits. 'Not for profit' firms aim to maximise their 'surplus' |
| Firms act in a holistic way – the firm as a reactive entity | Firms react in different ways to changes in the environment – the firm as a proactive entity |
| Firms have full and certain information | Firms work with imperfect and asymmetric information |
| Global rationality | Bounded rationality |
| Homogeneity | Heterogeneity |

and the real world. Chapter 4 looks at the issue of profit maximisation in the context of firms trying to minimise costs and maximise revenue. Part II introduces a new cost element into the model, management cost, whereas Part III introduces a third cost, competitive costs, which extends the model even further by exploring how firms behave in their output markets.

The material covered in this chapter forms the core of any introductory microeconomics text on the theory of the firm such as Sloman and Sutcliffe (2003).

## 2.5 | Student exercises

### 2.5.1 Review exercises and points for discussion

1. Provide brief and clear definitions of the following key terms and concepts as used in this chapter.

 a. The physical flow of production
 b. The monetary flow of production
 c. Resources
 d. The entrepreneur
 e. Holistic behaviour
 f. Full information
 g. Certain information
 h. Global rationality
 i. Homogeneity
 j. The representative firm.

2. Identify and classify the factors of production used in the production of

 a. A haircut
 b. A washing machine.

3. Identify and classify the main costs of production incurred in the production of the above two products.
4. How do you think the producers of the two products in question 2 might determine their output prices?
5. A firm producing widgets is faced with the following cost and revenue functions:

$$\text{Total revenue} = pq = 20q$$

$$\text{Total cost} = 10 + 2q^2$$

 a. Calculate the profit maximising level of output.
 b. If the price/marginal revenue increased to 24 what would be the effect on the profit maximising level of output?

    **c.** If the variable cost increased to 4 what would be the effect on the profit maximising level of output?

    **d.** If the fixed cost increased to 15 what would be the effect on the profit maximising level of output?

## 2.5.2 Application exercise

One theme of this chapter has been how the neo-classical model of markets and the firm can be used as a framework for

- Presenting a simplified representation of real-world situations.
- Making predictions about how firms and markets may respond to environmental change.

**a.** Use the neo-classical framework to model the following real-world situations

- The effect on motor manufacturers of rising fuel prices
- The impact on bars of bans on smoking in public places
- The technological improvements that have led to the development MP3 players

**b.** Use your model to predict the likely short-term effects on firms involved in each of these three industries.

**c.** What might be the longer-term effects of the changes in these three industries?

**d.** In relation to the five neo-classical assumptions outlined in Section 2.2.1, how may your answers to questions b. and c. above alter if these assumptions did not hold?

# 3 Extensions of the Economists' Model of the Firm

## LEARNING OUTCOMES

On completion of this chapter the reader should be able to

■ Describe the key alternative approaches to the theory of the firm

■ Compare the neo-classical model with real-world firms.

## KEY NEW CONCEPTS

| | | |
|---|---|---|
| Satisficing behaviour | Managerial utility function | Organisational routines |
| Divorce of ownership and control | Core competencies | Contracting |

## KEY NEW MODELS

| | | |
|---|---|---|
| Sales maximisation model of the firm | The firm as a coalition | Principal–agent theory |
| Managerial discretion model of the firm | The evolutionary firm | |

## MODELS AND CONCEPTS DEVELOPED FURTHER

| | | |
|---|---|---|
| The neo-classical firm | Asymmetric information | Bounded rationality |
| The entrepreneur | Uncertainty and complexity | |

Brief summaries of four stories taken from the 19 July 2005 edition of the *Financial Times* are given below:

*Example 1 – Marks and Spencer.* 'M&S chief loses right-hand man' – this story relates to the resignation of Charles Wilson from the board of Marks and Spencer. Institutional shareholders were reported as being disappointed by the resignation as he had been a key figure in the firm's attempt to end a drop in sales, which had been declining for the previous seven quarters. It was also reported that Mr Wilson had been paid £1.41m in the previous year, but had not taken up the 576,367 share option open to him (worth another £2m).

*Example 2 – David Lloyd Health Clubs.* 'Pain amid the gain for private health club operators' – the main point about this story was that despite significant growth in the market for private health clubs (up 25 per cent since 2002), some clubs, such as the David Lloyd Health Clubs, were reporting drops in membership and facing possible financial difficulties.

*Example 3 – Guidant.* 'Pacemaker brings Guidant heartache' – Guidant are a maker of medical devices but, unfortunately, faulty seals had been discovered in 69 out of 78,000 pacemakers so far produced.

*Example 4 – Telecity.* 'Telecity taken private for £58m' – Telecity are an Internet hosting company who had been set up at the height of the dotcom boom in the late 1990s. They had been floated on the London Stock Exchange in 2000, when the market valued the firm at £1bn. Five years later they had never made a profit, nor paid a dividend, and have now been taken back into private ownership for £58m.

In Chapter 2, we looked at the standard neo-classical model of the firm as developed and used by economists. We also showed how the model can be used to try and predict what will happen if the conditions in which a firm operates change. The chapter concluded by sounding a note of caution by outlining the strong underlying assumptions that lie behind the neo-classical model of the firm. The four examples above, however, are different. These relate to specific real-world examples of the behaviour and issues faced by individual real-world firms. How does the theoretical neo-classical model of the firm outlined in Chapter 2 relate to the four real-life firms referred to in the *FT* stories above? Let us consider them each in turn.

The M&S story raises an immediate issue. The neo-classical model assumes that at the centre of the firm is a profit-motivated 'entrepreneur', who owns the firm and organises the production process. In the case of M&S, the roles of owner and organiser are split – the owners are the institutional shareholders, whilst Mr Wilson is one of several 'organisers', or managers, who actually run the firm. The question this raises is, if the firm is not managed by the owners, does this cause a potential conflict between the separate groups – those who own the firm and those who manage the firm? In particular, will the salaried managers (Mr Wilson was paid £1.41m in the previous year by the owners) still be motivated by the desire to maximise profits for the benefit of the owners? Would they not be more interested in maximising their own salary and other personal benefits? In other words, does this split not weaken the assumption of profit maximisation?

The second example raises the issue of why the David Lloyd Health Clubs have experienced a drop in demand, whereas the industry as a whole has experienced such a big growth in demand? From the perspective of the neo-classical model, all the firms in the health club market were faced with exactly the same demand and supply conditions, all have the same full and perfect information, so all of them should have reacted in the same way and maximised their profits. So why have some firms prospered and others not? The idea of a representative firm does not seem to hold in this industry.

The question raised by the third example is simply why did Guidant not know they were making faulty pacemakers? If the firm was working under neo-classical conditions then the management of the firm would be globally rational, and the mistakes that lead to faulty parts being manufactured would not have been made.

The final example raises a number of questions which are not easily accounted for by the neo-classical model as presented in Chapter 2. The obvious question is, given the underlying assumption that firms aim to maximise profits, how has this firm survived for so long without ever making a profit? A related question is why the firm was so over-valued in 2000, a reduction from a £1bn valuation to £58m in five years is an awfully big drop!

This chapter deals with some of the ways in which economists have expanded upon, and suggested alternatives to, the neo-classical model of the firm. The models below will be used to try and address some of the issues raised in the four examples discussed above.

## 3.1 | Managerial models of the firm

Central to the neo-classical firm is the idea of profit maximisation. The only motivation for the entrepreneur in organising production is to ensure that the revenue generated from the firm's output exceeds the costs of acquiring the firm's inputs. Even more than this, the entrepreneur will try to acquire inputs at minimum cost whilst selling output at maximum revenue, thus achieving the highest level of profit possible. The implication is that the entrepreneur is not only the owner of the firm, but is also the organiser of the production process. Berle and Means (1932), in the 1930s, challenged this image of the owner-manager. They pointed out that the owning of a firm and its management are actually two separate and distinct activities. Further, there is no reason why the organiser of the production process need necessarily be the same person who owns the firm and is, therefore, entitled to any profits that might be made. In the UK, joint-stock companies (Ltd) and public limited companies (PLC) are owned by shareholders who are entitled to a share of the profits made. However, often the shareholders employ managers to organise and control the firm on their behalf. This is clearly the situation in the case of Marks and Spencer as shown in Example 1. The owners of the firm are represented by the institutional shareholders, whereas Mr Wilson is one the managers employed to run the firm.

The recognition of the possible divorce of ownership of the firm from its control has some potential implications for the assumption that firms have one profit maximising objective. The motivation for the owners of a firm may well be to maximise the value of their shareholding, which is directly linked to the profits being made. However, what about the managers they employ to organise the production process on their behalf? What is Mr Wilson's motivation for trying to maximise profits for his institutional shareholders? During the 1960s, a series of models were developed which tried to explore the implications of this divorce of ownership of a firm from its control. The main aim of these 'managerial' models was to examine the possibilities that the divorce of ownership from control of the firm may lead to the pursuit of non-profit maximising objectives by the managers of a firm. Later, another strand of theory led to the application of principal–agent theory to the firm, which again examines the possible implication of the divorce of ownership from control, but placed in the context of an uncertain and complex environment (see Section 3.3). These managerial models are summarised below.

### 3.1.1 Baumol's sales revenue maximisation model

The first model to be examined is the sales revenue maximisation model developed by Baumol (1967). In this model, the assumption is that the organisers of the firm – the managers – aim to maximise sales revenue, not profit. Profits are still a consideration, but only to the extent that sufficient profits are generated to keep the owners happy. This is referred to as 'profit satisficing' behaviour rather than profit maximising behaviour.

Why do managers do this? Baumol suggests five possible reasons why managers may act in this way:

1. The salaries and earnings of managers are more closely linked to sales than to profits.
2. Finance is linked closer to future sales growth.
3. Employees gain more pay, and other non-pecuniary benefits, when sales grow. Sales growth also reduces internal conflicts, and hence helps with the management of the firm.
4. Sales growth gives more prestige to managers, whereas profits just go into the pockets of shareholders.
5. Managers are generally risk averse; they prefer steady sales growth and the security that the resulting market share gives. Profit maximisation may lead to more risks having to be taken, and hence a greater threat to their own job security.

In mathematical terms, the profit maximising objective function of the firm (Equation 2.4 in Section 2.1.2) is replaced by the following sales revenue maximisation function:

$$\text{MAX } R = r(P, Q) \text{ w.r.t. } Q \tag{3.1}$$

The solution being

$$\delta r/\delta Q = 0$$

OR $\qquad$ (3.2)

$$MR = 0: \text{given that } \Pi \geq \Pi_s$$

where $\Pi_s$ is the satisficing level of profit. In other words, the firm aims to produce where MR = 0, the point at which sales are maximised, not at the profit maximising level where MC = MR.

Figure 3.1 shows the graphical representation of the sales maximisation model. From the diagram it can be seen that the firm maximises sales at quantity $q_r$ and price $p_r$. This gives a level of profit $\Pi_r$, which is greater than the satisficing level $\Pi_s$. We can also see that the sales maximising firm's output level of $q_r$ is higher than the profit maximising firm, $q^*$. Also, the price of the profit satisficing firm is lower than the profit maximising firm, $p_r$ as opposed to $p^*$. Thus the sales maximising firm produces more and at a lower price. Baumol also suggested that in the long run, profits will always be at the profit-satisficing level $\Pi_s$. Any short-run profits

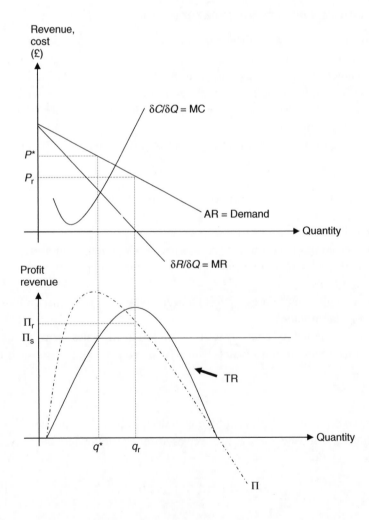

**Figure 3.1** The sales revenue maximising firm

in excess of $\Pi_s$ will be retained by managers to try and boost sales even further, by, for example, increasing the advertising budget.

## 3.1.2 Williamson model of managerial discretion

The Williamson model of managerial discretion (Williamson, 1963) begins with the same premise that the firm is a profit satisficer, and that the organisers of the firm – the managers – pursue alternative objectives once the minimum level of profits has been achieved. Williamson's assumption is that managers are interested in status, power and prestige, as well as, of course, their salary. From this, Williamson develops an indifference curve framework to define the equilibrium of the firm.

The assumption is that the managers have a utility function that they maximise against the minimum level of profits required by the shareholders. Williamson builds an indifference map for managers, which contains two elements. The first variable Williamson refers to as discretionary profit ($\Pi_d$). This is defined as

$$\Pi_d = \Pi - \Pi_0 - T \tag{3.3}$$

where $\Pi_0$ is the minimum profit requirement of the shareholders, and $T$ is tax.

As with the Baumol model, there is an assumption that the shareholders require a certain minimum level of satisficing profit if they are to keep their money in the company, and the managers to keep their jobs. The managers are interested in the 'excess' profit ($\Pi_d$) as it gives them funds to invest in their own pet projects. This 'discretionary investment' is over and above the requirement for the efficient running of the firm; however, Williamson relates this directly to a manager's status and power. A manager's ability to direct and manage funds enhances the utility a manager gains from his position.

The second element in the manager's utility function is staff expenditure ($S$). The manager is assumed to gain increasing levels of utility from increasing levels of expenditure on staff. Status and power are seen as being linked to the number of staff managed. The size of the manager's department within the firm leads to increasing levels of not only salary but also status and power.

From these two variables Williamson constructs an indifference map, with $\Pi_d$ and $S$ on the two axes. Each indifference curve indicates combinations of discretionary profits and staff expenditure to which managers are indifferent. In effect, each indifference curve is giving the manager a certain level of power and status. For example, combination ($\Pi_1$, $S_1$) in Figure 3.2, where a manager has a relatively high level of discretionary spending power but only a small department, gives the same level of power and status as ($\Pi_0$, $S_0$), where the discretionary spending is lower, but the manager heads a much larger department. As you move from indifference curve $P_1$ to $P_2$ the manager has increased power and status. For example, ($\Pi_1$, $S_{1'}$) shows the same degree of spending power, but the manager is heading a larger department.

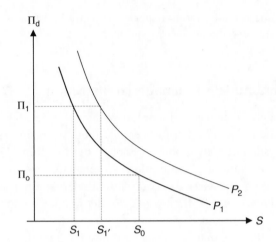

**Figure 3.2**
Managerial
indifference map

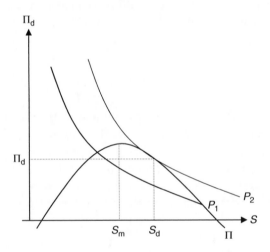

**Figure 3.3** The
equilibrium of the
firm

By superimposing a discretionary profit function on the utility map we reach the equilibrium point for the firm (Figure 3.3).

In the diagram, the points where the profit function crosses the $y$-axis represent the minimum level of profit required for the shareholders. Total profit increases to a maximum at the level of staff expenditure ($S_m$). Profits start to drop if staff expenditure is increased further beyond this point. The model suggests that managers will continue to increase staff expenditure until they reach $S_d$, where the profit function is tangential to $P_2$. This represents the limit to a manager's status and power, given the level of profit.

Thus, we can see that as with Baumol's sales maximisation model, Williamson's model also leads to non-profit maximising behaviour, but also highlights the inefficiencies this creates. Given the shape of the indifference map, managers will always increase staff expenditure beyond a level equating to profit maximisation. The model, therefore, suggests that firms will tend to be inefficient in terms of being over-staffed, and making unneeded investments.

### 3.1.3  The Marris growth model

The final managerial model to be considered was developed in the mid-1960s by the British economist Robin Marris (1964). It shares many of the features of the Baumol and Williamson models – the divorce of ownership and control, the potential for non-profit maximising behaviour – but also differs in a number of important respects. First, Marris explicitly models the shareholders' utility function rather than simply saying that there is a level of profit which will satisfice their expectation, which is a major weakness of both Baumol's and Williamson's models. Secondly, the model is concerned with the internal growth of a firm; there is a time dimension which, again, is so obviously lacking from the static models of Baumol and Williamson.

The assumption is that the firm's objective is to achieve a level of balanced growth through product diversification. Product diversification may be achieved through the creation of new products (differentiated growth) or substitutes for existing products (imitative growth). The equilibrium or 'balanced' rate of growth being that which satisfies both the managers and the shareholders and thus removes any conflict that may arise through the divorce of ownership and control.

The manager's utility function ($U_m$) has two elements, the growth of demand ($G_d$) and job security ($s$). Formally,

$$U_m = f(G_d, s) \tag{3.4}$$

This is similar to Williamson's model, suggesting that a manager's salary, status and power are directly, and positively, linked to the level of sales achieved by the firm. The second element in the utility function, job security, is threatened by either dismissal by the shareholders if their requirements are not met or take-over by another firm if the company becomes undervalued in the eyes of the capital market.

The additional element in the Marris model is the inclusion of a shareholders' utility function ($U_s$). Marris contends that shareholders' utility depends upon the growth in the asset base of the firm, which he refers to as the growth of supply-of-capital ($G_s$)

$$U_s = f(G_s) \tag{3.5}$$

The argument put forward is that the shareholders are interested not only in profits (as reflected in dividend payouts) but also capital gain (as reflected in the raising value of their shareholdings). Thus, to a shareholder their utility arises not only from the profit levels of the firm but also from the value of the firm's asset base and its subsequent valuation by the capital market.

The aim for the firm is, therefore, to achieve a rate of growth ($G$) which balances out both the growth in demand of sales and growth in supply of capital. Put another way, it equates the manager's desire for sales growth with the shareholders' desire for asset growth.

$$G = G_d = G_s \tag{3.6}$$

The model suggests that there are four possible constraints on the growth of firms:

1. A demand constraint – the diversification of a firm is achieved by using retained profits to develop new products and production processes. But this must be done in such a way so as to preserve a manager's job security, which means maintaining sufficient profits for the shareholders, and preserving the stock market valuation of the firm.
2. A managerial constraint – as a firm grows in size the ability of managers to efficiently control the firm deteriorates.
3. Financial constraint – over-quick expansion will be reflected in too high a level of retained profits and lead to a firm becoming undervalued and hence a potential take-over target.
4. Management objectives – to some extent the management's attitude to risk may affect the rate of growth of the firm; a more risk averse management will be inclined to have lower levels of retained profits, hence lower levels of diversification.

### 3.1.4  Managerial models and neo-classical theory

The three models discussed briefly above recognise the possibility of the divorce of ownership and control in a firm, and the ensuing problems this may cause when the owners' profit-maximising objective is not matched by their managers. Each leads to a model of profit satisficing rather than profit maximising (in the Marris model this is subsumed within the broader objective of achieving balanced growth). The managers of the firm aim to create a sufficient level of profit to keep their employers (that is, the shareholders) happy, whilst pursuing their own desire for income, status and power. The main weakness of the Baumol and Williamson models is the lack of a clear explanation of what determines this satisficing level of profit. In the Marris model, this is tied in with a broader consideration of the firm's relationship with the capital market and a recognition that this can act as a further constraint on a manager's actions.

However, all three models remain essentially neo-classical in nature – the other four neo-classical assumptions still remain largely intact. The firms are still represented as a series of mathematical equations, the objective function may vary in each case, but how they respond to any environmental changes can still be predicted by using a mathematical model. The environment is still one of full and certain information, managers know the level of profits the shareholders require, for example, or, in the Marris model, the capital market knows the true value of the firm. Managers and shareholders have global rationality, they always aim to maximise their various utility functions and are always able to achieve their aims. Finally, the resources and, in the Baumol and Williamson models at least, outputs of a firm are regarded as being homogenous and perfectly divisible. Also none of the models really throw much light on the Marks and Spencer example – the shareholders did not want Mr Wilson to leave, indeed they were happy that he was appearing to increase sales.

## 3.2 | Behavioural models of the firm

One of the main criticisms levelled at economics from other areas of social science such as sociology and psychology is its lack of a 'people element'. In neo-classical theory, the transformation of inputs into outputs is carried out according to a firm's production function (Figure 2.3). In addition, this production function also predicts how a firm will behave to any changes that may occur in the environment. For example, a natural disaster may reduce the supply of a particular raw material, which will be reflected in a higher price having to be paid in the factor input market. This increase in the price of one of their inputs will be reflected in the firm's production function and they will adjust their mix of inputs, and production level, accordingly to maintain their profit-maximising equilibrium. Similarly, an increase in demand for a firm's output due to rising consumer incomes is reflected in the production function, and the required adjustments are made to the input mix and production levels so as to, again, maintain the maximum profit level.

This is often referred to as the 'black box' approach to the firm – inputs go in one end, outputs come out of the other. What actually happens inside the firm is not worth looking at, as the firm's behaviour is predetermined by a mathematical model which constantly reacts to any external changes in such a way as to ensure that the objective of maximising profits is always met. Sociologists and psychologists argue that this is a gross misrepresentation of a firm – a firm is not a series of mathematical equations, but a complex structure of people, each with their own individual thoughts, abilities and objectives. Also, in any situation where you have groups of people interacting, you will see these groups developing patterns of group behaviour and their own internal cultures.

One response to this criticism has been for a series of economists to develop models of firms that focus on their internal workings. These models draw heavily on organisation theory, but use the concepts from this area in a context that is appropriate to economists. They are still interested in how firms turn inputs into outputs, and also what drives efficiency, but try to look at what lies underneath the production function in terms of how a firm actually operates. In other words, they try to lift the lid on the 'black box' and shed some light on what happens inside. These approaches are commonly referred to as behavioural models of the firm. In the following section, two of these models are discussed. First, the Cyert and March model, which dates from the early 1960s and, secondly, the work of Nelson and Winter from the 1980s which develops a view of the firm derived from evolutionary biology.

### 3.2.1  Cyert and March and the behavioural firm

Cyert and March (1963) were not really interested in examining the objectives of the firm and the implications these may have in terms of the most efficient way of achieving them. What Cyert and March were concerned with is how these objectives, and decisions, are actually arrived at in the first place.

Cyert and March suggest that the internal decision-making processes of a firm exhibit three general features,

1. Localised decision-making
2. Decisions based on 'rules of thumb'
3. Endogenously determined expectations.

### 3.2.1.1 Localised decision-making

Firms do not allocate resources so as to minimise costs across the board in accordance with some predetermined production function. What we actually see is a much more localised approach to resource allocation. Thus, within a firm the major functional areas such as marketing, personnel, finance and production will be allocated budgets from the centre, within which they are expected to operate. Cyert and March argue that this approach leads to localised problem solving. When falling sales are identified as a problem, this may lead senior managers to look closely at one specific area, the effectiveness of their sales force, for example, rather than looking at the problem within the context of the whole firm. This is a very different situation from the purely reactive decision-making implied by the firm based on neo-classical production function.

### 3.2.1.2 Decisions based on 'rules of thumb'

Firms tend to make decisions based upon 'rules of thumb', approximations based on past experience, not on the marginalist principles of neo-classical theory. Again, these decisions tend to be locally based. Thus, the problem of falling sales does not, as neo-classical theory predicts, lead to a firm re-assessing its output levels and re-adjusting them so as to bring marginal cost back in line with marginal revenue. What is more likely to happen is that the firm will gather information on why sales are falling and, maybe, reduces the price and sees what happens, or employ more sales staff. In other words, localised decisions based upon 'rules of thumb' – 'if we increase our sales force by 10 per cent then surely we will increase sales by roughly the same amount'.

### 3.2.1.3 Endogenously determined expectations

Expectations of the firm's objectives are not given exogenously, but are determined endogenously. What this means is that in neo-classical theory the expectations are predetermined in that firms aim to maximise profits. In the Cyert and March model, the expectations of the firm partly depend upon the people and groups of people who make up the firm. These groups have their own objectives based upon their aspirations, their past achievements and the nature of the information they have. Only one group, the shareholders, may have profit maximisation as their primary objective.

### 3.2.1.4 The firm as a coalition

These three assumptions lead to a firm not based upon a mathematical function, but on a coalition of different groups of people. Each of these groups (shareholders, managers, workers, customers, suppliers, etc.) has their own objectives or, as Cyert and March refer to them, 'aspiration levels'. The objectives of the firm and the manner, and efficiency, with which they transform inputs into outputs become determined by the ongoing relationship between the different groups within the firm.

On one level, the Cyert and March approach bears a similarity to the managerial models discussed in Section 3.1, in that the objectives of these various internal groups are bound to conflict. However, Cyert and March view these conflicts, and how they are resolved, as defining the nature of the firm itself. The aspiration levels of each group are based upon the group's past achievements and also their past, current and future expectations. Thus, for example, the workers on the production line may have experienced a period of relative stability with annual pay rises slightly above the rate of inflation and six–eight hours of overtime per week available if they wish to do it. They may reasonably assume that this will continue in the future. However, a fall in sales may bring the production line workers into conflict with the management whose own aspiration is to keep their jobs and income levels, but this may involve cutting back on production in an effort to maintain the profitability of the firm for the shareholders. The probable resulting conflict between management and production line workers is likely to be resolved through the process of bargaining, negotiation and compromise.

Thus, Cyert and March regard the firm as a coalition but with constant power struggles between the different groups which make up the coalition. Each group has its own aspirations that lead to conflicts that are resolved through the process of negotiation. This combined with local rule-of-thumb decision-making leads to profit satisficing rather than profit maximising behaviour. It also presents a very different view of the production process from that defined by the neo-classical production function. The model also opens up the possibility that firms can make mistakes. Decisions are no longer made only by all-seeing, all-knowing managers but they emerge from the internal interaction between groups from within the firm. Sometimes, as in the case of Guidant in Example 3 and the faulty pacemakers, the firm gets things wrong.

## 3.2.2 Nelson and Winter and the behavioural firm

Another strand to the behavioural view of the firm is represented by the work of Nelson and Winter (1982) and Nelson (1991). As with the earlier work of Cyert and March, the concern is with the internal workings of the firm. However, the emphasis is not just on how the firm works, but also on how a firm interrelates with its external environment. Unlike in neo-classical theory this external environment is seen as constantly changing. The approach draws heavily on various related areas from the social sciences, particularly business strategy, organisation theory and contingency theory. However, there is also a strong link with evolutionary theory from biology and, indeed, the approach is often seen as one of several evolutionary theories of the firm.

At its simplest level, the firm is regarded as being equivalent to a biological organism, and as biological organisms change and adapt to their habitat, so a firm constantly adapts and develops in response to its changing environment. Following the metaphor through, those biological organisms that adapt best to their habitat are those that survive; similarly, those firms which adapt best to their environment are the most successful. In contrast, those firms that are least successful at adapting eventually go out of business. As can be seen, this paints a different picture of the firm from that found in neo-classical theory. Here we have a constantly evolving firm which is struggling for survival in a constantly changing environment. This is very different from the neo-classical firm which is a purely reactive mathematical machine equating MC and MR in a static environment.

The evolutionary approach also implies that even though all the firms in a market may face the same external environment the way each firm responds and adapts as the environment changes may differ. Nelson (1991) suggests that these differences are reflected in three main aspects of a firm:

- The firm's strategy
- The firm's structure
- The firm's core capabilities.

Nelson defines 'strategy' as

a set of broad commitments made by a firm that define and rationalise its objectives and how it intends to pursue them. (Nelson, 1991)

The difference between this definition and the traditional 'maximise profits' assumption is the second part of the definition, 'and how it intends to pursue them'. This brings in a behavioural aspect implying that the firm's managers and not a mathematical equation called a production function decide how the objectives are met. Given that people are now involved in the objective function, a group of strategic decision makers in one firm will read a particular industry environment differently from those in another firm, and make different decisions regarding strategy. The assumption being that those firms that eventually survive are the ones whose managers chose the successful strategies.

Nelson defines a firm's 'structure' as

how a firm is organised and governed, and how decisions actually are made and carried out, and thus largely determines what it actually does given the broad strategy. (Nelson, 1991)

In other words, structure is how a firm actually organises itself to carry out the process of transforming inputs into outputs to meet the strategic objective of the firm. As with strategy decisions, a firm's structure is determined by people, and thus each firm's structure will vary. There is a long-running chicken and egg debate in the strategic management literature concerning the relationship between a firm's strategy and its internal structure. Does the strategy of a firm determine the structure required for carrying the strategy through, or does the structure of a firm largely determine the strategy adopted? Returning to our earlier example, does the structural feature of a large sales force out in the field reflect a marketing strategy based upon personal contact and cold calling, or does the fact that you have a large sales force determine the marketing strategy of personal contact and cold calling? However, the main point for our purposes is that firms will adopt different strategies and structures to cope with the environment as they see it, and will hence evolve along different paths as the environment changes.

This view of the firm throws some light on Example 2 and the problems faced by the David Lloyd Health Clubs. The idea that a firm is defined by a production function which ensures that any change in the environment results in the firm adjusting its position so as to maintain the optimal profit-maximising position is clearly at odds with this case. The David Lloyd Health Clubs faced the same 25 per cent increase in demand as their rivals, but, unlike other firms in the industry, failed to adjust their position to take advantage of the increase. From the viewpoint of the evolutionary model of the firm, one explanation for this failure may be that the structure and strategies adopted by David Lloyd Health Clubs appear not to have been as successful in coping with the environment as the alternatives adopted by their more successful rivals.

The final feature of firms which leads to differences is what Nelson calls 'core competencies'. These he defines as 'a hierarchy of organisational routines' (Nelson, 1991). By routines Nelson means all regular and predictable behaviour by firms or, put another way, the actual mechanics of the production process by which firms turn their inputs into outputs. Thus, for example, a manufacturing firm will have a whole series of routines relating to how it organises the production line, starting with a routine for getting components to the production line from the stores all the way to quality checking the finished product. Also, there will be another set of routines that need to be established for acquiring components and paying suppliers. Similarly, the personnel department will need a series of routines for hiring staff for the production line relating to, for example, identifying needs, authorising the new staff appointments, and the selection and interview process. All these could be regarded as low-order routines. High-order routines will govern areas such as strategy determination, for example what to actually produce on the production line, or the decision to introduce a new production line or introduce a new shift on an existing production line. Thus, if the firm's structure is the overall shape of the firm and the strategy determines the firm's direction, then the firm's core competencies are the means by which the firm actually moves in the direction fixed by the strategy.

The firm's routines become part of what Nelson referred to as 'organisational memories' which the firm learns by doing the routines over and over again. In the same way as an animal learns how to walk or fly, so a firm learns how to turn inputs into outputs. What is developed is an organisational culture which will be different for each firm. Again, this may link back to the relative failure of the David Lloyd Health Clubs. The core competencies developed by the firm, and the internal culture, may not have been as successful as its rivals had been in coping with the external market faced by the firm.

Nelson characterises a successful firm in the following terms:

> (it) must have a coherent strategy that enables it to decide what new ventures to go into and what to stay out of. And it needs a structure in the sense of mode of organisation and governance that guides and supports the building and sustaining of the core capabilities needed to carry out that strategy. (Nelson, 1991)

Thus, the evolutionary view of the firm combines the elements of behavioural theory in 'lifting the lid' on the black box and looking inside the firm, but also introduces behavioural elements into the determination of the setting of a firm's objectives and how the firm is structured. The firm is no longer a holistic entity acting in a purely predetermined reactive way to changes in its environment, but is a conscious entity making decisions in response to both internal and external factors. Some firms make the right decisions and survive; some make the wrong decisions and become extinct.

The view that the firm is organised around a series of routines, or competencies, and the notion of organisational memories is an important aspect of the resource-based view of the firm that will be considered in detail in Chapter 7.

## 3.3 | The principal–agent model of the firm

Principal–agent theory has its origins in the financial economics literature of the 1970s (Jensen and Meckling, 1976); however, the approach has been used in many contexts since. In one respect, principal–agent theory, when applied to the firm, continues with the same concerns as the earlier managerial models of Baumol and Williamson in that the start point is the problem of the divorce of ownership from control. However, principal–agent theory has a more generic applicability to any situation where two people, or groups of people, have some type of explicit or implicit relationship. The major difference over the earlier models is that the approach recognises, and explicitly deals with, the fact that the world is complex and uncertain and that people have bounded rationality.

Let us return to the problem of the divorce of ownership from control. The relationship between the shareholders and managers is, in fact, a principal–agent relationship. The shareholders, the owners of the firm, employ managers to act on their behalf in the running of their firm. The shareholders are the principals and the managers are their agents. However, the managerial models of Baumol and Williamson suggest that there might be a mismatch between the objectives of the shareholders and the objectives of their managers, and that this mismatch may prevent the maximisation of profits. The shareholders' main concern is to maximise the return they receive from their shareholding, whether in the form of their share of the profits paid as dividends or the possible capital gain they may make if the share price rises. The manager's objective is to maximise their own personal remuneration and, as suggested by the Williamson model, enjoy the benefits of position and power. The objectives of the owners and shareholders differ and, as we saw in the sales maximisation and managerial discretion models, may conflict. By a manager pursuing their salary, power and position objectives they may not be achieving the maximisation of shareholders' returns. Figure 3.4 summarises this mismatch of objectives.

The question might be asked, if the managers are in effect the employees of the shareholders, why do the shareholders not sack them if they are not achieving the objective that they are employed to achieve? The answer is, because the shareholders do not actually know whether the managers are achieving their (the shareholders) objectives or not. There is an 'observability problem', or, put another way, there is asymmetric information. The shareholders of a company cannot directly observe what their managers are doing on a day-to-day basis. They cannot observe the efforts being put in by the managers into the running of the business, nor how committed those managers are to the maximising of shareholder value. The shareholders have to make judgements on their manager's performance based upon limited information, such as the annual company accounts and the stock market value of the firm. Thus, in Example 1 at the beginning of this chapter we are told that the shareholders of Marks and Spencer were happy with Mr Wilson's performance based upon the apparent turnaround in sales. However, what we and they, do not know is whether this can be put down to the efforts of Mr Wilson, or whether Mr Wilson is benefiting from the actions of other senior managers, or even whether the market has simply changed and the improvement would have happened any way.

As with the sales maximisation and managerial discretion models, the likely outcome is that the manager/agent will exhibit satisficing rather than maximising behaviour. The managers will ensure that the firm performs sufficiently well in terms of dividend payouts and stock market valuation (or sales growth for the M&S shareholders) for them to get through the annual general meeting without getting the sack.

However, the principal–agent approach offers a solution. The solution lies in the employment contract of the manager. What is required is an enforcing contract that is designed to try and bring the manager's objectives closer to that of the shareholders. There are many examples of how shareholders try to resolve this problem. In the real world, many senior managers' remuneration package, for

**Shareholders (principals)**  **employ**  **Managers (agents)**

Objective
Maximise return on
shareholding (dividends and
capital gain)

Objective
Maximum reward with power
and position

**Figure 3.4**
Shareholders and
Managers

example, is partially dependent on stock market performance or profit levels. This is the case for Mr Wilson and Marks and Spencer. We are told in the report that Mr Wilson has a share option open to him for 576,367 shares. This is clearly an example of the owners building into Mr Wilson's remuneration package an incentive to try and maximise the share value of the company – the higher the share price the higher the value of his shares option to Mr Wilson.

Generally, what the principal–agent model suggests is that the problem of asymmetric information in any principal–agent relationship is overcome by a legal contract. The introduction of the idea of legal contracts to overcome the problems caused by the uncertainty and complexity of the environment is pursued in more depth in Chapter 6.

Let us consider another example of a principal–agent relationship found within a firm – that between managers and production line workers (Figure 3.5).

In this case, the managers are the principals that employ people to work on the firm's production line. As in the shareholders–managers example, we have a conflict between the objectives of the managers and the workers – the managers want as much output as possible for minimum cost, whilst the workers want as much pay as possible for the least effort. Let us assume that each production worker works independently on a production line producing widgets. The manager's problem is, again, how to align the workers' objective with his or her own. The solution lies in the contract of employment. Unlike the previous shareholder–manager example, the amount of effort put in by each worker is, in this case, directly observable by the manager – they can simply count how many widgets have been produced. Therefore, we can say that the information is symmetric – the managers and the workers have the same 'information'. Therefore, the solution for the manager to the conflict of objectives is via what is known as an enforcing contract; the workers are paid by piece rate – so much reward for each widget produced. Therefore, in this example the workers' reward is directly, and positively, related to the amount of effort put in. The objectives of the manager are 'enforced' upon the worker.

However, many workers' output is not amenable to this type of contract. Where workers are part of a team, or their output is not directly observable (such as in many service jobs), then the problem is the same as that for shareholders monitoring managers – there is asymmetric information. By paying a team on a piece rate basis you cannot be sure whether the effort put in by all members of the team is equal because all you observe is the final output of the team, not each member's contribution. A different type of contract may be required rather than the straightforward piece rate type, for example the team may have to be monitored directly by a manager.

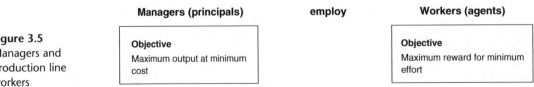

**Figure 3.5**
Managers and production line workers

Thus, principal–agent theory suggests that the means by which a firm overcomes the problems caused by uncertainty and complexity, and the resulting asymmetric information, is through the use of legal contracts. Therefore, the principal–agent approach gives yet another perspective on the firm. The firm is presented as a complex network of principal–agent relationships, of which only two have been highlighted above. There will be similar principal–agent relationships between managers and their administration staff, between the firm and its suppliers, between the firm and its bankers. In fact, there will be many more relationships, both inside and outside the firm, all governed by a contract aimed at reducing the uncertainty and complexity in the particular relationship. From this perspective, the firm is said to be at the centre of a 'nexus of contracts'. This is a view of the firm that will be developed in more detail in Chapter 6.

## 3.4 | Review and further reading

This chapter began with four short extracts from news reports in the *Financial Times*. Let us return to these examples and see how the models discussed in this chapter can help us to understand better what they are telling us about the real world.

1. ' "M&S" chief loses right-hand man' – this story (and a more detailed analysis a couple of pages on) related to the resignation of Charles Wilson from the board of 'Marks and Spencer'. Institutional shareholders were reported as being disappointed by the resignation as he had been a key figure in the firm's attempt to turn around a drop in sales that have been declining for the last seven quarters. It was also reported that Mr Wilson had been paid £1.41m in the last year but had not taken the 576,367 share option open to him (worth another £2m).

As we have seen, this example clearly shows the divorce of ownership and control, first noted by Berle and Means, and also illustrates some of the features discussed in relation to the principal–agent model. In common with most large firms in the UK Marks and Spencer is mainly owned by large City institutions who invest funds on behalf of many small investors (for example, Investment funds, Pension funds). Mr Wilson and the rest of the board act as the agents of the institutional investors who are the principals. As also discussed, the share options referred to are a common device by which the owners try to partly align the objectives of the managers to their own – the value to the manager of the share options depends upon the performance of the company in the eyes of the stock market.

2. "Pain amid the gain for private health club operators" – the main point about this story was that despite significant growth in the market for private health clubs (up 25 per cent since 2002) some clubs, such as the 'David Lloyd Health

Clubs', were reporting drops in membership and facing possible financial difficulties.

As discussed in Section 3.2, this report throws into the confusion the idea of the 'representative firm' approach adopted by neo-classical theory – the idea that one firm in an industry can be used as a proxy for all firms in the industry. What the behavioural and evolutionary models of the firm tell us is that every firm is different. Firms in the real world differ in terms of their internal structures and cultures and also in their perceptions of the external environment. Therefore, firms' strategies differ – some firms develop strategies that are more suited to their environment than others. Likewise, some firms' internal structures are better suited to adapting to the external environment. In this case, the suggestion is that the David Lloyd Health Clubs were not adapting to their environment as successfully as some other firms in the industry.

3.  'Pacemaker brings Guidant heartache' – Guidant are a maker of medical devices, but unfortunately faulty seals had been discovered in 69 out of the 78,000 so far produced.

This example illustrates that a firm can, and does, make mistakes. Guidant is not a set of mathematical equations, but a coalition of groups of people led by a management faced with bounded rationality. Somewhere within the complexity of the firm and its production process, a mistake has been made and some of the firm's output is faulty.

4.  'Telecity taken private for £58m' – Telecity are an Internet hosting company who had been set up at the height of the dotcom boom in the late 1990s. They had been floated on the London Stock Exchange in 2000, when the market valued them at £1bn. Five years later, they have never made a profit nor paid a dividend and have now been taken back into private ownership for £58m.

This final example has several interesting features. First, the idea that a firm could survive for six or seven years without ever making a profit is something that neo-classical theory would find hard to explain. It does raise a related question – are firms in the real world always expected to maximise profits? This is actually a difficult question to answer. Most private sector firms, which are not in the voluntary sector, certainly aim to make profits and to sustain these profits into the future, but whether they maximise profits is a different matter. In the real world, the concept of 'profit' is not as clear-cut as might be expected. Profit and loss accounts of firms will have a number of items that appear as 'profit' – for example, profit before tax, profit after tax – which one is the firm trying to maximise? There is also a time dimension. Are we talking about short-run, medium-run or long-run profits? In this example, it could well be that the expectation is that Telecity will eventually make profits, but only over the medium to long term.

However, if Telecity does eventually make a profit, how will we know if they are actually maximising profits? In theory they will know because their marginal cost will equal their marginal revenue. In practice, multi-product firms operating in a range of uncertain and complex markets means the calculation of marginal costs and marginal revenues, is virtually impossible. In theory, the stock market has a role to play here. Firms whom the stock market judge to be under-performing will tend to be undervalued on the stock market and thus may be liable to takeovers. The stock market may, therefore, act as some sort of guide to whether firms are generating sufficient profits, but this is a long way from the textbook firm that maximises profits by equating MC and MR. In this case, also, the stock market in 2000 appears to have massively over-valued Telecity, so relying on this as a means of assessing whether a firm is under- or over-performing is not necessarily very reliable.

What all of the examples show is that the neo-classical assumption of full information is very difficult to square with reality – the Marks and Spencer investors' inability to foresee the resignation of Mr Wilson; the David Lloyd Health Clubs' inability to react to the increase in demand; Guidant not knowing about problems in their production system; and the stock market's inability to see the true value of Telecity in 2000. There are very few markets where all the participants have all the information about the market immediately available when they make a decision to buy or sell. The one market that perhaps comes closest is the foreign exchange market where the single price is constantly being revised in response to changes in demand and supply, and the exchange dealers have instant access to the information. However, even in this market, away from the dealing floors, the average customer when obtaining foreign exchange for a holiday still does not have full information. Commission rates will vary, as do the actual exchange rates offered by different suppliers.

In addition, in the real world, we have to cope with information that we may not be too sure of the validity of – information may be uncertain, not certain as in the neo-classical world. As was pointed out, the Marks and Spencer shareholders assume that Mr Wilson had been responsible for a turnaround in sales; however, they cannot be sure. As with decision-making, the fact that a lot of the information we receive comes from other people leads to problems of uncertainty. The idea that information is certain implies that we believe everything we are told by other people – if bank X is offering an exchange rate of €1.60 per £ we accept that this is the rate. However, in reality Bank Y down the street may be offering a rate of €1.65 per £. In addition, what our foreign exchange customer cannot know is what the rate is going to be the next day, it may rise to €1.67. Our inability to see the future is another source of uncertainty.

What we deal with in the real world is limited information, where we all have different bits of information (asymmetric information) and the information we have may be uncertain. We can improve the quality of information we have before we decide whether to take part in a market, but this incurs an opportunity cost. Our purchaser of foreign exchange, for example, could spend their afternoon walking around town comparing all the rates on offer and then go into the public library and read the *Financial Times* to try and decide whether rates are likely to improve tomorrow or not. However, this then becomes a trade-off between improving our information and the opportunity cost of the time involved in searching out the information. As suggested in Section 2.3, the idea of global rationality is closely linked to the assumption of full and certain information. The fact that in the real world, information is asymmetric and uncertain implies that the decision makers within firms will only have bounded rationality.

Therefore, as we have seen, economists have developed a number of extensions to the basic neo-classical models of the firm, plus suggesting some alternatives, that seem to help with our understanding of what we observe happening to firms in the real world. The next chapter completes our discussion regarding the economist's model of the firm by looking in more detail at the mechanics of maximising and, equally importantly, sustaining profits.

### 3.4.1 Reading

The most comprehensive treatment of the managerial models of the firm is to be found in Koutsoyiannis (1979). Cyert and March (1963) and Nelson and Winter (1982) are the standard sources of the various behavioural models discussed. For a fuller consideration of the principal–agent problem, see Milgrom and Roberts (1992) plus Alchian and Demsetz's (1972) original article on the issues raised by team production is also worth looking at. Nelson (1991) is a good introduction to the more behavioural approach to the firm, but see also the references at the end of Chapter 7 in relation to the resource-based view of the firm. Rowlinson (1997) provides a good overview of the relationship between economics and organisation theory. Much of the material in this chapter presents economists' slants on models, concepts and theories drawn from the other social sciences such as organisational behaviour, sociology and strategic management. Readers interested in pursuing these in more depth are directed to some of the standard texts such as Mullins (2004) or Johnson, Scholes and Whittington (2005).

## 3.5 | Student exercises

### 3.5.1 Review exercises and points for discussion

1. Provide brief and clear definitions of the following key terms and concepts as used in this chapter.

   a. The divorce of ownership and control
   b. Sales maximisation
   c. Profit satisficing
   d. The managerial utility function
   e. The 'black box' view of the firm
   f. 'Rule of thumb' decision-making

    **g.** The 'coalition' view of the firm

    **h.** The evolutionary firm

    **i.** Organisational routines

    **j.** The principal–agent problem

    **k.** The observability problem.

2. Consider Figure 3.1, which shows the equilibrium for the sales maximising firm as being at price-output combination $(P_r, q_r)$. What would be the effect on the equilibrium price and quantity for this sales maximising firm in each of the following cases:

    **a.** An increase in demand.

    **b.** An increase in costs.

    **c.** A fall in the profit expectation of shareholders below $\Pi_s$.

    **d.** An increase in the profit expectation of shareholders to above $\Pi_r$.

3. As remarked upon in the text, the managerial models presented in Section 3.1 all rest quite firmly on the neo-classical assumptions outlined in Chapter 2.

    **a.** Clearly identify these neo-classical assumptions for each of the three managerial models discussed.

    **b.** Do these assumptions make these models of purely theoretic interest? (Remember the comments made on the purpose of an economic model in the exercise section in Chapter 2).

4. As quoted in Section 3.2, Nelson and Winter define a firm's strategy as 'a set of broad commitments made by a firm that define and rationalise its objectives and how it intends to pursue them'. What issues might a firm's management have in implementing strategy if the internal workings of the firm do indeed correspond with Cyert and March's coalition view of the firm?

5. Section 3.3 introduced the principal–agent problem using the firm to illustrate the basic concepts and ideas involved. How do you think these concepts could be applied to the relationship between a landlord and their tenants?

## 3.5.2 Application exercises

Consider the following three short reports.

*Example 1 – BAA.* BAA, who owns seven of the major airports in the UK, reported a 1.3 per cent drop in passenger volumes for March 2006. Growth for the year was only 2 per cent, lower than had been expected. BAA also reported a number of factors that had contributed to this shortfall on expected growth – poor weather in the UK, ongoing effects of the July 2005 bombings in London, strike action at Heathrow during the year and a late Easter holiday. (*Financial Times*, 12 April 2006)

*Example 2 – Matalan.* The BBC reported on 3 May 2006 that the budget clothes retailer Matalan was suing the company which had advised them to spend £20m on a new computer system. The reason given was that Matalan had discovered that they did not need a new system; an upgrade to the existing system would have sufficed.

*Example 3 The Economist* reported, in its edition of 20 May 2006, that 37 per cent of Britain's top 350 companies used shareholder return as the main measure of senior executive performance, this was down from 47 per cent the year before. ('Lowering the bar', *The Economist*, 20 May 2006, p. 31).

a. Use the examples above to illustrate the limitations of the underlying assumptions of the neo-classical model (profit maximisation, holistic behaviour, full and certain information, global rationality and homogeneity).

b. Can any of the models in this chapter help us to explain the issues raised in these examples?

# Costs, Revenues and Profit

## LEARNING OUTCOMES

On completion of this chapter, the reader should be able to

■ Assess the process by which firms generate profits

■ Explain why some firms are able to sustain profits in the long run

## KEY NEW CONCEPTS

| | | |
|---|---|---|
| Normal profits | Monopoly rent | Resource entry barriers |
| Abnormal profits | Structural entry barriers | Endogenous demand variables |
| Ricardian rents | Strategic entry barriers | Exogenous demand variables |

## KEY NEW MODELS

| | | |
|---|---|---|
| Perfect competition | Monopoly | Contestable markets |

## MODELS AND CONCEPTS DEVELOPED FURTHER

| | | |
|---|---|---|
| Management costs | The neo-classical firm | Opportunity cost |
| Competitive costs | Profit | Revenue |

In the mid-1980s, two companies were formed, namely Direct Line Insurance and Ryanair, that were to transform their respective industries. Both companies entered industries that were dominated by long-established incumbent firms – Direct Line Insurance into the motor insurance business and Ryanair into the short-haul airline business. There was a large degree of tacit understanding amongst the incumbent firms about the way in which business was done in these industries, with processes and business practices that had not changed for many years. However, Direct Line Insurance and Ryanair radically altered these industries by not only the introduction of completely new business structures and processes but also new means of engaging with customers.

*Direct Line Insurance and the UK insurance industry.* Peter Wood established Direct Line Insurance in 1985 under the umbrella of the Royal Bank of Scotland group (RBS). The company was set up to sell motor insurance and, within ten years, this newcomer not only was one of the most profitable businesses in the UK, but had also totally changed the whole motor insurance market. What was radical about Direct Line Insurance was the means by which they chose to sell insurance. In the mid-1980s, people bought their motor insurance in much the same way as drivers had always insured themselves – through an insurance broker. Typically, you would visit an insurance broker on your local high street. The broker would then offer you insurance quotes based on the prices they could obtain from Lloyds in London, as well as a commission to cover the cost of running their premises and income for themselves.

What Direct Line Insurance did though was to do away with the middleman broker and to make the buying of car insurance much easier. How they did this was by saving potential customers the time, and hassle, of visiting an insurance broker, by giving the customers the opportunity to buy their car insurance over the telephone. In effect, Direct Line Insurance set up one of the UK's first call centres. Not only was the service Direct Line Insurance offered more convenient, but they were also able to offer motor insurance at much reduced rates than the incumbent firms. This was due to a combination of factors, but principally because the Direct Line Insurance business model enabled them to operate from a much lower cost base than the incumbent firms in the industry. The selling of insurance directly over the phone from a single call centre meant an entire cost layer was removed – there was no need for a network of insurance brokers each with their own premises to maintain. Secondly, the rapidly evolving computer technology of the late 1980s enabled the firm's operators to connect directly to the insurance market, to make a quote to customers and then accept their payment – all in a single phone call.

By the early 1990s, Direct Line Insurance was one of the most profitable companies in the UK and the founder, Peter Wood, regularly appeared in the press as one of the wealthiest businessmen in the country. In addition, as a direct result of the business model used by Direct Line Insurance, the selling of insurance (of all types, not just motor insurance) was changed for ever.

*Ryanair and the European short-haul airline industry.* The year after Peter Wood set up Direct Line Insurance, two brothers from the Irish Republic, with the surname

Ryan, founded a new airline called Ryanair. Ryanair was set up as an airline flying passengers from Dublin to London in direct competition with British Airways (BA) and Aer Lingus, the two national carriers. Initially, Ryanair adopted a business model that was similar to all the incumbent firms in the short-haul market, not just BA and Aer Lingus but also the other national carriers operating around Europe such as KLM, Lufthansa and Air France. This was based on the idea that you had two classes of passengers, business and economy, whom you charged differential fares. However, the assumption was that your customers required a standard set of service – a meal, free drinks, a reclining seat and a flight between the two main airports in Dublin and London. The customers flying business class received an enhanced level of service – a better meal, for example, and a larger seat. As with the motor insurance industry, this had been the accepted business model almost since passenger air travel had first been established in the 1930s.

Not surprisingly, in its early years Ryanair struggled to compete against the two well-established national carriers. However, in the mid-1990s two events happened that were to change Ryanair, and the short-haul European airline business, forever. First, the Ryan family brought in a new chief executive by the name of Michael O'Leary and secondly, the European air industry was deregulated by the European Union (EU). Up until this time, the European airline industry had been heavily regulated, with national governments dictating who could fly into their airspace and where they could land. Inevitably, the national (and in most cases still Government-owned) flag carriers received preferential treatment and, in some cases, near monopoly rights within their home markets. With deregulation and the establishment of the so-called 'open skies' policy, Michael O'Leary seized the opportunity to radically alter the business model of Ryanair. Ten years previously an open sky's policy had been adopted in the USA. This had led to the development of budget, or 'no frills', airlines, the most successful of which had been Southwest Airlines. Michael O'Leary copied the Southwest 'no frills' model and, in a matter of five years, transformed Ryanair from a small single-route struggling airline into one operating across western Europe and one of the fastest growing businesses in the EU.

The basic idea of a budget airline is to focus on driving costs down to an absolute minimum, this then being reflected in the ability to offer vastly reduced seat prices (some Ryanair flights are offered for as little as 99p). In terms of the actual flight, this is done by removing all the previous taken-for-granted services – no free meals or drinks, a basic non-reclining seat, no dual class of passengers and flights to smaller secondary airports. However, Ryanair went beyond the 'no frills' flight as a means of reducing costs and looked at the entire process from buying a ticket to getting on the plane. Wherever costs could be saved they were – from the fact that tickets could only be bought online (hence no travel agent costs or even the cost of a paper ticket) to not paying the host airport for the use of an air bridge to get on the plane. Another means of reducing costs was by ensuring that the company's largest asset, its fleet of Boeing 737 aircraft, was kept in the air carrying paying passengers for as long as possible – the typical turnaround time for a Ryanair flight is just 20 min. The result of this cost-focused, no frills strategy was so successful that in 2003 Ryanair flew 23 million passengers, was the third largest airline in Europe and, in an industry where profits have always been hard (or even impossible) to come by, was an extremely profitable business.

*Direct Line Insurance and Ryanair compared.* Therefore, we can see that there are many similarities between Direct Line Insurance and Ryanair. Both entered mature industries and transformed the way in which these industries operated. Both used changes in technology to good effect and both were led by charismatic chief executives. The other similarity is that after introducing the different business models, both quickly became the most profitable firms in their respective industries. In economic terms, both firms were able to enter a market and, in a short space of time, generate high levels of abnormal profit which, in this context, can be taken to mean profits significantly above the industry average.

However, what is interesting is if we compare the subsequent development of these two pioneering companies to the present day. By the late 1990s, Direct Line Insurance was (and still is) a profitable company and remained the largest seller of motor insurance in the UK. However, the large abnormal profits seen in the early 1990s had disappeared. Profit levels, whilst still respectable, were much more in line with the industry norm. Ryanair, however, is currently at a similar distance in time from their change to a 'no frills' airline as Direct Line Insurance was in the late 1990s from setting up their first call centre. However, Ryanair is still growing and still making abnormal profits when compared to most other airlines (the other exception, of course, being the other major budget airline Easyjet). In other words, whereas Ryanair has been able to sustain its level of abnormal profits eight years after its switch of business models, Direct Line Insurance, at a similar eight-year point of their development, had largely lost their abnormal profits. Put another way, both companies, for similar reasons, were initially able to generate abnormal profits, but of the two only Ryanair has managed to sustain these abnormal profits nearly a decade after their operational innovations took place. The big question is why is there such an apparent difference in the two innovating companies' performance? Why has Ryanair been more successful in sustaining profits over the long run?

## 4.1 | An expanded model of the transformation process

The aim of this chapter is to provide a framework that will help to answer the more generic question posed by the above examples. Why it is that some firms, in some industries, not only appear to be able to generate short-run abnormal profits, but also appear to sustain these high levels of profits in the long run? In order to set about answering the question posed above, we will need to look in more detail at the profit equation from Chapter 2 that we generally assume a firm is trying to maximise:

$$\text{Profit} = \text{Revenue} - \text{Cost}$$

The equation implies that if a firm is to make profits then the revenue gained must exceed the costs incurred. More specifically, if the profits gained from a transformation process are to be maximised, then the revenue gained from selling the output must be maximised. Both Direct Line Insurance and Ryanair dramatically increased the revenue they took from customers, not just because they reduced the price of the product on offer, but also because they offered their products to customers in a manner that matched the customers' changed lifestyles and needs. Similarly, to ensure profit maximisation, not only must you try to maximise revenue, but you should also aim to minimise costs. As we have seen, both Direct Line Insurance and Ryanair managed to considerably lower the cost base of both their industries. They achieved this by the use of new and developing technology and by removing all unnecessary ancillary costs not related to the provision of the basic product.

Section 4.2 looks at the elements of the profit equation in more detail and considers how firms can generate abnormal profits. The discussion in this section also leads to a widening of the traditional notion of costs as being only incurred as a direct result of the production. Figure 4.1 reproduces the model of the firm introduced in Chapter 1. The model incorporates three types of costs:

1. Direct production costs ($D$) – the costs directly associated with producing a good or service

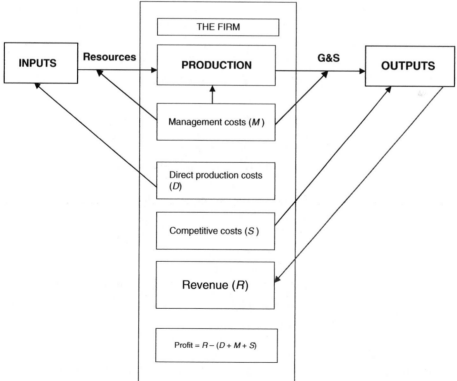

**Figure 4.1**
Expanded model of
the firm

2. Management costs (*M*) – the costs associated with the management and organisation of the firm
3. Competitive cost (*S*) – the costs associated with competing in a firm's output market.

Section 4.2 considers this wider definition of the costs incurred by a firm, which leads directly onto the issue of the generation and sustaining of profits in Section 4.3. In this section, we will look at the idea that the generation of profits is only the initial stage in the profit maximising process. Once the profits have been generated in the short run, firms need to try to sustain them in the long run.

## 4.2 | The generation of profit

### 4.2.1 Profit maximisation in the neo-classical model

As discussed in Section 2.1, in the neo-classical model of the firm, profit is regarded as the residual left after the firm has completed the transformation process and sold the resulting goods and services on its output markets. This residual belongs to the entrepreneur as the organiser and risk taker of the production process. If we accept the five assumptions of the neo-classical model (Section 2.3) then the transformation process is represented by Figure 2.2 – reproduced over the page.

Thus, all the costs (outflows of money) incurred by a firm come directly from the factor markets that supply the industry with resources. Similarly, revenue (inflows of money) comes from the markets the firm is supplying with goods and services where the prices obtained are based solely on the firm's costs of production. If the firm can generate more revenue than it incurs in costs, then the residual left is referred to as profit and belongs to the entrepreneur.

#### 4.2.1.1 Normal and abnormal profits

As discussed in Section 2.1, the firm has the single objective of maximising profits and this is achieved when MC = MR (Figure 2.4). However, in economic theory, an important distinction is made between 'normal' and 'abnormal' profits. To illustrate this difference, let us return to our window cleaner used in Chapter 2. Assume that our window cleaner makes on average £200 per week from his window round. This we can refer to as his total income, which represents the revenue he has generated from his customers minus his direct costs of production (his bucket, leathers and ladders). However, prior to becoming a small businessman and setting up his window-cleaning business, our window cleaner was a labourer on local building sites making, on average, about £150 per week. This £150 represents the window cleaner's next best wage – it is his 'opportunity cost'. Opportunity cost is one of the core concepts of economics and is cost in terms of the next best alternative forgone, in this case the £150 wage from the building work. This 'cost' will appear in Figure 4.2 as part of the cost of labour, it is the cost to the firm of acquiring the skills of the entrepreneur. The entrepreneur's opportunity

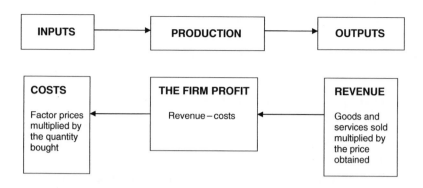

**Figure 4.2** The neo-classical transformation process

cost represents the minimum weekly income that he must make from his business; anything less than this and the most rational thing to do would be to return to his previous occupation. If, for example, our window cleaner experiences a drop in takings and he is only being left with £120 per week from his round, the rational thing to do would be for him to shut down his window-cleaning business and return to labouring.

In economics, this opportunity cost of the entrepreneur's next best wage is included in the cost of acquiring labour. In fact, all the inputs would have similar opportunity costs attached to them. The combined value of these opportunity costs equates to what is referred to as 'normal profit' and would be excluded from any residual made after taking production costs from revenue. What economists usually mean by 'profit' is actually 'abnormal' profit – the residual of revenue minus both the direct production costs and the opportunity costs of the inputs.

To illustrate, consider our window-cleaning example above (for the sake of illustration we shall assume the capital costs involved have zero opportunity cost):

> Total weekly income (revenue – production costs)
> from the window-cleaning round = £200 = TWY

Potential weekly income from next best occupation = £150 = PWY

Therefore

> Abnormal profit = TWY – PWY = TWY – normal profit ⇒
> Abnormal profit = £200 – £150 = £50

What we are saying is that although the window cleaner makes a total of £200 from his round, only £50 of this would be regarded by economists as profit – the extra income he makes from window cleaning that he would not make from labouring.

In the real world, precise calculations such as these are very difficult to make and the usual practice is to look at a firm's profit levels in terms of its relative level – relative to other firms in the industry or to other industries. Thus, in the Direct Line Insurance and Ryanair examples used in Section 4.1, we referred to both these firms making 'above-normal industry returns' in their early days – this is in effect saying that they were earning abnormal profits. How we can try and relate the idea of normal and abnormal profit to the real world is an issue we shall look at in more detail in Chapter 11 when discussing the idea of efficiency.

### 4.2.1.2 Profits in the model of perfect competition

Neo-classical theory has developed the benchmark model of perfect competition to illustrate a utopian situation whereby firms and consumers, by pursuing their objective functions, bring about a situation where all resources are allocated to their best possible use. Figure 4.3 summarises the outcome of this model.

The perfectly competitive model will be discussed in more detail later in this book, particularly in relation to its use as a benchmark model (Section 4.3) and the implications it has in relation to efficiency and public policy (Chapters 13 and 14). However, for our purposes here, it does provide a means for exploring the differences between normal and abnormal profit within the neo-classical model of the firm.

The perfectly competitive model leads to an equilibrium point where no abnormal profits are made; the only profits made are 'normal' and these are subsumed within a firm's cost curves. The explanation for this lies in the fact that the firm can sell as much output as it likes, but only at the prevailing market price. In other words, the firm has no control over price. The reason for this lies in the four assumptions made about the nature of the market:

1. There are many small firms and many individual consumers.
2. There are no entry barriers to the market or industry.
3. All inputs and outputs are identical (the homogeneity assumption).
4. There are no economies of scale.

Given these assumptions, the only means by which a firm can respond to changes in market price in order to maintain its profit maximising position is by adjusting

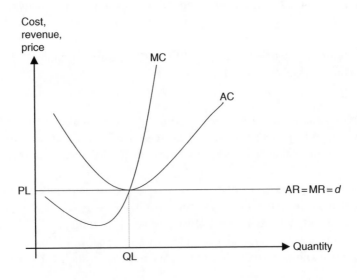

**Figure 4.3**
Perfect competition with only normal profits

output. The fact that the price is constant means that the revenue from each unit of output sold is identical and will be equal to the market price. In other words, the marginal revenue (MR) (revenue from the last unit sold) will always be the same as the prevailing market price. This can be seen in Figure 4.3, which shows the long-run equilibrium of the perfectly competitive model. PL is the constant market price that the firm is faced with and has no control over, and this is equal to the MR. The long-run outcome of the perfectly competitive model is that the profit maximising condition of MC = MR happens at the point where MC = AC, or at (QL, PL) in Figure 4.4. In other words, there are no abnormal profits.

As explained previously, the AC curve includes the opportunity cost of the entrepreneur's next best occupation. In terms of our window-cleaner example, this is the price that would provide the normal profit of £150 per week. If the price falls below PL, then the entrepreneur is not making sufficient profit (the window cleaner's normal profit falls below £150 per week) and will switch to the next best occupation – the firm will leave the market (the window cleaner gives up his round and goes back to his £150 per week labouring job). The other important point about the MC = MR long-run equilibrium in Figure 4.3 is that marginal cost also equals the price – the cost of the resources used in the last unit produced exactly matches the value put on that unit by society. In other words, in equilibrium, we also have the most economically efficient outcome (for a fuller discussion of economic efficiency, see Section 11.3).

Figure 4.4 shows the short-run equilibrium in perfect competition before the market has reached the long-run efficient position shown in Figure 4.3. The short-run price (PS) the firm is receiving for each unit of output sold exceeds the cost of making that unit (AC'), thus the firm is making an abnormal profit of (PS – AC') on each unit of output sold. In our example, the window cleaner is now earning more than £150 per week from his round. However, the whole point about perfect competition is that, given the four conditions under which the market operates, this short-run abnormal profit cannot be sustained. New firms are attracted to the

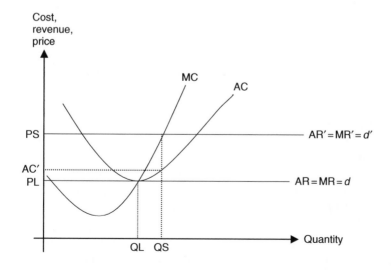

**Figure 4.4** Perfect competition

market; this increases supply which forces down the market price, as a result firms respond to this by cutting individual output levels so as to maintain their profit maximising position. Eventually, the market settles into the long-run economically efficient equilibrium as shown in Figure 4.3.

### 4.2.1.3  Sustaining abnormal profits in the perfectly competitive model

This model of perfect competition is regarded in neo-classical theory as a bench-mark – the ideal market structure that leads to the most economically efficient outcome. However, neo-classical theory also suggests that there are two general means by which deviations from the perfectly competitive model can lead to abnormal profits being made in the long run, as well as the short run. First, the existence of scarce resources in a production process can lead to abnormal profits in the long run. Scarce resources break the assumption that all inputs are available in unlimited and identical quantities. In other words, the assumption of homogeneity is broken. If resources are not identical and are limited, then early entrants into a market will have access to cheaper and hence more productive resources, allowing them to operate on a lower set of cost curves – and therefore at a higher level of abnormal profit.

A simple numerical example will serve as an illustration. Two firms earn revenues of £100 from a market. However, firm A was an early entrant and acquired more productive scarce resources that allow its costs to be £80 compared with firm B whose costs are £100. Thus, firm A makes abnormal profits of £20 whereas firm B makes zero abnormal profits.

This idea of the non-homogeneity of resources goes all the way back to David Ricardo in the early nineteenth century. The context used by Ricardo was related to agricultural land. The most suitable land for growing a particular crop, such as wheat, would be used first. However, if the demand for wheat continues to grow then the land used to grow the extra wheat may not be as suitable, and the crop yields per acre would begin to decline. Declining productivity leads to rising average costs. In other words, the costs to the early entrant farmer of growing wheat would be lower than the later entrants who are being forced to use the less-productive land. This situation could arise with any of the inputs into a production process; for example, if the process requires skilled labour then the firms that are first into the market would pick up the best and highly skilled workers, the later entrants would have to recruit less-skilled workers with lower productivity levels. Alternatively, it could be that Ryanair, being one of the first into the 'no frills' airline business, acquired the best of the limited landing slots available at the secondary airports it chose to operate from.

This type of abnormal profit arising from the ownership of scare resources is referred to as Ricardian profit or 'Ricardian rent'. In effect, the late entrants face an entry barrier to the market caused by their having to use less productive and hence more costly resources. In the case of the use of agricultural land, the Ricardian rent could be maintained over the long run, some agricultural land will always be better suited for the growing of wheat than other land. However, in some instances the Ricardian rent may only last for a short period of time. If it is possible for the low-productive resources to be upgraded, then the abnormal profits being earned by the high-productive resource will gradually disappear. This is common in some labour markets when a new production method requires particular skills. Initially, there may be a limited number of workers with the required skills and the firms employing them will earn abnormal profits. However, over time, other workers will gradually acquire those skills and increase their productivity accordingly and the market will adjust.

The second source of abnormal profits in the neo-classical model comes from the existence of restrictions to the market that are not related with access to resources, but allow one or more firms to sustain abnormal profits in the long run.

Figure 4.5 shows the familiar situation of abnormal profits being made through the existence of a firm with some monopoly control over the market. The essential difference between Figure 4.5 and the perfectly competitive market of Figure 4.3 is the fact that the monopolist is not a price taker. The restrictions on the market that could come from, for example, patent rights or maybe legal restrictions, give the monopolist some control over price – they are no longer price takers. This is reflected in Figure 4.5 by the downward sloping demand curve. Unlike the perfectly competitive firm, the monopolist has a choice over how to achieve maximum profits: it can fix either a price or an output level. The profit maximising outcome is $(P_m, Q_m)$ that generates a profit of $(P_m - AC_m)$ on each unit of output. Because of the restrictions on the market, which prevent the entry of new firms, these abnormal profits are earned not just in the short run but in the long run as well. This type of abnormal profits is referred to as 'monopoly rent'.

Therefore, we can see that the neo-classical model gives us a benchmark model where all the profits made in the long run are normal profits and this equates with the most economically efficient outcome. The ability of firms to sustain abnormal profits in the long run depends upon either the existence of Ricardian rents due to

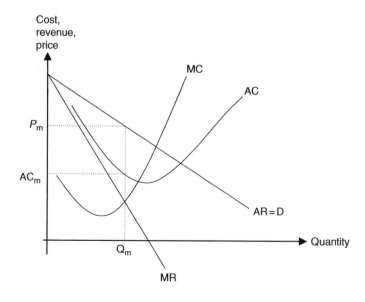

**Figure 4.5**
Monopoly rent

heterogeneous resources or the possibility of monopoly rent due to some restriction on the market preventing free entry. In general terms, the source of these abnormal profits, in both cases, is due to the existence of entry barriers. New firms (usually referred to as 'entrants') cannot enter the market and compete on the same terms as the firms already inside the market (usually referred to as 'incumbents'). As we shall see in Section 4.3, entry barriers are the key to firms, not only generating abnormal profits in the short run, but being able to sustain them in the long run.

However, before we look in more detail at the issue of entry barriers, let us switch our attention to the other side of the profit equation and look at revenue and costs. As explored in Chapter 2, in order for a firm to maximise profits the firm should be trying to minimise its outgoings to the input markets (costs) and maximising its incomings from its output markets (revenue).

## 4.2.2 Revenue maximisation

Firms generate income from selling their output onto the next stage of the production chain, which may be other downstream firms or the final consumer. The income gained is revenue that is simply the quantity of output sold multiplied by the price obtained ($P \times Q$). If the firm is to maximise profits then this is a positive inflow of money into the firm and needs to be as big as possible – in other words the firm needs to maximise its revenue.

In the discussion of the neo-classical firm in Section 2.1, it was suggested that the ability of firms to generate revenue was constrained by the state of the output market. The constraints are embodied in the familiar downward sloping market demand curve. Let us just review what exactly a demand curve indicates. The demand curve itself shows how much can be sold at each given price, with the exact slope of the curve being determined by the price elasticity of demand. The actual position of the demand curve in this price–quantity space depends upon a whole range of variables that influence the consumer's decisions as to whether to buy a particular product or not. Each demand curve reflects a certain combination of these factors; if any of the factors change then the demand curve shifts position within the price–quantity space.

The familiar downward sloping demand curve is drawn on the basis that all the factors influencing demand are fixed – the 'ceterias paribus' assumption that 'all things remain equal'. The factors that can influence demand for a firm's output are commonly referred to as 'factors influencing demand'. A typical list may be as follows:

- Price
- Price of substitute and complementary goods
- Marketing (usually referred to as 'advertising')
- Tastes and fashion
- Government policy
- Research and Development
- Income
- Demography.

In introductory microeconomic theory, the focus is on how changes in these factors affect the position and, in the case of price, the shape of the demand curve. However, from a firm's point of view what is important is not how the factors fix the position and shape of the demand curve, but how the factors impinge on the firm's ability to generate revenue. In particular, how the firm can influence and manipulate the demand factors to its own benefit. As stated previously, these factors of demand are the constraints on the firm in its bid to maximise revenue, and firms need to manipulate and control these factors as best as they can if they are to achieve their aim. Figure 4.6 illustrates this point.

In the left-hand diagram, it can be seen that total revenue from the same fixed price of £10 increases as the demand curve progressively shifts rightwards. D1 gives total revenue of £1000, D2 gives £2000 and D3 gives £3000. Therefore the firm, in trying to maximise revenue, needs to try and shift the demand curve rightwards. The right-hand diagram shows the effects of price elasticity. D1 shows a perfectly elastic demand curve where the firm can sell as much as it likes, but only at this one fixed price (as is the case in the model of perfect competition). In other words, the firm has no control over price at all and is therefore severely restricted in terms of trying to increase revenue from the market. The other extreme to this is D2 which shows a perfectly inelastic demand curve. In this situation, quantity is fixed and the firm has total control over price. This situation is the most desirable one for the firm in terms of revenue maximisation. However, as D2 for most markets is difficult to attain, most firms aim for the more common intermediate situation as shown by D3. Here the firm has some control over price and thus escapes the undesirable situation of D1, but does not have the total control of D2. Generally, we can say that the more price inelastic a firm can make its demand curve, the more control it gains over price.

Therefore, for a firm to try and maximise revenue it needs to try and influence both the position and the shape of its demand curve. Returning to the factors influencing demand, closer examination of the list shows that there are two broad types: those factors over which the firm has some direct control through decisions it can take and those factors over which the firm has little or no control. We shall refer to the factors that are open to direct influence by a firm's decisions as 'endogenous factors' and those over which the firm has little or no influence as 'exogenous factors'. Under the heading of endogenous factors would normally

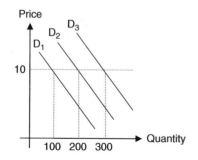

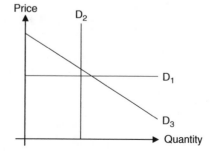

**Figure 4.6**  Demand constraint on revenue

come price, marketing and research and development, whilst exogenous factors would normally include income, demography, Government policy, price of substitutes and complements and tastes and fashion.

As always, there are likely to be grey areas. The whole point of marketing, for example, is to influence tastes and fashions and as we shall see, the price of substitutes can be heavily influenced by the prices a firm sets for its own products. However, the factors listed in Table 4.1 as endogenous are those over which any firm needs to make decisions in pursuit of revenue maximisation. For example, a successful marketing campaign will shift the demand curve outwards and, at the same time, increase consumer loyalty and hence make the demand curve more inelastic. Research and development may have the highly desirable effect of giving you a perfectly inelastic demand curve, at least for a short space of time if, for example, as a pharmaceuticals firm you discover a new drug. Firms need to make decisions on prices, marketing expenditure and R&D expenditure, as these are the variables open to firms to try and manipulate the demand curve in its favour as they try to maximise revenue. These are themes we shall return to in more depth in Chapter 9.

Let us see how this can be related to Ryanair. In the case of Ryanair, the initial key demand factor was not actually an endogenous factor, but the exogenous factor of the change in EU policy in relation to the deregulation of the airline sector. Prior to this change, many national airlines had been in the position of being a near monopolist in their own markets and having the ability to determine how many flights to offer.

This original situation is shown in Figure 4.7 as being represented by demand curve D1. After deregulation, however, the situation changed as the national carriers' monopoly was removed. As a result, the demand curve for the industry pivoted to the downward sloping shape as shown by D2. As discussed previously, Ryanair chose a strategy based on cost minimisation. This enabled them to use the strategic weapon of price to force down the market price from the old pre-deregulation price of $P_r$ to a much lower $P_d$. As a result, the number of flights rose from $Q_r$ to $Q_{r1}$. Therefore, we can say that Ryanair did not actually change the shape of the demand curve; this was done through an exogenous change in public policy, but it certainly exploited the change using the endogenous variable of price.

**Table 4.1** Endogenous and exogenous variables

| Exogenous variables | Endogenous decision variables |
| --- | --- |
| Income | Price |
| Demography | Marketing |
| Price of substitutes | R&D |
| Price of complements | |
| Tastes and fashions | |
| Government policy | |

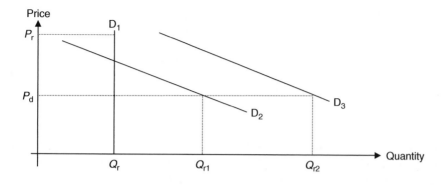

**Figure 4.7** Ryanair and demand

To add to this, we can also reasonably assume that the market experienced an outward shift in demand. This was partly due to the prolonged growth of the UK economy of the 1990s causing the exogenous factor of raising consumer income and partly because of a change in tastes and fashions. Ryanair's low-cost flights changed people's attitudes towards flying, which previously had been regarded as something you did once a year to go on a holiday. Therefore, the demand curve not only pivoted to D2 in Figure 4.7, it may also have shifted to D3, leading to a further increase in demand (and revenue) to $Q_{r2}$.

### 4.2.3   Cost minimisation

The other side of the coin from the maximisation of revenue is, of course, the minimisation of costs. As discussed in Chapter 2, firms in the neo-classical model incur costs in the acquisition of inputs for the transformation process. These costs represent an outflow of money and need to be kept to a minimum if the firm is to achieve its aim of maximising profit. However, in the real world, these are not the only types of costs incurred by a firm; the firm incurs a whole range of costs that are not directly related to the acquisition of inputs for the production process. These types of costs we shall refer to as indirect production costs, but first we need to look more closely at the types of costs found in the neo-classical model which we shall refer to as direct production costs.

#### 4.2.3.1   Direct production costs

As with revenue, neo-classical theory imposes a constraint on the ability of firms to minimise costs that can be summarised as the current state of technology. The firm's supply curve embodies this constraint defining how much the firm is willing to produce at any given price, with the slope of this curve being determined by the elasticity of supply. As with demand, there are underlying factors that determine the actual position of the firm's supply curve within the price–quantity space and its responsiveness to price changes. Introductory microeconomic texts are less uniform in defining these than they are with the factors of demand; however, two general factors can be identified.

1. The price of inputs
2. How the inputs are combined in the transformation process.

In the neo-classical model, the cost of the inputs, as reflected in their input market prices, can be regarded as being exogenously determined (that is, largely beyond the control of the firm) by their respective factor markets. As we shall see, however, in the real world a firm actually may have a lot of influence over the price of its inputs, particularly if it is in a monopoly position or in a strong 'hostage' position as will be discussed in Chapter 5. Even so, the price of inputs is still not the decision of the buying firm and hence can still be regarded as exogenous. In order to achieve the aim of minimising costs, the firm will obviously try to obtain its inputs as cheaply as possible.

The second factor of supply is how efficiently a firm combines these inputs in the transformation process, which is quite clearly an endogenous factor. Each potential output may have a number of transformation processes by which it can be achieved. Take, for example, the trivial example of producing a hole in the ground. One method to achieve this output is to employ a large number of men with shovels to dig the hole or, alternatively, you could employ one man with a stick of dynamite to blow a hole in the ground or finally you could employ a man with a mechanical digger to dig you a hole. The method adopted depends initially on the state of technology. About 500 years ago, only the first method was available; dynamite and mechanical diggers were not technologically possible. About 150 years ago, dynamite was available so that the firm would have a choice between either of the first two methods. Today, any of the three methods are technically possible. The actual method chosen will depend upon the relative price of inputs and their efficiency.

Both Ryanair and Direct Line Insurance had a very clear strategy from the outset: to minimise their costs of production. However, as previously explained, what they both did in the process was to change the transformation process within their respective industries. In effect, by driving down costs they were able to produce a higher quantity of output at each price – three £100 'no frills' flights compared to one £300 'traditional' flight to the same destination. In demand and supply terms, they shifted the supply curve to the right.

### 4.2.3.2 Indirect production costs

In the real world, however, the cost base of a firm is far more complex than suggested by the neo-classical model. Consider Peter Wood and Michael O'Leary, the two entrepreneurs behind Direct Line Insurance and Ryanair, respectively. Neither of these two actually take part in the direct production of the services their companies are producing – Peter Wood does not answer the phone in the Direct Line Insurance call centre, neither does Michael O'Leary fly a Ryanair jet. What they did initially was organise the whole production process, a function they gradually handed over to a team of managers as their companies grew. The original entrepreneurs and their managers are paid, they are a cost to the firm but they are not a cost that is directly associated with the production of their firm's services. If Ryanair wishes to fly more planes, then it is no good employing more managers, what it needs to incur is the direct production cost of employing more pilots. Having said that if Ryanair keeps growing then the cost of employing more managers will need to be incurred, but only to manage the increased size of the firm, not to directly increase the number of flights being made. Therefore, in the real world, firms have to bear the costs related to employing managers who organise and direct the transformation process without actually getting involved directly in the process.

Secondly, firms in the real world also incur costs in competing in their output markets; these costs are again not directly related to the transformation of inputs into outputs. As identified above, the firm has various strategic tools available with which to try and maximise the revenue it can gain from selling its output. However, in using these tools a firm may incur costs whether it is running a marketing campaign, financing a R&D department or maybe even incurring short-term losses by using products as loss leaders to build up consumer loyalty. Direct Line Insurance over the years have built up a strong marketing brand with their red telephone on wheels (now also with their red mouse for online sales) that has appeared in Direct Line Insurance advertising campaigns since the late 1980s. The development of a Direct Line Insurance marketing campaign incurs additional costs for the firm that does not lead to an immediate direct increase in output. The hope is, of course, that once the campaign is launched it will lead to an increase in output, but if this happens then the firm will also have to incur extra direct production costs as it will need to increase the number of people answering the telephones.

Therefore, the cost side of a firm in the real world is in fact more complex than traditional microeconomic theory would have us believe; there are not one set of costs to be minimised but three, namely:

1. Direct production costs: the costs associated directly with the transformation process
2. Management costs: the costs associated with the need to organise and manage the transformation process
3. Competitive costs: the costs associated with competing for revenue in output markets.

### 4.2.4 The generation of profits

Figure 4.1 at the beginning of this chapter summarises the model of the firm to be used throughout the rest of this book. Across the top is the physical flow of the firm taking in resources from the industry's input markets, transforming them into goods and services and selling them onto its output markets. Related to this physical transformation process are the related monetary flows of costs leaving the firm and revenue coming into the firm. The costs are of three types: first, the costs associated directly with the transformation of inputs into outputs ($D$); secondly, the costs associated with the management of the firm's market links ($M$); finally, we have the competitive costs that are incurred in the output markets as part of the process of trying to generate revenue in competitive markets ($S$). The inflow of money into the firm is represented by the revenue generated from the selling of goods and services produced on the firm's output markets.

As in the original presentation of the neo-classical model, the firm still generates profits by ensuring that the inflow of money exceeds the outflow, $R > C$. However, $C$ is comprised of three distinct types of costs – $C = D + M + S$. Thus, to generate profits the firm must ensure that $R > D + M + S$. The profit maximising position of the firm remains as before (Section 2.1); however, what have changed are the constraints on the cost function. Previously, the only constraint was the current state of technology. This is still a constraint, but only in relation to the direct production costs. What we also have now are two other sets of constraints. First, there is a constraint relating to the management costs faced by a firm – an examination of these types of costs is the subject of Part II of this book. Secondly, there is a constraint that relates to the competitive costs ($S$). This constraint arises from the nature of the output markets that the firm is involved in. Highly competitive retail markets are likely to lead to a firm incurring a higher level of $S$ than for a firm supplying a capital component to another firm with whom the former has a long-standing contractual relationship in a fairly static market. In Part III of the book, we will deal in more depth with issues surrounding a firm's competitive costs and how they relate to the maximisation of revenue in markets.

## 4.3 | Sustaining profits

The previous section looked at how firms aim to generate profits through the process of minimising costs and maximising revenue. However, generating profits is only the beginning, what firms aim to do is not just to create profits, but to sustain these profits into the future. In the illustrative example of Ryanair and Direct Line Insurance, both companies were able to initially generate abnormal profits; however, only Ryanair has been able to sustain these profits over a significant period of time. Indeed, it is often the case that industry innovators (both in terms of products and processes) are able to generate abnormal profits; however, more often than not, they prove unable to sustain these profits beyond a relatively short space of time. Hoover and Xerox both made significant product innovations (the vacuum cleaner and photocopier, respectively) even to the extent that their names are still synonymous with the product they invented (people still talk about 'doing the Hoovering' or 'Xerox copies'). However, as with Direct Line Insurance, they were unable to sustain their large abnormal profits for very long.

Section 4.2.1 identified the two potential sources of sustainable abnormal profits that may occur in the neo-classical model – those arising from a scarcity of a particular input (Ricardian rent) and those arising from some sort of restrictions being placed on the market (monopoly rent). What both of these have in common is that they create obstacles for new firms who wish to enter the market, such as higher costs or restrictions on access to output or input markets. In other words, potential new entrants do not face a level playing field; incumbent firms enjoy advantages not available to the new entrants. These obstacles are referred to as entry barriers and, as we shall see, the creation and maintenance of entry barriers is the key to the creation and maintenance of abnormal profits.

### 4.3.1 Definition of entry barriers

The most widely known, and used, definition of an entry barrier comes from *Barriers to New Competition* written by the American economist Joe Bain (1956). Bain defined entry barriers in the following terms:

> The advantage of established sellers in an industry over potential entrant sellers, these advantages being reflected in the extent to which existing sellers can persistently raise their prices above a competitive level without attracting new firms to enter the industry.

This definition breaks down into two assertions. First, the fact that the entry barrier represents some 'advantage' which 'established sellers' (now commonly referred to as incumbents) have over 'potential entrant sellers' (now commonly referred to as new entrants). What these advantages might be will be considered in Section 4.3.2. In this section, we are going to examine the second part of the definition. At this stage, it should also be noted that the Bain definition makes no judgements about whether entry barriers are efficient or inefficient.

According to Bain's definition, the result of the existence of entry barriers is the ability of incumbent firms to 'persistently raise their prices above the competitive level without attracting new firms to enter the market'. Figure 4.8 translates this statement into diagrammatic form.

In the figure, $P_c$ represents the competitive price. This is the price that would be achieved in the long run when the market is perfectly competitive, in other words,

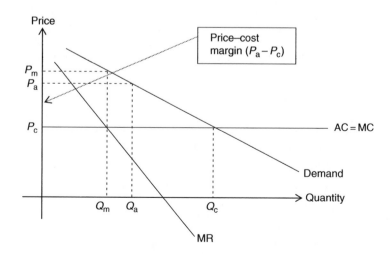

**Figure 4.8**
Price–cost margins

it is the price that equates with marginal cost (see Section 4.2.1). At this level the market is efficient, there is no wastage of resources and only normal profits are made or, put another way, there are no abnormal profits. The resulting level of output, $Q_c$, also shows the maximum output possible, given the level of demand and the costs, which firms can produce without incurring losses. $P_c$ is, therefore, the lowest possible price that could be charged; any price below $P_c$ would lead to firms leaving the market as they would be incurring losses.

$P_a$, however, shows a price that is above this minimum price. At price $P_a$, the firm is making abnormal profits equal to $P_a - P_c$ per unit sold or $(P_a - P_c)Q_a$ in total. This gap between the competitive price $P_c$ and a price above $P_c$, such as $P_a$, is referred to as a 'price–cost margin' – how far above the competitive price the actual market price is.

As discussed in Section 4.2.1, in the perfectly competitive model the price $P_a$ would not be sustainable; the fact that incumbent firms were charging a price above $P_c$ (and hence earning abnormal profits) would attract new firms into the market forcing the price down to the competitive price $P_c$. The abnormal profits disappear. If, however, the price $P_a$ was sustainable with no new firms being attracted into the market, then this would fit with Bain's definition of an entry barrier being present in the market – firms are able to 'persistently raise their prices above the competitive level without attracting new firms to enter the market'.

What is also implicit in Figure 4.8 is that the size of the gap between $P_c$ and $P_a$ shows the extent of the entry barriers present in the market. The extreme case is that of monopoly, where the entry barriers are so great that a single incumbent firm is able to charge the profit maximising price in the knowledge that no new firm can enter the market. Thus, in Figure 4.8, $P_m$ is the profit maximising price, and the gap between $P_m$ and $P_c$ represents the maximum price–cost margin. However, $P_m$ represents a maximum price achievable only by a monopolist; if any incumbent firm is able to charge a long-run price somewhere between $P_c$ and $P_m$, such as $P_a$, then it is in the position whereby it is not only creating abnormal profits, but also able to sustain these profits into the future. In strategists' terms, they have created a sustainable competitive advantage. The amount of abnormal profits made depends upon the price–cost margin that can be achieved which, in turn, depends upon the entry barriers present in the market.

## 4.3.2 Sources of entry barriers

Bain's definition of entry barriers refers to 'advantages of established sellers' as being the source of their ability to create entry barriers. In his book, Bain gives four potential types of 'advantage':

1. Absolute cost advantage
2. Economies of scale
3. Product differentiation
4. Discretionary expenditure.

### 4.3.2.1 Absolute cost advantage

By absolute cost advantage, Bain refers to cost advantages an incumbent firm might have over entrant firms. These cost advantages could take one of several forms. The incumbent firm may, for example, be enjoying monopoly rents arising from possession of patent rights or having access to secret processes. Alternatively, the type of monopoly rent arising from the sole ownership of a key source of inputs will also give rise to an absolute cost advantage for an incumbent firm. In all of these cases, an entrant firm will have to incur additional costs to try and overcome these incumbent-specific advantages. Absolute cost advantage would also cover the underlying reasons for incumbents enjoying Ricardian rent, namely incumbents having access to lower cost sources of inputs.

Another source of absolute cost advantage could be the existence of learning economies. The very fact of already being in the market producing output could mean that the incumbent firms have 'learnt' key features and aspects of operating in the market. They may, for example, know who the most reliable suppliers are or the most effective distribution system to use; in addition, they will have a workforce who have acquired the skills needed for production and who know how to operate in the input and output markets. All of this accumulated knowledge can give a cost advantage to incumbent firms over entrants who will take time to acquire the same level of knowledge that the incumbents have. Whatever the source of the absolute cost advantage, the result is the sort of disparity in cost curves reflected in Figure 4.9.

Because of the absolute cost advantage enjoyed by incumbents, new entrants would face the higher cost curve, $C_{min}^e$, as opposed to the cost curve of the incumbent, $C_{min}^i$. Therefore, the minimum price that the incumbent could charge is equal to $P_i$, whereas the lowest price an incumbent could charge is $P_e$. This disparity in costs allows the incumbent firm to charge a price anywhere up to just below

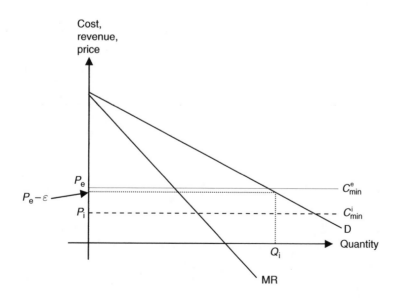

**Figure 4.9** Absolute cost advantage

$P_e$ (shown as $P_e - \varepsilon$ in Figure 4.9) without experiencing entry. The absolute cost advantage is creating an entry barrier equivalent to the price–cost margin $(P_e - P_i - \varepsilon)$. If the incumbent charged the highest possible price without attracting entry, $P_e - \varepsilon$, then it would earn an abnormal profit of $(P_e - \varepsilon) - P_i$ per unit, or $((P_e - \varepsilon) - P_i)Q_i$ in total. This is below the minimum average cost that an entrant would face and would thus be sustainable in the long run.

### 4.3.2.2 Economics of scale

Economies of scale can also be a source of advantage for the incumbent leading to the creation of an entry barrier that allows monopoly rents to be created. If the incumbent firm is supplying a large proportion of the market demand, it may well be that a new entrant will not be able to supply enough output to take full advantage of the economies of scale present in the industry.

In Figure 4.10, assume that the incumbent firm is already producing at the level of output required to take advantage of all the economies of scale available in the market, in other words it is producing at output level $Q_{mes}$. $Q_{max}$ represents the maximum output level that can be produced given the level of demand in the market. This means that for a new entrant, the most it could produce is the equivalent of $(Q_{max} - Q_{mes})$. $Q_e$ shows this level of output $((Q_{max} - Q_{mes}) = (Q_e - 0))$. At this level of output, the entrant is not producing enough to take advantage of all the economies of scale present in the market, the lowest price it can charge and cover costs is $P^e_{min}$. However, the incumbent can charge a price as low as $P^i_{min}$. Therefore, the incumbent can potentially charge any price up to just below the entrants' minimum price $(P^e - \varepsilon)$ without attracting entry. The economies of scale are creating an entry barrier and a price–cost margin equal to $(P^e_{min} - P^i_{min})$.

This type of entry barrier is commonly found in many manufacturing industries. The mass motor car industry is an extreme case where the $Q_{mes}$ figure is now so high (about one million units) that to sustain output at this level motor manufacturers have to be producing for a global market.

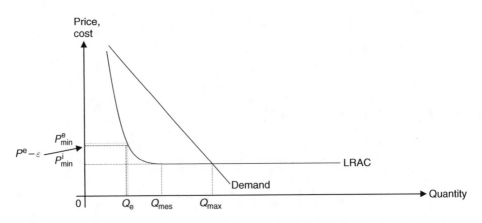

**Figure 4.10**
Economies of scale

### 4.3.2.3  Product differentiation

Product differentiation will be considered in much more detail in Chapter 9. Suffice to say for the moment that the ability of firms to differentiate their products is translated into consumer loyalty and hence gives the incumbent some control over the price charged. A new entrant with an unknown new brand of the product may have to enter the market at a lower price to overcome any consumer loyalty attached to the incumbent's brand that allows the incumbent to charge a price premium (see Section 9.1). This again gives the incumbent a price–cost margin and hence a source of abnormal profits.

### 4.3.2.4  Discretionary expenditure

The final entry barrier identified by Bain is discretionary expenditure. Discretionary expenditure in this context refers to funds made available for allocating to non-productive activities such as research and development and a marketing budget. The effect is to help support and create product differentiation and/or creating an absolute cost advantage. Take the case of an incumbent firm which has devoted large sums of money to its marketing budget to help create strong brand names for a particular product, Coca Cola, for example. The product differentiation created and the strong consumer loyalty give the Coca Cola company some control over price and create an entry barrier as discussed above. However, the continued level of marketing expenditure also creates an entry barrier for a new entrant who would have to invest heavily in marketing its own brand if it is to get a foothold in the market. Coca Cola's only serious rival is Pepsi, but Pepsi have to maintain a similar heavy commitment to marketing to stay in the market. Research and development budgets can play similar roles in some industries, such as pharmaceuticals, for example, where the rate of product change is fast and requires heavy investment in R&D to enter and stay in the market.

## 4.3.3  The contestable market hypothesis

During the 1980s, Baumol, Panzar and Willig (1982) developed the contestable market hypothesis. Whilst not specifically aimed at taking Bain's work on entry barriers a stage further, it does actually subsume Bain's work and also provides a clear theoretical basis for the analysis of entry barriers. In addition, the contestable market hypothesis also provides a broader and more realistic benchmark model of an efficient market than that provided by the model of perfect competition.

　The key to understanding the different perspective on efficiency offered by the contestable market hypothesis is actually found in Bain's original definition of an entry barrier as being 'The advantage of established sellers in an industry over *potential* entrant sellers'. Bain's definition talks about potential, not actual, entrants and this is also one of the main differences in achieving efficiency in a perfectly competitive market and in a perfectly contestable market. As discussed in Section 4.2, in the perfectly competitive market if abnormal profits are made in the short run then this attracts new entrants into the market, which in turn leads to an increase in supply which eventually forces down the price until the efficient outcome is reached and no abnormal profits are made (see Figure 4.4). In a perfectly contestable market, the outcome is the same, an efficient allocation of resources and no abnormal profits. However, there is one crucial difference in the way by which this is achieved. In a perfectly contestable market, the efficient outcome is not achieved by new firms actually entering the market, but by the market conditions being such that there are firms outside the market who could *potentially* enter the market.

### 4.3.3.1 Conditions for perfect contestability

As with a perfectly competitive market, there is a set of conditions that need to be met before we can say that a market is perfectly contestable. These are as follows:

1. Same technology
2. Zero sunk costs
3. Fully informed rational consumers, slow responding incumbent firms.

The 'same technology' assumption refers to incumbent firms having no (in Bain's terms) absolute cost advantage. New entrants into a market would face exactly the same costs as incumbent firms. The second condition concerns the costs involved in setting up production. Sunk costs are sometimes referred to as non-recoverable costs – costs incurred before production can take place or depreciation costs that are lost when production is terminated. The second condition, therefore, means that all costs are incurred only during production. In the original formulation of the model, it is emphasised that the condition refers to sunk costs, not economies of scale. However, in practice it is difficult to envisage a situation where the existence of sunk costs does not lead to the existence of economies of scale, so this second condition is usually taken as meaning there are no economies of scale present.

Finally, for a market to be perfectly contestable, assumptions are made about the behaviour of incumbent firms and market consumers. In terms of the incumbent firms the assumption is that, for whatever reason, they cannot respond quickly to entrant firms whereas consumers are assumed to be completely rational and have full and perfect information. Thus, when a new firm enters the market and charges a lower price, consumers will automatically switch to the entrants' product; however, the incumbent firms cannot respond immediately and so there is a time lag before they can lower their prices.

### 4.3.3.2 Contestability and efficiency

When the above three conditions hold in a market, then the market is said to be perfectly contestable and, as a result, the only long-run equilibrium possible is the efficient outcome with price equal to marginal cost. Why does this come about? Consider Figure 4.11.

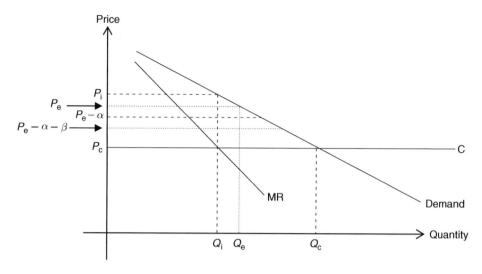

**Figure 4.11**
Hit-and-run tactics

In a market which demonstrates the three conditions outlined above, the only possible price an incumbent can charge is $P_c$, the competitive and efficient price. If the incumbent behaved like a monopolist and charged the profit maximising price $P_i$ where MC = MR, then it would be subjected to what is referred to as 'hit-and-run' tactics. Condition 1 ensures that the incumbent monopolist has no cost advantage over new entrants – entrants would face the same cost curve C in Figure 4.11. Condition 2 also ensures that the costs to entrants of entering and leaving the market are zero. Given these assumptions, a new entrant could simply enter the market and slightly undercut the incumbent by charging a price $P_e$. Condition 3 ensures that all consumers know about the new low-priced entrant and act in a rational manner by switching to the new entrant's product. Condition 3 also assumes that the incumbent firm cannot respond immediately. The result is that during the time lag before the incumbent responds and lowers their price, the entrant takes on the market and makes abnormal profits of $(P_e - P_c)Q_e$.

Assume that eventually the incumbent responds and charges $(P_e - \alpha)$ under-cutting the price of the entrant. All that will happen is that the entrant simply lowers its price again to say $(P_e - \alpha - \beta)$ and, again, takes all the abnormal profits. Only when the incumbent charges the competitive price $P_c$ and there are no more abnormal profits to be made will the entrant leave the market (that is, 'run'). What the model shows is that when faced with a perfectly contestable market the only price an incumbent can charge is the competitive price $P_c$, and the only profits that can be made are normal profits. If it tries to charge a price above $P_c$ in an attempt to generate abnormal profits then it will be subjected to the hit-and-run tactics by entrant firms, as outlined above, and forced back to $P_c$.

There are several significant consequences that come out of the perfectly contest-able model. First, the efficient outcome is arrived at irrespective of the number of firms in the market. Even when the market is a monopoly, provided the three conditions for a perfectly contestable market hold, the market will be economic-ally efficient; the monopolist will only earn normal profits. This is, of course, in direct contrast to the perfectly competitive model. The driving force behind perfect competition is the number of firms in a market with there being a direct inverse relationship between the number of firms and the efficiency of the market: the fewer the firms, the less efficient the market will be. However, by way of contrast, the driving force behind the perfectly contestable market is the potential for entry and not actual entry. What drives efficiency in the market is the ease with which entrants can practice hit-and-run tactics or, put another way, how easy it is to enter and leave the market. The efficiency of a market relies not on the number of firms, but on how easy it is for potential entrants to enter the market. Indeed, we can say that the perfectly competitive market is, in fact, a special case of a perfectly contestable market.

### 4.3.3.3   Contestability and entry barriers

These efficiency issues and the resulting implication for competition policy will be discussed in more detail in Chapters 13 and 14. What is of more interest in the present context is a second consequence of the perfectly contestable market in that it provides us with benchmark model for a market with no entry barriers. In effect, the three conditions lead to a market where there are no obstacles for firms who wish to enter the market. The three conditions for a perfectly contestable market actually provide us with a means for the classification of sources of entry barriers.

When one of the conditions for a contestable market does not hold, then there will be entry barriers present which incumbent firms can exploit to create and sustain abnormal profits. Thus we have potentially three classes of entry barriers that are directly related to the three conditions for a perfectly contestable market. Entry barriers can arise from

1.  Differences in technology (Class 1)
2.  Existence of sunk costs (Class 2)
3.  Irrational imperfectly informed consumers – slow responding incumbent firms (Class 3).

If any of the above situations exist in a market, then the market is not perfectly contestable and an entry barrier will be created which will be reflected in a price–cost margin and the incumbent firm will enjoy the benefit of sustained abnormal profits.

As stated earlier, the contestable market model and its resulting implications for entry barriers do not replace the work of Bain but rather subsume it. Bain's four class of entry barriers fits into the framework. Absolute cost advantage is obviously closely linked with the first class of entry barrier above. Economies of scale is also closely aligned with the second class above; as discussed previously it is difficult to conceive of a case where there are economies of scale present without the existence of sunk costs. Bain's third and fourth sources (product differentiation and discretionary expenditure) are subsumed in the third class above. The use of product differentiation to generate consumer loyalty can be regarded as trying to ensure that consumers act in an irrational way by not choosing the lowest priced product on offer (see Chapter 9). Similarly, the use of discretionary expenditure to, for example, develop new products can be viewed as the incumbents trying to keep ahead of potential entrants to avoid the time lags required for condition 3 of a perfectly contestable market.

### 4.3.4 Generating and sustaining profits

In Section 4.2, we discussed the creation of profits or, strictly speaking abnormal profits by firms in terms of the need for firms to minimise their costs and maximise their revenues and hence, hopefully, creating a positive monetary inflow. Figure 4.1 summarised the model of the firm that has been developed through the last three chapters. As discussed in Section 4.2, the firm generates profits if Revenue > Costs, where $C$ has three elements: costs associated directly with the transformation process ($D$); costs arising from the need for a firm to 'manage' its market relations ($M$); and costs arising from the competitive strategies adopted in its output markets ($S$). However, the generation of profits is only part of the story; a firm's aim is not only to generate profits, but to be able to sustain them in the long run.

The theoretical issues discussed in this section have revolved around two models of an efficient market: the model of perfect competition and the contestable market hypothesis. Both models lead to the conclusion that the source of long-run abnormal profits is entry barriers, whether of the Ricardian or of the monopoly type. The idea of a price–cost margin was introduced and used as a proxy measure of the height of entry barriers: the further the market price is above the efficient price the greater the entry barriers to the market. The major difference between the two models of market efficiency is the means by which price–cost margins can be reduced. In the perfectly competitive market, this happens by increasing the number of firms entering the market, whereas in the contestable market it is achieved by ensuring that the conditions are such that new firms may enter the market if incumbent firms are making abnormal profits. The perfectly contestable market, in effect, provides us with a model of a market with no entry barriers. The three conditions for a contestable market translate into the three classes of entry barriers discussed above.

Therefore, to summarise, if a firm is making long-run abnormal profits then, by definition, it must be generating more revenue from its output markets than incurring direct and indirect costs. In addition, it is operating in a market where there are entry barriers preventing the market from being perfectly contestable. Section 4.3.3 established three classes of entry barriers based upon the conditions for a perfectly contestable market. However, let us look at potential sources of abnormal profits from the perspective of the firm.

If you were a manager of a firm how could you see your firm generating abnormal profits? Consider again the simple equation we suggested at the end of Section 4.2.4 as defining our condition for a firm making abnormal profits:

$$R > D + M + S$$

This simple equation suggests two immediate sources of abnormal profits:

1. By being a lower cost producer (minimising costs)
2. By generating higher revenue (maximising revenue).

In addition, a third which arises from the whole transformation process:

3. By undertaking the transformation process more efficiently.

However, what Section 4.2.4 has shown is that if you wish to protect and sustain these abnormal profits then you will need to create entry barriers that allow you to protect your cost–price margin. Let us consider each potential source of abnormal profits in turn.

### 4.3.4.1   The firm is a lower cost producer

This source of abnormal profit relates back to the input/supply side of Figure 4.1. If, for some reason, the firm is enjoying an absolute cost advantage over other firms then it will be operating on a lower cost curve than its rivals and, as a consequence, will be earning a higher level of profits. In other words, for the firm enjoying an absolute cost advantage the $D$ element of the cost function in Figure 4.1 is less than that for other firms. Reasons why a firm may have an absolute cost advantage have been discussed in Sections 4.2 and 4.3 (for example, declining productivity of inputs, economies of scale, learning economies).

### 4.3.4.2   The firm is generating higher revenue

Another source of abnormal profits comes from the other side of the firm's transformation process, from the output/demand side. If a firm is able to generate higher levels of revenue by, for example, charging higher prices than its rivals, then this may also be a source of abnormal profits. The link between higher revenue and higher levels of abnormal profits may, however, not be as straightforward as that between production costs and abnormal profits. In order to generate the extra revenue from, for example, charging higher prices, the firm is likely to incur the indirect cost $S$, the competitive cost. The ability of a firm to charge a higher price may be the result of product differentiation and a supporting marketing campaign. To ensure this translates into higher levels of abnormal profit, the firm must ensure that the cost $S$ is less than the resulting increase in sales revenue – it is no good spending £2m on an advertising campaign if only £1.7m of extra revenue is created.

### 4.3.4.3   The firm is undertaking the transformation process more efficiently

The final potential source of abnormal profit comes from within the firm itself. If the firm is able to undertake the transformation process more efficiently than its rivals, then this may also lead to abnormal profits. The reasons for being more efficient are many and varied, for example, the firm may organise the transformation process more efficiently and hence reduce $M$, or the internal culture of the firm allows the production of more reliable products that command premium prices. This source of abnormal profits will be explored in Chapter 7.

However, as raised earlier, if the abnormal profits created are to be sustainable in the long run then there must be entry barriers in place that are preventing the creation of a contestable market. Specifically, there will need to be one or more of the following:

1. Industry/input entry barriers to protect sources of lower production costs
2. Market/output entry barriers to protect sources of higher revenue
3. Firm-specific entry barriers that protect a more efficient transformation process.

The rest of this book makes use of the distinction between three different general types of entry barriers that are open to, and used by, firms in the real world in order to sustain levels of abnormal profits, namely

1. Structural entry barriers
2. Strategic entry barriers
3. Resource entry barriers.

### 4.3.4.4 Structural entry barriers

The ability of firms to sustain abnormal profits by being a lower cost producer suggests that there are entry barriers on the input/supply side that are preventing the entry of new firms. One major source of industry entry barriers arises through the actual structure of the industry itself creating what we shall refer to as structural entry barriers. These have already been discussed in detail in Sections 4.2 and 4.3 – Ricardian rent, economies of scale and learning economies are all examples of this type of entry barrier. Structural entry barriers allow for absolute cost advantages enjoyed by a firm to be sustained in the long run.

The distinguishing feature of structural entry barriers is that they can be regarded as 'innocent' in that they arise through firms trying to operate more efficiently. All of the types of structural entry barriers listed above arise from the firm trying to operate more efficiently, they are not put in place deliberately by a firm to make entry into the industry more difficult. A firm will try to operate at the lowest point of the long-run average cost curve to take advantage of the cost savings afforded by economies of scale, the fact that it may make it more difficult for another firm to enter the industry (Figure 4.10) is an innocent (but potentially favourable) by-product. In relation to the class of entry barriers, most structural entry barriers relate to Classes 1 and 2 – absolute cost advantages and economies of scale.

### 4.3.4.5 Strategic entry barriers

Strategic entry barriers can occur on both the input and output sides of Figure 4.1. What distinguish them from structural entry barriers are that they are deliberate restrictions put on entry into a market by an incumbent firm. In other words, the entry barriers do not arise through firms trying to be more cost efficient but through firms consciously trying to protect sources of abnormal profits by preventing entry to the market or industry. There are a whole variety of ways in which firms can do this using the endogenous decision variables identified in Table 4.1.

The imposition of these strategic entry barriers in its output markets is the source of a firm's competitive cost $S$ in Figure 4.1. Most of the entry barriers used in this strategic manner are of a Class 3 type. The creation of strong brand names, for example, to create consumer loyalty, thus enabling the incumbent to charge higher prices than new entrants, has all the hallmarks of a strategic entry barrier: the firm incurs a marketing cost ($S$). The brand name has nothing to do with improving cost efficiency; in addition, the decision to develop the brand name is a conscious strategic decision by the firm motivated partly by the wish to prevent entry into the market by new firms. Strategic entry barriers will be looked at in more detail in Chapter 9 when we consider the strategic behaviour of firms.

### 4.3.4.6 Resource entry barriers

As discussed above, a firm may be creating abnormal profits through its ability to undertake the transformation process more efficiently than its rivals. If this is to become a source of sustained profits, then the source of the efficiency must be unique and not able to be imitated by the firm's competitors. If, for example, the advantage was coming from an ability to achieve a lower $M$ cost which was based on the firm's managers having a long-standing and close relationship with some suppliers, then this may be difficult for a new entrant to achieve. The new entrant may be treated with more suspicion than the incumbent and may therefore incur higher transaction costs in the arrangement of supply contracts. The whole issue of resource entry barriers is closely tied in with the resource-based view of the firm that will be developed in Chapter 7.

## 4.4 | Review and further reading

This chapter has extended the review of the neo-classical firm begun in Chapter 2 to look at the concepts of cost, revenue and profit in more depth. The analysis has focused on the idea that firms are seeking not only to create profits, but also to sustain these profits in the long run. The conclusion reached is that firms achieve sustained profits by the erection of entry barriers based on low cost, internal efficiency or strategic behaviour. Returning to the two firms discussed at the outset of this chapter, it is obvious that both Ryanair and Direct Line Insurance achieved their initial high levels of abnormal profit through the achievement of significantly lower costs of production and the creation of a structural entry barrier. In terms of the type of entry barriers, the abnormal profits were achieved through gaining an absolute cost advantage (type 1). However, as noted previously, only Ryanair was able to sustain abnormal profits, suggesting that it also managed to create an entry barrier which was more enduring than that of Direct Line Insurance. Put another way, the market for motor insurance proved to be more contestable than the short-haul European airline industry. The reasons for this will be looked at in Chapter 7.

This chapter has also presented an expanded model of the firm that recognises that firms incur not only direct production costs, but also indirect costs associated with the running of the firm (management costs) and competing in output markets (competitive costs). Parts II and III explore the sources of, and issues that arise from, these non-direct costs. Part II develops the notion of management costs and the underlying areas of transaction cost economics and resource-based theories of the firm. Part III looks in more detail at the idea that a firm can be both proactive and interdependent in its behaviour causing it to act strategically in its input and output markets.

As with Chapters 2 and 3, all introductory microeconomics texts will deal with the detail of costs, revenues and market structure – again Sloman and Sutcliffe (2003) and Begg, Fischer and Dornbusch (2003) are good starting points. For contestable market theory, see Baumol, Panzar and Willig (1982).

## 4.5 | Student exercises

### 4.5.1 Review exercises and points for discussion

1. Provide brief and clear definitions of the following key terms and concepts as used in this chapter:

   a. Normal profit
   b. Abnormal profit
   c. Ricardian rent
   d. Monopoly rent
   e. Endogenous demand variables
   f. Exogenous demand variables
   g. Entry barriers
   h. Price–cost margin
   i. A contestable market
   j. Hit-and-run tactics
   k. Non-direct production costs
   l. Structural entry barriers.

2. For many years Amy has been working as a reporter on her local newspaper. She currently earns £2000 net per month. She is increasingly frustrated by the constraints imposed on her by working for a small local newspaper and feels that she has sufficient experience and contacts to begin working for herself as a freelance reporter and writer. By doing so, she estimates that she could increase her monthly income to about £2500 per month net.

   a. What would Amy's normal and abnormal profits be if she was to freelance?
   b. What non-direct production costs might be involved if Amy was working as a freelance?

3. Figures 4.3–4.5 show the familiar equilibria for the market structures of prefect competition and monopoly. How would these diagrams alter if each of the five underlying neo-classical assumptions did not hold?

4. Section 4.3.3 classified entry barriers by source (differences in technology, sunk costs and informational issues) and Section 4.3.4 by type (structural, strategic resource). How do these apply to Ryanair and Direct Line Insurance?

5. What are likely to be the non-direct production costs for both Ryanair and Direct Line Insurance?

## 4.5.2 Application exercise

Apple computers introduced the iPod portable MP3 music player in 2001. Other MP3 music players existed at the time but they tended to rely on the use of flash memory and hence their flexibility and the number of songs that could be held were limited. The iPod had a number of features that set it apart. First, it had an integral hard drive which allowed many more songs to be stored (initially 1000). Secondly, from the second model onwards, a unique 'wheel' system was incorporated for operating the iPod replacing the old system found on other MP3 players which had hardly changed since the Sony Walkman of the 1980s. To further support the iPod, Apple also invested heavily in their iTunes website which allowed users to (legally) download individual music tracks for as little as 99 cents (67p). The iPod became an instant success. According to a report in the *Financial Times* in August 2006 Apple sold nine million iPods in the USA alone between April and June 2006 and had a 75.6 per cent share of the US market for MP3 players. The effect on Apple's profits has been dramatic. The table below summarises Apple's fourth quarter profits since 2002.

| Year | 2002 | 2003 | 2004 | 2005 | 2006 |
|---|---|---|---|---|---|
| Profits ($m) | –43 | 44 | 106 | 430 | 546 |

*Source*: apple.com website

The above is a brief outline of the iPod story; you may wish to supplement this by further research on the Internet.

a. Identify the sources of Apple's success in creating an overwhelming market share for the iPod in the USA.

b. What types of entry barriers do Apple appear to have created?

c. Is Apple going to be able to sustain their current level of market dominance, and the high levels of profits, into the future?

# Managing the Transformation Process

# Transaction Costs 5

5

## LEARNING OUTCOMES

On completion of this chapter the reader should be able to

- Define and explain the concept of transaction costs
- Explain the concept of a governance structure in relation to a chain of production
- Identify the sources of transaction costs and how they help explain the existence of firms

## KEY NEW CONCEPTS

| | | |
|---|---|---|
| Chain of production | Governance structures | Specific assets |
| Transaction cost | Moral hazard | Value chain |
| Vertical integration | | |

## KEY NEW MODELS

Organisational failure framework          Transaction-specific hostage model

## MODELS AND CONCEPTS DEVELOPED FURTHER

| | | |
|---|---|---|
| Opportunism | Bounded rationality | Transaction cost economics |
| Asymmetric information | Uncertainty and complexity | Transformation process |

The Bear Factory is a firm that sells teddy bears and various teddy bear accessories such as costumes, sunglasses and snorkelling kit. Their shops have a very interesting way of organising the sale of their principal product. When you go into one of the shops to purchase a teddy bear, you do not simply pick a complete bear off the shelf. What happens is that you select from a range of three basic bear types, but at this point all you have is an unstuffed bear body and head. What you have to do is first, take your bear to another part of the shop where an impressive looking machine will stuff the body of the bear (you have three choices: soft, squiggy or hard). Once the bear is stuffed, you move to another part of the shop where the bear is stitched up (and you can, if you wish, insert a red-cloth heart). Finally, you move to the checkout where your new bear is given a birth certificate and is boxed and, of course, you pay for him.

What is interesting from an economics point of view about the way the Bear Factory shops are organised is that they illustrate a simple linear production system that has three distinct processes – stuffing, stitching and boxing. We can also see many of the features of the neo-classical firm discussed in detail in Chapter 2. Each of the production processes has a set of inputs (there are no raw material inputs used): shop assistants (labour); the semi-complete bear and the stuffing machine, stitching needle and thread and the box (all capital). Figure 5.1 shows this simple production system.

We begin at the top of the diagram with the unstuffed body and head of the teddy bear, this then goes through three separate transformation processes until, at the bottom of the diagram, we have the final finished product which the customer takes from the shop.

The costs of the system are reflected in the unstuffed bear, the wages of the shop and checkout assistants, the cost of purchasing and running the stuffing machine,

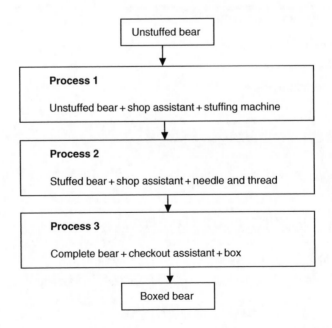

**Figure 5.1**
Production system in a Bear Factory shop

the needles and thread, the box and birth certificate as well as the rent and running costs of the shop. The revenue from the system is, of course, the price paid by the customer. From the point of view of the owners of the Bear Factory, the hope is that the costs of running the production system is less than the revenue gained from the sale of the teddy bears.

However, this example also illustrates the features of the expanded model of the firm as developed in Chapter 4 and represented in Figure 4.1. Each Bear Factory shop will have a shop manager who will hire the shop assistants, oversee the ordering of stock, oversee the organisation of the shop floor and undertake many other activities connected with running a busy city centre shop. What the shop manager is unlikely to do is to operate the stuffing machine, stitch the bear or box the bear – in other words they are not a direct part of the production system shown in Figure 5.1. What the shop manager does is organising and enabling the production and sale of bears to take place – his salary would count as an indirect management cost ($M$ in Figure 4.1). Similarly, we can also see the other indirect cost, $S$ or competitive cost, in the fact that the Bear Factory shops all have a strong brand image, have eye-catching displays as well as run an entertaining website. Again all of these costs are not directly related to the production system shown in Figure 5.1.

In a neo-classical world, both $S$ and $M$ would be zero – all costs would relate directly to the transformation process. However, in the real world inhabited by the Bear Factory, the five neo-classical assumptions do not hold. The need to incur the competitive costs, $S$, arises from several sources. First, the consumers do not have perfect knowledge. When they decide they wish to purchase a teddy bear, they will not necessarily know all the firms that sell teddy bears or the prices they charge. Typically, they will go to a local town and search for a shop selling teddy bears – the Bear Factory needs to promote their product so that the customer knows they exist. Indeed, it may well be the case that many customers do not know they wish to buy a teddy bear until they enter the Bear Factory shop itself. This, again, is a function of the promotional activity of the shop to persuade passing customers to enter the shop and purchase a teddy bear, even though 10 minutes before they did not even know they wanted one! Another source of the competitive cost $S$ is the need to differentiate the Bear Factory teddy bears from their rival teddy bears – the products are not homogenous.

The indirect costs related to competitive and strategic behaviour of firms is the subject of Part III of this book. What we are concerned with in this chapter and the next is the other type of indirect cost – management cost or $M$ in Figure 4.1. Consider Figure 5.1 again. We have clearly identified three distinct and separate production processes – stuffing, stitching and boxing. From our perspective, it is obvious why it makes sense for these three production processes to take place in close proximity to each other within the confines of a single shop – they are three closely related activities and it is part of the attraction of buying your bear from the Bear Factory. However, in theory, each of the three production processes (stuffing, stitching and boxing) could take place in separate firms with the customer purchasing the semi-complete bear from each firm and taking it to the next firm in the chain. In this case, there would be no need for the shop manager – each stage of the production process would be organised by the persons operating the stuffing machine, doing the stitching and boxing the bear. This raises a number of questions. What is different about the real world that makes more sense to co-locate these three processes in a shop with a shop manager? Also, why does the Bear Factory only include these three processes in their shops? Why not go further back in the production system to the processes involved with the cutting of the fabric from which the bear is made and the attaching of the head?

The answer to these questions rests on recognising that the neo-classical assumptions do not always hold in the real world and that firms have other types of costs to minimise other than their direct costs of production. The source of management costs lies within the area of economics referred to as 'transaction cost economics', an explanation of which is the main purpose of this chapter. As we shall see, transaction cost economics provides us with not only an explanation of management costs (the subject matter of the next chapter), but also a rationale for the existence of firms in the first place.

## 5.1　The firm and the chain of production

In Chapter 2, the firm was presented as being at the centre of the production process taking in inputs and transforming these into outputs. In most cases, however, each individual firm is part of a network of other firms. Each capital input, and some land and labour inputs, will be the output of another firm. Similarly, each firm's output becomes an input for another firm, unless the customer for the output is in fact the final customer, as we saw in Figure 5.1 in relation to the semi-complete teddy bear passing through the Bear Factory shop. Various analogies have been used to describe this interlocking network, the final outcome of which is a consumer good or service. One common analogy is to refer to a stream of production. The stream begins at its source with the basic raw materials and flows down from this start with tributaries adding to the flow or the stream splitting off into separate streams, finally reaching its destination that is the final product sold to the consumer at the end of the stream. Another analogy commonly used in the strategic management literature is of a chain, or more specifically a value chain. Each stage within the production network adds value, meaning the output from each stage is worth more than the sum of the inputs. The idea of value creation is briefly discussed in Section 1.2; the value chain is an extension of Figure 1.3 across the whole production network from source to outlet. Chapter 12 will look in more depth at the idea of value and the value chain.

For our purposes, in this chapter, we are going to use a different analogy. The network that produces a final consumer good or service can be regarded as a chain of production. The strategists' value chain is a monetary flow, whereas the chain of production is a physical flow, it shows how different transformation processes link together to produce the final product at the end of the chain. Further, we are going to deconstruct the network down into its individual production processes, which may or may not correspond with individual firms. Figure 5.1 shows just such a chain of production, or more accurately the latter end of a chain of production as the stages prior to the three processes that take place within the shop are not shown.

### 5.1.1    A simple chain of production – the production of bread

To illustrate the basic concepts of transaction cost economics, we shall leave the Bear Factory on one side for now and use a simplified production chain relating to the production of bread. At the start of this production chain is the production process 'growing wheat'. Using the input–production–output framework of Chapter 2, this production process may be represented as shown in Figure 5.2.

The next stage in the chain of production is to produce the flour, with the wheat output of Process 1 becoming one of the inputs (land) into this second stage of production. The third production stage is baking the bread (where, again, the output of Stage 2, flour, becomes the capital input) and finally Stage 4 at the end of the production chain is the shop selling the bread to the final customer. Figure 5.3 shows the full production chain for the production of bread.

The full chain is made up of four separate and distinct production processes: wheat growing, flour milling, baking and retailing. Each production process has its own set of inputs that are transformed into the desired output by a specific and different production function, as shown in Figure 5.3. What links the chain together is that the output of the four processes – wheat, flour, bread and the retailing of bread – feeds into the next stage of the chain of production as an input. The output at the end of the chain is the final good which is then consumed by the purchaser of the bread from the retail outlet.

Figure 5.3 shows this chain of production as a linear progression; however, all that is represented here is the central chain of core processes that are related to the production of bread. In fact, each input into each of the four production processes on the left-hand side of the diagram will have a separate chain of production associated with it. Take, for example, the inputs into Process 2, milling the flour. Apart from Process 1 in the diagram that produces the wheat, there will be a separate production chain that had led to the building of the flour mill. In addition, the millers themselves will be the output of an education production chain which has provided them with the knowledge and skills necessary to operate the flour mill.

Similarly, some of the outputs on the right-hand side of the diagram may actually become inputs in another production chain altogether, for example, the wheat

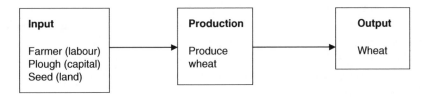

**Figure 5.2** Wheat production process

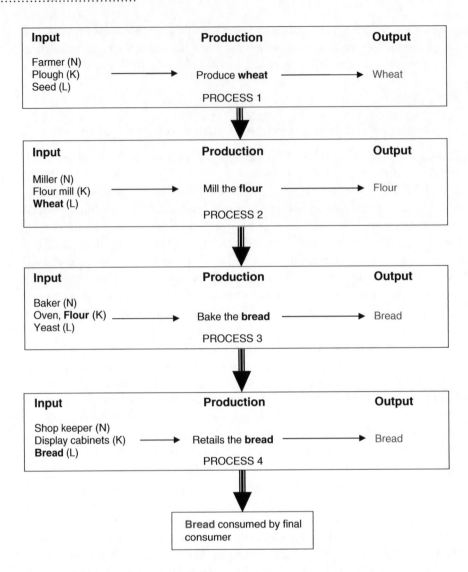

**Figure 5.3** Chain of production for bread making

may enter a chain where the final output is chocolate biscuits. Hence, even though Figure 5.3 represents a linear chain of production, this is only a part of what, even in this highly simplified example, is in fact a much more complex network of production processes, all feeding into this central core aimed at producing bread.

### 5.1.2 Transactions – the links in the chain

However, there is a question that arises from Figure 5.3, how does the wheat from Process 1 become the input into Process 2 or, indeed, the input into another production process altogether? More generally, how do all the inputs become involved in this production chain and what determines where the outputs go? In other words, what form do the links, or 'transactions', in the production chain (both the vertical and the horizontal) take?

This takes us to the core of what is known as 'transaction cost economics'. What, in this context, is actually meant by the term 'transaction'? Williamson, one of the key writers in the area, defined a transaction in the following terms:

> A transaction occurs when a good or service is transferred across a technologically separable interface. (Williamson, 1985, p. 1)

In our example, there are four 'technologically separable' processes and four corresponding 'transfers' or transactions: transfer of wheat from the farmer to the miller; transfer of flour from the miller to the baker; transfer of bread from the baker to the shop; and finally transfer of bread from the shop to the final consumer. In other words, the links in our bread-making chain of production are transactions – the means by which the output from one production process becomes an input into another.

Figure 5.4 represents a more generalised version of Figure 5.3. Any chain of production can be represented as a series of distinct production processes linked by a series of transactions.

Transaction cost economics is concerned with examining the nature of these transaction links and what they can tell us about the nature of a firm. The rest of the chapter examines what determines the nature of the individual transaction links and how these relate to the nature of the firm and finally, the next chapter provides us with a source for our management costs in Figure 4.1.

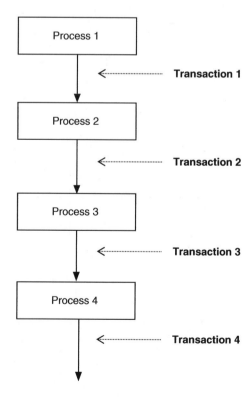

**Figure 5.4** Generic chain of production

## 5.2 Governance structures and the chain of production

### 5.2.1 Possible governance structures

There are three general means by which the four production processes in Figure 5.3 can be linked to form the production chain for the selling of bread:

1. A market transaction
2. An internal transaction within a firm (intra-firm transaction)
3. A market transaction governed by a contract (contractual transaction).

Williamson refers to these as being transaction governance structures, the means by which the output of one production process becomes the input into another. Figure 5.5 summarises the nature of each of these three governance structures.

#### 5.2.1.1 Free-market transactions

The first type of governance structure is where the transaction takes place over a free market. The firm producing the output (the seller) supplies the market to meet a corresponding demand for this output, either by another firm as an input into its production process or by the final consumer. Thus, in our example, the farmer producing the wheat through Process 1 supplies his output onto the wheat market. On the other side of the transaction, the miller enters the market looking to buy wheat to use as an input into his production process. The transaction takes place at a price determined by the relative levels of supply and demand which in turn rely on the two sides of the market maximising their respective objective

| Governance structure | | |
|---|---|---|
| **Free market** | **Intra-firm** | **Market contract** |
| Independent buyers and sellers | 'Buyers' and 'sellers' within the same firm | Independent buyers and sellers |
| Co-ordinated by market price | Co-ordination by management within the firm | Co-ordination by mutually agreed contract |

*Nature of the transaction*

**Figure 5.5**
Different types of governance structures

functions – if both buyer and seller are firms then they are maximising profits, if the buyers are the final consumers then they are maximising their utility.

The whole process outlined above is completely decentralised and anonymous, the farmer and the miller may never actually meet or even know who each other are. The price at which the transaction takes place (which becomes the farmer's revenue and one of the miller's costs) is determined where the market demand equals the market supply. This is the market process described by Adam Smith as the 'invisible hand' and is usually represented by the familiar method of demand and supply curves.

### 5.2.1.2  Intra-firm (internal) transactions

An alternative governance structure is for the transaction to take place within a single firm. In this case, the output produced by one production process becomes the input for the following production process, but the whole transaction takes place within the same firm. Managers within a firm co-ordinating the link between the two production processes replace the co-ordination of buyers and sellers that previously took place by the market fixing a price. In effect, the internal management of the firm directing the transaction replaces the decentralised market transaction. In contrast to the market transaction, the internal transaction is a planned and conscious decision taken by the management of the firm. The level of output produced by the first production process will be determined by the firm's management in response to that required as input into the second production process. There may be a price but this is likely to be purely based upon the cost of production and will be known and used only within the firm for internal accounting purposes.

Returning to our example, assume that the miller also bakes his own bread, thus production Processes 2 and 3 in Figure 5.3 take place within the same firm. The amount of flour produced by the milling process will be determined by the miller, not in response to the price he can obtain by selling the flour on an external market, but by the quantity of bread he wishes to produce. The transaction of making the output of Process 2 into an input for Process 3 is done within the single combined miller/baker firm, the functions of 'buyer' and 'seller' are carried out within the firm. Coase (1937) contrasted these intra-firm transactions with Smith's famous 'invisible hand' description of market transactions by referring to them as the 'visible hand'.

### 5.2.1.3  Market-contract transaction

The final means of governing a transaction lies somewhere between the other two, a contract. In this case, the link between two production processes does take place via an external market, but the transaction is governed by a legal agreement between the output sellers and the input buyers. Thus, the providers of the two production processes remain independent firms, but the link is coordinated via a negotiated agreement that, at a minimum, will determine the quantity exchanged and price. Thus the transaction between milling and baking in Figure 5.3 could take place between an independent miller and an independent baker, but be governed by a contract specifying the quantity of flour to be delivered to the baker, when it will be delivered and how much the baker will pay the miller. However, this minimal contract does leave both parties open to possible abuse by the other; the miller may not deliver on time or the baker may not pay on time. Therefore, in practice even a simple contract of this type is likely to have additional safeguards built in, such as specifying penalties for late delivery and, similarly, for late payment.

The decentralised free market is the governance structure found in neo-classical economics and lies at the heart of any course in microeconomic theory. However, to operate as effectively as described above the five assumptions of the neo-classical framework, as explained in Chapter 2, have to hold – maximising behaviour, holistic action, global rationality, full and perfect information and homogeneity. If any of these assumptions does not hold then the establishment of a single market-clearing price becomes harder to achieve. For example, the miller in Figure 5.3 may be faced with hundreds of potential farmers as suppliers of the wheat he needs, as a result it is unlikely that he will know all the prices on offer and he may make a mistake and buy from a farmer who is not actually the lowest cost supplier. In the real world, the completely free market found in neo-classical theory is almost non-existent, transactions tend to be governed by either market contracts or take place within a firm. Even apparently free-market transactions undertaken by consumers every day, such as buying groceries or clothes, are governed by implicit contracts; you can return goods that prove to be substandard, for example.

### 5.2.2 Configurations of the chain of production

The three different types of governance structures shown in Figure 5.5 when applied to a particular production chain give rise to a range of possible configurations of that chain of production. For the moment, we will treat the free-market and market-contract governance structures as one 'market' transaction. Figure 5.6 gives three possible configurations for our production chain relating to the core processes involved in the production of bread.

#### 5.2.2.1 Configuration 1 – all transactions governed by a market

Here, all the links in the chain of production are governed via external markets. Thus, the miller obtains his wheat input from the wheat market that is supplied by a wheat-producing farmer. The miller then supplies his output to the flour market where it is purchased by the baker who supplies his bread to the bread market where it is purchased by the bread shop. Finally, at the bottom of the chain of production the bread is sold over another market to the final consumer. Thus, each of the four production processes equates to an independent firm, run by an owner-manager who organises that firm's particular product process and the whole chain of production is organised via a series of external market transactions.

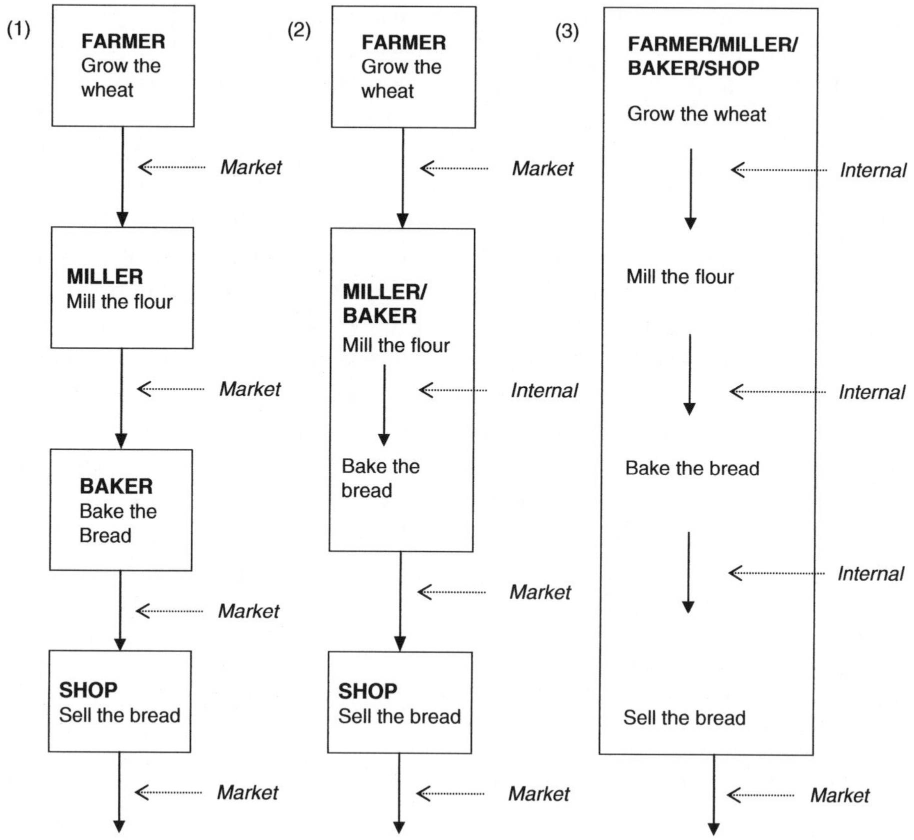


**Figure 5.6** Possible production chain configurations

### *5.2.2.2 Configuration 2 – transactions governed by mixture of market and internal*

Configuration 2 gives a different arrangement for the governance of the same chain of production. This time the link between the milling and baking processes is carried out within a unified miller/baker firm. The unified firm still obtains its wheat from the wheat market and still sells its bread to the bread market, but the transaction linking the milling and baking processes is now internal within the unified firm. Thus, configuration 2 has three firms as opposed to four in configuration 1, the milling and baking firms have become vertically integrated.

### *5.2.2.3 Configuration 3 – transactions internalised within single firm*

Finally, consider configuration 3. In this configuration, the entire production chain has been vertically integrated into one combined farmer/miller/baker/shop firm. All four production processes are carried on inside the single firm with all the transaction links being internalised within the combined firm. The only market transaction left is that at the bottom of the chain where the bread is bought by the final consumer.

Other configurations for the production chain are possible. However, the big question that needs to be answered is what will determine the actual configuration of the bread-making production chain shown in Figure 5.6? More generally, why are some chains of production fully vertically integrated as in configuration 3 whereas others are totally disaggregated as in configuration 1. One answer from neo-classical theory relates to monopoly power and the desire of firms to try and control the supply of vital inputs for the purposes of restricting entry to their markets or keeping costs lower so as to maximise monopoly rent (Chapter 4). This behaviour can also be viewed as being strategic and will be looked at in more detail in Part III of this book. However, the rest of this chapter focuses on the transaction cost approach to answering the question of what determines the configuration of a particular chain of production. The transaction cost approach presents the final configuration of a production chain as being determined by the familiar economists' principle of efficiency. Whether our bread-making chain of production is governed by a series of markets or by a fully vertically integrated firm, or some combination in between, depends upon which configuration is actually the most cost effective.

### 5.2.3 Production configurations in the UK biscuit and cake industry

However, before moving on, let us look at an interesting real world example of how production chain configurations may differ, even within the same industry. United Biscuits and Anthony Alan Food are two firms who supply biscuits and cakes to the UK market. Even though they belong to the same industry the two firms are very different in the size and the way in which they configure their production chains.

United Biscuits are a large multi-site firm who cover the broad market of biscuit and cake production in the UK and own many of the most familiar brands in the UK (for example, Jaffa Cakes, Hula Hoops, Penguin and KP nuts are all United Biscuits brands). They employ over 11,000 people and, in 2004, generated over £1.3 bn of revenue and £204 m of profit. They own 11 factories in the UK split between their three main broad brands – Jacobs (2), McVities (5) and KP (4). By way of contrast, Anthony Alan Food supply the niche market of low-fat biscuits and cakes having acquired the license for the Weight Watchers brand name from the US owners in 2001 (see the *Financial Times*, 8/9 April 2006). The firm has quickly come to dominate this market with a 57 per cent market share in 2005 and revenue of £30 m. The firm employs only 20 people in its headquarters in Barnsley who undertake the research and development, in addition to the marketing function for the firm. All the production is undertaken by about a dozen bakeries around the UK, who also undertake the local distribution to shops and supermarkets.

Therefore, we have two firms in the same industry adopting different production chain configurations.

Figure 5.7 shows a simplified summary of the production chain configuration for United Biscuits. As can be seen, United Biscuits combine four distinct processes within the firm: the direct production processes of manufacturing and distributing the biscuits and cakes and the support processes of R&D and Marketing.

By contrast, Figure 5.8 shows the different production chain configuration as adopted by Anthony Alan Food. In this case, only the support processes of R&D and marketing are internalised within the firm. The processes connected to the actual production of biscuits and cakes rely on a market relationship between Anthony Alan Food and the bakeries producing the Weight Watchers cakes and biscuits. Thus, we are back at the question as to why we see two different configurations of essentially the same production chain?

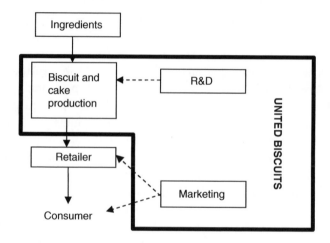

**Figure 5.7** United Biscuits production chain configuration

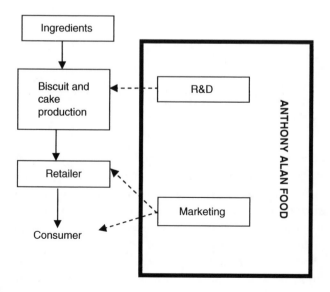

**Figure 5.8** Anthony Alan Food's production chain configuration

## 5.3    The costs of using the market

The previous section broke down a production chain into a series of discrete production processes and looked at the possible means by which these separate processes could be linked together. In general terms, the choice for a firm was either organising the transaction by itself or leaving the market, usually governed by a contract, to organise the transaction. In the neo-classical world, discussed in Part I, markets would be the governing structure for all the transactions in our chain of production. Even more than this, they would be free markets of the form discussed in relation to Figure 5.5. One of the outcomes of the five neo-classical assumptions (maximising behaviour, a holistic perspective, full information, global rationality and homogeneity) is the conclusion that the most effective and efficient means of organising transactions is via free markets. This is the outcome of the perfectly competitive market structure in the long run (see Section 4.2).

However, there is a paradox at the core of neo-classical theory. If markets are the most effective means of organising resources, how do we explain the existence of firms? As presented in Section 5.1, firms in effect replace markets by intern-alising transactions. In configuration 2 of Figure 5.6, the combined miller/baker firm has internalised the market transaction for flour. Similarly, as we have seen in Section 5.2.3, United Biscuits internalise the production of cakes and biscuits whereas Anthony Alan Food use a market transaction. In other words, markets and firms are alternative means of organising production chains. But why do firms exist if markets are, in theory, the most efficient means of organising transactions? The work of two economists has laid the theoretical foundations for explaining this apparent paradox and has led to the development of transaction cost economics. Ronald Coase and Oliver Williamson both start from the premise that markets are the natural order in terms of the governance of transactions and set out to explain why, in many instances, firms end up internalising transactions and in effect replacing markets.

### 5.3.1    Coase and marketing costs

The issue of why a firm might replace a market was discussed by Coase in his classic 1937 article 'The Nature of the Firm' (Coase, 1937). Coase formulates the problem in the following terms:

> Outside the firm, price movements direct production, which is co-ordinated through a series of exchange transactions on the market. Within a firm, these market transactions are eliminated and in place of the complicated market structure with exchange transactions is substituted the entrepreneur co-ordinator who directs production. It is clear that these are alternate methods of co-ordinating production. Yet, having regard to the fact that if production is regulated by price movements, production could be carried on without any organisation at all, well might we ask, why is there any organisation? (p. 388)

In other words, neo-classical theory assumes that firms exist, which they quite obviously do, but offers no real explanation as to why. Further on in the article, Coase elaborates on this apparent paradox at the heart of neo-classical theory:

> what appears to be a gap in economic theory between the assumption (made for some purposes) that resources are allocated by means of the price mechanism and the assumption (made for other purposes) that this allocation is dependent on the entrepreneur-co-ordinator. (p. 389)

Coase's point is that in terms of Figure 5.3, not only the links between each process, but also the horizontal links within each process could be a market. Thus, production Process 1, producing the wheat, could, in a pure neo-classical world, be co-ordinated not by a farmer obtaining and then ordering the inputs, but by a series of markets co-ordinated by the price mechanism. To Coase, the firms are the 'visible hand' in contrast to the 'invisible hand' of the market. To illustrate further, Coase quotes DH Robertson who graphically describes firms as 'islands of conscious power in this ocean of unconscious co-operation like lumps in a pail of buttermilk' (Coase, 1937, p. 388).

At the root of this apparent problem as to why firms exist in a neo-classical world lie our five assumptions upon which neo-classical theory is based. In the neo-classical world, markets operate on the basis of full information and global rationality, nothing is hidden and everybody knows everything. Consumers are rational and never make mistakes and hence always allocate their income so as to maximise their utility. Similarly firms, for the same reasons, always maximise profits, but, in addition, when we add the homogeneity assumption, each firm in an industry is identical with the next and faces the same production function. In terms of the operation of markets, prices within a market will co-ordinate the utility functions of consumers and the production functions of firms so as to bring about a market-clearing price at which both the utility and profit functions are maximised. Underlying this model is the assumption that the world is inhabited by what Williamson refers to as 'economic man'. 'Economic man' is open, honest, all knowing, entirely rational and only interested in maximising the utility function.

### 5.3.1.1 Real-world transactions

What does this mean in practice? How would a pure neo-classical market actually operate in the real world? Assume you are buying replacement windows for your house. In a neo-classical world, this would be a simple and almost instantaneous transaction. Once you decided you wished to purchase the windows and entered the market as a buyer you would immediately know all the types of windows available and their prices (full and perfect information). You would not be interested in the individual firms as they will all be identical (homogeneity). Being a rational consumer, you would choose the lowest price to suit your need (global rationality). Indeed, if the market were operating at its long run perfectly competitive equilibrium there would be only one price anyway. Once ordered, the windows would be fitted perfectly first time and, due to your having full information, you would have no concerns over the quality of the windows or the fitting, in fact in the long-run equilibrium position all the inefficient firms would have been eliminated from the market.

If you carry Coase's logic to its conclusion, then in buying your windows you would not be actually dealing with a firm at all; you would be at the end of a series of production processes co-ordinated entirely by market transactions. The making of the glass, the making of the frame, the design and fitting and also all their associated production chains would be co-ordinated by markets to provide you with perfect windows which maximise your utility function. All of this would simply happen and the only opportunity cost to you is the cost of the production of the materials involved, which would be reflected in the price that you pay.

The five underlying assumptions of the neo-classical theory lead to markets operating in what has been described as a 'costless' manner. The transactions linking our production chain in Figure 5.4 do not 'cost' anything in the sense that there is no opportunity cost involved. In practice, of course, this is simply not the case. Returning to our example of buying replacement windows, the first cost you incur will be search costs due to the fact that you do not have full information. You need to gather information on styles, prices and materials by looking at newspapers, catalogues or on the Internet or from even sales reps from companies visiting you. The same also applies to the window replacement firm. They also have to overcome the imperfect information problem by providing the information through newspaper, magazines and employing salesmen.

There is another set of problems to be faced, also relating to you having only limited, or asymmetric, information. How do you know that the firm you choose is actually reputable? Will they do as they say? Are the windows of good quality? Will they actually be fitted correctly? These questions reflect that a transaction in the real world may involve a certain amount of uncertainty and risk. The way you may try and overcome this is by trying to minimise the risk. Therefore you may not, for example, go to the cheapest supplier. You may decide to actually pay slightly more, possibly through ignorance (you may have missed a cheaper supplier in your initial search) or deliberately by choosing a reputable firm (on the advice of a previous customer, for example, or maybe a report in Which magazine). In addition, you would also require a written guarantee from the company saying that the windows would last ten years or be replaced. There is also a risk from the firm's point of view which is non-payment by the customer. This may be mitigated via an initial deposit, as well as legal action, if necessary.

### 5.3.1.2 Marketing costs and the existence of firms

Therefore, what we see is that when the neo-classical assumptions are relaxed, a market transaction may not operate in the frictionless and costless manner assumed by neo-classical theory. There are informational and risk problems to be overcome on both sides of the transaction which may incur both parties having to take on extra costs (both monetary and opportunity) beyond the direct cost of the production of the good or service. Each of our transactions in the production chain in Figure 5.3 may have additional costs beyond that of the product being exchanged. As in the replacement windows example, each of our four participants in the bread-making chain of production may be faced with search problems and also potential risk based around quality, delivery and payment. Coase referred to these as 'marketing costs' – the costs of using the market. Coase (1937) uses this idea of marketing costs to provide a theoretical justification for why firms sometimes replace markets:

> The question always is, will it pay to bring an extra exchange transaction under the organising authority? At the margin, the costs of organising within the firm will be equal either to the costs of organising in another firm or to the costs involved in leaving the transaction to be 'organised' by the price mechanism. (p. 404)

In other words, firms exist as a means of reducing the costs that may be associated with the linking of two production processes in a production chain by a market. Thus, returning to Figure 5.6, configuration 2 may arise if the cost of maintaining the external market transaction link between the miller and the baker became too great. For example, the quality of the flour produced may be poor or the costs of transporting the flour from the mill to the bakery are too high or possibly the delivery of the flour to the bakery is erratic. Each of these could lead to the miller and the baker deciding to internalise the transaction, in effect replacing the market link with an internal firm link.

However, the internalising of the transaction does not eliminate the transaction cost entirely. What it creates are 'management' costs – $M$ in Figure 4.1. The controls over quantity and quality of flour produced and the paying of the miller all still take place; however, these are 'organised' by the internal management of the firm rather than by external markets. As discussed in Chapter 4, these management costs are not contributing directly to the production, in this particular case, of bread. Thus, the potential costs involved in using the market are replaced by the actual cost of employing a manager (or incurring an opportunity cost by taking up some of the productive time of the miller or the baker) to oversee the transaction link between the miller and the baker. Coase's point was that firms expand by internalising production processes until the internal management cost of co-ordinating the links between the production processes is equal to the cost of using an external market co-ordination link. In other words, firms minimise not only their production costs, but also their 'marketing' costs in search for efficiency.

In Figure 5.6, if the chain of production took the form of configuration 3 the entire production process would be organised within one fully vertically integrated firm. This firm would need to employ managers to co-ordinate the various transactions, managers that would not be needed in configuration 1 where external markets undertake the co-ordination role. However, if this additional management cost is less than the combined non-production costs of using markets then configuration 3 is the more efficient way to organise this bread-making chain of production.

Therefore, in Coase's view the existence of firms comes down to a market being less than perfect or, as it is more commonly referred to, market failure. The response to market failure is for firms to take over the co-ordinating role of the market when they can organise the transaction more efficiently inside the firm.

### 5.3.1.3   Marketing costs and United Biscuits and Anthony Alan Food

However, when looking at the case of United Biscuits and Anthony Alan Food the two companies have obviously come to different conclusions about the relative costs of the biscuit and cake production process. United Biscuits have internalised the cake production processes, whereas Anthony Alan Food use an external market transaction. In other words, for United Biscuits the internal management costs of biscuit and cake production are less than the potential 'marketing' costs, but for Anthony Alan Food the reverse is true.

Why this difference? Part of the reason is historic. Anthony Alan Food are a relatively new firm (founded in 2001) and the use of local bakeries for production and distribution enabled the firm to climb over two of the significant structural entry barriers to the industry, namely the sunk cost of setting up a biscuit- and cake-making factory and a distribution network for the finished output. United Biscuits are a much older firm dating back to the nineteenth century and hence have not only the factories in place, but also the knowledge required to manage a multi-site biscuit- and cake-making firm. Therefore, one difference may be due to history. However another may be due to size. As Anthony Alan Food grow and mature, the costs of relying on market transactions for the production of their low-fat biscuits and cakes may begin to exceed the cost of internalising the production within the firm. To understand this, we need to move on to look in detail at what the actual sources of 'marketing' costs are.

## 5.3.2   Williamson and transaction costs

Coase's article, discussed in the previous section, appeared in 1937 and during the following 35 years was, as Coase himself commented, 'much cited and little used'. Further development of Coase's idea of marketing costs as a means of exploring the nature of firms had to wait until the 1970s and the publication of Oliver Williamson's book *Markets and Hierarchies* in 1975 (Williamson, 1975). This book, along with Williamson's subsequent book *The Economic Institutions of Capitalism* published ten years later (Williamson, 1985), forms the basis of what has become known as transaction cost economics.

Williamson's start point, as was Coase's, is to assume that the links in our simple production chain used in Section 5.1 should be market links ('in the beginning there were markets' (Williamson, 1975, p. 20)). This is what neo-classical theory tells us is the most efficient means of linking production processes together. However, as discussed above, this assumes that the market operates costlessly or, using Arrow's description, in a manner that is 'frictionless' (Williamson, 1975, p. 21). Like Coase, Williamson disputes this and sets out what he calls three 'transaction costs' – three sources of possible friction that may arise when using a market to link production processes in the chain of production.

Williamson's 'transaction costs' are roughly analogous with Coase's 'marketing costs' and may, in the same way, lead to the internalising of transactions within the firm as a more efficient means of organising parts of the chain of production. The underlying cause of the transaction costs comes from the nature of the real world itself where we are dealing with human nature which may not be as open and honest as the 'economic man' of neo-classical theory and an environment which does not allow for perfect knowledge to be achieved. Williamson identifies three sources of transaction costs:

1. Bounded rationality
2. Opportunism
3. Asset specificity.

### 5.3.2.1   Bounded rationality

The concept of bounded rationality was briefly discussed in Chapter 2 in the context of the five underlying assumptions to the neo-classical theory. The concept originates from the work of Herbert Simon who refers to human behaviour as 'intendedly rational, but only limitedly so' (1961). The neo-classical assumption is of global rationality. Under this assumption, decisions are taken based upon the decision maker being able to process all the information relating to a given situation and always producing the correct and optimal solution. For example, in our simple bread-making production chain in Figure 5.3 each of the four decision makers (the farmer, the miller, the baker and the shopkeeper) is able to recognise and assimilate all the information in the environment and always act in an entirely rational and correct manner. In the case of theory of the firm, this means they will always equate marginal cost with marginal revenue and thus maintain a profit maximising position.

Simon's view is that although each of our actors may try and act in this way ('intendedly rational'), they will not actually fully achieve their aim ('limitedly so'). According to Simon, there are two reasons that prevent the farmer, the miller, the baker and the shopkeeper from achieving global rationality:

a. Mental capacity
b. Language.

The potential problems caused by uncertainty discussed in Section 2.2.1 in relation to an ice cream manufacturer apply in exactly the same way to our baker in the bread-making production chain – uncertainty about levels of future demand, possible unforeseen interruptions to supply. As with the ice cream manufacturer, the baker will do his best to anticipate what may happen, usually based on his past experience – in Simon's words he will do his best to act rationally, but this may be limited by uncertainty about the future.

The issue of complexity also arises as the number of variables which a manager/entrepreneur have to take into account begins to increase. Assume, for example, that the shopkeeper owns a string of shops across the country. In this case, the issue of changes in the weather and uncertainties over supply multiply as the number of shops increases. A point will come where the amount of information to be assimilated becomes too great for the individual owner-manager to take in and, again, this causes bounded rationality. He will take decisions based only on partial information, not full information, thus decisions may not be optimal and can lead to mistakes (remember the Guidant case in Chapter 3). Thus, Simon's main contention is that the actual mental capacity of humans is limited, therefore we can never achieve the global rationality assumed by neo-classical theory.

The other source of bounded rationality identified by Simon is language. Language acts as a filter for our thoughts and feelings, but it is an imperfect filter. Language is open to misinterpretation and is another source of uncertainty and complexity. An embarrassing example of this relates to a recent project at the US space agency NASA. Quite late in the project to build a space probe, scientists realised that some teams working on the probe had been using imperial measurements, whereas others had been using metric measurements.

### 5.3.2.2 Opportunism

The neo-classical market system rests on the assumption that it is populated by agents (consumers and firms) who comply with Williamson's 'economic man' as discussed in the previous section. However, once the neo-classical assumptions are relaxed, then there is a possibility of agents operating in a less than open manner or manipulating situations and information to their own ends. The underlying assumption that people still pursue their own self-interest is the same but, as Williamson puts it, 'this involves self-interest seeking with guile' (Williamson, 1975, p. 26). Once an uncertain and complex environment, coupled with agents' bounded rationality, exists then information becomes imperfect and asymmetric. This makes what Williamson refers to as opportunistic behaviour a possibility, or even a probability.

To illustrate, take the situation where you have your car serviced. This is a situation that may, potentially, involve asymmetric information, particularly if you have very limited knowledge of car maintenance. In the neo-classical world, this exchange would take place at a price that reflects the cost of the parts and the labour involved. There is full and certain information, thus you would know if the car mechanic was lying or trying to cheat. However, in the real world you may have only imperfect information – you may not have the knowledge or skills required to check the mechanic's work. The mechanic knows what work he has done, but you may not (asymmetric information). In some instances, this may lead to the mechanic acting in an opportunistic manner – he may charge you for work that has not actually been done. This is what Williamson referred to as 'self-interest seeking with guile', manipulating the imperfect and asymmetric information that may be involved in a transaction to your own benefit.

In terms of market transactions, Williamson sees this aspect of human behaviour as being linked with the problem of 'small numbers' as another source of friction in the market system. By 'small numbers', Williamson is referring to the number of parties involved in a transaction. For example, let us take our baker in the simple chain of production from Section 5.1. One of the key inputs to their production process is flour. In a neo-classical world, the flour would be produced by a large number of small millers, which, in the long run, would be identical in terms of quality and price (that is, the market would be perfectly competitive). In this case, there is no room for one individual miller to act opportunistically because if he did then not only would the baker know, but also as the baker has many other sources of supply for his flour, he could simply switch suppliers. However, if we assume that there are only a limited number of millers in a world without full and certain information, then the baker is in a more difficult position and may find he is open to some sort of opportunistic behaviour in his dealings with the miller. The miller, for example, may experience a drop in the price of wheat from the farmer due to a glut, but this may not be reflected in the price charged to the baker for the flour.

Potential opportunism is one of the possible transaction costs that Anthony Alan Food may become increasingly vulnerable to as they grow in size. The risk is that the bakeries producing and distributing Anthony Alan Food's low-fat products reach a point where they use the knowledge gained and start producing their own competing brands. In other words, Anthony Alan Food, by not undertaking production themselves, may simply be creating potential future competitors. This is a transaction cost that is avoided by United Biscuits, of course, as the production is internalised. However, there is also a risk for the bakeries used by Anthony Alan Food in that they could become overreliant on production for Anthony Alan Food, who may then act opportunistically by reducing the price they pay the bakeries.

### 5.3.2.3 Asset specificity

The third source of friction in the market system is caused by what Williamson refers to as transaction-specific assets or idiosyncratic assets. In general terms, a specific asset is an asset that is owned by a firm but it can only fulfil a limited number of uses, for example, a highly specialised piece of machinery. The use of the specific assets may be reliant upon the demand for its output by a firm further down the chain of production. In other words, the usefulness of the asset is linked directly to a particular transaction; outside of this transaction it has no use at all. For example, our shopkeeper in 5.1 may be based on the ground floor of an old windmill and, as a promotional tool, wishes to sell loaves in the shape of windmills. This, however, would require the baker supplying the shop investing in windmill-shaped baking tins. These baking tins when purchased by the baker represent an asset for the baker; however, they have no alternate use outside of baking bread in the shape of windmills, and the only customer for such bread is the shop in the windmill. The windmill-shaped baking tins are therefore an example of a transaction-specific asset, their usefulness to the baker relies entirely on his continuing to supply the shop in the windmill.

### 5.3.2.4 Specific assets and the 'hostage' problem

This situation, often referred to as the 'hostage' or a 'hold-up' situation (Williamson, 1983), is another source of friction in the market system and may lead to the transaction between the baker and the shopkeeper being difficult to conduct via a market. The problem in our windmill-shaped loaves example could potentially lead to some doubts about the transaction from both the baker and the shopkeeper's perspective. For the baker, the issue is the security of the relationship with the shop and the financial risk involved in the purchase of the windmill-shaped bread tins. The windmill-shaped bread tins represent a sunk or non-recoverable cost, they are an investment that has to be undertaken before production can commence, but they will have no resale value.

The risk to the baker is twofold. First, there is the risk that the bread shop he is supplying with the windmill-shaped bread may, for some reason, stop demanding the windmill bread before the baker has recouped the value of his investment. Secondly, there is the risk that once the investment has been made the shopkeeper may engage in opportunistic behaviour. The shopkeeper knows that the baker has made a transaction-specific investment in the windmill-shaped bread tins and may use this information to his own advantage. The shopkeeper may try to negotiate a lower price for the bread in the knowledge that if the baker pulls out of the transaction then he is left with a worthless asset on which he will make a loss. In this case, the shop is holding the baker hostage; the baker may be forced to continue supplying the bread, even at a loss, simply to offset the sunk cost of the investment in the windmill-shaped bread tins.

However, the shopkeeper is also faced with a number of potential risks. Given the specialised nature of the windmill-shaped bread tins, he may find that only one baker is willing to make the investment. This then becomes a small numbers problem for the shop – this time it is the baker who could hold the shop hostage. Being the single source of the windmill-shaped bread, then the baker could, potentially, increase the prices he charges the shopkeeper, particularly if the shopkeeper has incurred some sunk costs of his own by, for example, running an advertising campaign promoting the windmill bread.

Therefore, the requirement for a transaction-specific asset in this relationship between the baker and the shopkeeper presents all sorts of potential risks for both parties involved. Both the baker and the shopkeeper are going to need some assurances from each other about how long the relationship is to last and agreement on a fixed price. In other words, what is required is a contract between the baker and the shopkeeper. Alternatively, the shopkeeper may decide to bake the windmill bread by himself. This immediately eliminates the problems over price and length of time. In other words, one solution to the problem of transaction-specific assets is to internalise the transaction. The choice between the transaction being governed by a contract between two independent firms or being internalised within one firm becomes, as we shall see in the next chapter, one of cost.

There is also a potential hostage problem for Anthony Alan Food and their bakery producers. One of the reasons for the bakeries not to act opportunistically and start producing their own brand of low-fat biscuits and cakes is the fact that Anthony Alan Food own the license to use the well-recognised Weight Watchers brand name. One way of looking at the brand name is as a specific asset – it is unique and could only be used within this industry for the promotion of low-fat biscuits and cakes (although it is used to promote a wide range of other products in other industries). If the bakeries wish to be part of this growing and profitable market, then they need to remain attached to Anthony Alan Food. What may happen is that as sales grow, instead of Anthony Alan Food needing the bakeries to produce their product, as in the early days, the bakeries come to rely on Anthony Alan Food to maintain their production levels – the balance of power shifts to Anthony Alan Food. One potential risk for the bakeries in this scenario is that Anthony Alan Food may hold the bakeries hostage when the time comes to renegotiate their contracts.

### 5.3.2.5 Types of specific assets

Williamson identifies four general types of specific assets that may lead to the types of problems with using market transactions as discussed in the above examples. (Williamson, 1985, p. 95):

a. Site specific. This relates to situations where successive production processes in a chain of production often requiring largely immobile units of capital which, due to cost in transporting the output from one process to another, need to be located close to each other. Thus, the assets may become interdependent; the continued use of one depends upon the continued use of the other. This is the situation in the Bear Factory shops. Although not involving large amounts of fixed capital, the costs of transporting teddy bears in various states of completion between different shops is simply too high when compared with locating the stuffing, stitching and boxing processes under one roof.

b. Physical asset specificity. This is the investment in specific capital which has a limited number of uses, such as the windmill baking tins in the example used previously.

c. Human asset specificity. Specialist skills and knowledge developed by employees can become a potential hostage situation if the employees' knowledge is vital to the firm's operation. However, this could work the other way around as well if the employees' knowledge becomes too firm specific and has little use outside of that firm, in this case the employee may become a hostage of the firm.

d. Dedicated assets. These are general assets rather than specific assets. A firm may expand a particular asset in response to the demands of a firm further down the production chain. For example, a firm may invest in additional productive capacity in response to a promise of increased demand from a customer.

### 5.3.2.6 Transaction costs and the existence of firms

Figure 5.9 is taken from Williamson's book (Williamson, 1975) and summarises the development of his transaction cost theory at that time. What is not explicit in the diagram is the role of specific assets, a concept that was only developed after 1975. However, the diagram is worth considering as it does bring together many of the issues developed so far and brings in two new elements: 'impacted information' and 'culture'. The framework summarises the sources of transaction costs that may be found to greater or lesser degrees in all markets. The existence of these costs may lead to market failure and the internalising of transactions and, by implication, the creation of firms (or 'hierarchies' to use Williamson's terminology in the book). As can be seen, Williamson divides the factors into two categories, those which can arise in the environment and those that arise through human nature.

The environmental factors are complexity and small numbers (of firms), and the human elements are bounded rationality and opportunism. The diagram shows the two-way link between complexity and bounded rationality. The complex and uncertain environment within which most firms operate is a source of bounded rationality; it limits the ability of firms to know and assimilate all the relevant information and take the correct rational decision. However, this bounded rationality also contributes to the complexity of the environment. A firm not acting in a purely rational manner adds to the uncertainty faced by its rivals in the market place. The opportunism – small numbers link works in a similar way. This two-way link is in fact the source of the 'hostage' problem and underlying problems caused by specific assets, therefore the third source of transaction cost, specific assets (physical and human) are implicitly hidden away in the diagram. Where there are a limited number of potential suppliers of a particular input or buyers for the output, this could lead to opportunistic behaviour such as sudden price rises

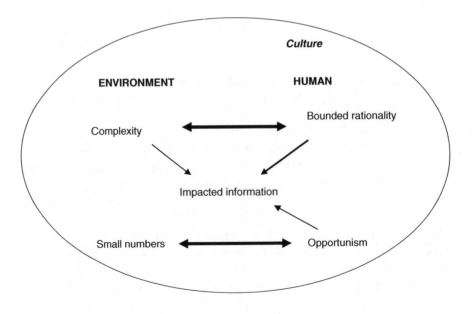

**Figure 5.9** The organisational failures framework

(by either party) or breaks in supply, particularly when specific assets are involved. As we have seen, one solution to this problem is to replace the market transaction by taking the transaction inside a single firm.

Two other features in Williamson's original 1975 diagram are worthy of note. In the framework, the existence of complexity, bounded rationality and opportunism creates what Williamson refers to as 'information impactedness'. Information impactedness 'exists when the true underlying circumstances relevant to the transaction … are known to one or more parties but cannot be costlessly discerned by or displayed for others' (Williamson, 1975, p. 31). In other words, there is a problem of asymmetric information, people involved in the transaction have different information sets in relation to the transaction, the information is not transparent and, for the hidden information to be found, may incur additional cost. The problem of the car mechanic making repairs to your car used earlier is a problem of impacted information. The impacted information is caused by a combination of your bounded rationality, the mechanical complexity of a modern car and the possible opportunistic behaviour of the mechanic. All of this makes verifying that the work has actually been done extremely difficult – the only way may be to employ an independent expert check the work done, but this is an additional cost required to remove the information impactedness.

The second feature to note is that surrounding the whole framework is what Williamson refers to as 'atmosphere' (shown in Figure 5.9 as 'culture') which he defines as 'attitudinal interactions and the systems consequences that are associated therewith' (Williamson, 1975, p. 37). In modern parlance, this would be referred to as business culture, in particular the level of trust that was present in the relationship between the parties. The issues surrounding opportunism and bounded rationality and the likelihood of their causing market failure do depend upon the level of trust that exists between the parties involved in the transaction. Take the example of the windmill-shaped bread and the possible hostage problems involved between the baker and the shopkeeper. If the baker and the shopkeeper were brother and sister then this may remove most of the potential for opportunistic behaviour and the transaction is more likely to remain as a market transaction. The higher level of trust that exists in the relationship reduces the information impactedness, as less information is hidden. Similarly, the problem of impacted information in the mechanic example would be reduced if the mechanic was a personal friend.

Much of the work done by economists using the transaction cost framework has largely ignored this element of Williamson's original framework. However, the concept of culture in relation to transaction costs can be part of the explanation for the differences in business structures we see around the world. For example, the typical business structure seen across much of South East Asia is networks of small-interlinked firms. This may be explained by the high-trust environment in SE Asia brought about by a variety of factors such as close family ties and religious and moral factors. The high-trust environment reduces opportunistic behaviour and the potential 'hostage' problems and hence reduces the transaction costs, which in turn leads to more transactions being left to the market. By way of contrast,

US firms operate in a business environment with a much lower level of trust. Therefore, more transactions are internalised to remove the problems caused by opportunism, bounded rationality and specific assets – hence the relatively larger and more vertically integrated nature of many US firms.

## 5.4　Review and further reading

The question asked at the outset of this chapter in relation to the Bear Factory shop was why is there a need for a shop manager, with his associated indirect cost, to organise the simple three-stage production system? Why not leave the market to organise the production of the teddy bear? The answer, as we have seen, lies in the idea of transaction costs as developed initially by Coase and then subsequently by Williamson.

To begin to answer the question we initially focused on the actual links in a production chain, the means by which the various production processes are linked together or, put another way, how the output of one production process becomes the input to another (Section 5.1). These links we defined as transactions. In the neo-classical world, free markets of the type defined in Figure 5.5 would govern all the transactions in a particular production chain. However, as we saw, when the underlying neo-classical assumptions begin to be relaxed, then the workings of the free-market mechanism begin to be impaired and may eventually breakdown altogether. The reason for this is that the transactions between production processes begin to incur costs that are not present in the neo-classical world. At the extreme, the costs associated with maintaining an external market transaction becomes so great that they outweigh the benefits of internalising the transaction within the firm, thus removing the transaction costs altogether.

However, internalising a transaction may remove a transaction cost, but it also creates another cost – a management cost. The transaction still has to take place, but instead of the market governing the transaction the firm has to govern the transaction. Take the United Biscuits and Anthony Alan Food example. In Section 5.3.2, we identified some of the transaction costs that Anthony Alan Food may be faced with given that they rely on an external market transaction to govern their production of biscuits and cakes – possible opportunistic behaviour by the bakeries. This is not a potential cost faced by United Biscuits as they undertake their own production. However, in its place, United Biscuits face the management costs involved in organising the production of their range of biscuits and cakes for themselves. In effect the firms face a trade-off between transaction costs and management costs. United Biscuits view the transaction costs of external production as higher than internal management costs whereas for Anthony Alan Food the potential internal management costs outweigh the existing external transaction costs.

The best introduction to the whole area of transaction is still Coase's original 1937 article. Williamson (1975, 1985) is the main source of current transaction cost economics and the fast-growing related area of New Institutional Economics – but they do not make for easy reading! For a shorter introduction to Williamson's approach see Williamson (1981). Information on United Biscuits can be found at www.unitedbiscuits.co.uk and Anthony Alan Food at www.aafood.eu.com.

# 5.5 | Student exercises

## 5.5.1 Review exercises and points for discussion

1. Provide brief and clear definitions of the following key terms and concepts as used in this chapter:

   a. A chain of production
   b. A transaction
   c. Governance structure
   d. Bounded rationality
   e. Opportunism
   f. Asset specificity
   g. The 'hostage' problem
   h. Impacted information
   i. Transaction cost.

2. Sarah's Pencils is a small family business producing novelty pencils. The firm undertakes four intermediate production processes in the production chain for the pencils: cutting and shaping the wood (six employees); introducing the lead and gluing (four employees); painting the finished pencil to customer specification (two employees); and packing the pencils for transit to shops (two employees). Sarah acts as manager of the production process and her partner, Gary, looks after sales to potential customers, mainly gift shops.

   a. Represent the above information as an internal chain of production for the firm. Identify the external, contract-governed sources of inputs that will be needed at each stage of production.
   b. If the four internally governed production processes operated as separate externally governed transactions, what might be the transactions costs involved?
   c. Sarah and Gary represent non-direct management costs. Why are they needed?

3. Looking again at the bread-making example, most large UK supermarkets internalise the final two stages of the production process, that is, baking and selling the bread. Why do they not just sell the bread? Alternatively, why do they only undertake the final two stages, why not all four stages in Figure 5.6?

4. At the moment Anthony Alan Foods are a fairly small firm. If Anthony Alan Foods continue to grow do you think they will be able to continue not to

undertake the production of their product? Might there come a point when the management costs of the current configuration of their production chain (Figure 5.8) outweigh the transaction costs of maintaining production as an external contract-governed transaction?

### 5.5.2  Application exercise

Building your own house has a number of potential attractions, such as a sense of achievement and also the fact that in direct monetary terms it can be considerably cheaper than buying a ready built house. However, the vast majority of people still opt to buy a ready built house. Why?

Consider the chain of production involved in the building of a house:

a.  Identify, in broad terms, the main production processes involved in the chain of production.

b.  If you were undertaking the building of your own house, what would be the potential transaction costs involved at each stage in the chain of production?

c.  Why do most people opt to buy a ready built house?

# Management Costs 6

## LEARNING OUTCOMES

On completion of this chapter the reader should be able to

■ Explain the relationship between transaction and management costs

■ Demonstrate an understanding of the contractual basis to the firm

■ Link the contracting model of the firm to the principal–agent mode

## KEY NEW CONCEPTS

Contracting costs     Ex ante contracts     Nexus of contracts

Ex post contracts

## KEY NEW MODELS

Contracting schema

## MODELS AND CONCEPTS DEVELOPED FURTHER

Opportunism     Bounded rationality     Transaction costs

Asset specificity     Management costs

In Chapter 5, we looked at the production chain configuration of two firms in the same industry – United Biscuits and Anthony Alan Food. The interesting fact was that United Biscuits produced their cakes and biscuits within the firm, whereas Anthony Alan Food did not. Figure 6.1 presents a simplified view of how the two firms appear to be structured.

In Figure 6.1, 'management' refers to those people within the firms who are organising and allocating resources, in other words those who are taking on the role of the market. Support services refer to areas such as the HR department, finance department, technical support and purchasing department.

In Chapter 4, we split the cost side of a firm into three distinct types of costs. Applying this division to the two firms above, their costs would be split as follows:

Anthony Alan Food
    Management costs ($M$) – management, support services
    Competitive costs ($S$) – marketing
United Biscuits
    Management costs ($M$) – management, support services
    Competitive costs ($S$) – marketing
    Direct production costs ($D$) – production of biscuits and cakes

As noted above, the distinctive feature of Anthony Alan Food is that they do not actually take part in the main production process of making of cakes and biscuits – in our model of the firm, they actually have no direct production costs. The main purpose of this chapter is to take a closer look at the parts of the two firms we have labelled as 'management costs'. As was discussed at the end of the last chapter, there is a direct link between transaction costs and management costs.

*Management costs and transaction costs.* Williamson's contention is that the presence of transaction costs in the link between any two production processes means that

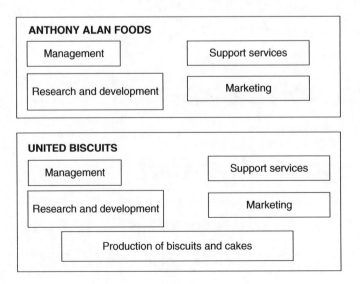

**Figure 6.1**
Internal structures of Anthony Alan Food and United Biscuits

the transaction cannot be governed by a pure market link of the type described in Section 5.1, summarised in Figure 5.5 as 'free market'. This was the conclusion we came to in the example of the baker and the shopkeeper. The product demanded by the shopkeeper (the windmill-shaped bread) required the baker to undertake investment in a transaction-specific asset (the windmill-shaped bread tins). As could be seen, this created a transaction cost due to the potential for either party taking advantage of the situation and acting opportunistically by holding the other hostage. The presence of transaction costs requires the transaction to be governed by either a contractual relationship ('market contract' in Figure 5.5) that removes some of the risk for both parties (by, for example, fixing the price and a minimum length for the supply contract) or by internalisation of the link within one firm ('intra-firm' in Figure 5.5).

The contractual solution can be regarded as a weaker form of a market link in that the two production processes remain separated in different firms, with the relationship being governed by a contract. The purpose of the contract is to try and mitigate the transaction costs of using the market. Given the original presumption that 'in the beginning there were markets', this is seen as preferable to the third, and final, solution the removal of the market altogether and the internalisation within a single firm of both production processes.

The big question of course is what determines the nature of the transaction link? At the end of Section 5.1, we considered three possible configurations for our bread-making production chain (summarised in Figure 5.6), but which one is most likely to occur? Or, in relation to the example above, how do we explain the fact that two firms in the same industry have different ways of organising their transactions? The transaction cost approach gives the answer that the actual configuration depends upon the transaction costs involved between each of the production processes and the feasibility of the parties involved being able to reach a contractual agreement that negates these costs. If this proves to be impossible then the external transaction link disappears, as the only solution is for the two production processes involved to be internalised within a single firm.

## 6.1 | The contractual basis to the firm

### 6.1.1 Contracts and management costs

Section 5.2 has outlined the transaction cost explanation for the existence of firms, as well as identified the source of the management costs shown in our expanded model of the firm as $M$ (Figure 4.1). This section looks in more detail at the nature of the contracts that may arise from the existence of transaction costs and provides a more rigorous theoretical explanation for when a firm may internalise transactions.

In the transaction cost view of the world, contracts drawn up between firms reflect the transaction costs present in their relationship; the contract is a means of trying to reduce these transaction costs. The need to try and overcome transaction costs via contract does reintroduce a more traditional perspective on 'cost' as a monetary cost. The process of setting up a transaction link as a contract involves the parties concerned in a range of expenditures. Williamson breaks these down into two types, ex ante and ex post (Williamson, 1985, p. 21).

### 6.1.1.1 Ex ante contracting costs

'Ex ante' refers to monetary costs incurred before the contract is agreed. These would include drafting, negotiating and safeguarding the agreement. This process may involve having to employ lawyers to draw up the contract. It would certainly involve the time of somebody in each of the firms to negotiate the contract and to ensure that the correct safeguards are incorporated. The actual cost of this would either be the opportunity cost of using an existing employee or the employment of somebody whose primary role is the managing of relations with suppliers and customers.

In our baker–shopkeeper potential hostage example, the baker and the shopkeeper would have to take time out from the running of their bakery and shop, respectively, to negotiate the contract for the supply of the windmill bread. To overcome the problems arising through the need for a transaction-specific asset by the baker, the contract would probably need to cover the price of the bread supplied, the quantity supplied each day and some specified time for the contract to run. The point is that the time taken to negotiate these terms represents a cost that is not directly related to the actual production process. The time taken to agree to the contract is time that the baker and the shopkeeper are neither baking nor selling bread, it can be called 'management time'.

In larger firms, there may be whole departments who deal with suppliers and customers; again the salaries of the people employed in these departments represent costs of the firm that are not directly related to the actual production process. For example, in the case of United Biscuits, they will have staff whose primary role is to deal with their principal suppliers of raw material ingredients that are the main input into their transformation process. In the case of Anthony Alan Food, they will have staff that has to negotiate and agree production contracts with the dozen or so bakers who are producing their products for them. All these types of indirect management costs would appear as $M$ in Figure 4.1.

### 6.1.1.2 Ex post contracting costs

The second type of costs, 'ex post', refers to costs incurred in enforcing the contract once it is up and running. In addition to the regular monitoring of the contract to ensure that its terms are being met, there may also be what Williamson refers to as 'maladaption costs'. These are costs that are incurred when contracts drift out of line. So there may be haggling costs to realign a contract or even adjudication costs, maybe in the courts. In our example, the windmill bread may prove so popular that the shopkeeper needs to renegotiate with the baker to increase the supply, the baker of course may take advantage to try and increase the price. However, again time is taken away from their main production-related activities and a management cost is incurred.

More generally, firms will need to employ managers to monitor the implementation of contracts and haggle if necessary. In the case of United Biscuits, there may be problems with the quality of some of the raw materials that need dealing with, or in the case of Anthony Alan Food, they need to ensure that the quality of the output from their suppliers is what is expected. In the extreme case, it may be decided that the contract has been broken and adjudication may be necessary and, again, firms may need to employ lawyers and possibly face court costs. The baker, for example, may consistently undersupply the agreed number of windmill loaves and the shopkeeper feels compelled to sue the baker for loss of earnings. As with the ex ante costs, these are all costs that may be incurred that do not relate to the transformation of inputs into outputs.

## 6.1.2 Transaction governance structures

Williamson combines the sources of transaction costs with the idea of being able to draw up contracts to negate their effects and identifies five possible governance structures depending upon the nature of the transaction costs present in a link between two production processes. Table 6.1 summarises the possible governance structures that may arise between two production processes (0 represents an absence of the transaction cost, + represents the presence of the transaction cost) (Williamson, 1985, p. 31).

The case where there are no transaction costs at the top of the table gives a transaction that is likely to be governed by a pure market of the type discussed in Section 4.1 and shown in Figure 4.5. The next three cases in the table involve two of the three types of transaction being present and lead to the transaction link being possibly governed by a contract; however, the type of contract varies with whichever of the transaction costs is absent.

**Table 6.1** Possible governance structures

| Type of transaction cost | | | |
| --- | --- | --- | --- |
| Bounded rationality | Opportunism | Asset specificity | Nature of transaction link |
| 0 | 0 | 0 | Market |
| 0 | + | + | Contract (complete) |
| + | 0 | + | Contract (self enforcing) |
| + | + | 0 | Contract (competitive) |
| + | + | + | Possibly internal |

Source: Based on Williamson (1985)

### 6.1.2.1 Complete contract

The first type of contract which Williamson calls a 'complete' contract is possible in the absence of bounded rationality. The absence of bounded rationality takes us back to a world where there is no environmental uncertainty; both the parties involved have full and certain information and take rational and consistent decisions based upon the information. Thus, even though there may be specific assets involved and possibly opportunistic behaviour, it is still feasible for the parties to draw up a 'complete' contract that will cover every possible contingency. With such a contract there will be no ex post costs, as the contract will be complete in the sense that every possible eventuality can be foreseen and clauses in the contract can be drawn up for each possible eventuality, thus avoiding any 'maladaption'.

### 6.1.2.2 Self-enforcing contract

The second type of contract identified by Williamson relates to a situation where there may be bounded rationality and specific assets but no opportunistic behaviour. The presence of bounded rationality now means that the complete contract discussed above is no longer possible. With the presence of bounded rationality, we are now back again in a world with asymmetric information and uncertainty; it is no longer possible to draw up a contract that covers every possible eventuality. However, in a relationship where there is no possibility of opportunistic behaviour the transaction will take place in a situation of complete trust between the two parties. Thus, even though there may be specific assets involved and there may be some ex post realignment costs due to environmental change, it may still be possible to draw up a contract. Williamson calls this type of contract 'self-enforcing', the lack of any opportunistic behaviour leads to the terms of the contract being adjusted when required with the complete trust and agreement of the two parties involved.

### 6.1.2.3 Competitive contract

Williamson identifies a third type of contract as being possible when there may be both bounded rationality and opportunistic behaviour but there are no specific assets involved in the relationship. With the absence of specific assets in a transaction, there are no ties between the two firms beyond the actual contractual relationship itself; the problem of one firm potentially being held hostage by the other does not exist. This makes for a competitive contracting process and probably fairly short-term contracts. The bidding firm has no additional transaction-specific cost to cover and likewise the tendering firm can switch easily to another supplier.

To illustrate, let us return to the case of the relationship between the baker and the shopkeeper. Williamson suggests that in a situation where the business environment is stable and any changes are entirely predictable the conditions may be correct for the agreeing of a complete contract, even though the baker still needs to invest in the specialised windmill-shaped bread tins and both are prone to opportunistic behaviour. The complete contract would specify what happens in every possible change of circumstance, for example, an increase in demand during the tourist season in the summer or an increase in the costs of the baker when flour is in short supply. The contract will cover the entire period required for the baker to recover the costs of the transaction-specific investment. If, however, the environment is not stable and hence less predictable then a complete contract for the length of time the baker requires to regain his transaction-specific investment may not be possible.

Williamson's second type of contract, the self-enforcing contract, might be possible in this situation if, for example, the baker and the shopkeeper were brothers and had a high degree of trust. In this case, if the external environment changed, such as increase in the price of flour, then the shopkeeper would accept as legitimate the need of his brother to increase his prices without recourse to costly renegotiation of the contract. The final type of contract might arise if the shopkeeper was simply selling ordinary-shaped bread and hence there was no need for the baker to invest in any specialised bread tins. There would still need to be a contract due to the existence of bounded rationality and opportunistic behaviour. The contract could, however, be fairly simple and short term specifying a price for the bread, the daily quantity and quality, also a time limit to the relationship to try and negate the transaction costs. However, the shopkeeper could put the contract out to competitive tender and take the cheapest source of supply. There is no potential hostage situation; if the baker suddenly increases his prices the shopkeeper simply switches to an alternative source of supply. Likewise, if the shopkeeper tries to force down the price then the baker simply stops supplying the bread at zero cost, as there is no transaction-specific investment that needs to be recouped.

## 6.2 | Internalising the transaction

### 6.2.1 Williamson's contracting schema

When all three transaction costs are present, this is the situation when the transaction may become internalised within one or other of the firms. None of the three types of contract outlined above are now possible, they cannot be complete because of bounded rationality – they cannot be self-enforcing due to opportunism and they cannot be competitive due to the interdependent relationship forced on the two parties by the presence of specific assets. The result is that the combined ex ante and ex post contracting costs involved in reaching and maintaining an agreement may be too high and force one of the firms to replace the external market transaction link with an internally controlled transaction. Some non-specialist economics readers may prefer to omit the rest of this section, which offers a fairly technical explanation of transaction costs, and move on to Section 6.3.

Two factors may force a firm to internalise a transaction in this manner:

1. The cost of safeguards required to overcome the hostage situation involved with asset specificity.
2. The frequency with which the contract needs to be renegotiated.

To illustrate the problem of the safeguards, which specific assets may lead to, Williamson developed a 'simple contracting schema' which forms the basis of Figure 6.2 (Williamson, 1985, p. 33). In the figure, $K$ represents the transaction-specific assets – the specialist capital that has limited use outside of this particular relationship. $P$ represents the breakeven price at which the transaction takes place. Williamson provides three possible outcomes to this relationship as represented by the nodal points A, B and C with a fourth, internalisation, node D implicit in Williamson's initial formulation. Nodal point A represents the situation where, due to the absence of any transaction-specific assets ($K = 0$), a competitive contract can be drawn up.

When transaction-specific assets ($K > 0$) are present, then two general contracting outcomes are possible depending on whether the parties take out contractual safeguards or not (represented by $S$). The purpose of the contractual safeguard is to try and overcome the possible hostage problem caused by the specific assets. The outcome at node B is the breakeven price for the contract when no contractual safeguards are provided ($P_2$). $P_2$ will need to be greater than the competitive price $P_1$ to take account of the potential risk involved to both parties due to the specific assets involved in the transaction. Therefore, $P_2$ is shown in Figure 4.9 as including an additional insurance element ($I$) to compensate for the risk attached to a potential hostage situation. Whereas at node C, the breakeven price is when there are contractual safeguards in place ($P_3$).

Williamson's contention is that the breakeven price for the contract without contractual safeguards ($P_2$) will be greater than with contractual safeguards ($P_3$). The reason is the same as the explanation as to why $P_2$ is greater than $P_1$. Without

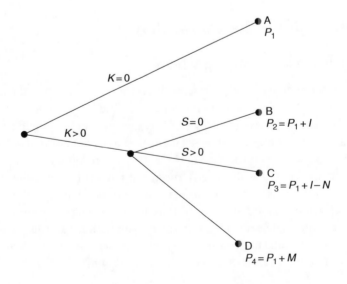

**Figure 6.2**
Specific assets and safeguard contracts

the safeguard, the parties involved are more vulnerable to opportunistic behaviour and, being held hostage therefore to offset the risk, they are likely to require a higher price before the contract is agreed. In Figure 6.2, $N$ represents the reduction in the non-safeguard price, $P_2$, achieved by the safeguard being in place; $P_3 = P_1 + I - N$. However, to achieve the lower price ($P_3$) there is a need to incur the extra costs associated with agreeing the safeguards, these extra costs are shown as $S$.

Therefore, when there are specific assets present there are two possible outcomes, the transaction is concluded either at $P_2$ with no safeguards or at $P_3$ with safeguards. Whether firms negotiate a contract with or without safeguards comes down to a straight cost decision. If the cost of negotiating the safeguard $S$ is less than the actual value gain in terms of the price reduction $N$, then the safeguard is not cost efficient – it is cheaper to conclude the contract at $P_2$ without safeguards.

$N > S$ then contract with safeguards (node C),

$N < S$ then contract without safeguards (node B).

To illustrate, let us return to our example of the baker requiring specialist windmill-shaped bread tins to meet the demands of the bread shop in the windmill. Node B would represent the situation where the shopkeeper simply places the order with the baker, who would then be expected to undertake the transaction-specific investment in the windmill-shaped bread tins. As discussed previously, this opens up the possibility of opportunistic behaviour by either the baker or the shopkeeper due to the transaction-specific investment – the shopkeeper has only one source of supply and the baker has costly unrecoverable investment in windmill-shaped bread tins. The baker is also likely to ask for a higher price to compensate for the risk involved in undertaking the transaction-specific investment.

However, the contract at node C is different in that it has some sort of safeguard built into it that tries to overcome or reduce the possible opportunistic behaviour by either party. For example, the contract may fix the price at which the transaction takes place and specify a minimum length sufficient for the baker to recover his investment with penalty clauses incurred if either party breaks the agreement. The outcome, in terms of the price of the contract, is that it is likely to be lower when the contract has some sort of safeguards built into it (provided, as shown above, the costs of the negotiation are not too high). Without the safeguard, the baker will want a higher price for his windmill-shaped bread to offset the risk he has taken by investing in the windmill-shaped tins. However, agreeing the safeguards means even more time away from the productive role of baking or selling bread or, put another way, more time spent managing and less time producing.

Figure 6.2 can also be related to the management costs incurred by the two firms involved in a relationship. The management costs involved in reaching node A are minimal, some ex ante costs to agree to the contract will be incurred but the transaction is largely 'managed' by the market (the free-market solution in

Figure 5.5). In fact, if the transaction not only has no specific assets involved, but also there is no bounded rationality or opportunistic behaviour, then the management cost would be zero – the entire transaction is 'managed' by the market. In reaching nodes B and C, however, more management costs are incurred as the contracts may have both ex ante and ex post costs. Both outcomes would incur the ex ante costs of drafting and negotiating the contract whilst C would have the additional cost of negotiating the incorporation of safeguards into the contract. However, the safeguards in the contract at C should reduce considerably the ex post management costs relating to the enforcement of the contract. The contract at B, without any safeguards, exposes both parties to the possibility of maladaption costs through opportunistic behaviour. There is, therefore, a trade-off involved when comparing nodes B and C, the lower price at C can only be gained by the higher management costs involved in negotiating $S$ or as Williamson put it 'parties to a contract should not expect to have their cake (low price) and eat it too (no safeguard)' (Williamson, 1985, p. 35).

Figure 6.2 leads us back to Coase's original suggestion as to why firms exist. Coase's explanation was that when the marginal cost of using the market for a transaction was greater than organising the transaction within a firm, then the market would be replaced by the firm (see Section 3.1). This can be illustrated by a closer examination of Figure 6.2. Williamson suggested three prices in Figure 6.2:

$P_1$: the price when there are no specific assets involved (the competitive price)
$P_2$: the price when there are specific assets, but there are no safeguards in place
$P_3$: the price when there are specific assets, but there is a contract which includes safeguards

To this we can add a fourth price:

$P_4$: the internal 'price' if the transaction was internalised within a single firm

The price when there are no specific assets, $P_1$, will be the lowest of the three prices and represents the baseline price in the sense that this is the price when minimal, and easily contractible, transaction costs are involved. $P_2$, the price with specific assets but no contractual safeguards, will be higher than $P_1$. As discussed above, this price needs to be sufficiently high to offset the potential risks involved in the transaction for both parties, in effect there will need to be an insurance value ($I$) added to the baseline price.

Let us look at a numerical example:

$$P_1 = 8$$

$$\Rightarrow P_2 = P_1 + I = 8 + I$$

$P_3$, the price with the contractual safeguards, will lie somewhere between $P_1$ and $P_2$. It must be higher than $P_1$ due to the need to negotiate a contract to overcome the transaction cost caused by the specific asset, but the safeguards negotiated ($N$) will offset some of the price insurance premium $I$. $P_3$ can be thus defined as $P_1$ plus the risk insurance ($I$) minus the benefit of the safeguard ($N$). For the purposes of exposition, we shall define $I-N$ as $X$.

$$P_3 = P_1 + I - N$$
$$P_3 = 8 + I - N$$
$$P_3 = 8 + X$$

Finally, we have $P_4$ which is the 'price' of the firm replacing the market transaction altogether. With the internalisation of the transaction, the costs associated with the specific assets disappears; the use and pricing of the output of the specific asset become a matter for internal direction within a single firm, not for negotiation between two firms. However, there is cost incurred in that, as suggested above, the transaction has to be managed – somebody within the firm will take on the role previously played by the market and will coordinate the transaction between the two production processes. Therefore, the internal price is the competitive transaction cost price, $P_1$, plus the internal management cost, $M$:

$$P_4 = P_1 + M = 8 + M$$

Returning to Figure 6.2, we can now clearly identify whether a transaction link will be left external to the firms involved or become internalised within one of the firms.

### 6.2.1.1 Node A – no specific assets

In this case, the transaction will always be conducted externally to the firm, the external price $P_1$ will always, by definition, be lower than the internal price, $P_4$:

$$P_1 < P_4$$
$$P_1 < P_1 + M$$
$$8 < 8 + M$$

### 6.2.1.2 Node B – specific assets and no safeguards

We now consider $P_2$ as the external price and $P_4$ as the internal price. Whether the transaction is internalised depends upon the cost of internal management, $M$, in relation to the price premium required as an insurance to cover the risks involved in the external price ($I$). In equilibrium, we would have

$$P_2 = P_4$$
$$P_1 + I = P_1 + M$$
$$8 + I = 8 + M$$
$$I = M$$

If $I > M$: transaction is internalised.

If $I < M$: transaction remains external.

### 6.2.1.3   Node C – specific assets with contractual safeguards

The comparison now is between $P_4$ and the external price $P_3$. This time, whether the transaction is internalised or not depends upon the relative cost of negotiating the safeguard contract, $S$, and the internal management costs, $M$:

$$P_3 = P_4$$

$$P_1 + X = P_1 + M$$

$$8 + X = 8 + M$$

$$X = M$$

If $S > X$: transaction is internalised.

If $S < X$: transaction remains external.

### 6.2.1.4   Renegotiation costs

The second cause of the internalisation of transactions relates to the number of times a contract needs to be negotiated. Put simply, the more often a contract needs to be revisited the greater the costs to the firm, both ex ante and ex post. Highly uncertain or complex environments, for example, tend to lead to significant levels of bounded rationality; firms are very unclear about the future. In these circumstances, it may be that firms are only willing to submit themselves to relatively short-term contracts, they do not want to be tied into a set of contractual conditions that may quickly become redundant. Short-term contracts will increase ex ante costs with a continual need for redrafting and renegotiating with the associated management and legal costs. Similarly, with the presence of a high degree of opportunistic behaviour, contracts may be constantly drifting out of line and hence need continual readjusting including possibly internal, or even external, arbitration leading to increasing ex post monitoring costs, managers' time and possible legal costs. In both these circumstances, the costs of a regular review, renegotiation and monitoring may exceed the cost of managing the transaction within a single firm. In other words, the transaction may become internalised.

## 6.2.2   An illustrative example – the case of General Motors (GM) and Fisher Auto Bodies (FAB)

To illustrate how the above framework for transaction costs may be used, consider the following extract from an article written by Klein, Crawford and Alchian:

In 1919 General Motors (GM) contracted with Fisher Auto Bodies for exclusive production of GM auto bodies. Because Fisher had to develop specialized production devices that could only be used for GM cars it was reluctant to sign a short-term contract because at renegotiation time Fisher would be at the mercy of GM. On the other hand GM was reluctant to depend so heavily on one supplier, fearing that, with a short-term contract, at renegotiation time GM would be at the mercy of Fisher. Because each party feared that a short-term contract would leave it at the mercy of the other firm, they signed a contract for 10 years, with the price to be set according to a special formula.

After 1919, however, demand conditions changed greatly and GM decided that the prices set by the contract formula were too high. GM finally merged with Fisher in 1926, thereby removing the costs associated with transacting in the marketplace. (Klein, Crawford and Alchian, 'Vertical Integration, Appropriable Rents and the Competitive Contracting Process', *Journal of Law and Economics*, 1978, pp. 309–10).

At the outset of the relationship, in 1919, both GM and FAB recognised the possibility of two of the three sources of transaction costs being a factor in their relationship – specific assets and potential opportunistic behaviour. The contract requires FAB to undertake transaction-specific investment in specialised production devices that can only be used to produce the GM parts. GM recognised that FAB would become the only source of supply for these parts and hence they could be held hostage by FAB when the contract came up for renewal. The solution was to agree to a long-term contract that incorporated safeguards regarding changes in price. Both the parties were happy with this: FAB had a ten-year period to recoup their investment in the specialised equipment and GM had some guarantees over the price of the components produced. The fact that the contract also contained various safeguards for both sides also suggests that the agreed price was lower than if, for example, it was for a shorter period of time or had a less sophisticated pricing formula. What FAB and GM tried to agree was a complete contract as in Table 6.1, a contract to cover all the eventualities as they saw them in 1919.

However, what FAB and GM failed to foresee was the enormous growth in demand for motor cars in the US during the 1920s that led to a rapid fall in costs as firms began to exploit the economies of scale present in the industry. In transaction cost terms, in 1919 all the three transaction costs were present at the commencement of the relationship, not just two as GM and FAB thought. The inability to foresee the future meant that in 1919 GM also suffered from bounded rationality in addition to being open to potential opportunistic behaviour and the requirement for FAB to undertake transaction-specific assets. The result was that GM became unhappy with the price, perhaps because they were tied into a long-term contract at a price that was higher for that particular component than the price being paid by their rivals who had not made such long-term commitments. In transaction costs terms, the contract became subject to maladaption and GM were faced with the problem of ex post renegotiation and, potentially, being held hostage by FAB for an even higher price, the exact situation they were seeking to avoid in the first place.

By 1926, GM had obviously decided that the cost of keeping the transaction external now exceeded the internal management costs of producing the component themselves and they merged with FAB. Thus, we can clearly see in this example a transaction link where all three transaction costs are present and, despite the attempt to maintain the transaction as an external contract-controlled market, the level of transaction costs involved became too great and the link became internalised. In terms of Figure 6.2, the firms are at node C throughout, there are specific assets and the firms initially negotiate a contract with contractual safeguards. In 1919, for GM, the cost of negotiating the contract was less than the cost of producing the components themselves, $X < M$. However over time, the baseline price $P_1$ fell. Thus, the baseline price in 1919 ($P_{1,19}$) when the contract was agreed was much higher than the baseline price in 1926 ($P_{1,26}$). In 1926, GM were still working on a contract based on the 1919 price. Add to this the extra ex post costs on renegotiation that increases the safeguard costs (from $S$ to $S^+$) and it appears that by 1926, the transaction costs of the external link now exceed the internal cost of managing the transaction within GM.

$$P_{1,19} + X < P_{1,19} + M: \quad \text{position in 1919}$$

$$P_{1,19} + X^+ > P_{1,26} + M: \quad \text{position in 1926}$$

where $P_{1,19} > P_{1,26}$ and $X^+ > X$.

GM took the decision to merge with FAB; in other words GM replaced the market as the transaction could now be managed more efficiently inside the firm.

## 6.3 | The firm as a 'nexus of contracts'

In Chapter 3, we looked at the principal–agent model of the firm which, like the discussion above, developed a view of the firm that placed the emphasis on the firm as essentially a contracting organisation. In the principal–agent model, the contract was used as a means of trying to align the objectives of the employing principals with the employed agents. In Section 3.3, we focused on the idea that the divorce of ownership from control leads to a principal–agent relationship between a firm's shareholders (the owners and principals) and the firm's managers (the firm's controllers and agents). During the course of the discussion, we looked at the problems surrounding the observability problem – the shareholders cannot always observe what the managers are doing. The solution was for the principals to construct the agent's contracts in such a way as to try and align the objectives of the agent with those of the principal. In the case of the firm's managers, this often leads to part of the manager's remuneration being based on the stock market performance of the firm.

The discussion in this chapter and the previous chapter leads to a similar view of the firm as primarily a contracting entity, this time the contracting though is to mitigate the transaction costs of using the market. The two views are, however, not incompatible. From the transaction cost perspective, the type of contract discussed above between a group of shareholders and their managers can be seen as trying to deal with potential opportunistic behaviour by the managers. Left to pursue their own objectives, they may well act opportunistically and aim to maximise their own managerial utility function as suggested by Williamson's earlier model of managerial discretion (Section 3.1.2). The contract which partly ties remuneration to the firm's performance is therefore a means of trying to negate this potential transaction cost.

The upshot of both approaches is the view that the firm ends up at the centre of a complex web of interconnected contracts, often referred to as the view of the firm as a nexus of contracts. Take, for example, a university such as my own. Within the university, every member of staff will have an employment contract of the type discussed in Section 3.3. By looking at the university in terms of our model of the firm, we can say that the academic departments are the main source of revenue as they produce the institution's output (teaching, research and consultancy) and hence represent the source of the direct production cost ($D$ in Figure 4.1). There will be within the university a series of contractual relationships between the productive academic departments and the non-productive source of the institution's management and competitive costs. In theory, the contracts will govern the transfer of funds to the non-productive units and the services the productive units can expect back. In practice, many universities operate, rather perversely, the other way round – the revenue goes to the non-productive unit first and is then transferred via contractual relationships to the productive units of the institution.

The staff within the university, who we can class as the source of management costs, will be split between those involved in managing the internal production process and those managing the external contractual relationships of the university. These external relationships break down into various types and would include

Professional services – banking, insurance, advertising, legal
Funding – funding council, research funding bodies, corporate clients, partner colleges
Suppliers – furniture, publishers, technology, travel

Each of these external relationships, and many more not included above, will be governed by a contract driven by the need to mitigate any transaction costs that might be present in the relationship. Figure 6.3 summarises how the university acts as a nexus of contracts.

Therefore the university, or indeed any firm, sits at the centre of a complex network of contracts – all of which need managing, both ex ante and ex post. As we have seen with the Anthony Alan Food and United Biscuits example, what firms decide to manage via internal contracts as opposed to external contracts can and does vary. Also, the nature of the internal and external contracts can vary from firm to firm. The internal contractual relationship between the productive

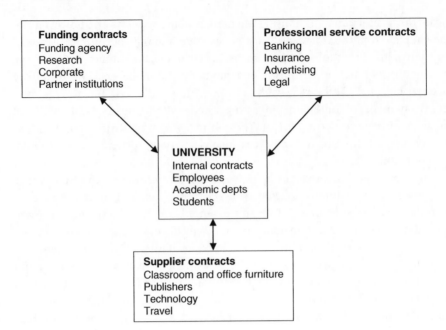

**Figure 6.3** The university as a nexus of contracts

and non-productive parts of a university, for example, varies enormously from institution to institution. Kay (1995) refers to the complex network of contracts each firm has as giving the firm a specific 'architecture' – and that each firm's architecture will be different. Accounting for the differences between firms is the subject of the next chapter.

## 6.4 | Review and further reading

During this chapter, we have built upon the idea that the existence of transaction costs in a firm's market relations provides an explanation for the non-productive cost that we have called management cost in Figure 4.1. The discussion at the end of Chapter 5 revolved around an explanation to the question as to which of the three possible configurations of our bread-making production chain shown in Figure 5.6 would actually occur. The answer, according to the transaction cost perspective, is the configuration that represents the most efficient ordering of the chain of production. On a more technical level, the Williamson contracting schema offers a theoretical means of determining this.

Applying this efficiency view to Figure 5.6, for example, assumes that the environment was stable and predictable, there were many firms at each stage of production and no specific assets were needed in any of the production processes (refer to Figure 6.1). This environment would imply a situation where there are minimal or possibly no transaction costs present, thus a free market may most efficiently govern each transaction in the production process – configuration 1 in Figure 5.6. However, as these conditions change, so may the configuration of the production chain. Configuration 2 implies that there are sufficient costs associated with the transaction from milling the flour to baking the bread to warrant the complete internalisation of the transaction. At the extreme is configuration 3 where the transaction costs are so great across all the four production processes that the most efficient configuration is for the entire production chain to become vertically integrated.

How a production chain is configured can also change over time. Changes in technology may, for example, lead to an increasing need for more, or indeed less, specific assets thus increasing, or decreasing, the transaction costs and hence possibly the configuration of the production chain. Alternatively as we saw in the GM–FAB example, changes in the business environment can have similar effects on the level of transaction costs. Looking at a wider macro-context, other factors can also affect transaction costs. The effect of business culture has already been discussed in relation to Figure 5.9. Another macro-factor could be the nature and efficiency of the legal system. A slow and/or corrupt legal system would make the agreeing and enforcing of contracts harder and hence more costly, making the internalisation of transactions more likely, ceteris paribus, than in a quicker fairer system.

To summarise, the transaction cost approach to economics reviewed in the previous two chapters provides an explanation for the apparent paradox of why firms replace markets when markets are, in theory, the most efficient means of allocating resources. Transaction cost economics argues that firms exist because, in certain circumstances, they are actually more efficient than markets in organising resources. The line of argument developed by Coase and Williamson goes as follows:

1. The transaction links that make up a chain of production may involve transaction costs that reduce the efficiency of these links being governed by markets.
2. The transaction costs may be traced to

   ▪ bounded rationality
   ▪ opportunistic behaviour
   ▪ transaction-specific assets.

3. The presence of one or more of the above requires the market transaction to be governed by a contract which tries to negate the inefficiency caused by the transaction cost.
4. A transaction link governed by a contract incurs management costs on the part of both the parties involved.
5. When all three types of transaction costs are present the costs of managing the external link rise considerably due to one, or both, of the following:

   a. the cost of frequent contract renewal
   b. the cost of ensuring sufficient contractual safeguards are in place.

6. When a + b is greater than the cost of managing the transaction internally, then the firm replaces the market.

7. By replacing the market, the firm necessarily incurs management costs related to the negotiation and monitoring of the internal and external contracts required to coordinate the transformation process.

The outcome of 7 is that the firm becomes a nexus of contracts which gives each firm its own particular architecture.

Thus, at the heart of transaction cost economics is a very neo-classical marginalist principle, 'at the margin, the costs of organising within the firm will be equal either to the costs of organising within another firm or to the costs involved in leaving the transaction to be "organised" by the price mechanism' (Coase, 1937, p. 21). What transaction costs also provide us with is a theoretical basis for the management costs identified in our expanded model of the firm – namely Coase's 'costs of organising within the firm'.

The readings for this chapter are essentially the same as for the previous, although the more technical approach of the contracting schema can be found in Williamson (1985). For a fuller discussion of the idea of a firm's architecture, please refer to Kay (1995).

## 6.5 | Student exercises

### 6.5.1 Review exercises and points for discussion

1. Provide brief and clear definitions of the following key terms and concepts as used in this chapter:

   a. Ex ante contracting costs
   b. Ex post contracting costs
   c. Complete contract
   d. Self-enforcing contract
   e. Competitive contract
   f. Safeguard contract
   g. nexus of contracts.

2. Let us return to the case of Sarah's Pencils from the exercises at the end of Chapter 5.

   a. What types of ex ante and ex post contracts may both Sarah, as manager of the production process, and Gary, as responsible for external sales, be involved with?
   b. For the example contracts generated in response to part (a), identify the transaction costs they are trying to counteract.
   c. What might the nexus of contracts look like for Sarah's Pencils (Figure 6.3)?

3. The issue of whether Anthony Alan Foods could maintain the production of their biscuits and cakes as an external transaction if they continued to grow

in size was raised in the exercises at the end of Chapter 5. Look again at your answer and see whether you can identify the nature of the management costs that may arise as the firm grows in size.

### 6.5.2  Application exercise

The application exercise at the end of Chapter 5 asked you to consider the transaction costs involved in the building of your own house.

a.  What might the ex ante and ex post 'management costs' be in doing this?
b.  How would you become your own nexus of contracts if you did try to build your own house?

# 7 Resource-Based Theory of the Firm

## LEARNING OUTCOMES

On completion of this chapter, the reader should be able to

- Explain the resource-based view of the firm
- Use the resource-based view of the firm to identify sources of sustained abnormal profits
- Explain Porter's value chain and relate it to resource-based view of the firm

## KEY NEW CONCEPTS

| | | |
|---|---|---|
| Threshold and unique resources | Threshold and unique competencies | Rare resources |
| Threshold and unique capabilities | Common resources | |

## KEY NEW MODELS

| | |
|---|---|
| Resource-based firm | The VRIO framework |

## MODELS AND CONCEPTS DEVELOPED FURTHER

| | | |
|---|---|---|
| The value chain | Resource entry barriers | Abnormal profit |
| The evolutionary view of the firm | Normal and abnormal profits | Value added |

In the preceding six chapters, a range of real-world examples have been used to illustrate many of the theoretical concepts and models that have been discussed. However, a number of the examples have raised questions that have not been addressed so far. Consider the following, for example.

Chapter 4 compared the development of the insurance company Direct Line Insurance and the no-frills airline Ryanair. The conclusion reached about these two firms was that they both achieved success in generating abnormal profits through industry-changing innovation that had allowed them to create entry barriers. However, as was also commented on, Direct Line Insurance proved to be incapable of maintaining their advantage, and the abnormal profits proved to be only a relatively short-run phenomenon, whereas Ryanair seemed to have been able to sustain its abnormal profits for a much longer period. Why is this? A further question related to Ryanair is how Ryanair managed to remain successful when other European airlines, both the traditional flag carriers and some of the newer 'no-frills' airlines, have been struggling to survive?

One of the extracts from the FT considered in Chapter 3 related to Marks and Spencer. The extract referred to the ongoing problems at Marks and Spencer in the UK retail sector. However, what the article does not say is that prior to the late 1990s Marks and Spencer had been one of the most profitable shops on the high street with an unmatched reputation for quality and efficiency – a position they had occupied for the best part of 50 years. How can a firm slide so quickly from an apparent position of being able to sustain abnormal profits over such a long period of time, to one of making significant sustained losses in a matter of few years?

Finally, consider a new example that has not been discussed previously, but one which raises some interesting new questions. British Gas is the main provider of gas in the UK and has held this position since being a nationalised industry before the 1980s. However you can, if you wish, also receive not only your gas from British Gas, but also your electricity and landline telephone services, despite there being similar dominant firms in these other industries. Why does a producer of gas also provide electricity and telephone services despite not producing either of the products themselves?

The purpose of this chapter is to provide an alternative perspective on the firm, which will provide some clues to the answers to the questions posed above. The previous two chapters have focused on developing the idea that firms incur not only costs directly associated with the transformation process ($D$ in Figure 4.1), but also indirect management costs ($M$). Chapter 6 concluded with a discussion of the view that the firm lies at the centre of a 'nexus of contracts' which, to use Kay's term, gives the firm a particular 'architecture'. This chapter takes a closer look at this internal architecture of a firm and expands the analysis to show how this 'architecture' can form the basis of the creation of sustained abnormal profits.

In the discussion in Chapter 4 about the means by which firms can not only create but also sustain abnormal profits, three broad sources of abnormal profits were identified:

1. Being a lower cost producer
2. Generating higher revenue
3. Undertaking the transformation process more efficiently.

Part III of the book will deal in detail with the second source of sustained abnormal profits. This chapter, however, will look at the third source: the creation and sustaining of abnormal profits that can arise from the nature and structure of the firm itself. To do this, we will develop a different perspective on the firm, one which is referred to as the resource-based theory (RBT) of the firm. Chapter 3 discussed a range of perspectives on the firm that have been developed over the last 50 years as people began to question the five assumptions that underlie the neo-classical model of the firm. The resource-based view of the firm has links to both the behavioural and the evolutionary models of the firm (Section 3.2) in addition to the principal–agent/nexus of contracts view of the firm referred to above. In terms of the five neo-classical assumptions, RBT of the firm rejects both the holistic assumption about a firm's behaviour and, more crucially, the homogeneity assumption.

*The resource-based view of the firm.* The starting point of RBT is to look at the firm not as a set of mathematical equations, but as a bundle of resources which are then organised and used to develop the ability to produce goods and services. The ability of a firm's resources to produce goods and services is commonly referred to as a firm's 'competencies'. In a pure neo-classical world, this view of the firm would not add anything to the analysis of the firm. This is due to the homogeneity assumption which means that the range and type of resources available to the firm would all be identical, as would be the capabilities of these resources. Further, the resources and capabilities would be the same across all firms in the industry, hence the idea of analysis being conducted by reference to the 'representative firm' (Section 2.3.1). How the firm's management used the resources would be dictated by the least cost combination discussed in Section 4.2.2 and would respond immediately to environmental changes (the holistic assumption). In addition, these decisions taken by the firm's managers would always lead to a firm maximising profit (the full and certain information as well as global rationality assumptions).

However, the resource-based view of the firm presents us with a perspective on the firm that enables us to explain why firms in the same industry differ not only in what they do, but also in how good they are at generating and sustaining profits – why Ryanair was able to outperform not only Direct Line Insurance, but also other airlines. The resource-based view starts from the assumption of heterogeneity, not the homogeneity view of the neo-classical firm. Each firm is considered to be a unique 'bundle of resources'. The uniqueness of each firm comes from two sources:

1. Resources differ – resources are not homogenous, they are heterogeneous. Each unit of human resource, for example, is unique and will have different skills, knowledge and potential to offer a firm.
2. Each resource has more than one use. Each worker, for example, could be used in a number of different jobs within the firm. In the real world of imperfect

information and bounded rationality, two firms may use the same unit of resource in different ways.

Taken together, these assumptions made about a firm's resources lead to the conclusion that when we look at an individual firm in a particular industry we are looking at just that, a unique individual firm. If you look at another firm in the same industry, it will be different because the resources will be different and the use to which the resources are being put will be different. The neo-classical idea of analysing one 'representative' firm and then drawing conclusions that will apply to all firms in the same market simply does not work. The sort of generic models that come out of neo-classical theory has to be replaced by examining each firm individually. This is the clue to addressing the questions raised at the beginning of this chapter. Each of the firms referred to – Ryanair, Direct Line Insurance, Marks and Spencer and British Gas – is a unique bundle of resources, and this uniqueness helps explain the issues raised in relation to each of these firms.

The next section explores the nature of the resource-based view of the firm further. RBT has been developed mainly in the strategic management literature where a number of writers have used the resource-based view of the firm to try and explain why some firms in a particular industry are more successful at creating and sustaining a competitive advantage in their particular industry. Section 7.2 shows how this strategic analysis relates directly back to the idea that the resource-based view of the firm also provides an explanation for a potential source of sustained profits for some firms. This section draws heavily on the work of Barney (1995), Wernerfelt (1984), Hamal and Prahalad (1994) and Peteraf (1993). Section 7.3 returns to the idea of a chain of production, as discussed in Chapter 5, but expands the idea by using RBT to develop the concept of a value chain.

## 7.1 | Resources, capabilities and competencies

The model of the firm that we have been developing throughout this book is one based on the view that a firm is essentially a transformer of inputs into outputs. The resource-based view of the firm does not deny this basic transformation role of the firm, but places greater emphasis on the nature of the inputs coming into the firm and how the firm uses these inputs. The following quote from Wernerfelt emphasises this point:

> For the firm, resources and products are two sides of the same coin … by specifying the size of the firm's activity in different product markets it is possible to infer the minimum necessary resource commitments. Conversely, by specifying a resource profile for a firm, it is possible to find the optimal product-market activities. (Wernerfelt, 1984)

The quote is actually describing the basic relationship between inputs ('necessary resource commitments') and outputs ('size of the firm's activity in different product markets') contained in the economists' production function. However, in RBT the relationship between a firm's inputs and outputs is not simply a matter of passing the inputs through a mathematical relationship defined by the production function. Central to the resource-based view of the firm is the distinction between the resources and the use to which they are put. One of the originators of this approach to the theory of the firm was Edith Penrose. She summarised the distinction in the following terms:

> The important distinction … lies in the fact that resources consist of a bundle of potential services and can … be defined independently of their use … while services cannot be so defined. (Penrose, 1957)

The point Penrose is making is that if we take one worker in a firm that worker has many potential uses. Take an employee of Marks and Spencer. With minimal training the employee could work on the tills or fill shelves on the shop floor or work in the warehouse. With more training, the same employee could work on the customer services desk or act in a range of supervisory roles within the store. In other words, the one unit of resource, the employee in this case, has many potential 'services' it could offer to the firm. In addition, the unit of resource (the employee) has an existence independent of the service it provides. This, however, is not true of the 'services' or roles required by the firm. Marks and Spencer need the roles of the checkout assistant, shelf stacker, warehouse worker, customer services assistant and supervisor to be undertaken if they are to produce their output.

Combining the Penrose and Wernerfelt views, we can also say that the resource, and the potential service it can offer, has a two-way relationship with the products the firm produces: the nature and amount of services required depends upon the products produced and, similarly, the products produced depends upon the nature and amount of the services available. Put another way, the number of employees and the nature of the services required by Marks and Spencer rely on the number of stores operated by Marks and Spencer but, conversely, the number of stores also depends upon the number of employees and the services they can provide. Traditionally, economists have taken this potential reciprocal relationship as actually working only one way – the services required depend upon the product produced, the economists' idea of derived demand. In other words, Marks and Spencer will employ the number of checkout assistants required to meet the demand within their stores. Put another way, the firm wants to incur the cost of employing particular workers not because they are pleasant persons, but because of the services they can offer as part of the transformation process.

However, as we shall see, RBT suggests that this relationship may sometimes be better thought of as working the other way round; what the firm can produce depends upon the resources available and services they can provide. If, for example, Marks and Spencer identified a demand for their output in a particular town where they did not currently have a store they may decide to open a new store.

If, however, there was no land available in that town for retail development then the demand for Marks and Spencer's output will go unmet – the unavailability of a resource limits the output that can be produced.

Penrose sets out her view of the firm as follows:

> it is … a collection of productive resources the disposal of which between different uses and over time is determined by administrative action. (Penrose, 1957)

This definition of the firm laid the foundation for what has now become referred to as the resource-based view of the firm. Figure 7.1 summarises the discussion so far about the nature of the resource-based firm.

In the figure, the firm has three different units of resources available for the production of widgets. Each resource, X, Y and Z, can offer one of three types of services, 1, 2 or 3. Each of the services is required in the production of widgets. On the output side, widgets can be produced in three different ways by using different combinations of services offered by the resources – $(X_{s1} + Y_{s2} + Z_{s3})$ or $(X_{s2} + Y_{s1} + Z_{s3})$ or $(X_{s3} + Y_{s2} + Z_{s1})$. The actual combination in which the resources are used to produce the widgets is, in Penrose's words, the result of 'administrative action' or, in more contemporary terminology, management. In the Marks and Spencer example, X, Y and Z could be three employees each of whom could provide one of three services – operate the till, stack the shelves or work in the warehouse,

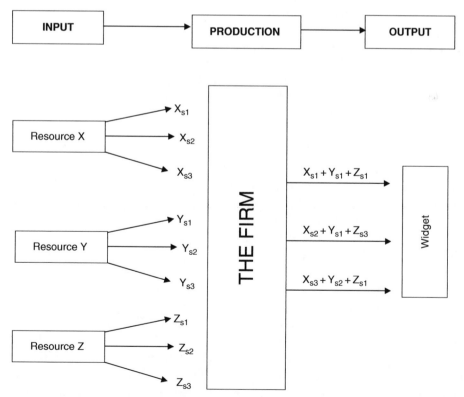

**Figure 7.1** The resource-based view of the firm

all of which are required if the store is to operate. Which role each employee carries out is determined by the store management.

The above explanation has obvious links back to the idea of transaction and management costs discussed in Chapters 5 and 6 – the allocation of resources being undertaken by a non-productive manager. However, the role of management described above goes beyond the mere allocation of resources; management also has to decide what services each of the resources is required to offer. Different managers may allocate resources to different roles – one supervisor in a Marks and Spencer store may allocate employee X to operate a till, whereas another supervisor may ask the employee to stack shelves. The ability of the management to organise their resources is one of the differences between firms – an aspect of the firm's architecture that may lead to abnormal profits.

Before progressing any further, it is important that we define clearly the terms to be used in the rest of this chapter. One confusing element of the RBT literature, particularly some of the earlier readings, is the lack of any single accepted set of terms. Set out below are the terms we shall be using.

### 7.1.1  Resources

Resources are the means available to a firm to help them achieve its objective. The original meaning of resources, as used by Penrose, for example, equated roughly with the economists' factors of production – human resources (labour), manufactured resources (capital) and natural resources (land). These we can think of as tangible resources – we can see and quantify them. However, other intangible resources are also available to a firm that adds to its ability to achieve its objective. This would include how the firm is organised and its internal organisational culture and may also include things such as the possession of brand names or the firm's reputation. In terms of Figure 7.1, these intangible resources would be included within 'The Firm' part of the figure.

### 7.1.2  Capabilities

By capabilities we will mean what Penrose referred to as 'services' – the different potential functions that each resource could carry out as part of the transformation process. As discussed above, some resources may have a number of capabilities. The most obvious resource that has a number of potential capabilities is human resource – as in the Marks and Spencer case. However, other types of resources may also have more than one capability. Take for instance the manufactured resource of a building. This could be used as a workshop or as offices or as storage. Even some of the intangible resources may have more than one use. Take, for example, the resource of an existing strong brand name. This could be used to create an ever-stronger association with a particular type of good (Coca Cola) or used as a means of developing new related, or even unrelated, markets. Virgin, for example, has used the brand name for products ranging from insurance to airlines to mobile phone to trains and many more. In Figure 7.1, each resource, whether a tangible resource such as an employee or a building or an intangible resource such as a brand name, is capable of undertaking more than one role.

One other important point to note about capabilities is that they are not static; the capabilities of resources can be changed either by training/redevelopment or by experience. Many employees when first employed will need to undergo some kind of training for the particular role they have been employed to perform. Similarly, a change in the use of a building almost always requires some refurbishment. However, the capabilities of particular employees will grow and develop over time as their experience in a particular role increases; indeed they may develop capabilities that allow them to take on a completely new role within the firm.

### 7.1.3  Competencies

Competencies refer to the actual uses to which the resources are being put – how the resources with their range of possible capabilities are actually used in the transformation process. As we have seen throughout this book, the transformation process requires the combining of resources (inputs) in order to produce outputs. By competencies, we mean the actual form that this combining takes. We have already come across the idea of competencies in Section 3.2 during our discussion of the work of Nelson and Winter (1982)(Nelson, 1991). In that section, we looked at the idea that there was a 'hierarchy of routines', or competencies, that a firm develops to enable it to undertake the transformation process. However, competencies refer to not only the actual routines themselves, but also how these routines are linked together – the linkage between the shop floor in a Marks and Spencer store and the warehouse which contains the stock, for example. As with the capabilities of resources, competencies can also develop over time as the resources involved become more familiar with them or the resources involved change. One other important point from Nelson and Winter for what follows is the idea that the competencies that a firm develops become embedded as 'organisational memories' and as such form an important part of the firm's internal organisational culture.

Firms also need to develop competencies for the use of their intangible resources. The brand name resource, for example, needs to be developed and used effectively as part of a firm's strategy for the maximising of the revenue taken from its output markets.

### 7.1.4  Threshold and unique resources, capabilities and competencies

The final definition we need to understand is the difference between what Johnson, Scholes and Whittington (2005) refer to as threshold and unique resources, capabilities and competencies. Threshold resources, capabilities and competencies refer to the resources and activities that a firm must undertake in order to produce a particular output for a particular market.

Take the example of the Baker's shop used in Chapter 5. In order to carry out this transformation function, the baker requires manufactured resources such as flour, an oven, display cabinets, a till, not to mention the actual shop premises. Similarly, the baker will require human resources to bake the bread and serve the customers and also natural resources such as sugar, water, milk and fuel. Without these resources the baker's shop cannot function, it will be unable to bake and sell bread to its customers. However, having the resources is simply not enough, they need to be deployed in such a way that the bread is baked and then sold to the customers. Some of the human resources, depending on their capabilities, will have to be deployed as bakers, and some as shop assistants. In addition, competencies by which these resources can produce and sell bread will have to be developed and put in place. Thus, opening times for the shop need to be determined, so do baking times and a routine for cashing up and transporting the day's takings to the bank, a routine for paying the staff, a routine for paying suppliers and so on. As discussed above, this process of deploying resources and developing the competencies that are needed to support the transformation process is the role of management. The main point is that all of the above resources, capabilities and competencies need to be in place if the baker's shop is to fulfil its function and produce and sell bread. The same applies to *all* bakers' shops, not just the one in our example.

Therefore, for a firm to take part in a particular production process there is a need for the firm to have a minimum set of resources with the correct capabilities, and the firm needs to develop a set of competencies to allow the transformation process to take place. These minimum requirements are what we shall refer to as the threshold resources, capabilities and competencies. As we shall see in the next section, possession of these threshold resources, capabilities and competencies is required if a firm is to make at least normal profits. However, to make more than normal profits the firm needs to possess unique resources and/or unique capabilities and/or unique competencies. Unique resources, capabilities or competencies are what sets one firm apart from its rivals and may enable it to make, and possibly sustain, abnormal profits.

## 7.2 | Resource-based entry barriers

In his article 'Looking Inside for Competitive Advantage' Barney (1995) develops a framework which he recommends for the use of strategic managers to help identify the sources of competitive advantage within their companies. In particular, he recommends that managers ask four questions in relation to their firm's resource and capabilities base (n.b. Question 3 has been slightly amended for reasons outlined below):

1.  The question of value ($V$)
2.  The question of rareness ($R$)
3.  The question of imitability (and, for resources, immobility) ($I$)
4.  The question of organisation ($O$).

In this section, we shall utilise the same Barney VRIO framework to help us explain how firms can use their resource and competencies to create resource-based entry barriers which are the source of competitive advantage or, in economists' terms, sources of sustained abnormal profit.

Returning for the moment to Barney's four questions – what do they actually mean? The first question relates to the strategists' idea of 'value', in particular, the idea of 'adding value'. This was discussed briefly in Chapter 1. The basic idea behind 'adding value' is that the sum of the individual parts should be of greater value than the individual parts – often presented as the idea that $2 + 2 = 5$. In this context, if you combine together two resources in a particular activity then the value, or income, they generate should be greater than the cost of combining the resources. If this is the case, then you have a value-adding activity. However, if the cost of combining the two resources is greater than the value generated, then the activity is taking value away from the firm. For example, if you employ a worker at £10 a day to operate a machine which cost £5 a day to run and the resulting output is worth £20 per day then you have a value-adding activity. If, however, the resulting output was only worth £12 a day, then you have a value-losing activity. This whole idea of value and value added is dealt with in detail in Chapter 12.

The second question relates to the availability of resources. What Barney is asking managers to consider is whether any resources or capabilities they may have within their firm are, in any way, different or unique. If so, then they may have a potential source of competitive advantage which, in turn, may be the basis for creating abnormal profits. The third question takes the rareness of resources and capabilities further by asking managers to consider whether they may have not only valuable and rare resources and capabilities, but also ones that are difficult for other firms to imitate. If this is the case, then Barney's argument is that their firm may have the basis not only for creating a competitive advantage, but also for sustaining that advantage – that is, sustained abnormal profits.

Barney's final question relates not so much to resource and capabilities but to competencies. Has the firm developed the competencies to organise and use its resource base to take advantage of any rare and/or non-imitable resources and capabilities? For our purposes (following Peteraf, 1993), we have expanded this final question to include resources. One other difference between resources and competencies is that resources are tradeable, they can be sold across resource markets. This even applies to intangible resources such as trademarks and brand names, even reputation can appear as an asset on a firm's balance sheet. Therefore, the final question in relation to resources is are they difficult to replicate, and can they be sold – are they mobile?

As can be guessed, these four questions and their implications for a firm's competitive advantage relate directly to our concern with the creation and sustaining of abnormal profits. However, before we proceed to look at this more closely we do need to slightly amend our notion of what is meant by 'normal' and 'abnormal' profits. The economists' notion of normal profit being that which equates with costs (including the entrepreneurs' transfer cost – see Section 4.2) does not easily translate when using the concept of 'value' rather than profit (as will be explained in Chapter 12, a firm's total added value does not equate with a firm's profit). What we mean in this context by 'normal' profit is the industry norm (as we did in Chapter 4 when discussing Ryanair and Direct Line Insurance) – the average profits being earned by other firms in the industry. In practice, this should roughly equate with the economists' normal profit; if it does not then there may well be a case for an investigation by the Competition Commission. Therefore, strictly speaking, 'abnormal' profit means a firm is earning profits in excess of the industry norm and, rather than saying the firm is making a loss, we shall refer to a firm as making below-normal profits – which in most cases would actually roughly equate with the economists' concept of 'loss'.

By combining the Barney approach with the idea of threshold resources and competencies, we can see that for a firm to make normal profits it must have

1.  The necessary threshold resources and capabilities.
2.  These resources and capabilities need to be combined in such a way that they are adding value.
3.  The firm needs to have developed the organisational competencies to ensure that the value-adding activities are actually taking place.

If the firm is generating above-normal profits then added to these three conditions is the need for some of the resources and/or capabilities and/or competencies to be rare. Finally, if the abnormal profits generated by the rare resources/competencies/capabilities are to be sustained in the long run then some element of this mix must be difficult for other firms to copy or imitate.

To summarise:

Normal profits ⇒ threshold resources/capabilities/competencies + adding value + efficiently organised

Short-run abnormal profit ⇒ conditions for normal profits + rareness

Long-run abnormal profit ⇒ condition for SR abnormal profit + non-imitability

The rest of this section will explore these conditions and show how they do in fact create resource-based entry barriers that allow some firms to enjoy sustained abnormal profits.

## 7.2.1 The basis of profit

As summarised above, in order to make any profit at all there are three factors that a firm must have in place. As explained at the end of Section 7.1, the most basic requirement is to have the resources with the required capabilities to be able to produce whatever product or service the firm is to offer. In the simple example of widget making used in Section 7.1 and summarised in Figure 7.1, without all three resources X, Y and Z the firm will not be able to make any widgets. However, just having the resources with the required capabilities is not enough in itself, these resources have to be organised and competencies developed and learnt that enable the transformation process that turns X, Y and Z into widgets to take place. Not only that, in the Barney framework this has been done in such a way that you are maximising the value added that you get from your resources. Figure 7.1 shows that there are three ways of using the capabilities of the resource base of X, Y and Z – all of which lead to widgets being produced. However, if you are to make at least normal profits then you need to be using the combination of X, Y and Z that gives you the most added value.

This leads on to the third basis for making profits – your resources need to be engaged in value-adding activities. There are two aspects to the total value of a particular resource – intrinsic value and value in use. For the moment, let us assume that we are dealing with what Barney refers to as 'common resources', by which he means resources that are easy to get hold of. In economists' jargon, we would say they are resources that are perfectly elastic in supply – there is an unlimited quantity available at the current market price. The intrinsic value of such a resource is its value in its own right which would be reflected in the cost of acquiring that resource from its particular resource market. The value in use, however, is the total value of the resource to a firm once it is combined with other resources within the firm; typically you would expect the value in use to exceed a resource's intrinsic value. Thus, resource X would have to be bought by the widget firm from the relevant resource market; the price paid would reflect the resource's intrinsic value. However, when the firm combined X with Y and Z in the transformation process, the value of X should increase (as would the value of Y and Z). In other words, the activity which combines X, Y and Z becomes a value-adding activity.

To illustrate, let us return to the Marks and Spencer example of the employee being used as a checkout assistant. Assume that there is an unlimited supply of potential checkout assistants and Marks and Spencer pay their checkout assistants £6 per hour. This £6 per hour represents the checkout assistant's intrinsic value – this is the value placed on this particular resource for this service by the market. If, however, when combined with the till at the checkout, the checkout assistant generates £10 of revenue then £4 of added value has been generated.

Figure 7.2 illustrates this; $X_p$ is the price of resource X in the marketplace (£6 per hour for the checkout assistant) and is shown as a vertical line reflecting the fact that supply of X is perfectly elastic. $X_v$ is the total value of X to the firm once

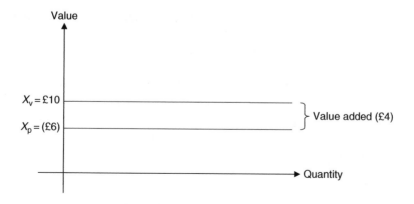

**Figure 7.2**   Common resources

it is combined in the transformation process with Y and Z (£10 in the case of the checkout assistant). Therefore, we can see that the distance $X_v - X_p$ represents the value added of the resource X (£4 is added by combining the checkout assistant with the checkout desk). What the figure shows is that the value added remains constant. The implication is that each unit of the resource is equally valuable to firms. In addition, there is an assumption that resources Y and Z are also common resources, as are the competencies developed, that is, there is an unlimited supply of checkout desks and all checkout assistants are equally competent.

So far, we have been assuming that this value added belongs to the firm; however, this might not be the case, some of the value added may be transferred back to the resource owner. The division of the value added $(X_v - X_p)$ becomes a process of bargaining between the firm and the resource owner, therefore the total value of resource X to a firm becomes:

$$V_x = X_v - X_p - X_t$$

where $V_x$ is the value of X to the firm; $X_v$, the total value of X; $X_p$, the cost of acquiring X; and $X_t$, the added value transferred back to X.

In a situation where all the threshold resources are common resources and with no collective action on the part of the resource holders (such as the existence of Trades Union) then the value of $X_t$ would actually be zero. Given that there is an unlimited supply of X there is no reason for a firm to transfer any of the value added back to the resource holder. If, for example, the resource holder demands some of the value added and threatens to withdraw its use, all the firm would have to do is go back to the resource market and obtain resource X from another supplier at the same market price. In other words, the holders of a common resource have very little power to influence the transfer back to them of any of the added value they help create. This is the case with checkout assistants. Marks and Spencer have no reason to transfer any of the £4 of value added in the example above back to the individual checkout assistant.

The example of the widget firm above with only common resources being used would mean that every widget-making firm would be faced with the same situation in terms of resources, capabilities and potential added values. Provided all the firms are organised efficiently and have therefore developed common competencies, then all the firms should make similar profits – normal profits. If a firm was not efficiently organised then the value added by X would reduce – $X_i$ in Figure 7.3. This lower level of value would be translated into a below-average profit level.

Thus, we can see that in a situation where there are only common resources required to undertake a transformation process, the opportunities for creating abnormal profits through the use of resources is difficult. However, it is possible to make below-normal profits if a firm is not organised efficiently. Therefore, the resource-based view of the firm, even in this simple case, is already offering reasons for differences in profit levels between supposedly very similar firms.

Marks and Spencer, as we shall see, are not the only one using common resources; many smaller retailers, by and large, are. The resources required to set

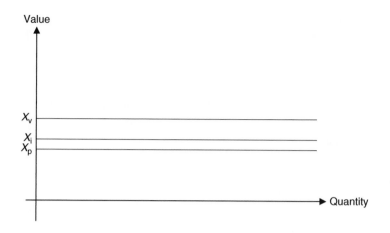

**Figure 7.3**
Below-average
performance

up a newsagents, for example, would mainly be common resources, as would the competencies required to operate the shop. The only unique distinguishing resource may be location. Other than this, opportunities for generating abnormal profits are very limited, the possibility of making below-normal profit through poor organisation is more likely.

## 7.2.2  Creating abnormal profits

In the Barney framework, above-average profits (abnormal profits) are created through a firm having rare resources or who have developed rare competencies. In this context, 'rare' refers to the fact that a particular resource or competence is not generally available and may be specific to a particular firm. Let us examine the case of resources first. In an economic sense, we can say that instead of a resource having a constant value in use, the resource or competency has a diminishing value in use.

In Figure 7.4, the value curve ($V$) is now downward sloping. This indicates that the value of the resource X is diminishing as more is used. Assume that firm A has the unit of the resource X shown as $X_a$, whereas firm B has $X_b$. If we assume

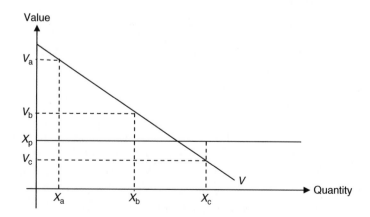

**Figure 7.4**  Rare
resource (short run)

that the market price for X is constant at $X_p$ then we can see that X is adding more value for firm A than for firm B. The value added by X for firm A is $(V_a - X_p)$ compared with only $(V_b - X_p)$ for firm B. If we assume that Y and Z are still common resources then we can see that the higher value added by X for firm A is going to translate into higher profit levels for firm A than for firm B. Firm C is in the worst position, its unit of resource X is actually taking value away from the firm but, as X is a threshold resource, C may simply have to accept this and take profits that are below normal.

This type of situation is one we have encountered before. It is the Ricardian rent example from Section 4.2.1. As discussed in this section, initially the best arable land would be used for growing wheat and would yield a high value $(V_a)$; however, as more land is brought into use then progressively less suitable land is used and value begins to fall $(V_b)$, until it becomes negative $(V_c)$.

The situation is similar for a firm that has developed a rare competence. In effect, the rare competence will mean that organisationally the firm is generating more value from its resources than a rival firm who has not developed the rare competency. This was the situation with Ryanair and Direct Line Insurance when they first entered their respective markets. Ryanair developed the competency of the 'no-frills' airline operation, whereas Direct Line Insurance developed the ability to sell insurance direct to the consumer without the need for agents. Both firms were able to generate more value from their resources than their competitors, many of which were using the same threshold resources.

However, a firm having a rare resource or competency is only a potential route to generating abnormal profits in the short run; these gains can disappear in the long run. There are three general reasons why this may happen. First, the rare resource may not continue to be rare, the rareness may only have arisen from a temporary shortage (for example, computer programmers at the end of the last century when there was a widespread fear about the so-called millennium bug). In this case, once the shortage has been addressed then the value advantage for firm A in Figure 7.4 will disappear and we will return to the situation in Figure 7.2. Put another way, the removal of the shortage turns the resource into a common resource and the potential value added from the use of the resource is the same for all firms (even firm C).

This is partly the explanation as to why the initial abnormal profits of Direct Line Insurance could not be maintained. The call centre concept, which was a new type of resource created by Direct Line Insurance for the selling of insurance, quickly became a common resource as other insurance firms set up similar call centres. In other words, the resource lost its uniqueness.

The second reason why the differential in the value in use between firms may disappear is related to the idea of value transfer raised in Section 7.2.1.

For some resources it may well be the case that the resource market adjusts the price of the resource to reflect the diminishing value of the resource. As shown in Figure 7.5, the price of the resource X varies directly with its value in use to firms. Therefore even though firm A's $V_a$ is higher than firm B's $V_b$, firm A is paying more for X than firm B $(P_a > P_b)$. The variation in price has also equalised the added values for firms A and B $((V_a - P_a) = (V_b - P_b))$. Therefore, the price adjustments

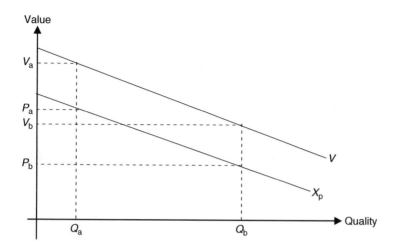

**Figure 7.5** Rare resource after market adjustment

made by the resource market has eliminated firm A's abnormal profits. This is what commonly happens with land prices, for example, the higher yielding arable land would cost more to acquire than the less suitable land. Using a more up-to-date example, rental values for office space in central London ($P_a$) would be more than in central Coventry ($P_b$).

Finally, there is a third reason why the abnormal profits made by a firm holding a rare resource may disappear. The resource holders may realise their value to the firm of their resource and take some of the value added for themselves ($X_t$ in Section 7.2.1 becomes positive).

Thus in Figure 7.6 the $V_t$ curve shows the value that the holder of resource X has transferred back to itself, thus reducing the value added that accrues to the firm. Firm A, for example, previously enjoyed the added value equivalent to ($V_a - X_p$); however, now $T_a$ of this added value has been transferred back to the resource holder and the value added to the firm is now only ($V_a - T_a$). Similarly, the value added for firm B was been reduced to ($V_b - T_b$) and again the short-run advantage enjoyed by firm A has disappeared: ($V_a - T_a$) = ($V_b - T_b$). This, for example, happens in occupations where the employee works on a commission basis.

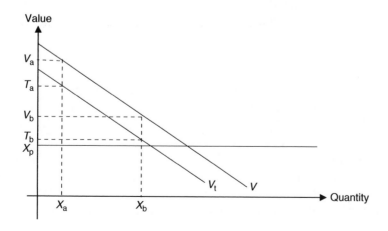

**Figure 7.6** Rare resource after value transfer

Therefore, the possession by a firm of rare resources, or rare competencies, only creates a short-run abnormal profit. For these abnormal profits to become sustained profits into the long run, then a fourth and final factor must also be present – the rare resources or competencies must be impossible to copy.

### 7.2.3   Sustaining abnormal profits

In order for a firm to create a sustained abnormal profit, in addition to the three features of value-adding, rarity and organisation there is a fourth element required:

1.  Some competencies need to be non-imitable

and/or

2.  Some resources need to be non-imitable and immobile.

Therefore, for both competencies and resources if they are to be a source of sustained long-run abnormal profit, then they must be non-imitable, that is, difficult for other firms to replicate. For competencies, this is a sufficient condition; however, for resources they must also be non-tradable or immobile. If they are mobile then any short-run extra added value a firm is able to generate may disappear, in the same way as discussed above in relation to a rare resource. The resource could be traded at a new high price reflecting its value or the value may be transferred to the resource owner. This is discussed further below.

#### 7.2.3.1   Non-imitable competencies

Barney (1995) identifies two sources of non-imitability for competencies:

1.  Competencies that are socially complex
2.  The development of tacit knowledge.

Socially complex resources are resources that emerge from the firm being part of, and engaging in, a range of communities. Firms belong to a range of different types of communities, for example, trade communities; they also create their own internal community and they also operate within a local external community. Through these interactions they can develop unique and difficult to imitate competencies such as a good reputation, trust, friendships and a unique internal culture. When used effectively, these unique resources can be used to reduce transaction costs and can be very difficult to copy. This was partly the source of Marks and Spencer's sustained above-average performance prior to the late 1990s. Marks and Spencer have a very strong brand image which was the source of a good reputation for quality and had also developed a degree of trust with their customers. Many firms try to establish a degree of trust based upon a reputation for service or quality – in transaction cost terms, they aim to reduce the perceived opportunism that may exist in the firm–customer relationship. Once gained, this can be a source of abnormal profits; as noted in Chapter 4, consumers are often willing to pay a price premium for the perceived reduction in risk attached to using a well known and trusted brand. However, socially complex resources of this type can be very fragile – if you lose your reputation then the abnormal profits can very quickly disappear.

The second of Barney's sources of non-imitability comes from the development of tacit knowledge. Firms do not exist in a static time frame; they grow and evolve as they respond to changes in the external environment and in the firms' resource base. As the firms evolve they develop and adapt the competencies required to turn inputs into outputs, they develop the myriad of routines, procedures and policies that anybody who has worked in an organisation will be familiar with (see the discussion of the work of Nelson and Winter (1982) in Chapter 3). Also, as anybody who has worked in more than one organisation will know, this complex structure of competencies will never be the same in any two organisations, even in organisations that carry out identical transformation processes. The way in which my university carries out its enrolment of students will vary from the way any other university enrols its students, in fact all of the 100 plus universities in the UK will enrol their students in a slightly different way. The differences arise through a combination of history and how the particular competency has evolved within the particular organisational setting which in turn reflects the resource base. As Nelson and Winter (1982) discuss, a firm's competencies in terms of its routines develop a life of their own, they become part of the organisational memory. The enrolment process used by a university is likely to have evolved over time as computer systems and the people involved have changed. As Barney points out, many competencies have also been influenced by a constant series of small decisions; the enrolment form, for example, tends to be changed incrementally each year.

Through this process, a firm will develop tacit knowledge, a way of doing things that becomes part of the firm's organisational structure and exists independently of the resources that might be currently used by the firm. This tacit knowledge is extremely difficult for another firm to duplicate and could be a source of sustained long-run profits if the competency developed is giving the firm a cost advantage in the market.

### 7.2.3.2 Non-imitable resources

Resources may be non-imitable for two reasons:

1. Legal restrictions
2. Uniqueness.

Legal restrictions refer to a situation where legal ownership over a resource is assigned to one firm. This would cover intangible assets such as brand names and legally held monopoly rights, both of which cannot be replicated by rival firms once property rights have been granted to a single firm. Uniqueness of a resource refers to more than a resource being simply rare; it also means that a resource is excludable. Once one firm has the resource no other firm has access to that resource. The footballer Wayne Rooney is a unique resource; once he signs for a particular club then no other club has access to his resource services.

### 7.2.3.3  Immobility of resources

However, a resource being difficult, or impossible, to copy is not a guarantee of the resource leading to a sustained long-run abnormal profit for the firm holding the resource. The additional complication for non-imitable resources that does not apply to competencies is that it is often possible for the additional value that is being created by a resource being transferred away from the firm. We saw this above with a rare resource, in the long run the additional value led to the resource being traded on the resource market at a higher price or the resource owner transferring some of the additional value back to them. As noted Wayne Rooney is a unique resource, but when he was transferred from Everton to Manchester United in the summer of 2005 much of the additional added value he could add to United was transferred to Everton through the £30m transfer fee paid and to Rooney through his contract negotiated with United.

Perfect resource immobility is actually quite difficult to find in a lot of industries. What are more common when looking for sources of sustained long-run abnormal profits based on resources are resources that are adding extra value, but where their value is location specific. As discussed previously, the only resource which may enable a newsagents shop to create abnormal profits is its location but even this may be reduced by the differences in rental value attached to different locations. Some resources may also be highly firm specific in that they fit the specific requirements of a particular firm, but their value would drop if they were used elsewhere in the firm or sold to another firm. This means that the firm is able to take the extra value gained from the resource and hence sustain long-run abnormal profits. The resource has a much lower value on its resource market, and the power lies with the firm in negotiating the value split with the resource owner.

## 7.2.4  Creating and sustaining resource entry barriers

Table 7.1 summarises how a firm's resource base and the competencies the firm develops may lead to a firm being able to create and sustain a resource entry barrier.

For a firm to sustain long-run profits all the elements in the table have to be present. In Barney's terminology (1995), competencies need to exhibit four characteristics:

1. Valuable – they need to be sufficient to enable the firm to transform inputs into the required outputs.
2. Rare – have a uniqueness that is not available to other firms.
3. Non-imitable – difficult for other firms to duplicate.
4. Organised – the need to be effectively organised to develop the competencies required to support the production process.

Also for resources

5. Immobility – the additional value created cannot be transferred away from the firm.

**Table 7.1** Resources, competencies and profits

| Resources | Competencies | Outcome |
|---|---|---|
| Minimum level of resources required to undertake the transformation process | Resources deployed effectively to develop the competencies required to support the transformation process | Firm operates at efficient level where costs equal price – normal profits made |
| Firm has unique resources as part of its resource base which arise through: | Firm develops unique competencies through either: | Short-run abnormal profit through either |
| ■ Scarcity<br>■ Strategic use | ■ Effective deployment of unique resources or<br>■ Development of unique competencies | 1. Lower production costs (scarcity, uniqueness)<br>2. Ability to premium price (strategic use) |
| Firm develops non-imitable resources through: | Firm develops non-imitable competencies through: | Long-run sustained abnormal profit through either |
| ■ Statutory restriction<br>■ Uniqueness<br>and Imperfect resource immobility | ■ Socially complex competencies<br>■ Development of tacit knowledge within the organisation which is difficult to replicate | 1. Lower transaction costs (socially complex resources)<br>2. Lower production costs (tacit knowledge)<br>3. Higher value added (resources) |

The absence of any one of these characteristics means the firm will be unable to create a resource entry barrier that leads to a sustained long-run profit.

## 7.3 | The strategists' view of the firm

As discussed earlier in the chapter, the resource-based view of the firm does have clear links back to the behavioural and evolutionary models outlined in Chapter 3. However, the major difference is that the resource-based model of the firm was principally developed within the strategy subject area, and not by economists. This is reflected in the language used in the previous section, we talked about 'value added' rather than 'profits' and 'competitive advantage' rather than 'sustaining abnormal profits'. The purpose of this section is to show how the resource-based view of the firm can be used to illustrate how strategists conceptualise firms from a different perspective than economists: the firm as a value-creating chain rather than a maximiser of profits. However, as we shall see, the strategists' view of the firm complements and adds to economists' view rather than replacing it.

### 7.3.1 Strategic entry barriers and resource entry barriers

Chapter 4 developed the view that the means by which a firm can not only generate but also sustain abnormal profits was through the existence of entry barriers. The suggestion was that these barriers came from three potential sources:

- Structural barriers through being a low-cost producer.
- Strategic barriers through incurring competitive costs and trying to gain more revenue.
- Resource entry barriers through holding, and using efficiently, unique and non-imitable resources.

As was discussed in Chapter 4, structural entry barriers arise from the nature of the supply/cost side of the industry the firm is involved in and simply require the firm to operate in an efficient cost-minimising manner. However, the other two sources of entry barriers require the firm to act in a more conscious manner, taking deliberate actions to try and create the entry barrier to protect and sustain its abnormal profits. The source of the entry barriers is, however, different.

In Part III, we will look at a range of ways in which firms can try and create strategic entry barriers as part of their attempts to increase and protect the revenue they take from a market. The common feature of all the means to be discussed (product differentiation, irreversible commitments, reputation, and so on) will be that the firm is looking for ways in which the market can be manipulated to its own revenue-raising ends. Similarly, Section 7.2 looked at the means by which a firm could use aspects of its resource base to create and sustain abnormal profits. The essential difference, however, is that strategic entry barriers arise from a firm looking to its markets whereas resource entry barriers arise from inside a firm, not from the external market.

This difference between strategic and resource entry barriers is referred to in the strategic management literature as the 'inside-out versus the outside-in' debate. The 'inside-out' view is that a firm should base its competitive strategy on its resource base. From this perspective, the firm's internal resource base is the source of creating a competitive advantage in the marketplace (our resource entry barriers). The older alternative 'outside-in' view is that abnormal profit comes from looking at your markets and developing effective competitive strategies that will lead you to gaining a competitive advantage in those markets (our strategic entry barriers).

The strategists 'outside-in' view will be returned to in Chapter 12, but we shall now examine the 'inside-out' perspective and how, by focusing on a firm's internal resources and competencies, it leads to a different perspective of the firm.

### 7.3.2 The firm as a value chain

Representing the firm as a value chain brings together the resource-based view of the firm and the strategists' view of the firm as a means of creating value. As discussed in Chapter 1, the term 'value' is used by strategists in much the same way as 'profit' is used by economists. The two concepts are not exactly the same (as will be explored in more detail in Chapters 11 and 12); however, for our purposes here value can be taken to mean the total monetary value of the output produced by the firm. The aim of the firm is to add value, which means the total value of output needs to be greater than the cost of producing that output. The value chain view of the firm represents firms as organisations that link resources via the development of competencies in order to produce goods and services with the ultimate aim of creating added value; the costs of the value chain are less than the value of the output produced. Figure 7.7 shows the most widely used representation of a firm's value chain, that developed by Michael Porter (1985).

The value chain shown in Figure 7.7 is a generic means of splitting the firm up into a series of activities and then using this dissected view of the firm to assess

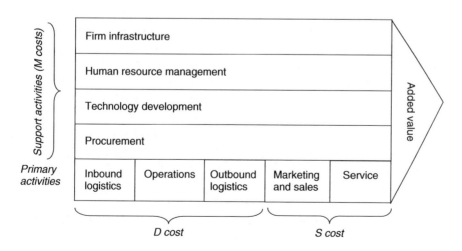

**Figure 7.7** Porter's value chain

where, within the firm, value is being created and, potentially, where value is being lost (that is, the value of the output of the activity is less than the cost of the activity).

As can be seen from Figure 7.7, the value chain splits into two sections: primary activities and support activities. The first three primary activities (inbound logistics–operations–outbound logistics) relate directly to the production of the good or service being produced by the firm (supplying inputs into the production process – the transformation process – getting outputs to the marketplace). As such these three activities taken together incur costs that correspond with our direct production costs $D$ in Figure 4.1. The other two primary activities (marketing and sales, after sales service and support), whilst still relating directly to the firm's output, do not relate to the actual transformation process itself. In terms of our representation of the firm, the costs incurred in these activities relate to competing in the marketplace and hence represent competitive costs $S$.

Porter identified four cross firm support activities. By the firm's infrastructure, he means the internal organisation structure of the firm as may be represented by a firm's organisation chart and the supporting decision-making and communication systems. The human resource management (HRM) activity will have two cross firm roles. First, the HRM activity will ensure the recruitment of staff and help and support for staff once employed. Secondly, the HRM activities will co-ordinate the training and skill development needs of the firm. Technology development relates to the need for firms to develop new products and processes in order to keep pace with rival firms and technological developments. The final support activity is procurement which relates to the acquisition of the firm's inputs for both the transformation process and all the non-productive primary and support activities. In terms of our model of the firm, all of these cross firm activities are not directly related to the transformation process, they are very much support activities that enable the production of the firm's output to take place. As such, they can be classed as management costs, $M$. The only possible exception may be in relation to the technological development activity. In some markets (pharmaceuticals, for example), the need to constantly develop new products may actually be a competitive cost as this is the principal means of competing in the marketplace.

Each of the activities in the value chain will use resources and develop competencies as described in Section 7.1. Similarly, some of these resources and the competencies developed will be threshold resources/competencies – required to undertake that activities' function – and some may be unique and hence be a potential source of competitive advantage and abnormal profit. However, another set of competencies is required to link the separate activities together. There needs to be a set of routines, for example, that co-ordinate the marketing and sales activity with the operations activity; it is no good having a very successful marketing activity if the extra sales generated cannot be then matched by the operations activity. Hence, another source of potential unique competencies is the linkage between the firm's activities.

The Barney model discussed in Section 7.2 readily fits into this value chain framework. If a firm is to create and sustain abnormal profits through its internal resource base and/or its competencies, then it needs to look inside and try to identify those value-creating activities which display the four characteristics of being valuable, rare, non-imitable and organised efficiently. These activities need to be nurtured and used to create sustained abnormal profits for the firm. However, the firm also needs to identify those activities that may be creating less value than costs and hence detracting from the overall value added by the firm – value-destroying activities. For example, a firm may find that it has a very effective sales team built on a wide range of good personal relations with customers that may be a potential source of sustained abnormal profits. However, if the firm has a poor outbound logistics activity and its customers are not receiving the product in the quantities they order, or on time, then this will offset the value added by the marketing activity. One solution for firms who find activities are destroying value is to stop undertaking the activity altogether – firms with poor outbound logistics activity may use a specialist distribution firm instead of trying to undertake the activity themselves.

### 7.3.3 The value chain – an illustrative example

Figure 7.8 shows a simplified value chain for a university. For the purposes of exposition, we shall focus on the teaching function only. The underlying resource base of the university will be its staff (academic and non-academic), students, the university's buildings, other physical resources (for example, the library stock), electronic resources (for example, electronic databases, a virtual learning environment) and its financial resources. A number of key activities have been identified within each of the generic activity boxes. Each of these individual activities requires the university to use its resource base and develop competencies that allow the activity to take place. Take the core activity of teaching, which is a bringing together of students, academic staff and physical resources. There is a series of competencies that need to be developed if students are to arrive in the correct room, at the correct time, with a lecturer who is teaching the module expected. To enable this to happen, there needs to be a timetabling competency which in turn needs to be communicated to both the student and the lecturer. This competency will involve other resources: a member of staff acting as a timetabler, computing services providing an online timetable system and financial resources to pay the staff involved and provide the computing system.

As with any firm, the university will be looking for resources and competencies that allows it to create a competitive advantage. This may come about through having unique resources such as academic staff that are well known and will attract research students or a set of staff able to put on a unique course offering. Alternatively, it may come about through having developed a very effective marketing and sales activity. Equally, the university will be keen to identify value-destroying activities. All universities, for example, will use a specialist advertising agency rather

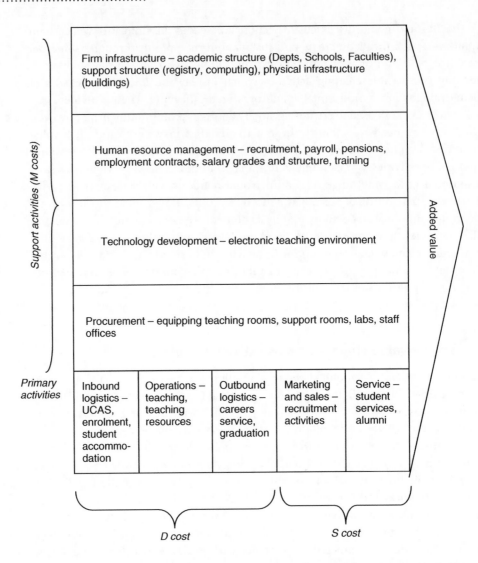

**Figure 7.8** The value chain of a university (teaching)

than undertake this function themselves. Some universities have also identified the provision of student accommodation as a value-destroying activity and have stopped providing accommodation themselves preferring instead to use private firms.

## 7.4 Review and further reading

This chapter began with a series of questions relating to three examples taken from the real world. Reference has been made at various points subsequently as to how taking a resource-based view of a firm helps to answer some of the questions raised. However, let us consider each in turn.

First, there is the case of Direct Line Insurance being apparently unable to sustain their high levels of profits. The problem here relates to the VRIO model discussed in Section 7.2. Direct Line Insurance achieved their initial success by developing new resources (the call centre) and new competencies (running the call centre and dealing directly with the Lloyds insurance market). However, the problem was that there was nothing Direct Line Insurance did which could not be readily done by other insurance firms. In other words, the resources and competencies developed were easily copied. Therefore, the abnormal profits gained by Direct Line Insurance were only short-lived; the rest of the insurance industry imitated the Direct Line Insurance approach and profits returned to the level of normal profits. In terms of the VRIO framework, Direct Line Insurance's resources and competencies were valuable, rare and organised effectively, but they were imitable. So far Ryanair has avoided this fate as it seems to be in a position to be able to sustain its levels of abnormal profit. This is partly because it was able to organise effectively around the single 'no-frills' approach whereas the older airlines are more diverse and have embedded organisational cultures to overcome.

The second example was the problems that have been faced by Marks and Spencer in recent years. For many years, Marks and Spencer were able to create and sustain abnormal profits, they were achieving all four of Barney's requirements – value, rare, non-imitability (the brand name as well as the close relationship with employees) and were effectively organised. One explanation for the sudden reversal in fortunes in the late 1990s was that they failed to recognise changes in the marketplace, particularly the arrival of new more flexible competitors such as Zara and New Look. These new chains reflected the changing patterns of consumer demands. For example, the new stores had the ability to restock with completely new ranges of clothes every six to eight weeks whereas Marks and Spencer were stuck in their tried and trusted biannual autumn/winter and spring/summer collections. The general view was that Marks and Spencer became complacent or, in the Barney framework, they failed to be organised effectively – senior management failed to recognise the changes in the marketplace and act accordingly. As the abnormal profits disappeared there was a knock-on effect on one of the non-imitability aspects of Marks and Spencer namely its brand name which was once the symbol of quality but quickly became the symbol of dowdiness.

Finally, the British Gas example illustrates an application of the idea that strategy may be driven by inside-out considerations rather than outside-in considerations, as was discussed in Section 7.3. Over many years, British Gas had developed the threshold competencies required to manage a large customer base and read meters and collect payments from households for gas services provided. With the opening up to competition of the other utilities markets, these same competencies could be used in the retail end of both the electricity and fixed line telephone industries; in fact there were economies of scale through, for example, the provision of a single website and payment system.

Many of the papers referred to in this chapter can be found in Foss (1997). Barney (1997) is also another important source for this approach to the firm. Fuller explanations of the value chain concept can be found in Johnson, Scholes and

Whittington (2005) and Lynch (2002). This chapter concludes Part II of the book. Part III moves on to look the revenue-maximising end of our extended model of the firm.

## 7.5 | Student exercises

### 7.5.1 Review exercises and points for discussion

1. Provide brief and clear definitions of the following key terms and concepts as used in this chapter.

   a. A resource
   b. Capabilities
   c. Competencies
   d. Threshold resources, capabilities and competencies
   e. Unique resources, capabilities and competencies
   f. Resource entry barrier
   g. Value of a resource or competency
   h. Rareness of a resource or competency
   i. Imitability of a competency
   j. Immobility of a resource
   k. Common resources
   l. Socially complex competencies
   m. Tacit knowledge
   n. The value chain.

2. One of the exercises at the end of Chapter 4 looked at the success Apple has been experiencing with the introduction of their iPod. As was seen this has led to a phenomenal growth in Apple's profits and a 75 per cent market share in the USA for MP3 players.

   a. From your research on Apple what do you think might be the main resources they use for the production of their MP3 player, and what competencies have they developed?
   b. Which of Apple's resources and competencies are unique? In other words, from a RBT perspective, what is the source of Apple's current high level of profits?
   c. The final question on Apple in Chapter 4 asked whether this high level of profits was sustainable. Reconsider your answer to this after applying the Barney VRIO criteria (summarised in Table 7.1) to the unique resources and competencies identified in (b) above.

### 7.5.2 Application exercise

Consider a firm with which you are familiar, maybe one you work for or have worked for in the past.

a. Detail what you consider to be the main resources of the firm. Are all of the resources threshold resources or do some appear to be unique resources?
b. Similarly, identify the main competencies of the firm. Are any of the competencies unique?
c. Construct a simple value chain for the firm. Distinguish clearly between activities that incur direct production costs, those which are strategic costs and those which are management costs.

# Firms and Market  Behaviour

# Game Theory and the Behaviour of Firms

## LEARNING OUTCOMES

On completion of this chapter the reader should be able to

■ Explain the structure of games

■ Define the core concepts used in game theory

■ Use some basic games to analyse the behaviour of firms

■ Explain the interdependent nature of a firm's decision-making

## KEY NEW CONCEPTS

| | | |
|---|---|---|
| Nash equilibrium | Credible threats | Pareto moves |
| Zero-sum/non-zero sum | Dominant strategies | The PARTS framework |
| The proactive firm | The reactive firm | Mixed motive games |
| Coopetition | | |

## KEY NEW MODELS

The prisoners' dilemma      Non-cooperative games

## MODELS AND CONCEPTS DEVELOPED FURTHER

Endogenous demand variables      Competitive costs      Value

In Part III of this book, we turn our attention to the output market side (Figure 4.1). As discussed in Chapter 4, the objective of a firm in its output markets is to maximise the revenue that it takes from those markets. At its disposal are the endogenous demand variables identified in Section 4.2.2 price, marketing and R&D (Table 4.7). As was also discussed in Chapter 4, the use of these variables can involve the firm in an indirect cost that we defined as being the competitive cost $S$ in Figure 4.1. Chapter 9 looks more closely at the nature of these competitive costs incurred by firms. However, before we can analyse the behaviour of firms as they try to maximise revenue, we need to develop an analytical framework that allows us to do this. For reasons developed below, the neo-classical theory of market structures is restricted in its applicability to the analysis of how firms behave in the real world. What we will discuss in this chapter is an alternative approach which uses game theory to analyse the behaviour of firms.

## 8.1 | The proactive behaviour of firms

Consider the selection of short reports taken from various financial journals:

- 'Freeview to take on BSkyB – Freeview to go head-to-head with British Sky Broadcasting'. (*Financial Times*, 19 May 2006)
- 'Chinese steeled for battle.... Chinese steelmakers appeared to dig in for a prolonged battle with the world's biggest iron ore miners'. (*Financial Times*, 19 May 2006)
- 'On the prowl for outsourcers – EDS and other software and services companies are snapping up back-office operations in India'. (*Business Week*, 17 April 2006)
- 'Will someone grab CSC? – While computer services companies are not exactly sexy, suffering stodgy growth and cutthroat competition of late, their long term contracts and steady cash flow make them juicy takeover bait'. (*Business Week*, 17 April 2006)

Each of these reports reflects some of the most common elements of the business world faced by firms – competition with rival companies, relationships with suppliers, mergers and acquisitions. Each of the reports also shows firms that are actively engaged in their business environments: introducing new products, trying to influence suppliers, looking for new markets, considering the takeover of existing firms. How does this square with the models of market behaviour found in neo-classical theory and summarised in Section 4.2?

### 8.1.1 The reactive firm

Neo-classical theory has developed various models of how firms behave in their output markets. At one extreme, we have the model of perfect competition. As we have seen in Chapter 4, in this model a firm's behaviour is totally driven by the need to maintain the correct level of output so as to always maintain its profit maximising position. The firm takes the price for its goods and services from the market and fixes the level of output that equates marginal cost and marginal revenue. The only decision the firm takes relates to the level of output to produce, and this decision is taken in complete isolation from the decisions taken by other firms, who are simply adjusting their output levels in exactly the same way. What is clear is that in this market structure, firms are taking independent decisions in a simple knee-jerk fashion to changes in the market price – the firm is a reactive firm.

At the other end of the spectrum is the model of monopoly where there is only one firm in the market. The behaviour of the monopoly firm is, like the perfectly competitive firm, purely reactive. Like the perfectly competitive firm, the monopolist is only concerned with maximising profits, except this time the firm has the choice between fixing its price and fixing its output. The monopolist may fix a price that maximises profit at the point where marginal cost equals marginal revenue; this then translates into a corresponding level of output. Alternatively, it fixes a level of output at the same profit maximising level that in turn translates, via the demand curve, into a price. Either way, it is acting in a similar knee-jerk reactive fashion to the market conditions in just the same way as a perfectly competitive firm.

## 8.1.2 The proactive firm

Firms in the real world, however, do not act in the reactive fashion of firms in perfectly competitive or monopoly markets as described above. As discussed previously, the models of perfect competition and monopoly rely upon the five neo-classical assumptions that in the real world may, at best, only partially hold. What we see in the real world are proactive firms. In each of the four short reports at the beginning of this section, the firms involved are not merely reacting to changes in their environment; they are proactively changing, or looking to change, the environment themselves. Freeview are developing a new product to compete with BSkyB; the Chinese steelmakers are trying to dictate the nature of the relationship they have with their suppliers; in the two final reports, firms are trying to change the structure of the industries by mergers and acquisitions. The real world is not dominated by perfectly competitive markets, monopolistically competitive markets or monopolies, but by oligopoly markets. Real-world markets tend to have a small number of dominate firms, often surrounded by a fringe of smaller firms serving specialised or niche markets. All the real-world firms used as examples in the book so far, and indeed those to be used in the following chapters, operate in oligopoly markets.

Neo-classical theory has developed a number of models to try and explain oligopoly markets, one of the more familiar being the Sweezy kinked demand curve. However, the major problem in trying to apply neo-classical models to real-world oligopolies is the model's reliance on independent decision-making – firms taking decisions based solely on their own cost and revenue functions. Decisions taken by firms in the real world are conscious decisions taken by the firms as they attempt to use the endogenous demand variables to try and maximise revenue. In addition, they are not taken in isolation of what is happening around them. In some of the short reports at the beginning of this section, the firms involved were reacting to decisions taken by other firms, the Chinese steelmakers, for example. Alternatively, the decisions taken by one firm would require other firms in the market to change their behaviour. BSkyB, for example, would have to respond proactively to the introduction of a rival product, they could not simply wait and reactively adjust their position once revenues started to go down.

In other words, what we are saying is that decisions taken by firms in oligopoly markets, and hence most real-world firms, are both proactive conscious decisions and interdependent on decisions taken by rival firms. In order to analyse and assess the behaviour of firms in the real world, we need an analytical framework that captures this deliberate interdependent decision-making that takes place in the real world. The game theory approach does exactly this and has, in recent years, become increasingly used to analyse the behaviour of firms in oligopoly markets. However, before we move to look at the game theory framework there is one more issue that needs highlighting which game theory also throws some light on.

### 8.1.3 Should firms compete or co-operate?

At the heart of both strategy and microeconomics is the idea that firms compete. The dictionary definition of 'compete' is 'strive in rivalry' (*Collins Shorter English Dictionary*, 1995). The very term 'strategy' is derived from the Greek word 'strategos' which refers to the 'art of war'. Look again at the language used in the short reports used at the beginning of this section. The terms used in these reports reflect this aggressive war-like/jungle view of the business world – 'take on', 'head to head', 'steeled for battle', 'a prolonged battle', 'on the prowl', 'snapping up', 'cutthroat competition' and 'juicy takeover bait'.

However, there is another view that is contrary to the war/jungle metaphor used almost universally in textbooks and the financial press. Consider these comments, one from the founder of modern economics, Adam Smith, and the second, written nearly 200 years later, by the Canadian economist John K Galbraith.

> People of the same trade seldom meet together, even for merriment and diversion, but the conversation ends in a conspiracy against the public, or in some contrivance to raise prices. It is impossible indeed to prevent such meetings by any law which either could be executed, or would be consistent with liberty and justice. (Smith, 1911)

> The convention against price competition is inevitable ... The alternative is self-destruction. (Galbraith, 1967)

Smith's quote is suggesting that the underlying motivation is not for firms to compete but quite the opposite, it is for firms to co-operate. Galbraith's quote suggests that this urge to co-operate is not only strong but essential. However, this perspective sits uneasily with the traditional view of market competition (with all the war and jungle metaphors), and the models and frameworks used to explain it, as the prime, and desirable, motivation behind firms' behaviour. Game theory, however, provides a theoretical perspective that supports the views expressed by Smith and Galbraith – the underlying instinct of firms may be indeed to co-operate not compete. This then raises the question of should firms co-operate, or should they compete with each other? This is a topic we shall return to at the end of the chapter as game theory throws some interesting light on the debate.

## 8.2 | The nature of games

Game theory grew out of the work of the mathematician John von Neuman who in the late 1920s became interested in whether there was any underlying theory that could explain the outcome of various parlour games (Backhouse, 2002), and help players of poker. Eventually, his ideas were presented in *The Theory of Games and Economic Behaviour* written along with the economist Oscar Morgenstein in 1944 (Neuman and Morgenstein, 1944). This book laid the foundation for modern game theory with contributions from a range of other writers, most notably John Nash, who formulated an equilibrium condition for games which has had far reaching consequences for how we view the behaviour of firms (the idea of Nash equilibrium will be discussed in Section 8.4).

### 8.2.1  The terminology of games

Like any academic subject area, game theory has developed its own terminology (or jargon) that is used to analyse and theorise about the area. The intention in this section is to try and demystify the game theory terminology by using three well-known games as illustrative examples – the three being:

- The card game patience (or solitaire found on any Microsoft Windows package)
- Chess
- Football.

Any game requires rules that define the game and set its parameters. In order to be an effective set of rules, there are three aspects of a game that need to be clearly defined at the outset:

1. The structure of the game
2. The nature of the game
3. The time frame for the game.

Let us consider each of these in more detail.

#### 8.2.1.1   The structure of the game

The structure of a game needs to identify who the players are and what the purpose, or objective, of the game is. The structure also needs to define what it is that a player wins from playing the game, or what the game's pay-off is.

The pay-off can be thought of as how the objective is quantified – the objective is how you win; the pay-off is what you win. An important aspect of the pay-off is whether you are playing for a fixed or variable amount of pay-off. If, for example, you enter a 'guess the number of sweets in the jar' competition and you are the only contestant to guess correctly, then you win the £100 prize, or, if somebody also guesses correctly then you share the prize and win £50. If you guess incorrectly, then you win nothing. When playing a pinball machine, however, the pay-off (points won) is not a fixed amount. In this case your pay-off, the number of points you score, depends upon how well you play the game. Games where the pay-off is a fixed amount are referred to as a zero-sum game (the 'guess the number of sweets in the jar' game); whatever one player wins is directly reflected in what the other player loses. On the other hand, games where the pay-off can be variable are referred to as non-zero sum games (like playing the pinball machine).

### 8.2.1.2 The nature of the game

The nature of the game needs to define various elements. First, the number of players involved is important – is the game a single-player game, such as singles tennis, or multiplayer, such as doubles tennis? A second important aspect of the nature of the game in relation to the players is whether the players are in direct competition with each other (as in singles tennis) or are they co-operating together to maximise the size of the joint pay-off (as in doubles tennis). Alternatively, some games have an element of both competition and co-operation. Most team games, such as cricket and football, are of this type of 'mixed-motive' game. In order to achieve the pay-off by winning the game, you need to compete directly against the other team; however, if you are to achieve the objective then you also need to co-operate with the other players in your own team.

The nature of the game also needs to be set out in the form of a series of rules defining how the game is to be played. The rules of the game need to specify the limits on the action of the players, what they can and cannot do in order to achieve the game's objective. One important aspect of the rules for our purposes concerns how the game is played in terms of moves made by the players. Is the game sequential, one player moves then another responds (as in tennis), or simultaneous, players move at the same time (as in a 100-m race)? Finally, there are assumptions to be made about the level of knowledge of the players and the informational environment within which the game takes place. The last two aspects define the degree of uncertainty there may be in the likely outcome of the game. A chess grandmaster will always beat a novice beginner simply because the grandmaster's level of knowledge is so much greater. However, whether you can predict the outcome before the game takes place depends upon whether you know that one of the players is a grandmaster and the other is not. In other words, with full information you will be able to predict the outcome of the game; however, with imperfect information this may not be the case.

### 8.2.1.3 The time frame

Time frame refers to how often the game is played; in practice there are three possibilities. First, the game is played once and once only, such as a game of pool between two friends in a pub. This type of game is referred to as a 'one-shot' game. Secondly, the game may be repeated ad infinitum, it is played once then repeated again and again and again with no end (the two friends, for example, play an ongoing sequence of pool games night after night). Thirdly, the game may be repeated but there is an end point to the sequence of games. Our two friends in the pub, for instance, may decide to play a best of five rather than a single game of pool.

In game theory, the distinction between the one-shot game and the repeated game (of either type) is important because in repeated games the players build up knowledge of how the other players react in certain circumstances. This accumulated knowledge (or history as it is commonly referred to) can become an important factor in the decision-making process of the two players during the game. For example, in the sequence of games between our two pool-playing friends it may become apparent during the first game that one of the players plays a risky game by always going for his shots and trying to pot the balls, no matter how difficult the shot may be. His opponent can use this knowledge in subsequent games by playing a more defensive type of game and forcing errors out of his pot-shot happy friend. The risk-averse player may lose the first game, and hence the match if the game was a one-shot game, but he may win the overall match if the match is a repeated series of five games.

The other issue in relation to repeated games is that as the game is repeated the starting situation for each game will change, this may then affect how the game is played. If, for example, one of our pool players had a 2–0 lead in the sequence of games he may play a more risky game than if the score was 2–2. When he is 2–0 up in the match he has less to lose than when the result of the match depends on the last frame.

## 8.2.2 Some illustrative examples

At the outset of any game these three aspects of the games – structure, nature and time frame – are set down and known by the players. In order to play the game and try to achieve the objective, and hence receive the pay-off, players need to decide how they are to play. In other words, they need to develop strategies that involve trying to determine the actions to take from the range of possibilities that may be open to them. Does the tennis player adopt a serve and volley game or opt for a base-line game? Which of the numerous chess openings does the chess player choose? Does a cricket captain include an extra batsman or pick a spin bowler? An important factor in each of these three cases may well be the strategy that you expect your opposing player to adopt. During repeated games, as discussed above, strategies may change as you discover more about how your opponent plays and perhaps more about how you or your team are playing. In addition, new strategies may have to be employed as the game is repeated and the situation and possible outcome of the games changes.

**Table 8.1** Summary of illustrative games' features.

|  | Structure | Nature | Time frame |
|---|---|---|---|
| Patience | ■ Objective – cards sorted into suites | ■ Single-player game, hence independent decision-making | One-shot game |
|  | ■ Pay-off – objective achieved or not | ■ Sequential moves |  |
|  | ■ Zero-sum game | ■ Rules specified |  |
|  |  | ■ Limited knowledge at the outset of the game |  |
| Chess | ■ Objective – capture opponents king | ■ Two players | One-shot game or repeated games if part of a tournament |
|  | ■ Pay-off – win game (one-shot game) or win points (repeated game) | ■ Pure conflict game with sequential moves |  |
|  | ■ Zero sum | ■ Interdependent decision-making |  |
|  |  | ■ Rules specified |  |
|  |  | ■ Complexity of the game leads to bounded rationality of players |  |
| Football | ■ Objectives – outscore the opposing team | ■ Two teams | One-shot game (cup games) or repeated games (league games) |
|  | ■ Pay-off – wins points (league) or progress to next round (cup) | ■ Mixed motives game with sequential moves |  |
|  | ■ Zero sum | ■ Rules specified and enforced by adjudicator during the game | |
|  |  | ■ Asymmetric information |  |

To illustrate how game theory terminology can be used, let us now examine the rules of three familiar games in the terms set out above. Table 8.1 summarises the set of rules for each of the three games.

### 8.2.2.1 The card game patience (the reactive firm)

The structure of the card game patience is that it is a single-player game with the objective of sorting the cards into a sequential order by suite. The pay-off is either you achieve the objective or you do not, and the game is therefore a zero-sum game. The nature of the game is that, being a single-player game, the player is taking independent decisions; the player does not have to take into account the actions of any other players. The rules specify how the cards are laid out and how the player should play the game, these are the limits placed on the player in trying to achieve the game's outcome. In terms of knowledge the player starts with very limited knowledge; all the player can see are the seven upturned cards that start the game. However, as the game proceeds the player's knowledge gradually improves as the cards are revealed during the play. The game is sequential, but not in the normal sense that players respond in turn to each other's moves. In this case, the single player responds at the end of each turn by making decisions based on the new information the move has revealed, the card showing at the top of the deck and/or the new cards showing on the table.

Finally, the game is a one-shot game. The game can obviously be played over and over again but each playing of the game is completely independent from the previous games; the cards are dealt at the beginning of each game in a purely random manner. The only slight bit of history that might be built up is in the experience of the player at playing the game. The development of strategies to play the game is very limited; given the randomness of the initial card dealt, the player simply tries to make the best response to the cards that are revealed as the game develops.

This type of game has all the elements of the reactive firm discussed in Section 8.1. The player makes decisions purely in response to the cards turned up; there is no interaction with any other players or any other aspect of the environment. This is exactly what the reactive firms in the perfectly competitive or monopoly models do – they make decisions on price or output based purely on the market conditions they find, without reference to other firms or the wider environment.

### 8.2.2.2  Chess (the proactive firm)

Chess is a two-player game where the objective is to capture the opponent's king. The pay-off depends on the time frame for the game. If the game is a one-shot game then the pay-off is simply winning or losing the game. However, if the game is part of a sequence of games in a tournament then the pay-off is points – one for a win, zero for a loss and half for a drawn game. In both cases, the game is a zero-sum game. The nature of the game is that it is competitive, with each player trying to beat his or her opponent, and decision-making is interdependent. The rules specify the limits of the players' actions by defining how the pieces move around the board, and the moves are sequential – one player makes a move and the other player responds.

On one level, knowledge is transparent, there are no hidden pieces and moves are made in the open. However, on another level, there is hidden knowledge in that the number of possible sets of moves is so large that no one player can ever achieve perfect knowledge of the game's possible outcomes. By comparison, in the game of noughts and crosses it is possible to achieve perfect knowledge. In noughts and crosses the number of possible sets of moves is limited, and it is possible to quickly learn all the possible sequence of moves and hence ensure that you never lose a game. Chess is too complicated to do this.

As indicated above chess can be played as a one-shot game or as a repeated game. If the games are repeated then the players will begin to learn how their opponent plays – their strengths and weaknesses or their favourite opening moves, for example. In other words the sequence of games generates a history that will begin to influence how players react when faced with situations that are similar to those that are arisen in the past. Tournament chess is of the type where the games have an end point, in that one of the players reaches the required number of points or the number of games played is specified by the rules. However games between the worlds' top players do have aspects of the other type of repeated games, those that are repeated over and over again. Although meetings may take place within the context of a tournament top players will already have a history of their opponents through previous games played, and recorded, against a range of other top players as well as themselves. Thus each game is part of an ongoing sequence that extends beyond the confines of the particular tournament they happen to be taking place in. The strategy a player adopts depends upon a whole range of factors such as the previous experience and the opponent's experience. However, during the playing of the game you try to adopt the best strategy given your opponent's move, but this best strategy will be limited by your own experience and ability at the game.

The game of chess with its moves and countermoves as players react to, and try to anticipate each other's moves, is one that reflects the behaviour of many firms when competing in their output markets. For example, the introduction of a new product into the market by Freeview (Section 8.1) would have involved Freeview in trying to anticipate the reaction of BSkyB. Likewise, after the introduction, BSkyB will have to adjust their strategy which, once revealed, Freeview would have to respond to – and so on. Over time the two companies would develop an understanding of how the other reacts in certain circumstances – do they always respond to price changes, for example? In other words, the market develops a history as the game is repeated – in the same way as the chess players develop an understanding of each other the more they play.

### 8.2.2.3 Football (proactive firms and co-ordinated behaviour)

Football is a multiplayer game, 22 players arranged into two teams. The objective is to outscore your opponents. As with chess, the pay-off varies depending on context. If the game is part of a league then the pay-off is points, three for a win, zero if you lose and one if the game is a draw. However, if the game is part of a cup competition then the pay-off is you either progress to the next round or you do not. Again in both instances the games are zero sum; if you lose the cup tie, your opponents go through; if you lose the league match you get zero points and your opponents get three. The pay-offs are fixed. In terms of the nature of the game, football is a mixed motive game, it has elements of both competition and co-operation. The 22 players are arranged into two teams of 11. The eleven players in a team act in a co-ordinated way to try and beat the opposing team. There is co-ordination within each team, but competition between the teams.

The limits on players' actions are specified by the rules which cover the length of the game, rules by which the game is played (throw-ins, free kicks, corners, penalty kicks, off-sides) and the number of substitute players allowed to be used and (of course) that only one outfield player per team is allowed to touch the ball up with his hands. Unlike the other two games considered, football has a team of adjudicators involved in the game – the referee and two assistant referees. The game is sequential, the ball moves between the players. As with chess the game would appear to be fairly transparent; all the players are known and moves are all in the open; however, there is also hidden knowledge relating to, for example, the tactics to be adopted by the team or the fitness of individual players.

The time frame can vary. Cup games are generally one-shot games, unless the game is drawn when the game is then repeated once. League games are, however, repeated games, but not always against the same opponents. The league games, however, do have an end point, when each team has played each other twice. However, elements of repeated games between opponents that transcend the single league seasons can develop their own ongoing history. This is particularly the case for games between local rivals. The first meeting between Manchester City and Manchester United, for example, was in 1902 and these derby games are often presented as being 'one off games' when in fact they are part of an ongoing sequence of games stretching back over 100 years with their own accumulated history.

As we shall investigate later in this chapter, and also in Chapters 9 and 10, elements of mixed motive games can be observed in some business behaviour. One example is the behaviour of cartels where groups of firms come together to fix prices or outputs – co-ordinating behaviour – but then compete with non-cartel members – competitive behaviour. Another interesting example of firms playing a mixed motive game is looked at in Chapter 9 where the firms inside a market compete with each other, but have a tacit understanding that they will co-operate with each other to prevent the entry of new firms.

### 8.2.3 Business and games

The games considered above may seem far removed from the real world of firms, markets and the competitive process. However, the interaction and behaviour of firms involved in the competitive process in markets can be readily assessed using the same game theory framework developed at the beginning of this section. Let us use the UK supermarket industry to illustrate how the market can be presented in a game theory context (this industry will be examined in more depth during Chapter 12).

### 8.2.3.1   The structure of the game

The players are the various supermarket chains and all of the hundreds of smaller locally based supermarkets. Their objectives are to make profits through the selling of, principally, food although some of the larger supermarkets offer a range of secondary goods as well. The pay-off is the money value of the profits made and the game is non-zero sum – there is no fixed amount of profit available to divide amongst the players.

### 8.2.3.2   The nature of the game

The game is a non-cooperative game. The implication is that the firms take independent decisions, there is no collusion and the decisions taken are interdependent; if Tesco instigates a price-cutting campaign then the other national supermarkets need to take a decision in response. Given the complexity of considering a whole real-world market as a single game, some moves will be simultaneous, day-to-day decisions on store layout for instance, or sequential, a response to a given strategic action by a rival firm such as an across-the-board price-cutting campaign. The move sequence depends to some extent on the moves that are made simultaneously.

The rules of the game have two broad elements. First, there are the formal restrictions placed on the behaviour of supermarkets by a whole host of rules and regulations covering everything from where they can build their stores in the first place to how they dispose of their waste. Secondly, as in any market, there tends to be a set of informal rules that reflects the prevailing business culture of the market, sometimes formalised in sets of voluntary codes of practice, but also often arising through custom and practice.

### 8.2.3.3   The time frame

The game is infinitely repeated; it is played over and over again with no obvious end in view. Therefore the supermarket game has accumulated a long and fairly transparent history, all the main players know how their rivals have acted and reacted to past changes in the market or changes in their own strategies. Thus when Tesco introduced loyalty cards a number of years ago they knew that all the other major supermarkets were likely to follow suit – and they duly did. The only possible uncertainty may be when a new player enters the market, most likely through merging or taking over existing players, hence the uncertainty created when Asda was taken over by the US giant supermarket chain Wal Mart. The new player has not played the UK supermarket game before, hence there is no history for the incumbent firms to assess how they are likely to act or react to changes in the market and rivals' strategies.

The means by which the players in the supermarket game play the game, the strategies pursued, relate directly back to the three sources of abnormal profits discussed in Section 4.4. They aim to increase revenue through a range of marketing strategies such as selective price cutting, loss leaders, buy-one-get-one-free (BOGOF offers), tie-in strategies (such as loyalty cards) and other strategies, all aimed at trying to create a strong brand image for the firm (an examination of these strategies forms the basis of Chapter 9). Similarly, they will also aim to minimise costs through trying to obtain the lowest cost suppliers, as well as maintain a size sufficient to achieve the full benefits of both economies of scale and of scope. Finally, they will try to ensure that they are operating as efficiently as possible in terms of the resources they have and how those resources are used. Thus they will try to obtain the best staff, have an efficient distribution system and make most efficient use of store space and all the many other aspects of resourcing and running a supermarket. To win the game the individual supermarket needs to create a sustained abnormal profit that is protected by entry barriers as discussed in Section 4.4. Game theory provides a means of modelling and analysing how firms try to create one of the types of entry barriers identified in Section 4.4, namely, strategic entry barriers.

Section 8.4 looks in detail at two types of business games, each of which reveal interesting aspects of business behaviour. Chapters 9 and 10 look in detail at some of the means by which firms develop and pursue strategies aimed at building and sustaining strategic entry barriers. However, before this we need to look at a deceptively simple game, the prisoners' dilemma game that, when applied to business, provides some of the key concepts and outcomes of the economics of game theory.

## 8.3 | The prisoners' dilemma game

### 8.3.1  Basic structure

The prisoners' dilemma game is a deceptively simple game. It was first used by the mathematician Professor A.W. Tucker in a lecture at Stanford University in 1950 to highlight some of the issues that arise from game theory. The game concerns the dilemma faced by two criminals arrested for a serious crime but, as we shall see in the next section, the issues raised by the game translate directly to the representation of the behaviour of firms in oligopoly markets. The game is presented below using the analytical framework developed in the previous section.

#### 8.3.1.1  The structure of the game

Assume that there are two criminals, Bert and Harry, who are arrested by the police for breaking and entering into a factory, a crime the police claim, quite correctly, they committed together. In addition, during the robbery a night watchman was attacked and suffered serious injuries. The game revolves around the decisions that Bert and Harry take during their separate interviews with the police as to whether to confess to the more serious crime of grievous bodily harm (GBH) or not. In making those decisions the objective of both Bert and Harry is to stay out of prison or at least to minimise the amount of time they have to spend in prison. The pay-off to the game is the length of the prison sentence Bert and Harry actually receive. The game is non-zero sum, as there is no fixed period of imprisonment that needs to be split between the two prisoners. The length of the prison sentence actually varies depending on the combination of decisions made by the two prisoners.

### 8.3.1.2 The nature of the game

The game is, initially, a non-cooperative game as the rules state that Bert and Harry are arrested separately and have no contact with each other before being interviewed by the police. In addition, the pay-off for Bert not only depends upon his own decisions, but also upon the decisions taken by Harry, and vice versa. The game is played in a simultaneous manner; the prisoners are interviewed in adjoining rooms at the same time by different sets of police officers. The police do not have quite enough evidence to convict both of the men of the more serious crime of GBH; they need at least one of the prisoners to confess and inform on the other in order to obtain the GBH conviction. If neither confesses to the assault then both Bert and Harry can only be convicted on a less serious charge of breaking and entering the factory. The police are, however, willing to do a deal by letting one of the men go free if they confess and informs on the other, provided the other person does not confess. Bert and Harry know of the situation and are also aware of the various pay-offs they might receive.

### 8.3.1.3 The time frame

The game is a one-shot game, the prisoners are interviewed once, then they are either charged with the crime or set free.

### 8.3.1.4 The pay-off matrix

The normal manner of representing this sort of two-person non-cooperative game is by means of a pay-off matrix that sets out all the possible outcomes to the game. Given the above specification of the game, Bert and Harry have to choose one of two strategies: either they confess to the more serious charge of GBH or they choose not to confess.

The matrix shows the four possible outcomes to the game given by the combination of decisions open to the two prisoners. In addition, the matrix also demonstrates the interconnected nature of the game (Figure 8.1).

Let us look at the payoff matrix from Bert's point of view (in reading the matrix the first number in each grid relates to the row, that is, Bert's pay-off). There are four possible pay-offs for Bert: 15 years in prison, 5 years in prison, 1 year in prison or he goes free. The actual outcome for Bert depends partly on his decision on whether to confess to the GBH charge or not, and partly on what Harry decides to do. If Bert confesses to GBH and so does Harry then Bert gets 5 years in prison,

Harry

|      | | Confess | Not confess |
|------|-|---------|-------------|
| **Bert** | Confess | (5, 5) | (0, 15) |
|      | Not confess | (15, 0) | (1, 1) |

**Figure 8.1** The prisoners' dilemma pay-off matrix

as does Harry (the north-west box on the matrix). However, if Bert confesses but Harry does not then Bert benefits from the police deal for informing on Harry and is rewarded by being set free (the north-east box). If neither Bert nor Harry confess to GBH then the police do not have enough evidence for the assault charge and both Bert and Harry are only convicted of the lesser crime of breaking and entering, and they go to prison for one year (the south-east box). The worst case outcome for Bert would be if he chose not to confess but Harry does the deal with the police and confesses to GBH in which case Bert would go to prison for 15 years (the south-west box).

What is the outcome of the game? If you were Bert what would you choose to do – confess or not confess? Let us look at your options. If Harry confesses to the assault charge then you are faced with two possible outcomes (shown in bold in Figure 8.2) – if you also confess then you go to prison for 5 years, but if you do not confess then you take the full blame for the assault and go to prison for 15 years. Obviously the best decision to take, if you think Harry might confess, is to confess. However, if Harry decides not to confess then the outcomes change (the italics outcomes in Figure 8.2). This time if you confess then you benefit from the police deal and are set free. If you also choose not to confess then you are convicted of the less serious crime of breaking and entering and you face one year in prison. However, in looking at the options the best choice for you seems to be, again, to confess.

Therefore, by applying rational analysis to the game you, as Bert, would conclude that the best strategy for you to follow, irrespective of whether Harry confesses or not, is to confess. The technical term for the 'confess' strategy is a dominant strategy, it is the best choice to make irrespective of what the other player decides to do. If you looked at the game from Harry's point of view then you would reach exactly the same conclusion that your dominant strategy is to confess. Therefore, both Bert and Harry would confess and the outcome of the game is the north-west box and both go to prison for 5 years.

Harry

|      | | Confess | Not confess |
|------|-|---------|-------------|
| **Bert** | Confess | (**5**, 5) | (*0*, 15) |
|      | Not confess | (**15**, 0) | (*1*, 1) |

**Figure 8.2** Bert's choices

## 8.3.2 Changing the outcome of the game

Close examination of Figure 8.1, however, shows that the (confess–confess) outcome is, from Bert and Harry's perspective, not actually the best outcome. There is another outcome, (not confess–not confess), that gives a better solution where both prisoners go to prison for only one year. This illustrates one of the key issues that arise out of the prisoners' dilemma game. By playing their dominant strategies Bert and Harry end up in a non-optimal equilibrium; if both played their non-dominant strategy of not confessing then they only go to prison for one year. However, as we have seen, this is a risky strategy because of the potential of receiving the 15-year sentence if the other prisoner chooses to confess. The safest strategy is to confess, even though they end up with the 5-year prison sentence rather than the 1-year sentence.

The question therefore arises as to whether there is any means by which the outcome of the game could be altered to give the preferred outcome. Could Bert and Harry avoid doing 5 years in prison and only do 1 year? The answer is that if we alter the nature of the game then a different solution is possible. As explained above the reason why Bert confesses is because this gives the best outcome for either of the strategies that Harry could play, and the same applies to Harry. What is needed is to move the outcome to the preferred (not-confess, not-confess) solution. In other words Bert and Harry need to act irrationally. However, this is not going to happen without some form of enforcing mechanism that convinces both Bert and Harry to choose the non-dominant strategy. Put another way, there needs to be some reason why both Bert and Harry act irrationally and choose not to confess.

One solution is to assume that there is some communication between the two men after their arrest. During their conversation Bert threatens Harry of dire consequences, such as physical violence, if he confesses. However, a simple threat of this type may not be enough; Harry may simply not believe Bert and still views the risk of not confessing as being too high. This highlights another key aspect of game theory: that for a threat to be effective it needs to be believed by the other players – the threat needs to be credible. If, for example, Bert is known to have friends who will carry out the instruction to harm Harry, then Harry may well do as Bert asks and not confess. The threat has become credible; Harry now believes that Bert means what he is saying. More generally the two players have agreed to co-ordinate their behaviour and the game has become a co-operative game rather than a non-cooperative game.

In fact the preferred outcome may also occur without the need for Bert and Harry to communicate after their arrest as Bert may have a long and well-known history of violent behaviour, particularly towards associates who double-cross him. In this case Bert's violent reputation may be enough to convince Harry not to confess. In game theory terms the game has been played before and one of the players has acquired a reputation – the game has a history.

Another solution may lie in the relationship between the two men. For some reason there may be a high degree of trust between the men; Bert and Harry may, for example, be brothers. Thus both men have a strong degree of belief that the other will not confess and this high level of trust therefore significantly reduces the risks involved in not confessing.

### 8.3.3 Some generic key features of games

The simple prisoners' dilemma game does serve to illustrate some of the key features of games that will become important when we look at game theory as a means of analysing the behaviour of firms in markets, in particular

1. The need to clearly specify the game
2. The possibility of non-optimal outcomes
3. The incentive for players to co-ordinate behaviour
4. Optimality relies on perspective.

#### 8.3.3.1 Clearly specified games

First, before analysing a game it has to be clearly specified in terms of its structure, its nature and the time frame. As we saw above if you alter the nature of the game by, for example, allowing Bert and Harry to communicate before they are questioned, this turns the game from a non-cooperative game to a co-operative game, and hence may change the outcome. The same could happen if you alter aspects of the structure or the time frame. This aspect of game theorising is also one of its main criticisms. Many economists have argued that game theory is non-robust; it is too specific and relies too heavily on a tight specification. If you change one element of the game then you potentially change the outcome and this makes the developing of any game theory-based general theory of firms' behaviour difficult. However, the counterargument to this is that the real world is not static and firms have to constantly adjust their strategies as the nature and structure of their particular game changes. Potentially, game theory provides a more dynamic representation of how firms behave in markets than the static neo-classical model.

#### 8.3.3.2 Non-optimal outcomes

The second key aspect of the game theory is, as we have seen, the possibility of non-optimal equilibrium points. Not only this, but you can construct games that have no equilibrium or even multiple equilibria. The importance of this aspect of game theory will become clear as we apply it to some simple business games in the next section, and also in the wider context of strategic behaviour discussed in the next chapter. Of particular importance for business behaviour is the possibility of moving from a non-optimal outcome to an optimal outcome. In the prisoners' dilemma game, we identified three possible means by which the outcome of the game could be changed:

1. The use of credible threats
2. Reputation
3. Trust

As we shall see, these three means of changing the outcome of a game away from the rationally determined outcome also have wide applicability in a business context.

### 8.3.3.3 *The incentive to co-operate*

In the introduction to this chapter it was suggested that some notable economists (Adam Smith and JK Galbraith) do not necessarily share the war/jungle metaphor view that predominates in the description of how firms behave towards each other in markets. The prisoners' dilemma game demonstrates the importance of the co-ordination of behaviour by one of the three means listed above. As we shall see, when applied to a business context the prisoners' dilemma game provides a justification for the view that a firm's most basic instinct is to co-operate with its rivals and not compete.

### 8.3.3.4 *Optimality relies upon perspective*

The final aspect of the prisoners' dilemma game that needs further comment relates to the concepts of 'optimality'. The optimal solution in the prisoners' dilemma game is only optimal within the context of the pay-off and objectives for the players as specified by the game. As discussed, within this context the optimal (not confess–not confess) outcome means that Bert and Harry only go to prison for 1 year for the lesser crime of breaking and entering. However, this is only optimal for Bert and Harry, not for the police or indeed for society as a whole. At the end of the day Bert and Harry have committed a more serious crime of GBH for which they are not punished. Similarly, the optimal outcomes of the business games to be discussed in the next section need to be related to their context; what is optimal for a firm need not be optimal for society as a whole.

## 8.4 | Business games

This section will present two business games which will serve to illustrate how the concepts and principles of the prisoners' dilemma game discussed in the pervious section can be related to the behaviour of firms in markets. The aim of this section is to present the basic ideas and games that will be used in the next two chapters to help explain and analyse the type of strategic behaviour we see in the real world. The assumption in all the games that follow is that there is full information, which in this context means that firms know the values in the pay-off matrix before they make their moves. The firms are also assumed to be rational in the sense that they will always choose the best strategy given the strategies they assume (and know) the rival firm will choose.

## 8.4.1  A market share game

Structure:

- Objective: maximise market share
- Pay-off: market share (per cent)
- Zero sum
- Non-co-operative.

Nature:

- Two players
- Strategic choice is between charging a high price ($H_p$) or a low price ($L_p$)
- Simultaneous moves.

Time frame:

- One shot.

The assumption is that the firms have only one strategic weapon open to them, namely price. The choice they have to make is whether to charge a low price ($L_p$) for their good or service or a high price ($H_p$). The pay-off matrix shows the percentage market share the firms achieve for each of the four possible combinations of prices (Figure 8.3). As with the prisoners' dilemma pay-off matrix (Figure 8.1) this matrix illustrates the interdependence between the two firms; the market share achieved by firm A depends not just on the pricing strategy it chooses, but also on the pricing strategy of firm B. The game is also an illustration of a zero-sum game. There are only two firms, so their total market share must add up to 100 per cent, thus a 10 per cent gain in market share for firm A represents a 10 per cent fall in market share for firm B.

What is the equilibrium? As before, put yourself in the position of one of the firms, say firm A. What is your best option if firm B charges a high price? What is your best choice if firm B charges a low price? The answer in both cases is a low price – the $L_p$ strategy gives you the highest market share in response to either strategy chosen by firm B. The $L_p$ strategy is therefore your dominant strategy, as it would also be for firm B. Therefore, in this market share game the dominant strategy for both firms is to charge a low price which leads to an outcome for the game in the bottom-right box of the matrix, and both firms have half the market each.

|        |        | Firm A | |
|--------|--------|--------|--------|
|        |        | $H_p$  | $L_p$  |
| Firm B | $H_p$  | (50, 50) | (30, 70) |
|        | $L_p$  | (70, 30) | (50, 50) |

**Figure 8.3**  Pay-off matrix for a market share game

The difference between this game though and the prisoners' dilemma game of the previous section is that the ($L_p$, $L_p$) outcome is not bettered for both firms by another possible outcome. There is another combination, ($H_p$, $H_p$), that gives the firms the same 50 per cent market share each, in fact the firms would be indifferent between the ($H_p$, $H_p$) and ($L_p$, $L_p$) combinations. Many students when faced with this game assume that the ($H_p$, $H_p$) combination would be the preferred outcome, but this is not so. The objective of the game is market share and not profit, and basic price elasticity tells us higher prices do not always equate with higher profits.

Given that ($H_p$, $H_p$) and ($L_p$, $L_p$) give the same 50 per cent market share why is ($L_p$, $L_p$) the most likely outcome? The reason is because the ($L_p$, $L_p$) outcome is, in fact, the game's equilibrium point. The dictionary definition of equilibrium is a point of rest between two opposing forces, or a point of steadiness or stability. This is the case with the ($L_p$, $L_p$) combination (and indeed the (confess, confess) equilibrium in the prisoners' dilemma game). Once the equilibrium ($L_p$, $L_p$) has been achieved there is no reason for either firm to switch strategy and charge a higher price, all they will do by this action is reduce their market share to 30 per cent.

In Figure 8.4 if firm A moved away from the equilibrium (shown in bold) by charging a $H_p$ then the game moves to the top-right box and their market share would drop to 30 per cent (shown in italics). Similarly, if firm B switched then the game would move to the bottom-left box and likewise their market share would drop to 30 per cent. The ($L_p$, $L_p$) equilibrium is said to be self-enforcing as neither firm has any incentive to do anything else other than charge a low price, which conforms to the point-of-rest dictionary definition of equilibrium.

To illustrate further consider Figure 8.5.

Assume that the game is at the ($H_p$, $H_p$) outcome shown in bold. This gives the firms the same 50 per cent share of the market but, however, this ($H_p$, $H_p$) outcome is not an equilibrium combination as it is not a stable point in the game. If firm A was to switch strategy then the game would move to the top-right box and A would increase its market share to 70 per cent (shown in italics). Similarly, a switch of strategy by B would move the game to the bottom left box and B's share would also increase to 70 per cent. Both firms therefore have an incentive to switch strategies or, put another way, both stand to lose market share if one remains at $H_p$ and the other firm switches to $L_p$. The ($H_p$, $H_p$) combination is not therefore a sustainable equilibrium outcome to the game.

This possibility of a one-shot game starting at an outcome that is not the equilibrium outcome may arise if there is imperfect information and, as a result, the firms did not know the pay-off matrix. If the game is not one shot, that is it

| | | Firm A | |
|---|---|---|---|
| | | $H_p$ | $L_p$ |
| Firm B | $H_p$ | (50, 50) | (30, 70) |
| | $L_p$ | (70, 30) | **(50, 50)** |

**Figure 8.4**
($L_p$, $L_p$) equilibrium

| | | Firm A | |
|---|---|---|---|
| | | $H_p$ | $L_p$ |
| Firm B | $H_p$ | **(50, 50)** | (30, 70) |
| | $L_p$ | (70, 30) | (50, 50) |

**Figure 8.5** $(H_p, H_p)$ non-equilibrium

was repeated, and the firms suffered from imperfect information then possibly the firms may start at a point away from the $(L_p, L_p)$ equilibrium. However, the logic of the pay-off structure of the game and the rationality of the firms mean that eventually the equilibrium point of $(L_p, L_p)$ will be reached, and, once attained will become the static point of the game. Assume the game in Figure 8.5 did start at $(H_p, H_p)$. The second time the game is played firm A switches strategy and the game moves to the top-right box, thus increasing its market share to 70 per cent, but at the same time, of course, reducing firm B's to only 30 per cent. During the next iteration of the game firm B takes the rational response by also switching strategy and the game gravitates to the equilibrium position in the bottom-right box.

In game theory, this self-enforcing equilibrium point is know as the Nash equilibrium, named after the American mathematician John Nash (and is the subject of the 2001 Oscar award wining film *A Beautiful Mind*). The definition of Nash equilibrium is that it represents the position in a game where all the players follow a strategy that is likely to give them the best outcome that can be achieved, given the likely decisions of the other firms involved in the game. Firms pursuing dominant strategies will, by definition, be following the best strategy they can, given the possible decisions taken by rival players, thus you will always end up at the Nash equilibrium point in the game.

## 8.4.2 A profit game

Structure:

- Objective: to maximise profits
- Pay-off: profit (£)
- Non-zero sum
- Non-co-operative

Nature:

- Two players
- Strategic choice is between charging a high price $(H_p)$ or a low price $(L_p)$ <
- Simultaneous moves

Time frame:

- One shot

As in the market share game, the strategic options open to the two firms is to charge either a high price $(H_p)$ or a low price $(L_p)$. This game is essentially the same

|  | | Firm A | |
|---|---|---|---|
|  | | $H_p$ | $L_p$ |
| Firm B | $H_p$ | (30, 30) | (0, 40) |
|  | $L_p$ | (40, 0) | (20, 20) |

**Figure 8.6**
Pay-off matrix for a
profit game

as the prisoners' dilemma game discussed in Section 8.2 but is now recast in the
form of two non-co-operative firms facing combinations of pay-offs in terms of £s
of profit rather than years in prison (Figure 8.6). The game is non-zero sum as,
unlike the market share game, there is no absolute level of profits that must be
shared between the two firms.

As before there is also a dominant strategy for both the firms – to charge
a low price. This therefore leads to the game's Nash equilibrium point of ($L_p$,
$L_p$) (shown in bold in Figure 8.7). This is the logical outcome if you follow the
same line of reasoning as in both the market share and the prisoners' dilemma
games. It is also the stable point in the game, the combination at which there
is no incentive for either firm to shift strategy. A shift in strategy by either
firm simply reduces profits from £20 to only £0. Also, as with the market share
game, if for reasons of imperfect information the start point was not at ($L_p$, $L_p$)
and the game was repeated, then the game would gravitate towards the stable
Nash equilibrium point of ($L_p$, $L_p$). If, for example, both firms initially chose a
high price then the chances are that one or both of the firms the second time
the game was played would switch strategies in the hope of increasing their
profits from £30 to £40, and also avoiding the possibility of making £0. Eventually you would end up at the ($L_p$, $L_p$) equilibrium and both firms would make
£20 profit.

However, unlike the market share game, but as with the prisoners' dilemma
game, the Nash equilibrium is not the optimal solution for the firms. If both
firms charged a high price then their profits would increase from £20 to £30 –
both firms would be better off. In economic terms the ($H_p$, $H_p$) combination is
said to Pareto dominate the ($L_p$, $L_p$) equilibrium, by which we mean that the
($H_p$, $H_p$) outcome represents a Pareto improvement over the ($L_p$, $L_p$) equilibrium
outcome. The definition of a Pareto improvement is that at least one party is made
better off without any other party being made worse off. This is the situation
shown in this profit game. Both firms would be better off by £10 if they were at
($H_p$, $H_p$) instead of at the Nash equilibrium ($L_p$, $L_p$). As discussed above though
the ($H_p$, $H_p$) combination is not a sustainable combination, both firms may find

|  | | Firm A | |
|---|---|---|---|
|  | | $H_p$ | $L_p$ |
| Firm B | $H_p$ | (30, 30) | (0, 40) |
|  | $L_p$ | (40, 0) | **(20, 20)** |

**Figure 8.7** Nash
equilibrium

the incentive to switch strategies and improve profits too great or, put another way, the risk of charging a high price is too great as you may end up with no profits at all.

This apparently straightforward dilemma is a rich source for helping to explain many aspects of firms' behaviour in the real world. The game suggests that if firms are to maximise profits then they are faced with exactly the same issue as Bert and Harry in Section 8.2. As with Bert and Harry, the firms need to find some way of coordinating their behaviour to avoid the $(L_p, L_p)$ Nash equilibrium and move the outcome of the game to the mutually beneficial, but non-equilibrium, $(H_p, H_p)$ outcome. The means by which firms try and achieve this market coordination and bring about the Pareto improvement is considered in more detail in Chapter 10. For now we need to recognise three related issues firms in this position face as they try to coordinate their behaviour:

1. How to agree on the preferred outcome? (Identification).
2. How to move to the preferred outcome? (Moving).
3. How to sustain the preferred outcome? (Sustaining).

The problem of agreeing to the preferred outcome is trivial in this simple game due to the fact that both firms know that $(H_p, H_p)$ is the Pareto superior position. However, in more complicated games with perhaps multiple equilibria, or where firms have different objectives, this may not be so straightforward. The second problem for the firms is how to move away from the equilibrium position to the preferred combination, given the logic of the Nash equilibrium combination. Finally if the firms do manage to get to the $(H_p, H_p)$ non-equilibrium combination how do they manage to stay there or, put another way, how do you stop firms, driven by the prospect of higher profits, from cheating? These issues and some potential answers are considered in more detail in Chapter 10.

# 8.5 | The game of business: co-opertition

The profit game at the end of the previous section illustrates the point made earlier about the nature of the relationship between rival firms – should they always compete or should they sometimes co-operate? The Nash equilibrium outcome of the game is at a point where firms are not making as much profits as they could. If they are to move the game to the non-equilibrium $(H_p, H_p)$ then the firms need to co-operate, not only to make the initial move but also to maintain the non-equilibrium point. Whether this is done whilst firms are meeting together for 'merriment and diversion' as suggested by Adam Smith or by some less overt means, it does support the Galbraith view of 'the convention against price competition is inevitable'. However, as noted by Adam Smith, what is good from the firm's point of view can also be viewed as 'a conspiracy against the public' who, in the game in Section 8.4.2, will end up paying higher prices. Protecting the public against the conspiracies of firms is one of the functions of competition policy to be looked at in Chapters 13 and 14.

The tension between firms, sometimes competing and sometimes co-operating, has also been examined by strategists using a similar game theory framework. One of the more interesting expositions of this is found in the work of Brandenburger and Nalebuff (Nalebuff and Brandenburger, 1996). Brandenburger and Nalebuff present what they refer to as the 'game of business' in terms of a value net as shown in Figure 8.8.

The horizontal axis of 'customer – company – suppliers' is, in effect, an alternative representation of the production or transformation process we have been using throughout this book. 'Competitors' are companies that make substitute products for the product produced by the central 'company', and 'complementors' are companies who make complementary products. The continuous lines show direct relationships between the players, thus customers will have a relationship not only with the central company but also with the producers of possible substitute and complementary goods. The same also applies to suppliers. The dotted lines linking the central company and the producers of substitutes and complements show a more implicit relationship, the actions of one are interdependent and interrelated on the actions of the others.

Brandenburger and Nalebuff identify five elements of the game of business that takes place within the value net that they (conveniently) refer to as PARTS:

**P**layers – the customers, suppliers, competitors and complementors.
**A**dded values – the value each player adds to the game.
**R**ules – that give the game its structure.
**T**actics – the moves undertaken by the players.
**S**cope – the boundaries of the game.

To illustrate let us return to one of the firms discussed in Chapter 4 – Ryanair. Figure 8.9 is a simplified representation of Ryanair's value net.

Brandenburger and Nalebuff's game of business is played out as a complex set of interrelationships between the players within the value net. The objective of the firm, Ryanair, in the centre of the game is to take as much value out of the value net for itself as possible (the idea of 'value' has been looked at briefly in Chapter 1

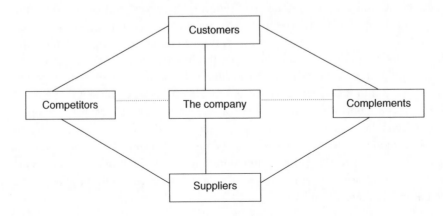

**Figure 8.8** The game of business

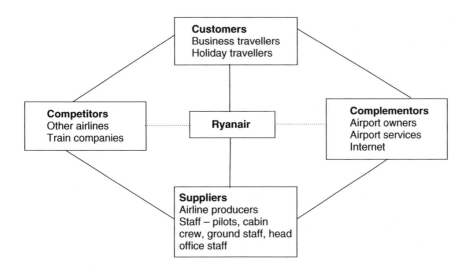

**Figure 8.9**   Ryanair's business game

and will be examined in a lot more detail in Chapter 12). As with the economists' game theory models, the Brandenburger and Nalebuff value net emphasises the importance of interdependence between the players; decisions taken by any one of the players affect the behaviour (tactics) of other players. Thus, any decisions taken by Ryanair have an impact on all the other players to a lesser or greater extent. For example, a decision to charge customers for all luggage other than hand luggage has an obvious impact on customers, and also on competitors (possible increase in demand), complementors (less work for airport services) and suppliers (less work for ground staff).

In addition, Brandenburger and Nalebuff also show that whilst some aspects of playing the game will be competitive, at other times there is a need for the players to co-operate. Thus, Ryanair will be competing with other airlines for customers, it may also co-operate with the other airlines in opposing increases in emissions taxes. Similarly, Ryanair and the airport operators will be in a competitive position when negotiating the operational contract for Ryanair using the airport, but have a mutual interest in attracting customers to use the airport. Brandenburger and Nalebuff refer to this mix of co-operation and competition as 'co-opertition'.

Thus, as with the price game in the previous section, for players to maximise their payoffs from the game of business there is a need for some coordinated decision-making. Brandenburger and Nalebuff referred to this as achieving 'win–win' outcomes.

## 8.6 | Review and further reading

The introduction to this chapter finished with a question – should firms compete or co-operate? The two quotes from Adam Smith and JK Galbraith, separated as they are by almost 200 years, suggest that the basic instinct of rival firms is to co-operate rather than compete. The games introduced in this chapter suggest that this is correct. The profit game settling at a non-optimal Nash equilibrium, for example, requires co-operation between the two firms if they are to move the game to the optimal outcome. Similarly, in the 'game of business' the suggestion was that to achieve the 'win–win' outcome a certain degree of co-operation was required between the firms. Thus the game theory approach provides a different perspective on the motivations behind interfirm behaviour – one based on co-operation rather than the normal assumption of competition.

More generally, the chapter has presented game theory as a means of analysing a firm's behaviour within the context of interdependence in decision-making. The approach also provides us with the basis to analyse strategic behaviour by firms which forms the subject matter of Chapters 9 and 10. The exposition of game theory in this chapter has been deliberately kept at a non-technical level; see also Kay (1995) for a very clear non-technical outline of the principles of game theory as applied to business. For a more technical treatment see Fudenberg and Tirole (1991). Brandenburger and Nalebuff (1995) provide a brief introduction to 'game of business' whilst their later book, Nalebuff and Brandenburger (1996), provides a much fuller exposition.

## 8.7 | Student exercises

### 8.7.1 Review exercises and points for discussion

1. Provide brief and clear definitions of the following key terms and concepts as used in this chapter.

   a. The reactive firm
   b. The proactive firm
   c. Pay-off
   d. Zero-sum game
   e. Mixed motive game
   f. One-shot game
   g. Co-operative game
   h. The prisoners' dilemma
   i. Dominant strategy
   j. Enforcing mechanism
   k. Nash equilibrium
   l. Credible threat
   m. Pareto optimal outcome
   n. Win–win outcomes.

2. Define each of the following games in terms of their structure, nature and time frame:

   a. Poker
   b. Draughts (Checkers)
   c. Golf.

3.

| Firm B | Firm A | |
| --- | --- | --- |
| | $H_p$ | $L_p$ |
| $H_p$ | (45, 45) | (0, 20) |
| $L_p$ | (20, 0) | (15, 15) |

In the profit game above, identify the Nash equilibrium. Is this the Pareto optimum point?

4. Construct a value net for Direct Line Insurance. Discuss how Direct Line Insurance may be both competing and co-operating with other players in the value net.

## 8.7.2 Application exercise

See the applications exercise on OPEC at the end of Chapter 10.

# 9 Firms and Competitive Behaviour

## LEARNING OUTCOMES

On completion of this chapter, the reader should be able to

■ Identify the source of a firm's competitive costs.

■ Outline a range of models that explain aspects of a firm's competitive behaviour.

■ Use the models to explain the revenue maximising behaviour of real world firms.

## KEY NEW CONCEPTS

| | | |
|---|---|---|
| Strategic moves | Predatory pricing | Irreversible commitments |
| Product differentiation | Market coordination | Switching costs |

## KEY NEW MODELS

| | | |
|---|---|---|
| Spatial models of product differentiation | Two- and three-stage entry games | Limit pricing models |

## MODELS AND CONCEPTS DEVELOPED FURTHER

| | | |
|---|---|---|
| Strategic entry barriers | Revenue maximisation | Mixed motives games |
| Competitive costs | Prisoners' dilemma game | Price-cost margins |
| Two- and three-stage entry games | | |

In this chapter and the next, we are concerned with examining the demand side of a firm's activities and, in particular, the means by which firms try to maximise their revenue. In many ways, it is the demand side of a firm's activities that is most immediately obvious to all of us. Every day of our lives we take part in the generation of revenues for firms, from the buying of our morning paper to the last drink we buy in the pub at night. What we are also surrounded by is the evidence of the proactive nature of firms as they seek to maximise the revenue side of their profit equation. A far from exhaustive list of the types of activities firms get involved in is given below:

- TV/radio/newspaper commercials
- Price wars
- Loyalty cards
- Branding, product differentiation
- Free tie-ins
- Competitor price matching offers
- Sponsorship of sports teams/events
- BOGOF (buy-one-get-one-free) offers.

Each of the above is an example of the second type of non-direct production costs – competitive costs ($S$) as shown in Figure 4.1. As with the management costs discussed in Part II the competitive costs incurred by a firm do not contribute directly to the production of the goods or services that result from the firm's transformation process.

## 9.1 | Competitive costs and strategic behaviour

Let us look more closely at one of the examples of competitive costs from the list, loyalty cards. Loyalty cards are increasingly used in retailing as a means of rewarding customers by giving money-off vouchers or cash-back payments based on the amount spent by the customer over a given period of time. The cost of a loyalty card system is significant; the firm incurs not only the costs in terms of the consumer benefits given back, but also the costs of setting up and administering the system. So what is the motivation for firms incurring the non-production-related competitive cost of loyalty cards?

As was discussed in Section 4.2.2, a firm's ability to maximise revenue is constrained by the state of the output market, as represented by the shape and the position of the demand curve for the firm's output. The purpose of competitive costs is to influence, to the firm's benefit, both the position and the slope of the demand curve. Figure 4.6 is reproduced below to illustrate the point.

One purpose of a loyalty card is to increase demand by shifting the demand curve to the right as shown in the left-hand diagram in Figure 9.1. By promising customers benefits for repeat purchases the hope is that demand increases at the expense of your rivals – the demand curve is progressively moved from $D_1$ to $D_2$ and $D_3$. The second purpose of a loyalty card is implied in the name, customers

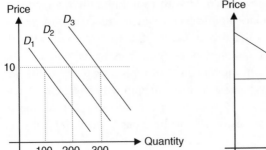

**Figure 9.1**
Revenue
maximisation and
competitive costs

develop loyalty for the provider of the loyalty card. In order to boost the bene-fits they receive, customers are more likely to return to make further purchases at the provider of the card's shops. In economic terms, this makes demand more price inelastic, giving the firm more control over price. In the right-hand diagram of Figure 9.1 loyalty cards aim to shift the demand curve closer to the perfectly inelastic $D_2$, the point where the firm has complete control over price. What the right-hand diagram also shows is that as the demand curve becomes steeper so the entry barriers into the market increase, the price–cost margin becomes greater (see the explana-tion to Figure 9.2, and how product differentiation has the same effect on elasticity). Thus, the loyalty card also helps create a strategic entry barrier into the market.

All of the examples at the beginning of this section could be analysed as a means by which firms are trying to increase revenue by changing the position and/or the shape of their demand curve. However, the other feature is that each of the actions taken and the resulting costs incurred are not taken in isolation, they are part of Nalebuff and Brandenburger's game of business. The introduction of a loyalty card and the costs involved are not something that a firm would choose to do unless they were part of a competitive interdependent game. If the firm was the first in the industry to introduce a card then its rivals would have to respond, either with their own cards or by some other means (for example, increased levels of advertising). Alternatively, a firm may feel the need to introduce a loyalty card because a rival firm already has. Either way we are in the game theory world, explored in the last chapter, of firms taking interdependent decisions based on how they perceive the market and their rivals' intentions and reactions – not the independent decision-making world of the neo-classical market structures. For firms the real world is a game of chess, not solitaire.

### 9.1.1 Strategic moves

As indicated above, the underlying reason for a firm incurring competitive costs is the need to try and maximise revenue as part of the firm's efforts to maximise profits. All of the activities listed can be regarded as evidence that firms are behaving proactively by trying to shape and change the markets they are supplying with output. An alternative representation is that the firms are acting strategically, in the sense that they are taking conscious decisions to try and maximise the benefit to them of taking part in the market. In the present context, each of the actions listed as examples of competitive costs could be said to be strategic moves, that is specific actions undertaken by firms as part of an overall strategy. Thomas Schelling (1960) in his book *The Strategy of Conflict* defines a strategic move as:

> any action which influences the other persons choice in a manner favourable to one's self by affecting the other person's expectations of how one's self will behave.

The definition emphasises the interdependent nature of strategic behaviour and is readily applicable to the types of strategic moves made by firms listed above.

The Schelling definition clearly has direct links back to the game theory framework discussed in the previous chapter. In the simple prisoners' dilemma game, Harry threatening Bert in order to change the outcome of the game is an example of a strategic move. The definition is also sufficiently broad enough to cover both competitive market behaviour discussed in this chapter and the co-operative behaviour which is the subject of the next.

Therefore, strategic moves and strategic behaviour in general, and the resulting competitive costs (*S*) incurred, are an everyday feature of firm's behaviour in their output markets. As discussed previously, the motivation for firms incurring *S* is to try and maximise revenue as part of their overall aim of maximising profits. Moving away from the specific example of loyalty cards, there are four possible means by which the activities resulting from the incurring of competitive costs can help a firm in its pursuit of revenue maximisation:

1. By providing information to potential consumers
2. To create strategic entry barriers
3. Competing with other firms in the market firms
4. Co-operating with other firms in the market.

### 9.1.1.1 Information to potential consumers

One of the most common sources of competitive costs to a firm is the need to advertise; indeed all of the examples listed above would need to be supported by advertising. Firms can undertake advertising through the various forms of media (TV, radio, newspapers, magazines, the Internet, flyers, information leaflets, travelling salesmen and many more). However, in the neo-classical world advertising would not be required as all consumers have full and certain information, they know everything on offer in the market. In reality, of course, consumers do not know everything on offer, hence firms have to inform them. Therefore, one view of the competitive cost incurred through advertising is to overcome the imperfect and asymmetrical information that is typical of real-world markets.

### 9.1.1.2  Creation of strategic entry barriers

In Section 4.3, we defined strategic entry barriers as barriers to market entry that do not arise from firms trying to be more cost efficient (which are structural entry barriers). They are the result of deliberate actions taken by firms to try and keep new entrants out of the market. All of the actions listed above as examples of competitive costs could be used as strategic entry barriers. Some are aimed at creating strong brand names (advertising, sponsorship), others at creating what are referred to as 'switching costs' – consumers incur a cost if they switch brands (free tie-ins, loyalty cards) – and others, such as product differentiation, to fill the market 'characteristic space' (see Section 9.2) to leave no room for new entrants. As was discussed above, all these actions are aimed at making demand less price-elastic by increasing the slope of the demand curve and hence increasing price–cost margins. Put another way all these actions would make entry into the market more difficult for potential entrant firms.

As was also discussed in Chapter 4, traditional economic theory lists a range of factors that influence the demand for a firm's product (see Table 4.1). This list of demand factors divides into those over which a firm has some control (endogenous factors) and those over which a firm has little or no control (exogenous factors). The endogenous factors (price, marketing and R&D) are the means by which firms can undertake strategic moves. All the examples listed above of types of competitive costs incurred by firms relate to either the demand factors of pricing (price wars, price matching, free tie-ins, BOGOFs) or marketing (branding, sponsorship, loyalty cards, advertising) or research and development (development of differentiated products).

### 9.1.1.3  Market competition

In a neo-classical world with homogenous products, there would be little point in firms wasting money on many of the types of competitive costs listed earlier. Each firm's output would be identical, therefore there would be little to actually compete on. In the real world, goods and services are heterogeneous. One reason for this is precisely to give a firm something to distinguish its product from its rivals, to allow competition for consumers to take place.

### 9.1.1.4  Market co-ordination

One of the themes of Chapter 8 was the notion that although firms appear to be essentially competitive in nature, in reality much of a firm's behaviour could be driven by the desire to co-operate with other firms. This provides a fourth possible reason for incurring 'competitive' costs, some of these costs could actually be 'co-ordinating costs' rather than 'competitive costs'. Strong branding by Coca Cola and Pepsi, for example, can be seen as the natural outcome in what is basically a duopoly market as the two firms compete for soft-drink consumers. However, it is also in the interest of both firms to have a market dominated by two strong brands as this creates a significant entry barrier to the market for new firms.

Consider again the loyalty card example. As was discussed, the introduction of loyalty cards by a firm in a particular market would require a response from other firms in the market. If all the firms in a particular market introduce loyalty cards, and hence cancel each other out, the question arises as to what has actually been the gain for the firms as a whole? They have all increased their competitive costs, but with no gain in revenue. One answer is that loyalty cards actually represent another strategic entry barrier for a potential new entrant to the market, in that they are another entry cost which needs to be incurred by a new entrant. The game has become a mixed motives game – competition within the market through benefits from the various loyalty cards, but co-operation between the firms to use the loyalty cards to prevent new entrants into the market.

## 9.1.2  Strategic behaviour

In summary, firms produce output that they sell into their output markets and hence generate revenue that forms the positive part of the profit equation that firms are trying to maximise (Figure 4.1). In doing so, firms incur competitive costs which can take a whole range of forms and a variety of possible objectives. What can also be seen from the above is the underlying game theoretic structure to real-world markets: firms take interdependent decisions with each firm trying to do their best, given how they think rivals may react. What has also been touched upon above is the conflict between the expectations that firms compete with each other but that the underlying urge may also be to co-operate. The rest of this chapter looks at aspects of competitive behaviour, the next chapter looks in more detail at co-operative behaviour.

In the sections that follow we shall deal with some of the models that have been developed to explain how firms can use their endogenous demand variables in the maximisation of revenue. As was discussed in relation to the loyalty card example, what firms try to do is change both the position and the shape of the demand curve so as to increase demand and to make demand more price inelastic in order to increase control over price. Less technically, we can say that competitive costs have a twofold and inter-related purpose:

1. To maintain and improve a firm's market position (market competition)
2. To prevent the entry into the market of new firms (strategic entry barriers).

In the rest of this chapter, we shall look at four areas related to a firm's competitive behaviour in its output markets:

1. Product differentiation
2. The use of irreversible commitments
3. Reputation
4. Some aspects of strategic pricing.

## 9.2　Product differentiation

If you are reading this book in a library or in a class or on a train or bus look at the people around you. The chances are that everybody you can see is wearing a different top, whether it is a shirt, t-shirt, blouse or sweat shirt. What you are observing is the outcome of one of the most common aspects of strategic behaviour by firms – product differentiation. Neo-classical theory assumes that all goods and services are homogenous, each widget produced is identical to the last and the next, irrespective of which firm produced it. However, what we are surrounded by all the time in the real world is quite the opposite, goods and services are not homogenous sometimes they come in a bewildering array of types, sizes, colours and shapes. In a neo-classical world, everybody who sits around you would have the same shirt or top, rather like in Mao Zedung's China where virtually everybody wore the same Mao suit. In other words, what we see in the real world is heterogeneous products not homogenous products.

Product differentiation is costly for firms. It would be much cheaper for a clothing manufacturer to produce a single design and colour of shirt rather than the range that we see around us. So the question is why do they do it? The rest of this section deals with how firms can use product differentiation as a strategic weapon, both within the market and as the basis for a strategic entry barrier. Seen from the neo-classical angle, however, product differentiation is wasteful and inefficient; the competitive cost $S$ in Figure 4.1 represents an inefficient waste of resources.

Figure 9.2 illustrates the effect that product differentiation has within the neo-classical model. $(Q_h, P_h)$ represents the familiar perfectly competitive equilibrium with homogenous products. As already noted, the whole purpose of product differentiation is to create some consumer loyalty and give the firm some control over its demand curve and, as a result, enable the firm to generate abnormal profits by being able to charge a price that is above the cost price $P_h$.

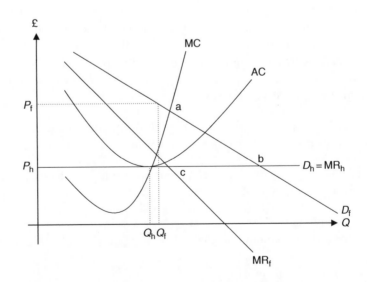

**Figure 9.2**
Product differentiation in the neo-classical model

In terms of Figure 9.2, by differentiating its product the firm is trying to move away from the perfectly inelastic demand curve $D_h$ where they are price takers to the downward sloping demand curve $D_f$ where they are price makers. If successful then product differentiation would give a firm some control over its demand curve, and hence the price it can charge for its product. In the figure, the product differentiating firm will fix a profit maximising price $P_f$ (where $MC = MR_f$) and generate abnormal profits of $(P_f - P_h)$ per unit. In the neo-classical world, this is inefficient. The area $(P_f - P_h)$ shows that a price–cost margin exists and the area $(abc)$ is the resulting deadweight or efficiency loss.

However, there is another perspective on the idea that product differentiation is wasteful and leads to inefficiency. When looked at from the point of view of the consumer, the fact that some of them are prepared to pay a higher price for the differentiated product suggests that they are actually gaining more utility than from purchasing the homogenous undifferentiated product. Mao suits are still available in China, but virtually all consumers prefer to buy the more expensive differentiated shirts and tops that are also available. The reason for this is that the differentiated product is a better match to the consumer's own personal tastes and preferences. In other words, consumers are heterogeneous as well as the products they buy, therefore they are all maximising their own differentiated utility functions.

## 9.2.1 Products as bundles of characteristics

To understand product differentiation better, it is helpful to think of a good or service (or product as we shall refer to them) as a bundle of characteristics, features of the product that when combined give the product its own particular distinctive quality. The characteristics of a product may vary in terms of:

- Quality
- Location
- Time
- Availability
- Design and packaging
- Services supplied with the product
- Attributes (for example, colour or shape)

Consider the familiar product of a pen. All pens perform the same function in that they enable you to write. However, there is a vast array of pens that differ in terms of quality, design, packaging and attributes. The bundles of characteristics that make up an expensive Mont Blanc fountain pen, for example, are very different from those that make up a disposable Bic biro, but they fulfil exactly the same purpose. This applies to just about every product that we buy and use.

In relation to the neo-classical model, product differentiation has three immediate consequences. First, it causes problems when defining markets. This will be discussed in detail in Chapter 14, but the underlying issues examined there come originally from product differentiation, particularly the fact that what may appear as a single market for pens may in fact be series of separate markets based upon the characteristics of pens and their respective cross elasticities. For example, could we really say that the Mont Blanc pen is in the same market as the Bic pen or do they belong to two separate markets?

Following on from this, once you divide a market up into a series of sub-markets you are increasingly likely to find yourself dealing with an oligopoly market. There are quite a number of pen producers, but only a relatively small number who make top of the range expensive pens. As you begin sub-dividing the pen market then, in terms of characteristics, what you end up with is a series of smaller sub-markets each served by a smaller number of firms. In broader terms, product differentiation is likely to lead to oligopoly markets with the sort of interdependence, and hence strategic behaviour by firms, discussed in Chapter 8.

The final consequence of product differentiation is that it does raise welfare issues that go beyond the immediate issue of efficiency loss. As discussed above, the positive side of product differentiation is that heterogeneous consumers can buy products that suit their own particular tastes, the idea that 'one size fits all' simply does not work in the real world. However, as we shall see below, producing differentiated products that help to increase consumer utility can also be used in a less benign manner to create strategic entry barriers to markets that may have a detrimental effect on welfare.

Product differentiation is usually split into two types:

1.  Vertical or quality differentiation
2.  Horizontal or range differentiation.

### 9.2.1.1  Vertical product differentiation

Vertical differentiation refers to products where the mix of basic characteristics is generally agreed, but product differentiation arises from quality. The higher the quality of the product, the more expensive the product is to produce and hence the higher the price. The pen market referred to above can be looked at as an example of vertical product differentiation. The resource cost required to produce an expensive Mont Blanc pen compared to the resource costs involved in producing a plastic Bic pen can explain much of the difference in price.

Successful vertical product differentiation relies upon the consumers perceiving the link between price and quality; they need to recognise that the higher price products are higher priced because they are better quality. Thus the highly priced Mont Blanc pen needs to be seen, and perceived, as a better quality product than the Bic pen. In effect, this type of product differentiation provides a basis for defining different market segments based upon quality and cost, as will be discussed in more detail in Chapter 14.

### 9.2.1.2  Horizontal, or range, product differentiation

What is of more interest in the current context is the product differentiation that takes place within the different quality bands, namely horizontal product differentiation. Horizontal, or range, differentiation refers to products that are of the same quality, but are differentiated by their mix of characteristics. This is the sort of differentiation that is shown in Figure 9.2. The higher price charged for the differentiated product, $P_f$, comes about by the firm developing some consumer loyalty through the mix of characteristics, not because they are producing a better quality product and hence operating on a higher cost curve than the undifferentiated product. For example, there are a number of other pen producers who also produce expensive pens, for example, Watermans and Cross. Mont Blanc needs to differentiate their pens from these other expensive pens not in terms of quality, the other pens are of equal quality, but in terms of styling, smoothness of the writing and so on.

In terms of our overall model of the firm, vertical differentiation involves a firm operating with a higher level of direct production costs ($D$) and relates to the input or supply side of the firms' operations. However, horizontal differentiation is where the firm incurs competitive costs ($S$). The costs incurred relate not to production but to the use of one of the endogenous demand variables, namely marketing expenditure. Successful horizontal differentiation relies upon successful marketing of the product.

To analyse horizontal product differentiation (HPD), we shall use the concept of a characteristic space. This approach comes from Hotelling (1929) who represented a city as a two-dimensional space between two end points that defined the limits of the city (usually referred to as Hotelling's linear city). Similarly the characteristics of a particular product can be represented as a linear space between two extremes.

Have you ever wondered why, when going to buy toothpaste, you are faced with such a wide choice of brands? You have different flavours, toothpaste that promises to whiten your teeth, toothpaste which is for smokers or people with sensitive teeth, toothpaste with red bits or green stripes – the list is almost endless. Figure 9.3 shows a characteristic space for one attribute of toothpaste – mintiness.

Assume that the taste of toothpaste can range between two extremes. At one extreme, it can be very minty and at the other completely tasteless. As you move away from the minty extreme of the space, the mintiness of the toothpaste gradually diminishes. A firm producing toothpaste needs to determine where in the characteristic space it is going to produce its toothpaste. Assume the firm decides to produce somewhere in the middle at point $i$ in Figure 9.4 and calls this brand A.

In the figure, $q$ represents the maximum amount that can be sold at each point along the characteristic space. Points on the characteristic space will represent consumers who range between the two extremes of those who prefer tasteless toothpaste to those who prefer minty. Thus, for the consumers at point $i$ in the space, brand A exactly matches their own particular tastes and the firm will achieve the maximum sales $q$ with this set of customers. However, as you move either side

**Figure 9.3** The characteristic space for the mintiness of toothpaste

Minty                                                                    Tasteless

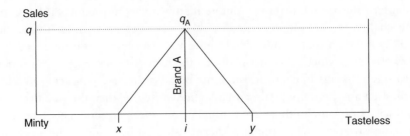

**Figure 9.4**
Demand for
brand A

of this set of consumers you move to sets of consumers who find that brand A does not quite match their taste in toothpaste. By the time you get to consumers at point $x$ you have reached those consumers who find the toothpaste is not minty enough and they will not buy it. Similarly, as you reach $y$, you reach consumers who find the toothpaste is too minty and likewise they will not buy brand A. Therefore, the total sales of brand A are equivalent to the triangle $(x, q_A, y)$ in Figure 9.4.

However, from a revenue maximisation point of view, selling one brand is not very effective; there is a whole range of consumers in the characteristic space beyond $x$ and $y$ who are not buying the firm's toothpaste at all.

The obvious response by the firm is to produce more than one homogenous brand of toothpaste; they need a brand which is less minty (brand B in Figure 9.5) and a brand which is mintier (brand C in Figure 9.5). In doing this, they will capture the entire market and, successfully fill the characteristic space with their three brands. For the consumers beyond $x$ there is now a mintier brand C and for those beyond $y$ there is the less minty brand B. From the consumers' point of view, the product differentiation appears to be beneficial as they all now have a brand of toothpaste which, to a lesser or greater extent, approximates with their own preferences. If you add in the other possible attributes over which toothpaste can vary then you have an explanation for the extent of product differentiation observed in the toothpaste market.

As pointed out above, HPD can be of consumer benefit; however, there is a potential less benign outcome in that this type of HPD can be used as a strategic entry barrier, particularly when used by a firm that is first into a market. Assume, the firm above was the first into the toothpaste market. By producing brands A, B and C in Figure 9.5, the firm is filling the characteristic space. If this was supported by the establishment of a strong brand name, by incurring the competitive cost

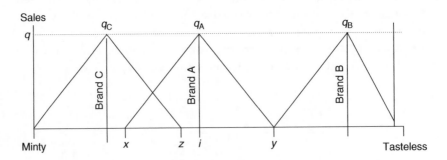

**Figure 9.5**
Demand for
multiple brands

of marketing, then it would prove difficult for another firm to enter the market. One classic example of this sort of strategic behaviour was the actions of the US chemical firm DuPont. In the 1930s, DuPont's R&D department produced the first synthetic material, nylon, which they promptly patented. However, what they realised was that there was a range of other synthetic materials, each with different attributes, that could also be produced using the same processes. DuPont therefore patented all the possible variants of nylon, thus effectively taking control of the entire characteristic space for synthetic materials.

What DuPont's action also did was create an entry barrier. However, the inventing and patenting of every variant on the new synthetic material nylon was not the outcome of trying to minimise costs; it was done deliberately to prevent any rival entering the new market for synthetic material. In other words, DuPont created a strategic entry barrier, not a structural entry barrier – it was a proactive decision, not a reactive action. More generally, filling the characteristic space usually needs supporting by an effective marketing strategy which is aimed at establishing a strong brand name if an effective entry barrier is to be created. Figure 9.6 summarises the position faced by an entrant into the market.

$C$ represents the direct cost of production faced by both the firms, the incumbent and the new entrant. $S_i$ is the competitive cost incurred by the incumbent firm and represents the marketing cost required to maintain the firm's brand image. Any new entrant into the market where there is no part of the characteristic space open, faces the problem of trying to establish its own brand image in direct competition to the well-established incumbent. The level of marketing cost ($S_e$) required by the new entrants is going to be higher than the incumbents. Thus, in the figure, the minimum price that an incumbent needs to charge in order to break even, Min $P_i$, is lower than that which a new entrant could charge, Min $P_e$. In effect, the incumbent has a competitive price margin of (Min $P_e$ – Min $P_i$). It could charge anywhere up to $P_e$ without attracting entry, and, of course, any price above Min $P_i$ is generating abnormal profits. The HPD combined with the use of the endogenous variable of marketing has been used to create a strategic entry barrier that can be used by the incumbent firm to generate abnormal profits.

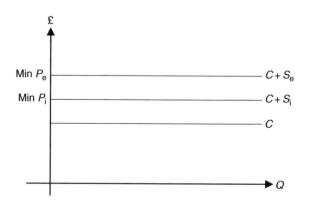

**Figure 9.6** HPD as a strategic entry barrier

If the incumbent is the first firm to exploit a new market then this can also be regarded as an example of first mover advantage. Let us return to Figure 9.5 and assume that our incumbent firm is slow off the mark and fails to fill the characteristic space, they leave a gap at the minty end of the space that is filled by another firm who produce brand C. The market for toothpaste is now a duopoly market. However, what the figure shows is that the two firms are only in direct competition for a small part of the characteristic space, those consumers between groups $z$ and $y$. This section of consumers could potentially buy either brand A or brand C, and it is only these consumers that the two firms would compete to gain from each other.

Figure 9.5 can also be used to explain another aspect of market behaviour, the existence of a duopoly but where the firms seem not to compete at all. Assume brand B is produced by a third firm. This third firm would not actually take part in any competitive behaviour with the other firms in the market, as there is no overlap in consumers. The firm supplying brands B and A would co-exist in the same market without any need for competitive behaviour.

The relatively simple model of HPD above illustrates not only the positive side of HPD, the providing of brands of a product to suit a range of consumer tastes, but also how they can be used as a strategic entry barrier. The above example is a fairly static example. In a more dynamic representation the entrant firm, or the duopolists, would seek to compete by either expanding the characteristic space or develop a new characteristic space. For example, the new entrant could expand the characteristic space by offering toothpaste with fluoride or develop a new characteristic of toothpaste in a pump action tube rather than plain tube. This aspect of HPD could be seen as a vital part of a competitive market in pushing forward product and process innovation.

As an example of the above, consider the market for wet razors. For many years up until the 1970s, the market in the UK was dominated by a duopoly, Wilkinson Sword and Gillette, who filled the characteristic space with their own products. However, in the 1970s Bic realised that the resources and competencies they had developed for the production of disposable pens could be readily used to produce disposable razors (an interesting example of the 'inside-out' approach to strategy discussed in Chapter 7). They therefore entered the market, not by competing with the incumbent duopolists in the existing characteristic space but by creating an entirely new characteristic space. Since that date, the market has been a highly competitive one with the original disposable razor being replaced by a succession of innovations and improvements that is still continuing today.

## 9.3 | Irreversible commitments

For the second example of how firms may incur competitive costs to try and maximise revenue, we shall examine another type of game – the entry game. Unlike the example of product differentiation used in Section 9.1, the entry game is focused solely on entry prevention through the use of what are referred to as 'irreversible commitments'. The entry game below, using the same format as was used in Chapter 8 to discuss the market share and profit games, is based upon the two- and three-stage game first discussed by Dixit (1982).

Structure:

- Objective: to maximise profits.
- Pay-off: profit (£).
- Non-zero sum.
- Non-co-operative.

Nature:

- Two players – one firm is already in the market and acting as a monopoly (the incumbent); one firm is currently outside the market, but considering entry (the entrant).
- The strategic choice differs for the two firms. For the entrant the choice is between entering the market or not ('in' or 'out'). For the incumbent, the choice is whether to fight entry or not ('fight' or 'share').
- The moves are sequential, with the entrant moving first.

Timeframe:

- One shot.

The situation in this market is that there is a monopoly firm inside the market that is enjoying monopoly profits of £5, but potentially a new entrant outside the market who is considering whether to enter the market or not. The pay-off matrix shows the various outcomes dependent upon the actions taken by the entrant firm and the response to those actions by the incumbent firm. Within the matrix three types of profit levels can be identified:

1. The monopoly profit level ($\pi_m$) of £5 (the bottom-right and bottom-left boxes of Table 9.1 where the entrant stays out of the market).
2. The shared or duopoly profit ($\pi_d$) of £1 (the top-left box).
3. The loss if the incumbent firm fights entry ($\pi_w$) of £1 (the top-right box).

Unlike the market share and the profit games looked at in Chapter 8, moves in this game are sequential not simultaneous; the entrant decides whether to enter the game or not, then the incumbent firm decides whether to fight entry or not. If no entry takes place (the entrant chooses the 'out' strategy) then the incumbent firm continues to enjoy its monopoly profits of £5. If, however, the entrant decides

**Table 9.1** Pay-off matrix for an entry game

| Entrant firm | Incumbent firm | |
| --- | --- | --- |
| | Fight | Share |
| In | (–1, –1) | (1, 1) |
| Out | (0, 5) | (0, 5) |

to come into the market (the 'in' strategy) the incumbent firm has to decide whether to fight entry or whether to do nothing (the 'share' strategy) and simply accept the new entrant into the market. The form that the 'fight' strategy takes is a price war. If the price war takes place then both firms end up making a loss (top-left box); however, if the incumbent does nothing then the market becomes a duopoly and both firms make £1 profit (top-right box).

For sequential games a game tree such as that shown in Figure 9.7 is a more useful representation of the game than the matrix of Table 9.1.

Representing the game in this format makes clear the sequence of moves in the game and the resulting pay-offs from each sequence of decisions. The entrant has the first decision to make whether to enter the game or not, the incumbent then makes a decision based upon the move made by the entrant. If the entrant stays out then there is no decision to be made by the incumbent, and the game resolves along the top branch of Figure 9.7 to the pay-off (5, 0); the incumbent continues in its monopoly position. However, if the entrant decides to enter the market the incumbent has to make a decision. Either it can simply allow entry as shown by the in-share branch in Figure 9.7 and the pay-off becomes the duopoly-shared profit of (1, 1). Alternatively, the incumbent can decide to resist entry by fighting a price war as shown by the in-fight branch of Figure 9.7. The resulting pay-off of this sequence of events is both firms make a loss, (−1, −1).

What is the Nash equilibrium? Will the new firm enter the market or not? The rational outcome is that unopposed entry will in fact take place and the market becomes a duopoly with both firms sharing profits of £1. The logic behind this conclusion is that the cost for the incumbent of fighting entry is too great because if it fights entry by instigating a price war then it ends up making a loss of £1 (in-fight). Compared to the £1 profit made if it does nothing and shares the market (in-share) then the rational choice is to choose the share strategy and share the market. The in-share combination is the Nash equilibrium. As with the Nash equilibria looked at in Chapter 8 this is the stable point in the game. The entrant has a choice between the 'in' strategy and the 'out' strategy. Given the assumption that the incumbent is a rational player and will not choose to make a loss the pay-off for the entrant is either £1 profit or nothing. Whereas the incumbent has a choice, post-entry, between −£1 ('fight') and £1 ('share') and chooses to share. As in the market share and profit games considered in Chapter 8, this equilibrium point is arrived at by the two firms pursuing the best strategy they can, given the likely strategies to be pursued by the other firm.

However, this is not the end of the story. The next question to be asked is whether there is anything that the incumbent firm could have done to prevent entry taking place and thus preserving its monopoly position in the market? The

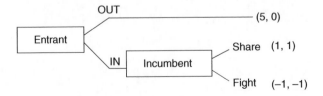

**Figure 9.7** The entry game

answer to this question is possibly, given the correct pay-off structure to the game. By changing aspects of the game, a range of potential options become open to the incumbent firm for the imposition of entry barriers to the market designed to force the entrant down the 'out' branch of the game tree. These entry barriers being consciously put in place by the incumbent firm fall firmly under our definition of strategic entry barriers.

### 9.3.1 The use of credible threats

One means open to the incumbent firm is to take control of the game by moving first and thus making it a three-stage game. The option here is similar to one of Bert's options in the prisoners' dilemma game, the use of a credible threat. In this context, the threat is rather subtler than the threat of physical violence and involves the use of strategic investments undertaken by the incumbent firm. The aim of the strategic investments is to change the pay-off structure of the game and convince the potential entrant that fighting entry will be the rational choice of the incumbent if entry takes place. To show how this might work consider Figure 9.8, a more generalised version of Figure 9.7.

Given certain conditions, the incumbent firm can change the outcome of the game by moving first (another example of 'first mover advantage'), this turns the game from a two-stage game into a three-stage game. What the incumbent firm can do is make a strategic move that convinces any potential entrant that its logical response to entry is to 'fight' and not to 'share'. Dixit referred to the strategic move as a commitment that is shown as $C$ in Figure 9.9.

$C$ represents some sort of commitment to fight a price war that is a cost to the incumbent firm, in fact in our model of the firm it is an example of a

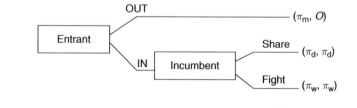

**Figure 9.8** The generic two-stage entry game

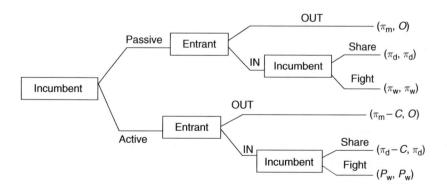

**Figure 9.9** The three-stage entry game

competitive cost ($S$). In the three-stage game, the incumbent takes the first decision of whether to undertake this strategic commitment or not, represented in the game tree as remaining passive or becoming active. If the incumbent remains passive and does nothing the game becomes the two-stage game as before. However, if the strategic commitment is made then this will change the pay-off structure at the end of the game. If the incumbent makes the strategic commitment $C$, but does not use it to fight a price war then the incumbent firm bears the cost of $C$ right through to the final pay-off of the game, and its final profits are reduced by the value of $C$. In Figure 9.9, this is either the (active–out) branch of the tree or the (active–in–share) branch. However, if a new firm enters the market and the incumbent uses the strategic commitment to instigate a price war then the same $\pi_w$ level of profits is achieved (active–in–fight). As with the two prisoners though, the threat to fight a price war by using the strategic commitment has got to be believed by the potential entrant firms – the threat has got to be credible.

Two conditions are required from within the structure of the game for a threat to use a strategic commitment to be regarded as credible. First, the pay-off for not using the strategic commitment to fight entry ( $\pi_m - C$ from the active–in–share outcome) needs to be greater than the shared profit (the two-stage equilibrium of $\pi_d$ from the passive–in–share branch). This condition makes the use of a strategic commitment rational in the first place. If you are going to receive a lower pay-off by undertaking the commitment than from simply sharing the market in the first place, then it is rational to simply remain passive and accept the two-stage outcome of $\pi_d$.

The second condition is the requirement for the profits from fighting the price war ($P_w$ from the active–in–fight branch) to be greater than the incumbent's profit of undertaking the strategic commitment, but then not using it ( $\pi_d - C$ from the active–in–share branch). This condition makes the threat credible because it makes the fighting of the price war the rational choice once entry takes place. To summarise, the conditions for strategic commitments to be made are

1. $\pi_m - C > \pi_d$
2. $\pi_w > \pi_d - C$

If these conditions hold then the incumbent firm, by moving first and undertaking the necessary level of strategic commitment, can prevent entry and keep its monopoly hold on the market, all be it with a lower level of monopoly profit than initially ( $\pi_m - C < \pi_m$).

A numerical example will help to illustrate this. Assume that in our original game, the incumbent firm decides to undertake a strategic commitment in the form of investing in excess capacity. This represents a sunk cost of £3. During the game, the incumbent has the option of using the excess capacity to flood the market and force the price down, in other words the excess capacity will be used as the means of fighting a price war. If the excess capacity is used in this way then the sunk cost is recovered in full by the incumbent firm. However, if the excess capacity is not used then the incumbent firm does not recover the sunk cost. Figure 9.10 shows the resulting three-stage game.

Do the two conditions hold? Should the incumbent firm choose to be active and move first by undertaking the investment in the excess capacity?

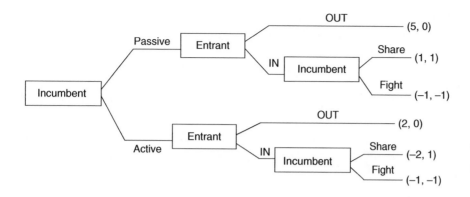

**Figure 9.10**
Three-stage entry
game example

1. $\pi_m - C > \pi_d$: $2 > 1$
2. $\pi_w > \pi_d - C$: $-1 > -2$

Both conditions hold. The monopoly profit minus the sunk cost is still greater than the duopoly profits; the incumbent can still make more profit from undertaking the investment and never using it than from the original shared outcome. The threat is also credible; the loss from using the excess capacity and forcing the price down is actually smaller than not using the excess capacity and sharing the market. Thus, by making the investment in the excess capacity the incumbent firm is signalling to potential entrants that entry will be fought, they (the entrants) will make a loss if they decide to enter the market. The incumbent has therefore successfully deterred entry; the strategic move to invest in excess capacity has created a strategic entry barrier. The level of the incumbent firm's abnormal profit is reduced from £5 to £2, but this is still better than the £1 profit if no strategic investment took place. The interesting thing to note about the reduction in abnormal profit is that, unlike in most cases, it does not increase efficiency. The decrease is brought about by the incumbent firm undertaking unnecessary and wasteful investment. The reduction in abnormal profit, and hence the implied reduction in the price–cost margin, arises from the incumbent's cost curve shifting upwards, not by the price moving downwards.

What would happen if the sunk cost of the strategic commitment was £5? In this case, the first condition is not met

1. $\pi_m - C > \pi_d$; $0 < 1$
2. $\pi_w > \pi_d - C$: $-1 > -4$

The sunk cost required is so big that the original two-stage in–share equilibrium is still the optimal outcome for the game. If the sunk cost is only £1 then we have the following situation.

1. $\pi_m - C > \pi_d$: $4 < 1$
2. $\pi_w > \pi_d - C$: $-1 < 0$

In this case, the threat is not credible, the rational option for the incumbent when faced with the choice whether to fight or not is not to fight and break even; fighting entry would result in a loss of £1.

In his original article, Dixit (1982) suggests the strategic investment undertaken by the incumbent firms could be investment in excess production capacity. The excess capacity is not used unless entry takes place. If entry does take place then the excess capacity is used and the incumbent firm floods the market and forces the price down to a level where the entrant is facing a loss. However, as with Bert and Harry, the threat by the incumbent firm has got to be credible, the entrant firm has to believe that the incumbent firm will carry out the threat and use the excess capacity. The threat becomes credible if the use of the excess capacity becomes the rational choice of the incumbent firm when this decision point is reached in the game tree.

## 9.4  Pricing strategies

One of the endogenous variables available to firms to deter entry is the actual price of the firm's output. Price can be used in a number of ways to try and maximise the revenue taken from a firm's output market. The most obvious is through the use of the concept of price elasticity, increasing the price in inelastic markets and decreasing the price in elastic markets (although this also increases costs, so may not lead to increased profits). An extension of this is through the use of price discrimination, splitting markets and charging different prices in markets with different price elasticities. However, as effective as these can be, they cannot really be regarded as strategic decisions, they are not designed to influence how competitors perceive and react to your decisions. In the following sections, we shall consider some other aspects of pricing which do reflect the interdependent strategic decisions we are concerned with in this chapter.

### 9.4.1  Limit pricing

Models of firms using price strategically go all the way back to Bain in the 1950s. Chapter 4 introduced the idea of price–cost margins as a reflection of the control a firm may have over a market. Figure 9.11 reviews the situation.

$P_c$ represents the competitive price, the price that achieves economic efficiency by being equal to the cost. $P_I$ represents the price charged by the incumbent without attracting entry to the market. In effect, the difference between $P_I$ and $P_c$ is the price premium that the incumbent firm has over any new entrants. As discussed in Chapter 4 the source of this price premium comes from at least one of three sources:

1. Differences in technology (type 1 entry barrier)
2. Existence of sunk costs (type 2 entry barrier)
3. Irrational imperfectly informed consumers, quick responding incumbent firms (type 3 entry barrier).

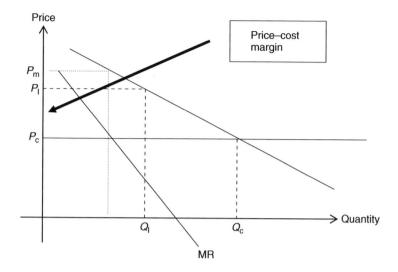

**Figure 9.11**
Price–cost margins

As also discussed in Chapter 4, the higher the entry barrier created the greater the price–cost margin, and the higher the abnormal profits the incumbent firm can extract from the market.

Bain refers to the $P_1$ as being the *limit price* (Bain, 1956). A limit price is the maximum price that an incumbent firm can charge without attracting entry into the market. Any price between $P_1$ and the monopoly price $P_m$ would attract new firms into the market. A limit price does not have to be confined to a monopoly market. In markets with more than one incumbent firm, the limit price could be the Nash equilibrium price or a price maintained collusively by the incumbent firms using methods discussed in the next chapter. In the market represented by Figure 9.11, the incumbents have two choices, either they charge the limit price, $P_1$, and prevent entry or they charge the monopoly price, $P_m$, and take a short-term profit. A number of factors will influence the decision. The first consideration will be the relative sizes of the potential profits. If the price–cost margin is small relative to the size of the potential profit then the incumbents may take the monopoly profit in the short run, accepting that entry will occur and the price will be forced down to $P_c$. Game theory considerations also influence the decision. If the market in Figure 9.11 represents a one-shot game then the incumbent firm will charge the monopoly price $P_m$. However, whatever the outcome, the price fixed by the firm becomes a conscious decision that is partly determined by strategic considerations, not simply in response to shifts in demand and supply functions.

Bain's basic model was quickly added to by various writers, most notably Sylos-Labini (1957) and Modigliani (1958). The extensions to Bain's basic model added two important elements:

1. The existence of economies of scale
2. Informational assumptions about the behaviour of the firms (the Sylos postulate).

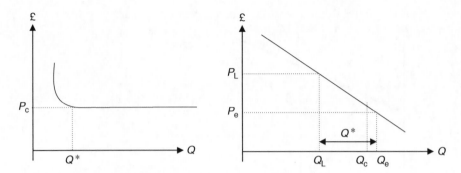

**Figure 9.12** The extended limit pricing model

The informational assumptions are that the entrant firm assumes that the incumbent firm will maintain its current level of output and the incumbent assumes that entrants will not enter the market if the post-entry price is lower than their average costs. Figure 9.12 summarises the extended model.

The level of output $Q^*$ is the minimum level of output which is required to be productively efficient, with the corresponding price $P_c$ being the competitively efficient price. $P_l$ represents the limit price of the incumbent firm. Why is this a limit price? The reason is that for an entrant to be able to compete in cost terms with the incumbent it must produce $Q^*$ level of output. However, the limit price $P_L$ leads to a level of output for the incumbent of $Q_L$. If a new firm enters the market at the efficient level, it is going to increase the output to $Q_e$ ($Q_L + Q^*$) and force the price below the cost price $P_c$. In other words, entry leads to the entrant making a loss and hence the rational thing to do is not to enter the market at all. By setting the price at the limit price the incumbent firm has effectively prevented entry to the market.

The limit pricing model described above was one of the first attempts by economists to explain what would now be referred to as strategic behaviour. It is essentially a static neo-classical model but does link together the idea of entry barriers and how firms set prices to maximise their potential revenue taken from a market.

### 9.4.2 Predatory pricing

Predatory pricing is closely linked to the limit pricing models discussed above but is more readily observable in the real world than the rather theoretic limit pricing model. Instead of the firm fixing a price such that entry into the market forces the price below $P_c$ in Figure 9.11, what the incumbent firm does is actually price below $P_c$ in the first place. In other words, the incumbent incurs a short-term loss on the basis that this will prevent entry into the market.

Predatory pricing is something which large multi-product firms are often accused of practising – the idea of 'loss leaders'. In practice, it is very hard to prove that this is actually happening. One case which was proven by the Office of Fair Trading (OFT), one of the institutions involved in the enforcement of UK competition policy (see Chapter 13), illustrates the issues involved. In 2002, the OFT published a report on a complaint of predatory pricing against *Aberdeen Journals Ltd* (OFT (c)).

What the OFT found was that *Aberdeen Journals* were using their dominant position in the local market for newspaper advertising space to undercharge for the advertising space in their publications. The reason for doing this was the arrival of a new potential rival, *Aberdeen and District Independent*. Thus the incumbent, *Aberdeen Journals*, were incurring the competitive cost of predatory pricing to create a strategic entry barrier to the market. The OFT fined Aberdeen Journals £1.3m.

### 9.4.3   The creation of switching costs

The creation of switching costs is another aspect of pricing behaviour that is common in many markets. The idea is that you tie-in consumers to your particular brand of a product by the use of complementary products that are only suitable for your product. Quite often the complementary product is priced below cost to entice the consumer to make purchase in the first place. Returning to our example of the wet razor market, one of the innovations referred to previously was the development of the 'combination' shaver. A combination shaver is when the handle and the blade head are sold separately. However, each manufacturer's handle is only suitable for its blade head, thus once a consumer purchases your handle they are tied-in to buying your blade heads. In order to switch the consumer must incur the switching cost of buying another manufacturer's handle. The firms tend to under-price the initial handle and blade head package, but over-price the blade heads when sold separately.

## 9.5 | Reputation

The previous three sections have highlighted various means by which a firm can use the endogenous demand variables of price/output, marketing and R&D as strategic weapons to prevent entry and/or enhance their own position in a market. However, there is one further weapon firms can use to try and influence the behaviour of their rivals and potential rivals, namely the perception other firms have of them. We have already seen this argument in Chapter 8 when we were considering a solution to the prisoners' dilemma game. If Bert had a well-known reputation for violence then Harry may well not confess for fear of what Bert may do to him.

Let us reconsider the entry game examined in Section 9.3. In the second of our numerical examples we concluded that the threat to use the strategic investment was not credible, instigating the price war would lead to a pay-off for the incumbent that was worse than sharing the market with the new entrant. As a result the rational decision for the incumbent was not to undertake the sunk cost and allow entry. However, if this was a repeated game there is another strategy that the incumbent firm can take. When first faced with entry the incumbent could act irrationally. It could move first and undertake the strategic commitment. This may not be enough to prevent entry though as, from the entrant's point of view, the threat to use the strategic commitment to flood the market and force the price down is not credible – it is not the rational option for the incumbent to take. However, if the entrant does enter the market then the incumbent may well act in this irrational manner and instigate the price war forcing both firms to incur losses (this is the (active–in–fight) branch of Figure 9.10). The entrant will be forced out of the market.

Thus, by acting irrationally the incumbent has established a reputation for fighting entry no matter what, this sends out a signal to other potential entrants that entry into the market will result in the incumbent acting irrationally. By the establishment of a reputation the firm can effectively prevent entry and the game settles to the (active–out) branch of Figure 9.10. The profits made by the incumbent are not the monopoly profits $P_m$, but the reduced monopoly profits $\pi_m - C$. This type of reputation-building behaviour in repeated entry games will only potentially happen if $\pi_m - C > \pi_d$.

One of the main weaknesses of the limit pricing model discussed in Section 9.4, pointed out by writers at the time, was the behavioural assumption that the incumbent firm would maintain its level of entry post-entry. By doing this, the incumbent firm not only forces the entrant firm below cost price but itself as well. However, again, this type of apparently irrational behaviour could be used to protect long-term profits by establishing a reputation for being prepared to take a short-term loss. This may well have been part of the reasoning behind the *Aberdeen Journals* motivation for their predatory pricing. The firms were not only creating an immediate short-term strategic entry barrier, but were also signalling an aggressive stance to any other potential entrants in the future. They were creating a reputation that might deter other potential entrants.

## 9.6 | Review and further reading

As discussed at the opening of this chapter, the activities undertaken by firms in their output markets surround us every day of our lives. This chapter has focussed on the competitive aspect of these activities, the next chapter looks at the possible co-operative aspects of a firm's output market behaviour. The main purpose of these activities, as we have seen, is for the firm to try and gain some control over either the position of its demand curve or its slope, or both, in an effort to maximise revenue. This is achieved through a range of strategic means using the endogenous variables of price, R&D and marketing to create strategic entry barriers (gaining control of the slope of the demand curve) and/or increase market share (shifting the demand to the right).

All of the activities discussed in this chapter incur costs for the firm. These costs, competitive costs, as noted at the outset, are another type of costs that are not directly related to the production process. They sit alongside the management costs which were discussed in Part II as the final component in our extended model of the firm presented in Figure 4.1. As management costs are necessary if a firm is to order its transactions efficiently, so competitive costs are necessary if a firm is to maximise its revenue take from its output markets.

The basic models of product differentiation and limit pricing can be found in Koutsoyiannis (1979). For a discussion of many of the other issues discussed in this chapter, see the parts of Clarke and McGuiness (1987) and Hey (1991).

## 9.7 | Student exercises

### 9.7.1 Review exercises and points for discussion

1. Provide brief and clear definitions of the following key terms and concepts as used in this chapter.

   a. Competitive costs
   b. Strategic moves
   c. Horizontal product differentiation
   d. Vertical product differentiation
   e. Irreversible commitments
   f. Strategic entry barriers
   g. Limit pricing
   h. Switching costs
   i. Predatory pricing.

2. Consider the following examples of competitive costs

   ■ Three for two offers in the larger chains of booksellers

   ■ Sponsorship of the world snooker championships by the on-line casino '888.com'

   ■ The purchase by Sky of exclusive rights to show Premier League football matches live in the UK

   ■ The introductory offer to new members of the Internet provider AOL of free wireless routers and one month membership free

   ■ The camera shop Jessops offering to match any Internet prices for products in their shops

   Which of the four means of trying to generate revenue, discussed in Section 9.1, do these examples relate to?

3. Consider the following products

   ■ Hairdressing
   ■ Laptop computers
   ■ Airlines
   ■ Shoes

   a. Which characteristics of these products do firms use to try and differentiate their own particular brand?

b. Do firms tend to practice horizontal or vertical differentiation in the provision of these products?

### 9.7.2 Application exercise

For the firm used as part of the application exercise at the end of Chapter 7, try to identify:

a. Competitive activities which are aimed at shifting the demand curve to the right
b. Competitive activities that are aimed at making the demand curve more price inelastic
c. Do any of the identified activities identified in a. and b. result in strategic entry barriers?

# Firms and 10
# Co-operative
# Behaviour

LEARNING OUTCOMES

On completion of this chapter, the reader should be able to

■ Identify aspects of co-operative behaviour

■ Demonstrate an understanding of the basis for co-operative behaviour

■ Outline the various forms that co-operative behaviour can take.

## KEY NEW CONCEPTS

| | | |
|---|---|---|
| Tacit collusion | Explicit collusion | Chain store paradox |
| Joint ventures | Strategic alliances | |

## KEY NEW MODELS

| | |
|---|---|
| Price and output fixing cartels | Co-operative games |

## MODELS AND CONCEPTS DEVELOPED FURTHER

| | | |
|---|---|---|
| Nash equilibrium | The prisoners' dilemma game | Strategic entry barriers |
| Coopetition | Revenue maximisation | |

The previous chapter began with a list of examples of competitive activities undertaken by firms in their output markets. The following is another list of activities undertaken by firms:

- Manufacturer trade catalogues
- The SMMT, the trade association for the motor industry
- The Nectar card
- The former Net Book Agreement (NBA)
- The Star alliance in the airline industry (the sharing of various routes and services by different airlines)
- The Airbus A380, the so-called 'superjumbo'
- OPEC
- The merger of the virtual learning environments (VLE) WebCT and Blackboard
- Price matching – 'we will match any price being offered elsewhere'
- Price leadership.

This seems to be a fairly eclectic list, but they all are linked by a common thread – they represent some of the various means by which firms co-operate. Trade catalogues and SMMT are about information exchange between firms; the Nectar card, the Star alliance, the NBA and the 'superjumbo' are examples of firms explicitly working together; OPEC is an example of a quantity-fixing cartel; the merger of the two leading providers of VLE creates a monopoly; price matching is an example of implicit collusion between firms. In other words, these activities represent the co-operative side of the competition/co-operation debate discussed in Chapter 8 – the 'coop' part of Nalebuff and Brandenburg's 'coopetition'.

The motivation is the same as it was for the competitive activities discussed in Chapter 9. Principally, they are about firms trying to maximise their revenue in their output markets, although some (the Star alliance and WebCT–Blackboard merger) also have cost minimisation aspects as well. They are activities aimed at either increasing the revenue taken from markets and/or the creation of strategic entry barriers. Theoretically, as with the competitive behaviour looked at in the previous chapter, they are aimed at either, shifting the demand curve to the right or making demand more price inelastic or both (see Figure 9.1).

The theoretical explanation for co-operative behaviour lies in the profit game derived from the prisoners' dilemma game discussed in Chapter 8. Let us review the outcome of that game.

Structure:

- Objective: to maximise profits
- Pay-off: profit (£)
- Non-zero sum
- Non-co-operative

Nature:

- Two players
- Strategic choice is between charging a high price ($H_p$) or a low price ($L_p$)
- Simultaneous moves

Timeframe:

- One shot.

The problem identified for the firms is that the self-enforcing Nash equilibrium for the game is at combination $(L_p, L_p)$; however, the non-equilibrium combination of $(H_p, H_p)$ is better for both firms as it gives them higher levels of profits. The $(H_p, H_p)$ outcome is said to Pareto dominate the equilibrium combination (see Table 10.1). As was discussed in Section 8.4.2, what is required is for the firms to undertake some sort of co-operation that co-ordinates their behaviour and moves the outcome of the game from $(L_p, L_p)$ to $(H_p, H_p)$.

However, the problem is that the desired $(H_p, H_p)$ outcome is not an equilibrium point, it is inherently unstable. As was discussed previously if, due to imperfect information, the firms actually started off at this point then both firms would see an opportunity to increase profits to 40 by switching strategies – if both firms did this you would end up at the $(L_p, L_p)$ Nash equilibrium. For the firms to successfully maintain the non-equilibrium $(H_p, H_p)$ then there are three issues that need to be addressed:

1. How to agree where they would prefer to be? (Identification)
2. How to move to the preferred combination? (Moving)
3. How to sustain the preferred combination? (Sustaining).

Only if all three problems can be resolved will the firms be able to move to, and sustain, the non-equilibrium position of $(H_p, H_p)$. In the rest of this chapter, we shall consider each of these three issues in turn. However, before we do this it is worth remembering that we are taking a very firm-specific view in this chapter and we should not forget Adam Smith's warning that co-operation can lead to 'a conspiracy against the public'. Just because the ability to co-operate and co-ordinate a market may lead to the best outcome for a firm does not mean the outcome is satisfactory for its consumers. Competition legislators in both the UK and the EU keep at best a wary eye on many of the co-operative activities of firms; at worst many co-operative practices are illegal. This will be discussed in greater detail in Chapter 13.

## 10.1 | Identifying the preferred combination

In the simple profit game shown in Table 10.1, the reaching of an agreement on what is the preferred outcome to the game does not pose any problems. Both the firms have full information; they both know the pay-off matrix and that the other firm is entirely rational in its behaviour. Both firms are also playing the same profit game. However, unfortunately, as has been discussed in previous chapters, the real world is not like this. Firms are more likely to be operating in a more complex world with imperfect and asymmetric information. Add to this the bounded rationality of the decision makers and the possibility of opportunistic behaviour, and the whole nature of the game changes. The pay-off matrix may be less transparent, the firms may not know for sure what the likely pay-offs for each combination of actions will

**Table 10.1** Pay-off matrix

Firm A

|  | | $H_p$ | $L_p$ |
|---|---|---|---|
| Firm B | $H_p$ | (30, 30) | (0, 40) |
|  | $L_p$ | (40, 0) | (20, 20) |

be, they may have to work on the basis of probabilities rather than certainties. The firms may also not be entirely sure about how the other firms are likely to react, particularly in one-shot games where there is no past history to the game to give any clues. Even if some sort of agreement can be reached, the firms may be leaving themselves open to opportunistic behaviour once the agreement is enforced, this again may reduce the likelihood of an agreement being reached in the first place.

In the real world, one of the key roles played by trade associations and trade catalogues is to try and reduce imperfect and asymmetric information in an industry. One of the largest such associations is the SMMT – the Society of Motor Manufacturers and Traders. The SMMT is funded by subscription from the firms that make up the motor industry in the UK and beyond. In return, the SMMT provides a range of services such as motor industry data, exhibitions and trade fairs, trade publications as well as representing the industry in various political and international forums. One of the more important services provided is the Motor Industry Directory which is a list of 5000 firms involved in the motor industry listing the main contacts and products produced. As can be seen, much of this activity carried out by the SMMT is designed to improve the information flow within the industry and to specifically reduce asymmetric and imperfect information.

Returning to the theoretical informational issues, there may be a more fundamental problem in some games in that the firms may not actually be playing the same game. For example, you could have the situation where firm A is playing the profit game set out above, but firm B is playing the market share game discussed in Section 8.4.1. The Nash equilibrium is the same in both games, $(L_p, L_p)$, so this is the combination that the game would reach. However, firm A would rather be at the combination $(H_p, H_p)$ that yields higher levels of profits. From firm B's perspective, both combinations yield the same 50 per cent market share so either is acceptable, but there is no particular reason why they should want to move to $(H_p, H_p)$ combination. The $(H_p, H_p)$ combination still represents a Pareto improvement as firm A would be better off, and firm B would be no worse off, but there is no agreement between the firms that $(H_p, H_p)$ is the preferred outcome. This would make market co-ordination to achieve the preferred outcome less likely.

## 10.2 | Reaching the optimal outcome

Assuming that the firms can agree on where they would like to be, the next problem becomes getting there. In the profit game, the problem, as explained, is that the market has reached its Nash equilibrium point, $(L_p, L_p)$, which is giving profit levels which can be bettered by moving to non-optimal combination, $(H_p, H_p)$. The problem for the two firms is how to move from the stable self-enforcing $(L_p, L_p)$ equilibrium to the unstable non-equilibrium point of $(H_p, H_p)$. To achieve this, there needs to be some sort of collusive agreement between the firms. These agreements can be of two types. The agreement between the firms could be an open and explicit agreement to co-ordinate the market to achieve the desired outcome. Alternatively, there could be a less obvious implicit agreement, but aimed at the same co-ordination goal. In both cases, there are three considerations that need to be taken into account when trying to reach a collusive agreement:

1.  The ease with which cheating firms can be detected
2.  The strength of the incentive to cheat
3.  Whether cheating can be prevented.

The motivation for cheating lies in the non-equilibrium nature of the combination that is reached by the collusive agreement. The problem with the $(H_p, H_p)$ combination is that if one firm cheated on the agreement and switched to the $L_p$ strategy then that firm would further increase its profits from £30 to £40, at the expense of the other firm whose profits would disappear. The first problem above is an information problem. In our simple game with only two players and full information, it would be easy to detect cheaters. However, as you increase the number of firms involved in the market then it becomes more difficult to co-ordinate the market and move to a non-equilibrium position. In food retailing, for example, it is much more likely that the four big national supermarkets in the UK could co-ordinate moving to a non-equilibrium point than the thousands of corner shops of the UK. Cheaters could be easily detected with only four national chains to monitor, whereas a single cheating corner shop in one specific location would be almost impossible to detect.

Secondly, the bigger the incentive to cheat, the less likely firms are to reach a collusive agreement. If in our game the $(H_p, L_p)$ outcome was (−20, 80) then agreement would be much less likely, the gains for the cheater are much higher as is the loss for the non-cheater. The final issue that potential colluding firms need to consider is if they did collude, could they actually do anything to prevent cheating? This is dealt with in detail in Section 10.3.

However, before considering the potential means by which market co-ordination can take place there are a number of more technical considerations relating to the construction of the game that may help or hinder firms in reaching a collusive agreement.

First, if the game is a one-shot game then the chances of the firms reaching a collusive agreement are minimal, the risks of not playing the $L_p$ strategy are simply too great. Either firm is risking not making a profit at all if they play the $H_p$ strategy. If they play the $L_p$ strategy, they are guaranteed at least £20 profit. In other words, in one-shot games the dominant $L_p$ strategy is the rational choice for both firms and the Nash equilibrium, but non-optimal, outcome will prevail. For the firms to reach a collusive agreement the game needs to be repeated; in fact more than that, the game needs to be an infinitely repeated game. As explained in Section 8.1, repeated games can be one of two types, they either continue indefinitely or they are repeated but finitely – they have an end point at some time in the future. The reasoning for collusive agreements being more likely only if the game is repeated indefinitely is due to the 'chain store paradox'.

To explain the chain store paradox, consider what happens the last time a repeated game is played. Rational firms will treat the last game as if it was a one-shot game, irrespective of what has gone before. Given that this is the last time that the game is to be played, the risk of not choosing the dominant strategy is too great. For the same reasons outlined previously, the rational decision in one-shot games is to play the $L_p$ strategy; both firms do this and the Nash equilibrium ($L_p$, $L_p$) results. However, this now has a knock-on effect in that the last but one time the game is played also becomes a one-shot game. The firms know that in the last period both of them will play the $L_p$ strategy; in the last but one game, the $H_p$ strategy now also looks too risky so both firms play the $L_p$ strategy and the Nash equilibrium is also the outcome of this last but one game. This process of backward induction happens in each period of the game back to the start of the game making collusive agreement very difficult to achieve.

This would also happen if an infinitely repeated game is suddenly given an end point. Assume that in our profit game there existed for some time a price-fixing ring; the firms have a long-standing agreement that they all charge $H_p$. If this market was investigated by the competition authorities and these authorities announced that the price ring was illegal and must stop in six-months time, then the chain store paradox predicts that the price ring would collapse immediately.

An example of this relates to the NBA which used to operate within the UK. Prior to 1995, books sold in the UK were sold at the publishers' price; the retailers had no scope for reducing book prices. In effect, the industry practised what is called resale price maintenance (see Chapter 13) – price fixing by the publishers. In 1995, the NBA was investigated by the European Court of Justice (ECJ) and was criticised as being anti-competitive. Under UK legislation, the NBA was finally outlawed in 1997; however, by that time the agreement had already collapsed. What happened between 1995 and 1997 was that a succession of large publishers withdrew from the NBA, thus allowing retailers to begin to offer discounted books to the public. In game theory terms, the 1995 ECJ ruling announced that what had previously been an infinite game had, almost certainly, become a finite game. The result was that the chain store paradox took effect and ended the NBA before the final legal end to the game in 1997.

### 10.2.1 Explicit formal collusion

There are various forms that explicit collusion between firms could take, we shall consider four broad areas.

1. Cartels
2. Horizontal integration
3. Joint ventures
4. Strategic alliances.

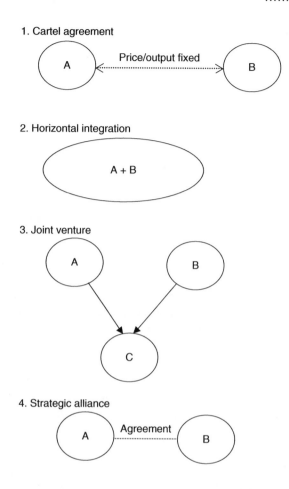

1. Cartel agreement

A ←·····Price/output fixed·····→ B

2. Horizontal integration

A + B

3. Joint venture

A    B

C

4. Strategic alliance

A ·····Agreement····· B

**Figure 10.1**  Types of explicit collusion

Figure 10.1 summarises the various arrangements in which explicit collusion can take between the two firms in our game matrix considered at the end of the introduction to this chapter. At one extreme, the two firms could agree to form a cartel and either fix the price or fix the output. At the other extreme, the two firms could actually merge together and form a new monopoly firm, firm C. The other options involve different types of working together, either forming a strategic alliance (a more benign form of agreement than a cartel) or actually creating a new jointly owned independent company to serve the market. Each of these is considered below.

## 10.2.2  Cartels

Cartels are formal agreements between firms to either fix prices or fix output. Thus, in the context of our profit game the two firms could either agree to charge $H_p$ or agree to fix output levels that will bring about the price $H_p$. The strength of a cartel depends upon the three factors considered previously; how many members there are; how strong the incentive is to cheat; and whether there is a means of enforcing the cartel agreement.

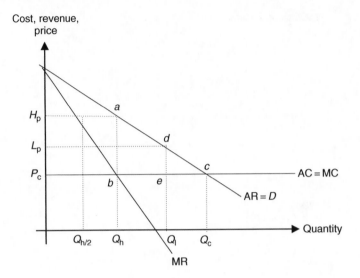

**Figure 10.2** A cartel agreement

Figure 10.2 represents the workings of a cartel and is an alternative representation of the game matrix shown in our profit game in Table 10.1. Assume initially that the market is a duopoly and has settled into the Nash equilibrium position at $(L_p, Q_l)$. To form a cartel and move the market to the preferred $(H_p, Q_h)$ profit maximising outcome the firms have a choice. Either they agree to fix the price at $H_p$ and produce half the output each $(Q_h/2)$ or they both reduce their output to $Q_h/2$ and the price would increase to the profit maximising price $H_p$. Whether the agreement is based on price fixing or quantity fixing, the outcome is the same – higher prices and lower output. The view taken by competition authorities is that due to this outcome cartels are undesirable and should be outlawed.

One of the best-known cartels is OPEC (Oil Producing and Exporting Countries). Although OPEC does not cover all the world's oil producers (neither the USA nor the UK are members, for example), it does cover those countries that primarily produce oil for export. OPEC is an output-fixing cartel. The OPEC members determine amongst themselves on the level of output each will produce, and hence determine their total supply to the world's oil markets. Given the importance of these countries to the overall world supply of oil, the level the OPEC countries fix plays a decisive role in fixing the world price of oil. The issues raised in relation to enforcing the price (via output levels) are largely overcome by their being a small number of easily monitored members. Cheating, however, does happen and needs to be remedied by negotiation among the member states, although more drastic action has taken place in the past with Kuwait's overproduction in 1991 being given as one reason for their invasion by Iraq and the subsequent first Gulf war (see Exercise 3 at the end of chapter).

As mentioned above, within the UK and the EU cartels are illegal. However, the competition authorities do still find them operating. The 'Office of Fair Trading' annual report for 2004/05 (OFT (d)) provides details of investigations into three cartels during the year. One involved the company UOP Ltd UOP are a supplier of insulated glass desiccant, a chemical which removes the moisture between double-glazed glass. The OFT found that UOP, the main supplier of the chemical in UK, and four of their main distributors were fixing the prices charged to customers. All received hefty fines.

### 10.2.3   Horizontal integration

Horizontal integration is a means of market co-ordination that changes the entire nature of the game. In our profit game, horizontal integration would mean the merging together of firms A and B to become a monopoly firm A + B (Figure 10.1). In effect, the game is brought to a close and the new monopolist would fix a price that maximises its profits. In this simple game, the three problems relating to cheaters disappear, there is only one firm. In more complex games with more firms, the horizontal integration of firms may not create a monopoly, but it may make co-ordination and collusive agreement more likely. As discussed above, reducing the number of firms in the market makes co-ordination easier.

One recent merger, which mirrors the discussion above, is that between WebCT and Blackboard. These two firms dominate the market for VLE across the world's higher education institutions. The merger of the two firms (although it looks more like WebCT 'merging into' Blackboard rather than 'merging with') in effect creates a new monopoly, firm C in Figure 10.1. The case against mergers from a consumer point of view is less clear-cut than with cartels. Whilst the aim is undoubtedly to increase revenue and hence profits, the firms involved often point out cost savings that can be achieved. This is the case with the WebCT–Blackboard merger with both firms pointing out not only cost savings, but also technological advantages with the mixing of the good features from each VLE. This may be so, but the temptation may also be there to increase prices to the equivalent of $H_p$ in our profit game.

### 10.2.4   Joint ventures

The third explicit form of collusion is a joint venture. The use of a joint venture in this context is for established firms avoiding competing with each other in a new, or secondary, market to their main area of activity. Assume that firms A and B in our profit game discover a new market that they both wish to enter. One way to avoid the problems they may be having to coordinate behaviour in their current market is to create a joint venture, firm C, which they co-own. Firm C is set up to operate in the new market, where, assuming there are no other entrants, it can operate as a monopolist to the benefit of the co-owners, firms A and B.

One example of how a joint venture can be developed is the history of Airbus, the European aircraft manufacturer. The aircraft industry, like the motor industry, discussed previously, is an industry with significant economies of scale. During the 1990s, it became apparent that some of the main manufacturers in Europe were becoming too small to compete with the big US manufacturers, particularly Boeing and McDonald Douglas. Therefore, four governments in the EU decided to create a joint venture – the Airbus consortium. The consortium was made up of four national companies; Airbus France, Airbus Deutsland, Airbus Espana and BAE Systems (from the UK). How the joint venture worked was that different companies in the consortium had the responsibility for different parts of the manufacturing process, with the complete planes being assembled in Toulouse in the south of France. The consortium proved to be very successful and in 2001 the decision was taken to merge the three national Airbus companies into one. The newly merged firm was called European Defence and Space Company (EADS) and the Airbus consortium was re-launched as a separate company, jointly owned by EADS (with an 80 per cent shareholding) and BAE systems (a 20 per cent shareholding).

What this example shows is some common features of joint ventures. First, in terms of Figure 10.1 the newly created company C is often an amalgamation of complementary resources and competencies taken from firms A and B, not simply a duplicate of firms A and B. Secondly, as with Airbus, if the joint venture firm is successful then quite often it will evolve into a firm in its own right.

One interesting variant of a joint venture is the loyalty card Nectar. We looked at loyalty cards in the previous chapter as an example of firms incurring competitive costs. However, the Nectar card scheme operated in the UK has more in common with a co-operative joint venture than as a competitive cost. The Nectar card is not a loyalty card for any one firm but a card which is operated by a separate company on behalf of a range of companies including Sainsburys, Vodafone, BP, Barclays and many more. In terms of costs, joining the Nectar card scheme has a number of benefits for a firm. First, you do not incur the costs of setting up and administering the scheme. Secondly, the attraction to the consumers is that points earned on their card in purchasing your products are pooled with those earned across a range of companies. Finally, if you look at the lists of firms attached to Nectar, there are no two companies from the same sector. Thus, from a strategic point of view, as a participating firm you send out the same signal to the rest of your market as with an in-house loyalty scheme, but forcing your rivals to incur the cost of setting up their own scheme if they wish to compete in this way with you.

### 10.2.5  Strategic alliances

The final explicit form of collusion is the strategic alliance. Strategic alliances, as collusive agreements, lie somewhere between cartels and horizontal integration. The firms remain independent and do not overtly co-ordinate prices and/or output, but they do agree to co-operate on other aspects of their operations. This sort of collusion can be seen in the international airline industry where there are several global strategic alliance groupings. One such strategic alliance is the 'Star alliance', which covers 16 airlines. The airlines within the 'Star alliance' agree to share or co-operate at certain operational levels such as check-in staff, ground crew and the provision of business lounges. Some members take this a step further by 'code sharing' flights and even co-ordinating schedules.

As with joint ventures, strategic alliances are co-ordinating mechanisms between competing firms, but they tend to operate on the same basis as joint ventures in the sense that they bring together complementary resources and competencies.

Thus, the members of the 'Star alliance' include airlines from every part of the globe which can provide customers with a more integrated and co-ordinated set of routes covering the entire globe – something no single airline could do on its own. Strategic alliances, unlike mergers, tend to create more benefits for consumers than potential anti-competitive problems. In many cases, as in the 'Star alliance' example, the bringing together of complementary resources and competencies tends to broaden consumer choice.

### 10.2.6 Explicit collusion and welfare

As stated previously, the aim of market co-ordination is to benefit the firms. The optimal combination is optimal from the point of view of the firms in the market, but not necessarily from the point of view of the consumers or wider society. In particular, as we shall see in Chapters 13 and 14, the first two forms of collusion outlined above, cartels and horizontal integration, are subjected to quite close scrutiny by the competition authorities in the UK and the EU.

The situation with joint ventures and strategic alliances, however, is less clear-cut, as discussed above. Most joint ventures and strategic alliances have the more benign intention of combining firms' complementary resource bases to produce or develop new products or processes – both of which contribute to the wider economic welfare rather than detracting from it.

### 10.2.7 Implicit tacit collusion

Given the legislative prejudice against explicit forms of market collusion, the more common form of collusion observed in the real world is the subtler implicit, or tacit, collusion. It is sometimes referred to as 'facilitating practices', many of which on first sight appear to have little to do with market co-ordination. We shall consider three of these:

1. Information exchange
2. Tit-for-tat behaviour
3. Contractual commitments.

### 10.2.8 Information exchange

Information exchange includes the publishing and exchanging of market inform-ation between firms through, for example, trade associations, trade journals, published price lists or notification of price changes. These types of practices can make market co-ordination more likely as they all reduce the uncertainties surrounding the market. In game theory terms, they make the game more trans-parent and the pay-offs more predictable, all of which act as an aid to co-ordination. The practice of publishing price lists, for example, can be used to co-ordinate prices across a market, as well as making the detection of cheaters easier. Likewise, trade associations and trade journals represent sources of information exchange that reduce the uncertainties about rivals' behaviour, as well as a means of broadcasting future changes in strategy such as price rises.

The role played by the SMMT in the motor industry was discussed earlier. As we saw, the SMMT fulfils a valuable function, carried out by many trade associations and helps reduce search costs, as well as reduces uncertainty and complexity, for firms in the industry – put another way it helps reduce transaction costs. However, on a less benign note, it also provides the opportunity for firms in the same trade to keep in contact with each other and, as Smith told us 230 years ago, 'People of the same trade seldom meet together, even for merriment and diversion, but the conversation ends in a conspiracy against the public, or in some contrivance to raise prices'. Trade associations may reduce transaction costs, but they also help facilitate the co-ordination of markets – not always to the benefit of their customers.

### 10.2.9   Tit-for-tat

Tit-for-tat behaviour is another form of implicit collusive behaviour. Tit-for-tat works by one of the firms, for example, firm B in Table 10.1, taking the risk at the $(L_p, L_p)$ equilibrium of switching strategy. The rational response for firm A is to follow the switch in strategy and so reaching the desired $(H_p, H_p)$ outcome. Why does firm A do this? The reasoning is that although the original switch by firm B leads to firm A increasing profits as they move to the $(H_p, L_p)$ combination, firm A realises that this is only likely to be temporary. Firm A is therefore faced with a choice: either stay at $L_p$ and return to the profit level of £20, as firm B switches back to $L_p$, or follow firm B and switch to $H_p$ and accept the £30 profit made at the $(H_p, H_p)$ combination. In the real world, this sort of behaviour would be typified by the idea of price leadership, one firm taking on the role of price leader putting up its prices in the knowledge that its rivals will do the same. Some industries are often accused of practising price leadership (the petrol retailers, for example) but in practice it is hard to prove.

### 10.2.10   Contractual commitments

Contractual commitments revolve around the idea that market co-ordination is achieved by one of the firms making some sort of credible commitment to its customers which forces the non-optimal Pareto outcome across the market. One of the more familiar of these is the so-called 'meet or release' clause. An example of this is the common claim by retail outlets to match the price charged by any of their rivals – 'if you find this cheaper anywhere else then we'll refund the difference'. On the face of it, this looks like a good deal for consumers; however, in practice, a firm may be using this as a means of forcing a non-equilibrium outcome on the game for its own benefit.

In our profit game, the $H_p$ firm offering the meet or release clause is sending a message to its rivals that there is no point in charging the $L_p$ as it will simply match the price difference and the rival firm does not make the sale. Indeed, there is no point in the other firm charging the $L_p$ at all; it might as well charge the same $H_p$ as the firm offering the meet or release clause. Thus, through the contractual meet or release clause the non-equilibrium Pareto outcome is forced across the market. Making this work does depend upon the factors outlined previously relating to cheaters; also, as with the threat in the prisoners' dilemma game, it must be credible. Rival firms must believe that the firm making the contractual commitment will actually carry this out. Also, in terms of the meet or release clause, the firm making such a contractual commitment needs to be sufficiently large in the marketplace to be able to communicate the message and to carry out the threat in a public manner that makes sure that all customers know.

### 10.2.11 Implicit collusion and welfare

Thus, as we can see, collusive behaviour by firms does not have to be of the obvious and explicit kind such as a cartel arrangement, it can take the form of a subtler and less overt type of co-ordination. However, the same welfare concerns arise. The firms may achieve their objective of sustaining a non-equilibrium non-optimal outcome to the game, but is it in the consumers' interests? For the very reasons of the collusion being implicit rather than explicit, it is actually very difficult for public authorities to legislate against implicit practices that might be against the consumers' interests.

## 10.3 | Sustaining the optimal outcome

Assuming that the firms can agree to outcomes and manage to move to the optimal non-equilibrium combination, the next problem becomes the ability of the colluding firms to maintain that outcome. Many of the problems in doing this relate to the same three issues discussed in relation to the achieving of the optimal outcome in the first place.

1. The ease with which cheaters can be detected, which depends upon:
2. The strength of the incentive to cheat
3. Whether cheating can be prevented, which is a combination of the elements above.

Similarly, many of the ploys discussed in Section 10.2 can be used to try and sustain the collusive outcome: credible threats, meet or release clauses, tit-for-tat and so on. Other means of sustaining the collusive outcomes involve the use of what are termed 'trigger strategies'. These involve firms reacting to cheaters in a way that ensures that any of the gains from cheating are only enjoyed on a short-term basis. Thus, for example, in our profit game if a firm cheats whilst at the $(H_p, H_p)$ optimal outcome and switches to the $L_p$ strategy, the other firm follows and both firms end up at the $(L_p, L_p)$ Nash equilibrium. In more complicated games, the cheating firms could be forced to combinations that actually lead to a pay-off worse than the Nash equilibrium pay-off.

## 10.4　Review and further reading

The chapter began with a list of seemingly loosely related activities and aspects of business behaviour which were linked by the fact they all related to the co-ordination of markets by firms. By the use of the profit game from Chapter 8 and its inbuilt prisoners' dilemma, we have shown how all the items in the list actually reflect different aspects of this game as firms try to bring about a co-ordinated, more favourable outcome. Table 10.2 summarises how the theory and examples used fit together.

As stated at the outset, the principal purpose behind firms trying to co-ordinate their markets is exactly the same as that behind the competitive aspect to firms' behaviour looked at in the previous chapter – the maximisation of revenue from their output markets. The difference though is that there is no equivalent to the competitive cost (S) to include in our model of the firm as shown in Figure 4.1.

This chapter finishes the development of the expanded model of the neo-classical firm first introduced in detail in Chapter 4. Early on in this chapter, and at various points in the previous two chapters, we have sounded a word of caution to beware of the firm-specific view that the games in Chapter 8 present. As has been discussed above, at various points, what is beneficial for the firm is not always beneficial for its customers. This issue forms one of the key themes for Part IV of this book as the concerns surrounding the wider welfare issues lead to the discussion on competition policy in Chapter 13. However, before we look at competition policy we need to return to the theme of Chapter 1, namely highlighting some of the

**Table 10.2**　Co-ordinating behaviour

|  | *Purpose* | *Possible means* | *Specific examples* |
|---|---|---|---|
| Identification | Reducing information asymmetries and complexity | Trade associations | SMMT |
|  |  | Trade directories | Motor Industry Directory (MID) |
| Moving | Shifting to a non-equilibrium outcome | Cartels | OPEC (quantity), UOP (price), NBA |
|  |  | Joint ventures | Airbus, Nectar card |
|  |  | Horizontal integration | WebCT–Blackboard |
|  |  | Strategic alliances | Star alliance |
|  |  | Information exchange | SMMT and MID |
|  |  | Tit-for-tat behaviour | Price leadership |
|  |  | Contractual Agreements | Price matching |
| Sustaining | Sustaining the non-equilibrium outcome | Detecting cheaters |  |
|  |  | Reducing the incentive to cheat |  |

differences and similarities between the strategists' and the economists' views of the firm. This is most pronounced when we move the focus of analysis from the individual firm to the wider market and industry context in which they operate. This is what we shall look at in Chapters 11 and 12.

The basic approach taken in this chapter follows Stiglitz and Matthewson (1986). For a more detailed discussion on the economics of co-operation see Faulkner and Child (2001).

## 10.5 | Student exercises

### 10.5.1 Review exercises and points for discussion

1. Provide brief and clear definitions of the following key terms and concepts as used in this chapter.

   a. Explicit formal collusion
   b. Implicit tacit collusion
   c. The chain store paradox
   d. Joint ventures
   e. Cartels
   f. Horizontal integration
   g. Strategic alliance.

2. Consider the following examples of co-ordinated behaviour by firms.

   ■ Sony Ericcsson is a joint venture firm owned by the electronics company Sony and the telecoms company Ericsson.

   ■ The TRIUM global MBA programme is run jointly, in the form of a strategic alliance among the London School of Economics (LSE), the Stern School of Business (based in New York) and HEC School of Management (Paris).

   ■ GAP Inc., the clothing retailer, has a history of growth by horizontal integration. Over the years they have successively merged with competitors such as Banana Republic, Old Navy and Forth and Towne – but continue to use the four separate brand names.

   What do you think are

   a. The motivations and benefits to the firms involved in each of these examples of co-ordinating behaviour
   b. The advantages and disadvantages to the customers of these firms.

3. The following is a brief outline of OPEC: you may wish to supplement this summary through other sources that are readily available on the Internet.

   The Organisation of Petroleum Exporting Countries (OPEC) is, in economic terms, an output-fixing cartel. OPEC represents 11 countries (12 from 2007) and between them control over 41 per cent of the world's oil reserves. The aim of

OPEC is to try and maintain the world price of crude oil within an agreed band. This is done by the countries agreeing output quotas which, in effect, fix their combined supply of oil and thus, through the normal workings of demand and supply, play a major part in fixing the world price for oil.

However, co-ordinating 11 counties is not easy. OPEC splits into roughly two camps: price 'hawks' and price 'doves'. The price hawks tend to be those countries with large populations and few other resources beyond their oil reserves – such as Iran and Nigeria. They tend to push for higher prices, through the setting of lower quotas, to generate income to help with debt repayments and to support the development of their countries. The price doves, Saudi Arabia and Kuwait for example, tend to be the smaller countries with large oil reserves that prefer lower prices to counteract the incentive that high prices may have on the development of alternative energy supplies. Given these pressures, maintaining discipline within OPEC is difficult. The most notorious example of one member trying to force another into line was the invasion of Kuwait by Iraq in 1990 due to Kuwait persistently overproducing and thus keeping the oil price down. The other increasing pressure on OPEC is the development of oil supplies from outside their member countries, for example Russia which currently has over 14 per cent of the world's reserves.

a.  Specify OPEC in game theoretic terms by defining

  i.   The structure of the game
  ii.  The nature of the game
  iii. The timeframe for the game

b.  Consider the issues that arise for OPEC in trying to sustain a position that may be optimal, but possibly not a Nash equilibrium. Consider the issues under the headings of:

  i.   The identification of objectives
  ii.  The moving to the non-equilibrium position
  iii. Sustaining the non-equilibrium position

c.  Is the optimal position for OPEC optimal for non-OPEC members and oil consumers?

## 10.5.2  Application exercise

Complete your analysis of a firm you are familiar with (exercises at the end of Chapters 7 and 9) by examining any signs of co-operative behaviour. This may include

a.  The existence of any trade associations the firm may belong to
b.  The existence of any trade journals the firm may subscribe to
c.  Evidence of any implicit or explicit collusion.

# The Firm and Its Environmental Context

# Environmental **11** Analysis: The Economists' Perspective

## LEARNING OUTCOMES

On completion of this chapter, the reader should be able to

- Explain the difference between 'profit' and 'value added'
- Outline the structure–conduct–performance (SCP) model of environmental analysis
- Explain the limitations of the SCP model as a means of analysing the environment
- Use the SCP model to assess industries/markets

## KEY NEW CONCEPTS

| | | |
|---|---|---|
| Measures of economic performance | Measures of market concentration | Consumer surplus |
| Rates of return | The Lehner index | |

## KEY NEW MODELS

Structure–conduct–performance

## MODELS AND CONCEPTS DEVELOPED FURTHER

| | | |
|---|---|---|
| Value added | The value chain | Profit maximisation |
| Exogenous and endogenous variables | Economic efficiency | Perfect competition |
| Monopoly | Price–cost margins | |

In the UK, in 2004, 42 per cent of the adult population read a national daily news-paper (Mintel, 2005a). As in the USA and other European countries, there are a range of regional newspapers in the UK, but what makes the UK market different is the high proportion of the population that read a national daily newspaper. The market is dominated by an oligopoly of four firms – 'News International', 'Trinity Mirror Group', 'Associated Newspapers' and 'Express newspapers' – that produce a range of titles which account for over 80 per cent of the national newspapers sold. The industry is one of the oldest and most mature within the economy, most titles have been around for over 100 years, for example, 'The Times', for over 200 years. The industry has also proved to be one that is remarkably resilient. Having survived the challenges posed by radio in the 1930s and then television in the 1950s as alternative sources of news coverage, now the industry has to cope with a new source of competition in the form of online news. However, as we shall see below, this has been turned by some newspapers from a threat-ening substitute good into a useful complementary good to the existing hardcopy print title.

So far in this book, we have been focusing on the analysis of the firm, like the four main firms involved in the national daily newspaper industry. However, in the rest of the book, we shall broaden out the analysis to deal with the wider context within which an individual firm operates. Instead of looking at the transformation process of one of the four firms involved in the national daily newspaper industry, we need to look at the industry as a whole. What is the demand structure of the newspaper industry? What is the supply structure? What is the nature of competition in the industry? Do the four firms earn abnormal profits? Is the industry efficient? In order to answer these questions, we need to have a framework within which to undertake the analysis. The purpose of the next two chapters is to present a range of frameworks that have been developed by both economists and strategists to help with trying to answering these questions.

The famous line 'no man is an island' applies equally to firms – no firm exists in isolation. Every firm exists as part of a chain of production, as outlined in Chapter 5 and expanded on in Chapter 7 in relation to the idea of a value chain. Take, for example, the Bear Factory shops used in Chapter 5 to illustrate a simple chain of production. These shops lie at the end of a complex set of interrelated production chains, perhaps better described as a production network, that produce not only the unstuffed fabric bears but also the shop fittings, the clothes and accessories for the bears, the stuffing machines, the needles and the thread, the scissors, the promotional material (including the website), even the training of the staff – the list is almost endless. Similarly, the firms involved in the UK national daily newspaper industry will be at the centre of a series of interlocking production chains involved in the production and distribution of their newspaper titles. The interconnectedness of firms was also a theme that emerged from Part III of the book which used game theory as the basis for assessing the strategic nature of a firm's revenue-maximising efforts. Any actions taken by, for example, 'News International' over the price of their titles would influence the pricing decisions of the other firms in the national daily newspaper industry.

So far in this book, the approach has been to use the ideas, concepts and models of strategists to enhance and expand upon the well-established neo-classical approach to the analysis of firms. However, as we move to look at the wider environmental context of firms we hit upon a fundamental difference in the perspective of economists and strategists. As discussed in Chapter 1, traditionally economic theory has been driven by the need for economists to advise and inform public policy, whereas strategic theory has been driven by the need to advise and inform company policy. Therefore, the purpose behind environmental analysis is different for economists than for strategists. The models developed by the economists are driven by the need to assess whether a particular production network is efficient – is it producing the final product by making the most economic use of resources. If not then there may be a need for intervention by the public authorities to ensure resources are used more efficiently (the subject of Chapters 13 and 14). Thus, in looking at the national daily newspaper industry, the economist would be looking for evidence of strategic entry barriers or signs of market co-ordinating behaviour by the four oligopolists that were generating and sustaining abnormal profits and hence economically inefficient price–cost margins.

However, the firm-focused strategists' models are directed at trying to help firms understand their environments better, so that they can extract as much value for themselves out of their own production network. To the strategist, the firm is still the focal point but 'efficiency' relates to the levels of profits a firm is making – the higher the level of profits the more efficient the firm is. Thus, the strategist would be looking at the firms in the national daily newspaper industry and assessing the levels of profits being made – the firms with the higher profits would be regarded as the more efficient. This is a very different view of efficiency, from that of the economist.

Where economists and strategists do not disagree, however, is on the fundamental need for firms to make profits, interpreted in the widest sense as a surplus of revenue over costs. This applies equally to the so-called 'not-for-profit' organisations, such as charities, and public sector bodies. Even these organisations need to generate a surplus. However, before moving on to look at the various models and methods of environmental analysis in this and the next chapter, it may be worthwhile just reminding ourselves of the essential difference between the idea of the economists' 'profit' and the strategists' 'value'. This was first discussed in Chapter 1 but has been developed and expanded as our analysis of the firm has progressed.

*The economists' perspective: maximisation of profits.* Figure 11.1 is a summary of the model of the firm developed in Chapter 4 and represented by Figure 4.1. Across the top of the figure, we have the fundamental production transformation of inputs into output by the firm. The costs involved in undertaking this transformation are the direct production costs ($D$), the management costs ($M$) and the competitive costs ($S$). These costs need to be offset against the revenue ($R$) that is generated from the sale of output in the firm's output markets. The aim of the firm is to minimise costs (all costs) and maximise revenue. Profit is the residual of revenue after the deduction of costs.

*The strategists' view: maximising value added.* By way of comparison, Figure 1.3 from Chapter 1 is reproduced. Across the top, we have the same transformation process, but this time, the corresponding flow is not in monetary terms but in terms of 'value'. As we shall see in the next chapter, 'value' can also be translated into monetary terms, but the calculation is a little more involved than the simple residual of revenue from costs used in Figure 11.1. However, at the end of the day, the underlying aim is the same – the value gained must be greater than the value lost, if the firm is to survive. Indeed, the firms aim to try and maximise this value added (Figure 11.2).

*Environmental analysis – the firm in its wider context.* As noted in Chapter 1, the concepts of 'profit' and 'value' are essentially the same, and indeed many writers use the terms interchangeably. However, the way in which economists and strategists have developed and used their respective 'profit' and 'value' concepts further emphasises the different foci of the two subject areas. We have already seen in Chapter 4 how the economist makes the distinction between 'normal' and 'abnormal' profits, and how abnormal profits are seen as being inefficient in the wider economic context. However, to strategists with their firm-specific focus, the idea that some profits may be viewed as 'abnormal' does not make any sense at all. The sole purpose of a firm is to generate as much profit as possible

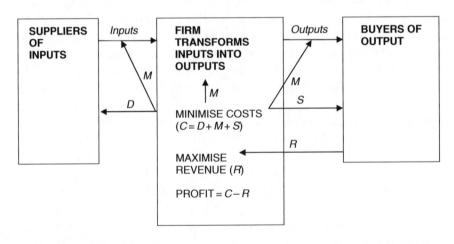

**Figure 11.1**
The maximisation of profit

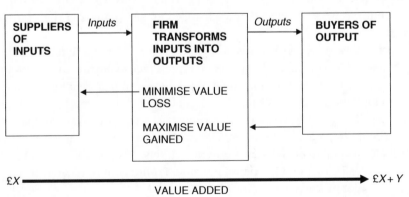

**Figure 11.2**
Adding value

or, in strategist-speak, to maximise the value added. What is missing from the strategists' perspective is the 'wider economic context' that the more public policy-specific economist has to consider. The two most widely used models of environmental analysis in the two discipline areas – structure–conduct–performance (SCP) (economists) and five forces (strategists) – further emphasise this difference in perspective, not so much in the way in which they are formulated (which is essentially the same) but the way in which they are used as analytical tools.

The SCP model dominated industrial economics (IE) throughout the 1960s and 1970s and, indeed, many economists, either explicitly or implicitly, still adhere to its basic tenets. As mentioned previously the IE economists' concern has been to inform public policy. Therefore, the model tries to provide a generic framework to explain how industries work and, in particular, how they can be made to work better or more 'efficiently'. Efficiency to an economist means obtaining the maximum output to meet society's demands from the resources available to that society. As we shall see, SCP is a neo-classical model resting on the familiar bedrock of full information, global rationality, homogeneity with holistic profit-maximising companies as described in Chapter 2. Thus, efficiency requires that industries make zero abnormal profits and operate at a point where price is equal to marginal cost (see Section 4.2).

The dominant model in strategy for analysing the environment has been, since the 1980s at least, Michael Porter's (1980) five-forces model. Porter was originally an industrial economist and the five-forces model is essentially a recasting of the SCP model to suit the more firm-specific needs of the strategists. However, the way in which Porter used the model was fundamentally different from how industrial economists were using SCP. Porter's concern, as a strategy convert, was not with public policy and market efficiency but with how firms could assess the potential profits to be extracted from industries. Efficiency to a strategist is how a firm can use its resources to extract as much profit as possible from the markets it is involved in or in which it may become involved in the future. Thus, abnormal profit is the desired outcome and indicates efficiency from the strategists' firm-centred perspective. To use the strategists' terminology, they are maximising the value added.

Thus, we can see that the neo-classical economists' and the strategists' differing perspectives on efficiency are reflected clearly in the two core models they have developed to analyse the environment. This chapter deals with the economists' SCP model in more detail, and the next chapter not only deals in more detail with the five-forces model, but also expands on the idea of 'value' and some of the other tools used by strategists to assess their environment.

## 11.1 | The SCP model

### 11.1.1 The basis of the SCP model

The SCP framework first came into wide use following the work of the American economist, Joe Bain, in the 1950s. The following quote from Bain encapsulates the underlying thrust of the SCP approach:

> Market structure may logically be expected … to influence the conduct of firms in maximizing profits, the interaction of the conduct of competing firms in maximizing profits, the interaction of competing firms in the same market, and the performance emerging from the industry. (Bain, 1956)

As can be seen from the quote, Bain identifies three separate elements that contribute to the determination of organisation of an industry – market structure, market conduct and market performance.

### 11.1.1.1 Market structure

In the SCP model, market structure relates to the operating environment of the industry, those factors that firms within an industry have to take as being given and beyond the control of any single firm. To use the terminology developed in Chapter 4, they are exogenous factors impacting on the firm. In the original exposition of the SCP approach, the key aspect of the market structure was the number of firms in the market or, as it is more commonly referred to, the market concentration.

### 11.1.1.2 Market conduct

Market conduct refers to how firms in an industry actually behave. Thus, market conduct relates to the decisions that firms take in relation to their three endogenous variables – price, marketing and R&D. It is within this part of the model that we would categorise all the strategic decisions and actions discussed in Part III.

### 11.1.1.3 Market performance

Market performance is the extent to which a particular industry meets the conditions of economic efficiency. In other words, how effectively the industry allocates resources and produces goods and services. As discussed in the previous section, this is what economists are interested in – how effective the industry is in organising the resources it uses to produce its output.

### 11.1.1.4 The basic SCP relationship

The basic premise of the Bain quote is that the industry environment the firms find themselves in determines how the firms behave, which in turn determines how economically efficient that industry is. In other words, we have a linear relationship from the market structure to the market conduct and finally the market performance as shown in Figure 11.3.

**Figure 11.3**
The SCP model

The model suggests that the performance of a particular industry is a direct function of the industry's structure or more formally: Performance = $f$(structure). In other words, for any given industry structure, you should be able to predict how efficient that industry will be. Thus, the message for the policy makers is that if you wish to improve the economic performance of an industry, then you need to look to changing that industry's structure. This, of course, begs the question which market structure gives the most efficient market performance?

### 11.1.1.5 The expanded SCP model

By the early 1970s, Bain's original model had been expanded and some of its limitation addressed (see, for example, Scherer/Ross, 1990). Figure 11.4 summarises an expanded version of the model.

The central element still remains the S–C–P linear linkage, but two new elements have been added, as well as the possibility of some feedback between the various components of the model. The new element 'basic conditions' refers to the factors influencing the demand and supply for the product being produced. These are essentially the exogenous demand factors discussed in Section 4.2.2 (demographics, income, tastes and fashions, substitutes and complements) and the supply factors (price of inputs, state of technology) from which a firm's demand and supply curves are derived. These are seen as the main determinants of the market structure. The other new element is a recognition that industries do not operate in isolation. All industries operate within a legal and regulatory framework imposed by national government and supranational organisations (the subject of Chapter 13), hence the need to include 'public policy' as a factor influencing the operation of an industry.

Market structure has been expanded by this time to include not only the number of firms in the industry but also such structural features as entry barriers, product differentiation and vertical integration. Thus, the strict linear relationship of Figure 11.3 needed to be relaxed with the possibility of feedback between the elements within the model recognised. As we have seen, the number of firms in a market, for example, can be influenced by the conduct of incumbent firms through the use of strategic entry barriers. However, the original underlying premise of the model that structure determines conduct determines performance remains in these later representations of the model.

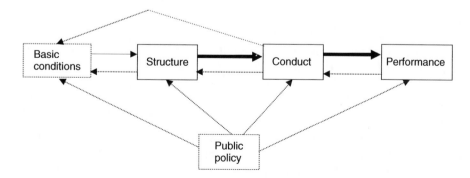

**Figure 11.4** The expanded SCP model

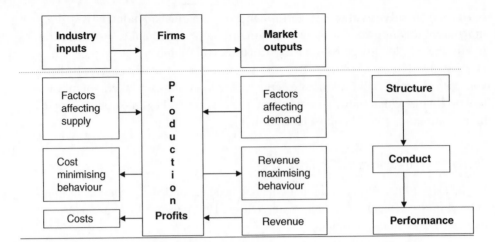

**Figure 11.5**
SCP and the
neo-classical firm

### 11.1.1.6 SCP and the model of the firm

Although SCP is an environmental assessment model used by economists to try and predict the efficiency of a particular industry, it is also reflected in the basic neo-classical model of the firm discussed in Chapter 2. Figure 11.5 illustrates the point.

A firm is faced with a set of exogenous factors affecting the supply of its inputs and the demand for its outputs, the basic conditions of Figure 11.4, which define the structural environment faced by the firm. It then uses the endogenous supply and demand factors to try to minimise industry costs and maximise revenue from its output markets, the conduct part of the SCP framework. The end result of this activity is a level of profits that the firm gains from the market, the final performance part of the framework.

## 11.1.2 SCP and the national daily newspaper industry

### 11.1.2.1 Basic conditions and structure

As discussed above, in the SCP model, the basic demand and supply conditions of a market help to determine the market structure. Table 11.1 summarises the exogenous demand (see Table 4.7) factors for the national daily newspaper industry.

The costs side of the industry is fairly capital intensive with the requirement to produce anything between half a million and 3.5 million copies per day depending on the title. There is also the need for an extensive national distribution network which ensures that copies of newspapers are available nationally from early morning. Both of these factors represent structural entry barriers based on economies of scale.

The market structure that emerges from the above is one where there are many buyers, about 13 million; however, this figure is declining, but the economies of scale required means there are few producers. On the face of it, there does appear

**Table 11.1**  Exogenous demand factors faced by the national daily newspaper industry

| Exogenous demand factor | National daily newspaper industry |
| --- | --- |
| Demography | The average readership across the age ranges was 42% in 2005. This is down from 49% in 2001. However, there is a noticeable divide between the 15–44 age range (approximately 33%) and the 45–65+ age range (approximately 51%) |
| Tastes and fashions | One possible influence on newspaper purchase is the means of travelling to work, with people travelling to work by bus or train, more likely, to buy a newspaper. In recent years, there has been an increase in the use of buses and trains for getting to work. Between 2001 and 2003, travel by bus has increased by 2.2% and by train by 4.3% |
| Substitutes | The national daily newspaper industry faces an increasing range of substitutes from long-established substitutes such as radio and television to newer ones such as free papers (e.g. the 'Metro') and online news. Television is the main substitute with 63% of adults saying this is their main source of news |
| Complements | The possibility of online news can also be used to complement a newspaper's main hard copy paper. An online version of the hard copy newspaper can be used as a means providing the opportunity for more in-depth and wider coverage than the space-limited hard copy |
| Government policy | Newspapers are subject to the laws relating to liable and there is a body, the Press Complaints Authority, which monitors newspapers. As with all of the UK economy, the industry is also subject to the UK and the EU competition legislations |

*Source*: Data from Mintel (2005a).

to be quite a range of newspaper titles (Mintel, 2005a, includes 12 titles as national daily newspapers); however, the four main firms in the industry each own a range of titles which gives them an 80 per cent market share (this will be considered in more detail in Section 11.2.1); therefore, we can say that the industry is an oligopoly. The declining readership is another structural feature faced by the industry, as is the relatively lower readership amongst the under 45s. These are both important factors as one of the main sources of income for newspapers is advertising, and fewer readers and a bias towards the 45+ age group reduce advertising income for newspapers.

### 11.1.2.2  Market conduct

As discussed previously, three of the factors that influence demand are endogenous – they are under the control of the firm. The decision a firm takes in

**Table 11.2**  Endogenous demand factors and the national daily newspaper industry

| Endogenous demand factor | National daily newspaper industry |
| --- | --- |
| Price | Price only has a short-term effect on sales, so is not considered to be a main factor in market conduct |
| Marketing | This is a major aspect of market conduct. Just under £116m was spent by the industry on advertising in 2004; this represents 2.72% of sales. In addition to advertising expenditure, the industry uses a whole range of other marketing tools, for example, free DVD/CDs, free holidays and a range of special offers from restaurant meals to air travel. Therefore, the total marketing expenditure will be even higher than 2.72% of sales |
| R&D | One of the main sources of competition is quality, both in terms of the physical appearance of the newspaper and the papers' content. In recent years, newspapers having invested heavily in the use of colour printing, 'cleaner' print and changes in size and format (all bar one title, 'The Daily Telegraph' have abandoned the broadsheet format). Another aspect of R&D has been the investment in the development of online versions of the hard copy version of the newspaper |

*Source*: Data from Mintel (2005a).

relation to these endogenous demand factors determines the firm's behaviour; in SCP terms, it defines the market conduct part of the model. Table 11.2 summarises the endogenous demand factors for the national daily newspaper industry.

Is this the market conduct we would expect, given the market structure described above? By and large, the answer has to be, yes, it is. The oligopoly market structure seems to lead to a market conduct that is dominated by non-price competition. Many of the strategic features of competitive behaviour discussed in Part III of the book are present in the market, particularly the high expenditure on marketing (competitive cost in terms of Figure 11.1) and the interrelated nature of the competition. Other aspects of market conduct can also be related directly back to the market structure. The almost total shift away from broadsheets, for example, reflects the growing importance of the travel to work market – a broadsheet is not easy to read on a crowded bus or train. Similarly, the development of online versions of newspapers is a response to the growing threat of the online news sources.

### 11.1.2.3  Market performance

In practice, the estimation of market performance for real-world industries is not easy. The evidence on market performance for this market is conflicting with the standard measure of profits (rate of return on capital employed, ROCE) open to different interpretations. This will be dealt with in more detail in Section 11.2.2.

### 11.1.3  SCP and the traditional models of market structure

Given the basic premise of SCP is that the performance of an industry derives from its structure, the question left unanswered from Section 11.1.1 is what set of market structure variables is going to give you the most efficient market? In order to answer this, we need to look no further than the neo-classical market structures of perfect competition, monopolistic competition, oligopoly and monopoly. Each of these familiar models is presented below but recast into the SCP framework (Figure 11.3).

One of the underlying assumptions behind the perfectly competitive model is that all firms face the same perfectly elastic demand curve and the same costs for all their inputs, hence the underlying basic conditions lead to the structural features as shown in Table 11.3.

As discussed in Section 4.2.1, a perfectly competitive firm's conduct is purely governed by the need to maintain a profit maximising position. The structure of the market means that the firm not only is a price taker (perfectly elastic demand curve) but also has no need to undertake marketing or R&D (homogenous product and no economies of scale). Thus, the only endogenous variable is output, which a firm adjusts in a knee-jerk type reaction to changes in price, so as to maintain its profit maximising position. The performance that this leads to, in the long run, is one where there is no abnormal profit, and the market ends up being economically

**Table 11.3**  Perfect competition

| | |
|---|---|
| Basic conditions | Perfectly elastic demand curve<br>Homogenous inputs<br>Identical costs for all firms |
| Structure | Low concentration<br>No product differentiation<br>No economies of scale<br>No entry barriers |
| Conduct | The objective is to maximise profits<br><br>1. Short run<br><br>Firms maximise profit where MC = MR: abnormal profit<br><br>2. Long run<br><br>New entrants reduce the price: Profit = 0<br>(normal profits) |
| Performance | Short run: abnormal profits made, price–cost margin Inefficient<br>Long run: normal profits made, price–cost margin = 0<br>Efficient |

**Table 11.4** Monopoly

| Basic conditions | Downward sloping demand curve<br>No close substitutes |
|---|---|
| Structure | One firm produces the entire output for the market<br>Product differentiation possible<br>Economies of scale<br>Entry barriers |
| Conduct | The objective is to maximise profits<br>Monopolists will either:<br><br>a. Maximise profits by fixing price where MC = MR making abnormal profits<br><br>or<br><br>b. Fix a limit price which prevents entry into the market<br><br>The monopolist may also practise price discrimination if the market structure allows |
| Performance | Short run and long run: abnormal profits made, price–cost margin<br>Inefficient |

efficient. The market performance is clearly linked directly back to the market structure (Table 11.4).

As with perfect competition, a monopoly's market structure leads directly to the market performance with the firm's conduct being entirely governed by the structure of the market and objective to maximise profits. The basic conditions lead to a market structure where there is a single firm in the industry. As with the perfectly competitive firm, the monopolist's conduct is wholly focused on maintaining its profit maximising position. The monopolist has no need to undertake marketing or R&D, so the only decision is over whether to fix price or output. The decision taken depends on the height of entry barriers. If the entry barriers are sufficiently high enough to allow a price to be fixed by the firm without attracting entry, then this is what the firm will do. If not, then the firm will fix a limit price (Section 9.4) that is just sufficient to prevent entry into the market (Table 11.5).

Oligopoly does not fit easily within the SCP framework. The elements can be identified as in Table 11.5, but the link from structure through to performance is not at all clear. Much of what oligopoly firms do under the conduct part of the model (erecting strategic entry barriers, product differentiation, tacit collusion, basically everything discussed in Part III) is deliberately aimed at influencing market structure, thus reversing the linkage flow of Figure 11.3.

The real problem with oligopoly within the SCP framework is that there is no one generic model of oligopoly. However, the element of oligopoly that is generic is the interdependent nature of firm's decision-making, hence its suitability for analysis using the game theory approach as presented in Part III. Within the SCP

**Table 11.5** Oligopoly

| Basic conditions | Downward sloping demand curve<br>Rest of the market conditions depend on the nature of the product being produced |
|---|---|
| Structure | High market concentration<br>Product differentiation<br>Entry barriers |
| Conduct | Possibility of non-profit maximising behaviour<br>Strategic behaviour to maintain market position and/or to prevent entry<br>Discretionary expenditure to support strategic behaviour (competitive costs) |
| Performance | Likely to be inefficient in SCP sense of efficiency |

context, this means that the behaviour of firms is more likely to be determined by the behaviour of other firms, not just by market structure. Put simply, the SCP linkage does not work for oligopoly. If the market is inefficient, it is more likely to be as a result of a firm's conduct and not the structure of the market. In particular, it is more likely to be as a result of a firm erecting entry barriers in an attempt to sustain the abnormal profits that it is making, all of which leads us back to the idea first raised in Section 4.3.3. It is not the structural feature of the number of firms that is important for economic efficiency but the removal of entry barriers that may partly arise from the conduct of firms. This is an issue that will be returned to in Chapter 13 when looking at the basis of competition policy.

## 11.2 | Does structure determine performance?

Despite the limitation of the SCP approach, particularly the problems it has with oligopoly markets, much effort has been put into trying to test its basic proposition namely: Performance = $f$(structure).

Given the relationship between SCP and the economists' traditional models of market structure discussed in the previous section, by testing the structure–performance link, we are in fact testing one of the bedrocks of neo-classical microeconomics. The traditional models of market structure emphasise the central importance of market concentration. At one extreme, we have perfect competition with its many small firms bringing about the economically efficient market performance. At the other, we have the single firm monopoly market which brings about the worst outcome in terms of market performance. The contention was that most markets lie somewhere in between with the defining structural characteristic being the number of firms in the market. Put simply, the fewer the firms in a market, the greater their ability to raise prices above cost and hence the higher the abnormal profits.

Many of the statistical models tested took the general form

$$\Pi = \beta_0 + \beta_1 C + \mu$$

where $C$ is market concentration (structural variable) and $\Pi$ is profit (performance variable).

In the equation, $C$ represents the independent variable and $\Pi$ the dependent variable. Profit is used in these models as a proxy for efficiency; the higher the level of profit, the greater the price–cost margin and the less efficient the market (see Section 4.3.1). If the theory is correct, then there should be a positive link between $\Pi$ and $C$, the more the output becomes concentrated in the hands of a small number of firms, the less efficient the market becomes. In other words, the further you move away from the perfectly competitive model towards the monopoly model, the less efficient the market should become. However, before we can consider what the empirical evidence tells us, we need to first consider the concepts and methods developed to measure market concentration and hence a testable value for $C$ and secondly to look again at the idea of market performance.

## 11.2.1 Measuring market structure

Over the years, a plethora of methods for measuring market concentration have been devised. The reliability of many of the measures has been challenged, particularly in relation to their static nature and inability to reflect changes in Market Structure. As an aid to assessing the validity of the concentration methods, Hannah and Kay devised some conditions that any measure of market concentration should be tested against. These Hannah–Kay axioms are set out below (Hannah and Kay, 1977):

1. The concentration curve ranking criteria – the measure should give a clear and unambiguous ranking.
2. Sales transfer principle – transfer of sales from one firm to another should increase concentration.
3. The entry condition – the entry of new firms should reduce concentration.
4. The merger principle – mergers between incumbent firms should increase concentration.
5. Brand-switching principle – random brand-switching by consumers should increase concentration.
6. Falling new firm share – as a new firm's market share falls, so should its effect on the concentration measure.
7. Random growth factors – random factors affecting growth should increase concentration.

We shall consider two of the more commonly used measures of market concentration:

1. The $x$-firm concentration ratio
2. The Herfindahl–Hirschman index (HHI)

**Table 11.6**  Concentration ratio for the UK newspaper industry (2004)

| Title | Circulation ('000) | Market share (%) | Cumulative market share (%) |
|---|---|---|---|
| The Sun | 3333 | 26.1 | 26.1 |
| Daily Mail | 2412 | 18.9 | 45 |
| Daily Mirror | 1830 | 14.3 | 59.3 |
| Daily Express | 939 | 7.4 | 66.7 |
| Daily Telegraph | 911 | 7.3 | 74 |
| Daily Star | 890 | 7.0 | 81 |
| The Times | 658 | 5.2 | 86.2 |
| Daily Record | 488 | 3.8 | 90 |
| Financial Times | 432 | 3.4 | 93.4 |
| The Guardian | 376 | 2.9 | 96.3 |
| The Independent | 260 | 2.0 | 98.3 |
| The Hearld | 79 | 0.6 | 98.9 |
| The Scotsman | 69 | 0.5 | 99.4* |

*0.6 error due to rounding of figures.
*Source*: Data from Mintel (2005a).

### 11.2.1.1  The x-firm concentration ratio

This is the most commonly found measure of market concentration used, mainly due to its simplicity. Formally stated the $x$-firm ratio is stated as

$$CR_x = \sum S_i; \quad i = 1 \ldots x$$

where $S_i$ is the per cent market share of the $i$th firm.

To derive the $CR_x$ measure, all you have to do is rank the firms in an industry in terms of market share and decide what value $x$ will take and then add the $x$ number of firms' percentage market share together. In the UK, usually the top three or five firms are included ($CR_3$ or $CR_5$) and in the USA, usually it is the $CR_8$ that is used.

Table 11.6 gives a detailed breakdown of the circulation data for the UK national daily newspaper industry for 2004. The cumulative market share for the three best selling titles shows that the market has a $CR_3$ of 59.3 per cent and a $CR_5$ of 74 per cent.

As can be seen, this is an easy method to use, but it does not fare very well when set against the Hannah–Kay axioms. The main weakness is the emphasis placed on the top three or five firms to the exclusion of all the other firms in the industry. Thus, looking at the first axiom, the measure does not always give an unambiguous ranking when comparing two industries. Consider Figure 11.6.

Using $CR_3$, it would appear that industry A is more concentrated (A3 > B3). However, if we used $CR_{10}$ as our measure, then industry B is more concentrated (B10 > A10). Thus, when we try to rank industries A and B in terms of concentration, we are getting ambiguous results. In fact, when you go down all seven of

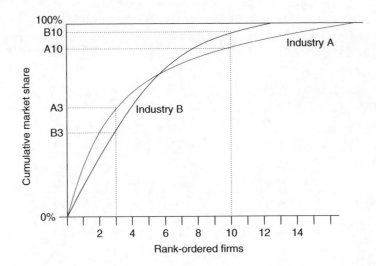

**Figure 11.6**
Concentration
curves

the Hannah–Kay axioms the $CR_x$ method does not meet any of them. Having said this, the method is still widely used, not so much by economic researchers but in many other sources.

### 11.2.1.2   The Herfindahl–Hirschman index

The HHI is another widely used method of measure of market concentration that is a more reliable method than the $CR_x$. The measure still uses a rank order of firms by market share, but this time all the firms in an industry are included and the measure is weighted to give added emphasis to the markets where a small number of large firms dominate. Formally, the measure is defined as

$$HHI = \sum_{i=1}^{n} S_i^2$$

where $S_i$ is the market share of the $i$th firm divided by the total market output and $n$ is the total number of firms in the market.

Therefore, we use the squared percentage market share of each firm and add them all together to give the HHI. The HHI will give a figure between 0 and 1 (although in the USA, they take the absolute share and multiply this by 100 to give a range from 0 to 10,000); the closer to 1 the more concentrated the market.

Table 11.7 shows the calculation of HHI for the same UK national newspaper industry data used in Figure 11.6.

This time, for the purpose of calculation, we use the absolute market share rather than the percentage market share. The HHI is 0.154. Something which is commonly done with the HHI is to divide the figure obtained into 1 to produce the 'numbers equivalent' figure. This shows the number of firms of average size required to fill the market. In this case, the numbers equivalent figure is 6.5. Compared to the concentration ratios calculated above, this appears to be fairly low. The reason being that, although the top three titles account for just under 60 per cent of the market, only one title has just over 25 per cent of the market.

**Table 11.7** The HHI for the national UK newspaper industry (2004)

| Title | Circulation ('000) | Market share | Squared market share |
|-------|--------------------|--------------|----------------------|
| The Sun | 3333 | 0.261 | 0.068 |
| Daily Mail | 2412 | 0.189 | 0.036 |
| Daily Mirror | 1830 | 0.143 | 0.02 |
| Daily Express | 939 | 0.074 | 0.01 |
| Daily Telegraph | 911 | 0.073 | 0.01 |
| Daily Star | 890 | 0.07 | 0.01 |
| The Times | 658 | 0.052 | < 0.002 |
| Daily Record | 488 | 0.038 | < 0.002 |
| Financial Times | 432 | 0.034 | < 0.002 |
| The Guardian | 376 | 0.029 | < 0.002 |
| The Independent | 260 | 0.02 | < 0.002 |
| The Hearld | 79 | 0.006 | < 0.002 |
| The Scotsman | 69 | 0.005 | 99.4* |
| | | | HHI = 0.154 |

*0.6 error due to rounding of figures

Thus, there is no one dominant title, a fact that is picked up by using a weighted calculation.

However, as noted previously, most newspaper titles are owned by one of four firms, they are not independent. By way of comparison, when the HHI is calculated by ownership of titles, as in Table 11.8, the HHI increases to 0.221 due to the 'News International Group' now owning over 30 per cent of the market. The numbers equivalent figure is 4.5, supporting the contention that the industry is in fact an oligopoly.

In terms of the Hannah–Kay axioms, this method gives a more valid estimate of the market concentration including, as it does, all the firms in a market. Therefore, any change in the market such as new entrants or the mergers of firms low down the market share ranking, should affect the market's HHI, not just if these changes happen in firms in the top 5 or 7.

## 11.2.2 Measuring market performance

Chapter 4 dealt in some detail with the creation and sustaining of profits, the idea of economic efficiency was introduced as part of that discussion. From the perspective of the current discussion, looking at the wider environmental context of a firm, the issue of economic efficiency is central – the ability of a firm to create and sustain abnormal profits means they create economic inefficiency.

To illustrate, consider Figure 11.7. Consumer $X$ represents the marginal consumer in the sense that the price he is prepared to pay for the product exactly

**Table 11.8** HHI by ownership of titles

| Title | Circulation ('000) | Market share | Squared market share |
|---|---|---|---|
| News International | 3992 | 0.313 | 0.068 |
| Trinity Mirror Group | 2318 | 0.182 | 0.036 |
| Associated Newspapers | 2412 | 0.189 | 0.02 |
| Express Newspapers | 1829 | 0.143 | 0.01 |
| Rest | – | – | > 0.001 for each company |
| | | | HHI = 0.21 |

matches the actual market price $P$. In other words, the marginal utility in monetary terms for customer $X$, $U_x$, exactly matches the price paid, $P$. For consumer $X + 1$ (to the right of $X$) the price $P$ is too high, the marginal utility gained in monetary terms ($U_x + 1$) is lower than the price $P$ of acquiring the good – so he does not buy the good. For customer $X - 1$ (to the left of $X$), the monetary value of the marginal utility gained ($U_x - 1$) is actually higher than the price he pays. Consumer ($U_x - 1$) would actually be prepared to pay a price up to the value of ($U_x - 1$), but only pays the market price $P$, he actually gains the monetary value (($U_x - 1$) – $P$) for nothing. This is also true for all the consumers to the left of $X$, the total area 1 being what is commonly referred to as consumer surplus.

On the other side of the market, the price $P$ is equal to the marginal cost of the product or, put another way, the price the product is sold for exactly matches the cost in resources used to produce it. If the price was above $P$ at $P_1$ then the cost of producing the last unit is less than the price and not enough is being produced. If the price is below $P$ at $P_2$ then the cost of producing the last unit is more than the price and too much is being produced.

To summarise, at price $P$, the cost of the last unit produced exactly matches the utility value, or the marginal benefit, of the marginal consumer and it exactly

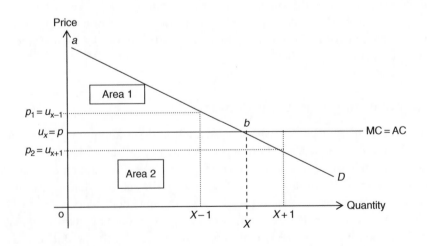

**Figure 11.7**
Economic
efficiency

matches the resource cost to society, the marginal cost. $P$ is therefore the economically efficient price for the market, and $X$ is the economically efficient level of output. It shows the price–output combination at which resources are being optimally allocated. This is the price and quantity combination that the model of perfect competition delivers in the long run. Thus, economic efficiency occurs when:

$$\text{Price} = \text{Marginal cost}$$

$$\implies \text{Marginal benefit} = \text{Marginal cost}$$

$$\implies \text{Benefit to the marginal consumer} = \text{The cost in resources to society}$$

In Figure 11.7 area 1 ($a$, $b$, $P$) represents the total consumer surplus and area 2 ($P$, $b$, $X$, o) represents the normal profits of the firm.

The economically efficient price of $P$ is unique, any other price would mean the market was operating inefficiently; it would not be allocating resources in such a way that maximises benefit. Figure 11.8 illustrates this.

Consider what happens to the areas of consumer surplus and the normal profits of the firm if the market is a monopoly market. The monopolist will maximise profits. Instead of equating marginal cost with price, they will move to the profit maximising position where marginal cost is equated with marginal revenue. The price rises to $P_i$ and the level of output produced falls to $Q_i$. Area 2 in the previous figure has now been split into two. Area 3 now represents the firm's normal profits, whereas area 5 represents resources that have been transferred to their next best use. Area 1 in the previous figure, the consumer surplus, has been split three ways. Area 1 in Figure 11.8 is the new reduced level of consumer surplus whereas area 2 is consumer surplus that has been transferred to the firm in the form of abnormal profits. What makes the market less efficient than previously is what happens to area 4. Area 4 was previously part of consumer surplus, but in the monopoly market, it simply disappears altogether, it is a deadweight loss or efficiency loss.

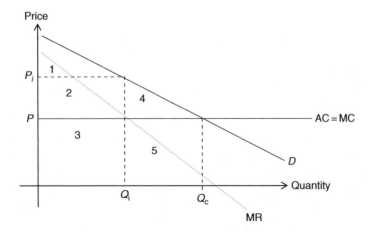

**Figure 11.8**
Economic inefficiency

**Table 11.9** Distribution of market value

|  | Efficient market | Inefficient market |
|---|---|---|
| Consumer surplus | 1+2+4 | 1 |
| Normal profits of the firm | 3+5 | 3 |
| Abnormal profits of the firm | None | 2 |
| Transferred resources | None | 5 |
| Deadweight loss | None | 4 |

Table 11.9 summarises how the distribution of the market value is split.

In the SCP model, measuring market performance requires the measurement of the size of the deadweight loss, which increases directly with the extent to which the market price rises above the cost price. In other words, we are back at the concept of the price–cost margin (Section 4.3), only this time not as an indication of the height of entry barriers, but as a measure of the efficiency of a market.

In practice, the determination of economic performance is no easy matter. Estimation of the level of abnormal profits being made by firms relies on the use of published accounting data. One problem with this is that the intended audience for these data is the company shareholders, their auditors and, if they are a public company, the stock market, and not an economist wishing to estimate economic efficiency. Additionally, anybody who has any familiarity with published profit and loss accounts will know that these include more than one line in the accounts that refer to 'profits'. Finally, many larger firms will operate in more than one market which are not separated out in terms of the presentation of accounts.

Economic researchers have tended to adopt two basic approaches to try and estimate abnormal profits for use in models investigating the link between structure and performance.

1. Measures of the rate of return.
2. Measures of the price–cost margin.

### 11.2.2.1 Measures of the rate of return

These are used to measure the extent of the abnormal profits earned by firms and thus gauge the magnitude of the producer surplus being extracted from the market. By rate of return, we mean the earnings per £ invested in a firm. Thus, we are calculating the return to the economists' theoretical 'entrepreneurs', the shareholders. The typical measure used is the ROCE as, again, this seems to match closest to the economists' idea of the risk-taking entrepreneur who provides the means for the transformation process to take place. Table 11.10 shows the ROCE for the four main companies in the national daily newspaper industry for 2004.

What the table seems to show is that at one extreme we have 'News International' where for every £10 of capital the return was £20, whereas, at the other extreme, we have 'Express Newspapers' where the same £10 of capital only

**Table 11.10**  Rate of return on capital employed

|  | Return on capital employed (ROCE) (2004) (%) |
| --- | --- |
| News International Newspapers | 100 |
| Trinity Mirror | 10.06 |
| Associated Newspapers | 9.36 |
| Express Newspapers | –6.07 |

*Source*: FAME database.

returned £9.40. Using the data in Table 11.10 to draw conclusions about market performance in the national daily newspaper industry is extremely difficult. Does this mean that 'News International' is abusing its market position to extract very high abnormal profits? Is 'Express Newspapers' about to exit the market due to the loss they are making? Does the ROCE of around 10 per cent for the other two firms indicate excessive abnormal profits? At first sight, the ROCE appears to be a very attractive performance measure. The means for the calculation are readily available for most big companies, as they publish accounts that are required to contain the relative information. It is also an easy calculation to make. However, interpreting the figures obtained, as shown above, is often not easy and there are various theoretical problems in using ROCE to comment on market performance.

The biggest conceptual problem with this approach is that the economists' concept of profit is: total revenue minus opportunity cost (see Section 4.2.1 for a discussion on the difference between normal and abnormal profits). The account-ants' (who produce the company reports) concept of profit does not take oppor-tunity costs into account. The result is that any profit levels that appear in the company accounts will be an over-estimate of the economic profit. The problem becomes determining how much of the return to the firm's shareholders is normal profit, the return required to keep the shareholders capital in the firm, and how much is abnormal profit, the return over and above the minimum required. As was commented on in relation to 'Ryanair' and 'Direct Line Insurance' in Chapter 4, quite often a more comparative measure would be used. Industries where on average the ROCE appears to be higher than in other similar or related industries may be an indication that abnormal profits are present. This, however, is an awfully long way from the precise definition of economic efficiency represented by Figures 11.7 and 11.8.

### 11.2.2.2  Price–cost margins

The other way to try and measure economic performance is to try and estimate the price–cost margin. As discussed in Section 4.3, the larger the gap between price and cost, the higher the level of the abnormal profits being made – and the more inefficient the market is. A method of determination of price–cost margins was developed by Lehner. This method is referred to as a Lehner index and has been used by industrial economists as a performance measure for markets. The equation is reproduced below.

$$L = P - MC/P$$

Therefore when $P$ = MC, or the market is efficient, then the value of the Lehner index will be zero (the top of the equation will be 0). As the gap between $P$ and MC gets greater then the Lehner index deviates further and further from zero. The further from zero the index deviates the greater the price–cost margin, the higher the level of abnormal profits and by implication the greater the efficiency loss to society.

However, in practice, using the Lehner index is fraught with problems. Many firms are multi-product producers (as are the firms involved in the national daily newspaper industry), so which price do you use? In addition, the calculation of marginal cost for a real-world firm is extremely difficult. Many researchers have opted to use measures based on average cost rather than marginal cost and sales revenue rather than profit. This could be defended on the assumption that real-world firms may be faced with constant cost curves, hence average and marginal costs will be the same.

## 11.2.3 The empirical evidence

Despite all of the issues discussed above, in relation to obtaining reliable measures for market structure and performance, many econometric studies were undertaken in the 1960s and 1970s testing whether there was indeed a relationship between market structure and market performance as indicated by levels of abnormal profits. Hay and Morris (1991) summarise the results of these studies. Of the 67 studies listed by Hay and Morris, all except two test a model of the general form

$$\Pi = \beta_0 + \beta_1 C + \beta_1 V_1 + \beta_1 V_2 + \cdots + \beta_1 V_x + \mu$$

where $C$ is the market concentration (the market structure variable), $V$ is the range of other structural variables and $\Pi$ is the estimates of profits (the market performance variable).

The studies use a range of profit measures, the most common being the ratio of $\Pi$ to sales (the definitions used for profit is not specified in the table), although some prefer the ratio of $\Pi$ to expenditure or capital. Virtually, all the studies include other variables in addition to concentration, particularly growth and advertising intensity. Of the 65 studies that include concentration as a structural variable, 30 found the predicted positive link between $C$ and $\Pi$, 28 found no link and 7 proved to be indeterminate. This suggests that the case in favour of the SCP linkage is at best not proved. In fact, given that SCP is supposed to be a generic model of market structure, it appears to be remarkably non-robust and too reliant on the variables used to define the model and, more importantly, the industry or firm being analysed. The reasons for this should be no surprise; SCP is a heavily neo-classical model with all the inherent limitations discussed at length in Chapter 2 and various other parts of this book. In particular, as shown in Section 11.1.2, the model simply does not accommodate oligopoly markets which, unfortunately for SCP, are the market structure that dominate the real world.

## 11.3 | Review and further reading

This chapter has reviewed the main model of environmental analysis used by economists – the SCP model. This is not the only model of analysis used by economists, but it is the method that most obviously uses the neo-classical perspective. Two other common perspectives are the Chicago school and the Austrian school. The Chicago school is, again, a neo-classical model, but central to this analysis is the role played by markets, and in particular prices. The view is that provided markets are left to function then any inefficiencies, such as monopolies, will only be temporary, as in the long run freely functioning markets will tend to be economically efficient. The Austrian school comes from a different tradition where the emphasis is placed on an entrepreneur operating in an environment of asymmetric information. From this perspective, competition is viewed as an ongoing process which never achieves the efficient market equilibrium of neo-classical theory – new information is constantly being discovered which shifts the equilibrium.

Scherer/Ross (1990) remain the definitive text written from the SCP perspective whilst Johnson (1988) shows how the methodology was applied to different sectors of the British economy during the 1980s.

## 11.4 | Student exercises

### 11.4.1 Review exercises and points for discussion

1. Provide brief and clear definitions of the following key terms and concepts as used in this chapter.

   a. Market structure
   b. Market conduct
   c. Market performance
   d. Market concentration
   e. Concentration measures
   f. Economic efficiency
   g. Consumer surplus
   h. Measures of rates of return
   i. The Lehner index

2. Section 11.1.3 presented the traditional models of market structure within the SCP framework. Carry out a similar exercise for the contestable market structure.

Does this market structure assume a linear link between market structure and market performance?

3. Consider the newspaper example used throughout this chapter. Is there a linear link from structure to conduct to performance, or can you see how there might be feedbacks as suggested in Figure 11.4?

4. Given the difficulties of measuring the real-world market performance of firms in terms that satisfy the theoretical concept of economic efficiency, does this invalidate the whole SCP framework (you may wish to refer back to the exercises at the end of Chapter 2 and the comments on the purpose of an economic model)?

## 11.4.2 Application exercise

In groups, select an industry/output market. The selection of the industry is probably best done with reference to the sectors used by 'Mintel' or 'Keynotes'.

a. Using some of the commonly available information sources (such 'Mintel', 'Keynotes', 'Fame' and internet searches) for your industry:

   i. Determine the main exogenous demand factors and factors influencing supply.
   ii. Comment on the resulting market structure.
   iii. Determine the main endogenous demand factors and how they reflect market conduct.
   iv. Comment on the market performance.

b. Can you determine whether the performance of the industry is determined by its structure?

# Environmental Analysis – The Strategists' Perspective

## LEARNING OUTCOMES

On completion of this chapter, the reader should be able to

- Explain the concept of value added
- Outline the methods used by strategists to analyse macro, industry and market environments
- Use SWOT analysis

## KEY NEW CONCEPTS

Value net

## KEY NEW MODELS/ FRAMEWORKS

PEST            Strategic group analysis          SWOT

Five forces

## MODELS AND CONCEPTS DEVELOPED FURTHER

Value added         Chain of production

The UK food-retailing market generated £93,589m of sales in 2004 (Mintel, 2005b). Like the national daily newspaper industry looked at in Chapter 11, the UK's supermarket industry is dominated by four national firms – Tesco, Asda (Wal Mart), Sainsbury's and Morrisons. In 2004, the $CR_4$ for the industry was 64.5 per cent. Tesco had the largest market share with over a quarter of the market (26.4 per cent), indeed it is estimated that one pound out of every eight spent in the UK is spent in Tesco. The other three supermarkets had market shares almost half that of Tesco – Sainsbury's with 14.4 per cent, Asda with 13.9 per cent and Morrisons with 11.8 per cent. There are other smaller national chains such as Aldi and Somerfields and a number of more regional chains such as Budgens and Waitrose. In addition, there are thousands of small convenience stores (corner shops), some being part of a loose confederation such as SPAR. However, the concentration ratio for the next six largest chains is only 16.9 per cent showing not only the importance of the so-called 'big four', but also the fact that the small convenience stores still account for about 20 per cent of the market.

The focus in this chapter switches away from the public policy orientated economists' models of environmental analysis to the firm-specific orientated strategist. As discussed at the beginning of Chapter 11, for strategists' the idea of efficiency relates to how well a firm is performing in the sense of the firm maximising its value added. Thus, the question for strategists when looking at the food-retailing sector is not whether the sector is creating abnormal profits and, if so, does this indicate the market is economically inefficient. Rather the question is how much value added is the firm creating and will it create more or less in the future. A closely related question of interest to strategists would be, if a particular firm is adding more value than its rivals, how is this being achieved and, again, can this be maintained. As discussed elsewhere in this book, this is essentially the same concern as explaining how firms sustain abnormal profits.

Although the most widely recognised and used model of environmental analysis by strategists is perhaps the five-forces model, this is by no means the only tool in the strategists' armoury of environmental analysis. The range of models and tools that have been developed betrays the diverse nature of strategy as a subject area and the range of influences that have been apparent in the subject area's development (see Section 1.2). However, three methods of environmental analysis seem to have become the standard core content of most strategy textbooks, each method being used to assess different aspects of the environment. Generally, strategists divide the environment into what Johnson, Scholes and Whittington (2005) describe as 'layers', like the layers of an onion. Figure 12.1 summarises this view.

At the centre of the onion lies the firm which is surrounded by three layers of environments: the immediate market environment where the firm competes and sells its output; the wider industry environment within which the firm operates and, finally, the macro-environment which is the broader general business environment within which the firm has to operate. The further out from the centre of the onion, the less influence the firm has over the environment it has to operate in. So, for example, the firm can have a direct influence over its immediate market environment via the strategic decisions it takes regarding prices or marketing, but

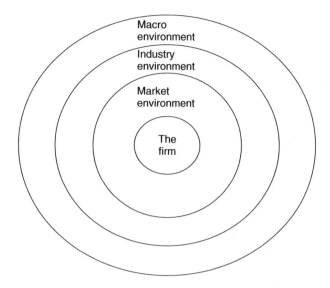

**Figure 12.1** The environmental layers

has no influence over the levels of interest rates or changes to competition policy that occur in the macro-environment.

This chapter will consider the three most common means employed by strategists to analyse these different layers of the environment namely:

1. STEP/PEST/PESTLE/SLEPT for the macro-environment
2. Five-forces for the industry environment
3. Strategic group analysis for the market environment.

However, before looking at these, we need to return to look again at the strategists' idea of value creation. Section 7.3 examined the idea that a firm could be represented as a value chain. We now need to expand this analysis to look at how a firm's individual value chain relates to the much larger surrounding production net.

# 12.1 | Value and value creation

## 12.1.1 The value net

Section 7.3 dealt with the concept of value and value creation within a single firm in detail. However, each firm is part of a much wider value-creating network. This relates directly back to the idea of a chain of production which we dealt with in Chapter 5 in relation to the transaction costs faced by a firm. Figure 5.3 in Section 5.1 showed a simple production chain for the production of bread. From the value-net perspective, each of the four processes identified in Figure 5.3 – growing the wheat, milling the flour, baking the bread and retailing the bread – represents a particular value-creating process. Similarly, the possible production chain configurations shown in Figure 5.6 could be shown as a series of linked value

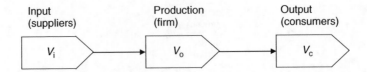

**Figure 12.2** The value net

chains of the type outlined in Figure 7.9 for a university. A generic representation of a value net is shown in Figure 12.2. This represents the value net in the input–production–output format used throughout this book as representing the basic transformation process which is central to understanding the economic function of the firm.

The box $V_o$ represents a particular firm's value chain, the supplier's and consumer's value chains are shown as $V_i$ and $V_c$. $V_i$ and $V_c$ are amalgamations of many value chains – most firms will have more than one supplier and more than one consumer – but for the purposes of exposition it is easier to represent these as single entities.

As we saw in Section 7.2, each value chain has two broad elements:

- The costs of the transformation process
- The value added.

Therefore, we can divide the three value chains in Figure 12.2 into these two elements – as shown in Figure 12.3.

### 12.1.1.1  The supplier's value chain

The supplier's value chain is at the start of the chain of production and therefore contains all the source input costs ($C_i$). In the case of the food-retailing industry, we would be talking, principally, about the farmers and food producers who supply the food retailers with their stock. However, there would also be a whole range of other firms supplying secondary inputs such as shop fittings, checkout machines and another set of firms supplying services such as insurance, marketing and banking. On top of each of these input costs would be the value added by each of the suppliers ($\pi_i$), therefore

$$V_i = C_i + \pi_i$$

### 12.1.1.2  The firm's value chain

The cost element of the firm's production is the price it has to pay its suppliers for its inputs, which in turn is the total value of the supplier's value chain – $V_i$. To this

**Figure 12.3** The value net and added value

Input (suppliers) — $C_i$ | $\pi_i$ — $V_i$ → Production (firm) — $V_i$ | $\pi_o$ — $V_i + \pi_o$ → Output (consumers) — $V_o$ | S — $V_o + S$ → TV the firm also adds its own value ($\pi_o$). Therefore:

$$V_o = V_i + \pi_o$$

or

$$V_o = (C_i + \pi_i) + \pi_o$$

### 12.1.1.3   The consumer's value chain

The consumer comes at the end of the production chain. The value added to the value net by the final consumer differs from that of the firms and suppliers in that it is not measured as profit but by the more abstract notion of consumer surplus ($S$) – the additional utility gained above the price actually paid (see the explanation to Figure 11.13 in Section 11.3.2). Therefore:

$$V_c = V_o + S$$

or

$$V_c = ((C_i + \pi_i) + \pi_o) + S$$

### 12.1.1.4   Total value added

The simplest way to calculate total value added (TV) is simply to look at the value at the end of the production chain. However, for what follows in the rest of this section, it is perhaps better to think of the total value as shown below:

$$TV = \overbrace{\underbrace{Ci + \Pi i + \Pi o}_{Vo} + S}^{Vi}$$

More usefully the above can be thought of as having two elements – the original costs of the suppliers ($C_i$) and the value added (AV).

$$TV = \overbrace{Ci}^{Costs} + + \overbrace{\Pi i + \Pi o + S}^{Added\ Value}$$

$$TV = Ci + AV$$

### 12.1.1.5   A numerical example

To illustrate the above, consider the simple production net shown in Figure 12.4.

Assume that we are looking at the bread-making production chain as used in Section 5.1. The configuration of the chain as shown above indicates that the three processes of milling, baking and selling the bread have been integrated into one firm. The supplier value chain ($V_i$) in this case is that of the farmer who grows the wheat. As shown in Figure 12.4, the farmer's value chain is made up of two components. As the farmer is assumed to be at the source of the production chain the total cost of the source inputs is 10. The farmer is able to sell the wheat to the miller/baker/shop for 12, hence the value added by the farmer is 2. The cost to

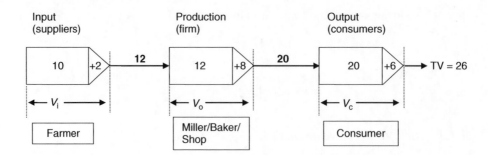

**Figure 12.4** The value net and added value (numerical example)

the combined miller/baker/shop of the input is also 12. However, this integrated firm is able to charge a price of 20, hence it adds another 8 to the total value of the production chain. At the end of the production chain are the consumers. They are charged a price of 20 for their bread, there is a consumer surplus of 6 gained by the consumers (that is, some consumers were willing to pay more than 20 for their bread). Thus, the total value of the entire production chain is 26 as shown in Figure 12.4. This total value could also be obtained by adding the value added at each stage of the production chain to the original input costs of the farmer: $10+2+8+6=26$.

Therefore we can see how the economists' chain of production links directly across to the strategists' value chain. Much of the strategic theory focuses on the added value part of Figures 12.3 and 12.4 – the original input source costs are essentially fixed. In particular strategy theory focuses on:

1. Maximising the size of the added value. This was essentially the topic of Chapter 7 and relates to the resource-based view of the firm.
2. How the added value created is divided amongst the three participants in the value creation process.
3. Protecting the total value of a production chain from external threats.

Points 2 and 3 form the basis of strategic analysis and is reflected in the frameworks and models to be discussed in the rest of this chapter. However, before moving on to look at these models let us return to the food-retailing industry and see how the above discussion can be used in practice.

## 12.1.2 Value added and the supermarkets

The Department of Trade and Industry in the UK produce an annual 'value added scoreboard' where they calculate and publish the value added by the top 800 firms in the UK (DTI (c)). The definition used by the DTI for value added is

> wealth created is measured as value added which is sales less the cost of bought-in materials, components and services. (DTI (c))

In terms of our representation of value added in Figure 12.3, the 'bought-in materials, components and services' represents $V_i$ – the total cost to the firm of

**Table 12.1**   Value added by UK food retailers 2004/05

| Supermarket | Value added (£m)* | Value added per store (£m) | Value added per Employee (£m) |
|---|---|---|---|
| Tesco | 5806 | 3.3 | 0.024 |
| Sainsbury's | 3092 | 4.3 | 0.021 |
| Asda/Wal Mart | 2309 | 8.1 | 0.016 |
| Morrisons** | 992 | 4.8 | 0.037 |
| Somerfield | 627 | 0.4 | 0.021 |
| Aldi | 105 | 0.35 | 0.021 |
| Average | – | 3.7 | 0.023 |

* Calculated as operating profits + employee costs + depreciation + amortisation
** Based on pre-'Safeways' merger data
Source: DTI (c), Mintel (2005b)

acquiring its inputs from suppliers. Therefore, the value-added calculation undertaken by the DTI provides us with $\pi_0$ as shown in Figure 12.3.

Table 12.1 shows the value added for the six supermarkets that appear in the DTI listing of 800 companies. What this is showing us is that Tesco added the most value out of the six supermarkets included in the list. In terms of Figure 12.3, Tesco was taking a larger share of the total value created by the food-retailing value net than any other of the five supermarkets in the list. Does this mean that Tesco is the most efficient firm? The rank order of supermarkets by value added is the same as by market share. However, the third and fourth columns in Table 12.1 are perhaps better indicators of comparative efficiency showing the value added by each store and by each employee. In terms of value added per store, Asda appears to be the most efficient, probably reflecting the much higher average size of their stores. Whereas the low figures for Somerfield and Aldi reflect their 'pile them high, sell them cheap' low value-added strategy. In terms of value added per employee most are close to the average for the sector. However, Morrisons are significantly above the average, therefore, on this measure at least, they were the most efficient of the national supermarkets, whereas Asda are significantly below the average and would appear to be overstaffed compared with the sector as a whole.

## 12.2 | Macro-environmental analysis (PEST/STEP/SLEPT/PESTLE)

The standard approach adopted by strategists to the analysis of the macro-environment shown in Figure 12.1 goes under a series of acronyms depending on how you divide up the environment. The most common is STEP (or PEST depending on how you order the letters). STEP stands for *Sociological, Technological, Economic* and *Political* with the variants adding *Legal* and *Environmental* (SLEPT/PESTLE). The approach adopted is to use the headings as a means of ordering the macro-environmental factors that may be of importance for a particular firm, or industry, in its pursuit of added value. The STEP method is not really a theory or model – it does not lend itself to empirical investigation nor does it produce testable predictions. What it does is provide a series of pigeonholes in which to group some of the key macro-environmental influences on a firm. By using the STEP method, a firm can try to place some order on the range of possible macro-environmental influences and enable the firm to try and make some sense of its macro-environment.

Once a STEP analysis has been undertaken the strategist will then try to identify the key drivers that are likely to be of most importance in the future development of the industry, and hence of importance for firms within the industry. Put another way, STEP is a means of trying to assess the likely future influences that will either add to, or detract from, the value created by the industry.

Table 12.2 shows what a simple STEP analysis of the UK supermarket industry may look like.

As can be seen, the method 'pigeonholes' various external factors which might be of importance in the future development of the industry. As can also be seen, just about all of the factors listed in Table 12.2 are beyond the control of the individual firms in the industry, as you would expect given that we are dealing with the outermost layer of the environmental 'onion' as shown in Figure 12.1.

To an economist, the STEP method is not a very satisfactory method for the analysis of the macro-environment for a number of reasons. The list of factors that may be of importance in determining the factors driving the UK supermarket industry, for example, is just that – a list. It does not lead to a model which can be tested and confirmed or refuted. What to include in a STEP analysis is also very subjective, as is the interpretation of the factors of importance to the industry. What to include in terms of the selection of data, the identification of the key drivers and the interpretation of the consequent action required by the firm are all

**Table 12.2** Simple STEP analysis of the UK supermarket industry

| *Political* | *Economic* |
|---|---|
| ■ Legislation on opening hours | ■ Income inelastic nature of core products – fairly static level of demand through economic cycle |
| ■ Consumer protection legislation | ■ Level of interest rates – affects consumer spending power and costs of firm |
| ■ Planning legislation – potential limits on new developments | |
| ■ Attitude of Office of Fair Trading (OFT) – potential investigation for contravening competition policy | |
| Social | Technological |
| ■ Spending behaviour of consumers | ■ Internet shopping |
| ■ Changes in lifestyle – for example, demand for 24-hour opening | ■ Electronic tracking of produce through the supply chain – improves efficiency |

subjective. Somebody else constructing the key factors driving the development of the UK supermarket industry may come up with a different set of factors, which may be just as valid as those shown in Table 12.2.

## 12.3 | Industry analysis (five-forces)

By far, the most widely known method of environmental analysis is the five-forces method developed by Michael Porter (1980). The method is widely used to assess the second layer of the environmental 'onion' – the industry environment. The method was originally devised as a means of helping to assess the potential profitability of an industry; however, since the mid-1980s the method has been adapted and adopted by a range of different writers in different contexts and subject areas.

### 12.3.1 The five-forces method

The underlying premise is that an industry is shaped by five different forces, acting simultaneously, to determine the profitability of the industry. The five-forces are

- The power of buyers
- The power of sellers
- Substitutes
- Entry barriers
- Competitive rivalry.

Figure 12.5 shows how the forces inter-relate together to form Porter's five-forces method. For a full description of the five-forces method, see Johnson, Scholes and Whittington (2005) or Lynch (2002).

In the diagrammatic form, it appears that there are in fact four forces at work that determine the fifth force – competitive rivalry. The stronger the four outer lying forces the more competitive the industry is likely to be. Consider Table 12.3.

Assume that both industries are oligopoly in nature. In industry A, the firms are selling to a small number of large firms which puts these buyers into a strong

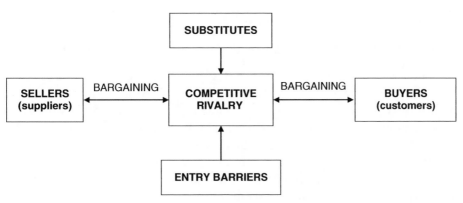

**Figure 12.5** Porter's five-forces

**Table 12.3** Industry competitiveness

|  | Industry A | Industry B |
|---|---|---|
| Buyers (customers) | Few large consumers | Many small consumers |
| Sellers (suppliers) | Monopoly suppliers | Many small suppliers |
| Substitutes | Many substitute goods | Few substitute goods |
| Entry barriers | Low | High |
|  | ↓ | ↓ |
| Competitive rivalry | Tends towards high | Tends towards low |

bargaining position. These large buyers are likely to account for a significant proportion of each firm's output, which puts the buying firms into a strong bargaining position when contracts come up for renewal. In terms of transaction cost, there is a potential hostage situation in favour of the buying firm. The industry also relies on monopoly suppliers for their inputs, thus again the bargaining power is not with the firms in the industry but with their suppliers. In addition, it is relatively easy for new firms to enter, and there are lots of substitute goods; then this means that the competition between the firms in the industry is going to be intense. In value added terms, you would expect the value added by the firms in industry A to be low – most of the value added is being taken by the buyers and suppliers. In economic terms, price–cost margins for firms in industry A are going to be fairly small.

In contrast, industry B has a large number of small consumers, which removes the potential hostage situation, but may still not give a lot of power to firms in the industry, especially if switching between firms' products is easily done. However, the large number of suppliers tips the balance of power in this relationship towards firms inside the industry, this time they are the potential beneficiaries from a hostage position. In addition, the high entry barriers and limited substitute goods and, on the face of it, the firms in industry B seem to be in much more attractive position in terms of taking more of the value out of the value net for themselves. Or, in other words, the potential price–cost margins, and hence abnormal profits, look to be much better than in industry A.

### 12.3.2 A five-forces analysis of the UK supermarket industry

In many ways, the UK supermarket industry looks more like industry B than industry A in Table 12.2. The supermarkets' customers are literally millions of individual consumers. In addition, switching between supermarkets is relatively easy (the only potential blocks are geographical location and the use of loyalty cards). Then the conclusion can only be that the bargaining power in this part of the five-forces method lies strongly with the consumer. However, the power most defiantly lies with the supermarkets in the other three forces. Entry barriers are high given the expense required to set up a national supermarket chain – the main entry in recent years has been through the acquisition of existing chains (Wal Mart buying Asda, for example). Competitors do exist, such as specialist shops (for example, butchers, bakers and fruit and vegetable shops), but they tend to offer a limited range and hence will not attract the weekly/monthly shop market. Thus, again, the supermarkets are in a strong position.

The relationship with suppliers is more complicated, however. The suppliers of fresh produce to the supermarkets tend to be many relatively small farmers and growers (not just from the UK but from all over the world), often supplying virtually all their output to one supermarket. In these relationships, the supermarkets hold all the power. This is clearly evidenced by the complaints coming from farmers about the low prices they are receiving for their output from the four big supermarkets. However, for the packaged part of a supermarket's stock they are mainly dealing with large multinational food producers, therefore the power tends to be more evenly shared.

Figure 12.6 summarises the above comments. So what about the fifth force – competitive rivalry? Any casual observer of the UK supermarket industry will tell you that it is one of the most competitive sectors in the entire economy, which does not match with the conclusion in relation to industry B in Table 12.2. In practice, the power of the buyers is so strong that, despite the balance of power lying with the supermarkets in relation to the other three forces, the industry is intensely competitive.

As with STEP analysis, the five-forces is not a model as understood by economists – it does not lead to testable conclusions. Just because the UK supermarket industry looks more like industry B than A in Table 12.2 does not mean we can predict that competitive rivalry will be low; in fact as discussed above, the opposite appears to be the case. As discussed in the previous section, STEP analysis allows us to make sense of the macro-environment, in the same way the five-forces method gives us a means of ordering and making sense of the equally complex industry environment. However, as with STEP, the factors included and their interpretation is both subjective and open to more than one interpretation.

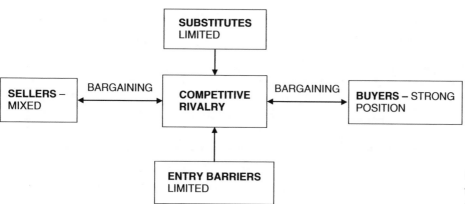

**Figure 12.6** The five-forces and the UK supermarket industry

### 12.3.3 Five-forces and the value net

As mentioned previously, the five-forces framework is usually used to help strategists to assess the potential profitability of a particular industry prior to entry. However, the framework does have an underlying structure which betrays Michael Porter's background as an industrial economist and helps to illustrate further the links between strategic analysis and economic analysis.

#### 12.3.3.1 Five-forces and division of added value

So far in this section, we have looked at the five-forces method as presented and used in a whole range of strategy textbooks. However, a close examination of the underlying structure of the standard representation, as shown in Figure 12.5, reveals that it does show the same input–production–output process that has been the core of the development of the model of the firm throughout this book. It can also be used to illustrate the strategists' concern with the division of added value between the three main players (see the end of Section 12.1).

Consider Figure 12.7. This is the same five-forces diagram but recast to show its economic basis. In the original Figure 12.5, it is clear that the central horizontal core of the diagram shows the relationships between the industry and its buyers and sellers. In economic terms, this central horizontal part of Figure 12.5 is simply another representation of the 'input–production–output' transformation process. In strategic terms, this horizontal axis is the same representation of the value creation process discussed in Section 12.1 (and illustrated in Figure 12.2) showing the three groups of participants that are involved in the creation of value and the potential recipients of any added value. However, the added element is the idea that the relationship between these three elements is not purely defined by a series

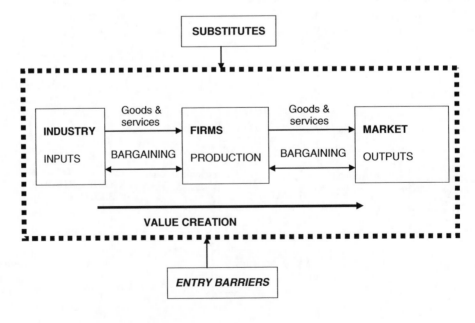

**Figure 12.7**
Five-forces and the
value added

of impersonal markets as in economics, but there is an element of bargaining that goes on between the parties involved.

The bargaining aspect of the central transformation process in the five-forces diagram is, in effect, a fight between the sellers, the producers and the consumers over how much of the added value they can grab for themselves. The five-forces working together determine the total value or, if you like, the size of the cake; the outcome of the bargaining process between the participants in the transformation process determines how big each participant's slice of the cake is. In practice, the size of the cake for a particular value creation process is difficult to calculate. In the supermarket industry, the total value of sales in 2004 was £93,589m (Mintel, 2005b); however this is not the total value created as we do not know the size of the consumer surplus enjoyed by the buyers.

To illustrate let us use the simple numerical example of Section 12.1– as shown in Figure 12.4. We represented the total added value in its generic form as

$$TV = C_i + (\Pi_i + \Pi_o + S)$$

or

$$TV = C_i + AV$$

or, for our numeric example,

$$26 = 10 + 16$$

The initial cost of the inputs $(C_i)$ is 10 with the additional value added by the end of the production chain being an additional 16, giving a total value of 26. In our original example, we apportioned the value added between the three participants in the following proportions:

Suppliers (the farmer) – 2
The firm (the integrated miller/baker/retailer) – 8
The final consumer – 6

However, what was not made clear is what determines the proportion of the AV that accrues to each participant. Why does the firm take 50 per cent of the value added from the production chain whereas the suppliers and the consumers have an uneven share of the other 50 per cent? The answer given by the five-forces method is the relative bargaining strengths of the suppliers, the firms and the consumers. If the firm is gaining more than its fair share of the AV created then it suggests it is in a strong bargaining position in relation to its suppliers and customers – it resembles industry B in Table 12.3. If the industry was closer to A in Table 12.3 then we may see a different division of the AV say

Suppliers (the farmer) – 6
The firm (the integrated miller/baker/retailer) – 2
The final consumer – 8.

It should also be noted that the division of the added value between the three participants can alter over time, either through changes in the industry environment or through the actions of the participants themselves. Earlier, the UK supermarket industry was used to illustrate the five-forces method. One of the groups in that production chain that commonly complain as being left with virtually none of the added value is the many small farmers who supply the supermarkets with their fresh produce. Recently, they have formed an association, or what may more correctly be described as a pressure group, to try and shift some of the bargaining power back to their members and take back some of the added value from the supermarkets for themselves. Unfortunately, they have not been very successful, presumably they suffer the same problems discussed in Chapter 10 in relation to trying to co-ordinate behaviour in a game theory context – too many small farmers are involved with the associated problem of detecting cheaters.

This strategists' view of firms trying to maximise the added value they can take from their production chain is essentially the same as the economists' view that firms try to minimise the outflow of costs to their suppliers and maximise the inflow of revenue from their customers. The difference has been in the approach taken, economists tend to use abstract models and theories of how product and factor markets work, whereas strategists have developed a range of practical methods and frameworks that try to help firms make decisions that will maximise their added value.

### 12.3.3.2 Five-forces and the protection of value

The third function of strategy, as outlined at the end of Section 12.1, was the protection of the value chain from external threats. In the five-forces diagram this is shown on the vertical axis of the five-forces (Figure 12.7). These forces of substitutes and entry barriers are external in the sense that they are not part of the central value creating production process, in fact they represent a possible threat to this core. Possible substitute goods and the possible entry of new firms represent a challenge to the added value to be carved up amongst the existing firms and their suppliers. Substitute goods threaten the available amount of value added; new substitutes may well attract consumers away from this particular production chain, thus reducing demand. Low entry barriers allowing new firms into the market may not reduce the size of the value added created by the production chain, but it may need to be split between more firms. In other words, substitutes are a threat to the size of the value-added cake to be divided up, whereas new entrants means the cake has to be more thinly sliced.

### 12.3.3.3 Five-forces and strategic behaviour

The other obvious link that can be made is between the five-forces method and the type of strategic behaviour discussed in Part III of this book. The split between the division of value and the protection of value clearly relates back to the material covered in Chapters 9 and 10, respectively: the split in competitive behaviour between firms (division of value) and market co-ordination (value protection). Overlying all of this is a strong reference back to game theory – the bargaining between the three groups involved (sellers, producers and buyers) lends itself to game theory analysis (Chapter 8). The other issue that is again evident is the conflict between competition and co-operation – firms and their suppliers will compete for added value, but there is an obvious incentive to co-operate to protect that added value from the external threats of substitutes and new entrants (Section 8.1).

However, it is worth repeating that despite its obvious economic basis and the clear link back to various earlier parts of this book, the five-forces method is not a model in the sense understood by economists – it is difficult to test empirically and is non-robust (it is too dependent on the variables included). As with the STEP method, it is generally used as a means of sorting information about the industry environment to aid strategic decision-making and it can be very descriptive and subjective.

## 12.4 | Market analysis (strategic group analysis)

The idea of a strategic group is one concept that has emerged directly from the strategic management literature rather than having been taken over and adapted from one of the related disciplines. A strategic group relates to a group of firms within an industry that are following similar strategies in a particular market which are clearly distinctive from other firms, or groups of firms, within that market. Thus, in the motor industry there are a group of large producers that produce the full range of vehicles from small urban cars to large 4 × 4 off road cars that may be said to belong to a different strategic group than the small producers only producing specialised and high performance sports cars.

The basis for a firm belonging to a particular strategic group is the resource base and competencies that the firm within the group has developed (see Chapter 7). Thus, Ford and Toyota have a cost base that depends upon economies of scale, and highly developed supply and distribution systems, which allow them to produce a full range of vehicles on a worldwide basis. Whereas the resource and competencies base of Ferrari and Morgan Cars are very different relying on a high-quality finish and a focus on a very narrow range of high-value cars which they produce in small numbers for a niche market.

### 12.4.1 The concept of a strategic group

Strategic groups present an alternative means of defining a market lying somewhere between the demand- and supply-based methods of market definition (market definition is to be discussed in more detail in Chapter 14). The strategic group links back to the input markets. Ford and Ferrari belong to the same industry in the sense that the industry defines the set of firms from which the strategic group is drawn. However, it also looks forward to the output markets in which the firms are to compete, with the firms being divided on the basis of the strategies they are pursuing. Of the categories of market definition to be discussed in Chapter 14, the strategic group actually fits best into the resource-based definition; the strategies pursued rely upon the resource base available to the firm (see Section 14.1). However, a strategic group is more than a simple means of trying to define a market, they can be regarded as an alternative unit of analysis to the normal 'industry', 'market' or 'firm'.

Central to strategic group analysis is the idea of a mobility barrier. McGee and Thomas (1986) define a mobility barrier as allowing firms to

> make strategic decisions which cannot be readily imitated by firms outside the group without substantial costs, a significant elapsed of time or uncertainty about the outcome of those decisions.

This definition has overtones of the Barney VRIO framework discussed in Chapter 7. However, the emphasis is on the strategies being pursued, not just the resource base of the firm. Firms with similar resource bases can decide to pursue very different strategies. The threshold resource and competencies required by Tesco and Aldi to run national supermarket chains are essentially the same. However, Tesco have gone for a strategy of a wide range of choice and stocking an ever increasing range of non-food goods, whereas Aldi have chosen a low price, limited range strategy (the 'pile them high, sell them cheap' approach).

Mobility barriers result in what are referred to as 'isolating mechanism' which, in effect, act in exactly the same way as the entry barriers introduced in Chapter 4. Indeed, McGee and Thomas split mobility barriers down into three types:

1. Market-related strategies
2. Industry supply characteristics
3. Characteristics of firms.

Table 12.4 provides further details. As can be seen from the table this division clearly reflects the entry barrier framework developed in Chapter 4 with our basic input–production–output transformation process evident in the table headings. The market-related strategies have a clear similarity to what we defined as strategic entry barriers, primarily focused on the maximising of revenue from a firm's output markets. But the industry-supply characteristics relate more to the input markets and the minimisation of costs (with the exception of R&D capability). Finally, the characteristics of firms reflect the internal organisation of firms and relate back to the idea of resource entry barriers.

However, the role of a mobility barrier is a little narrower than that of an entry barrier. An entry barrier's role is to protect a market from all potential entrants to that market, whereas the mobility barrier is to protect a group of firms' output markets from other firms within the same industry. However, the motivation is the same – to protect value added/sustain abnormal profits. The mobility barriers reduce the number of firms in the market segment and hence limit what may be a potentially competitive industry into an oligopoly strategic group where the sort

**Table 12.4**   Sources of mobility barriers

| Market-related strategies | Industry-supply characteristics | Characteristics of firms |
|---|---|---|
| Product line | Economies of scale: | Ownership |
| User technologies | Production | Organisation structure |
| Market segmentation | Marketing | Control systems |
| Distribution channels | Administration | Management skills |
| Brand names | Manufacturing processes | Boundaries of the firm |
| Geographic coverage | R&D capability | ▩ Diversification |
| Selling systems | Marketing and distribution systems | ▩ Vertical integration |
| | | Firm size |
| | | Relationships and influence groups |

*Source*: McGee and Thomas (1986)

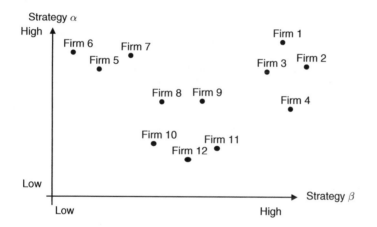

**Figure 12.8**
Strategic positions in the widget industry

of market co-ordination activities discussed in Chapter 10 are easier to carry out. Consider Figure 12.8.

There are 12 firms in the widget industry. If this industry existed in a neo-classical world then all the firms would be identical, and the industry would be reasonably competitive – it would not be possible for one of the firms to sustain a price–cost margin and hence generate a sustained abnormal profit. However, if we take a resource-based view developed in Chapter 7, then each of the 12 firms is not identical, they are each a unique bundle of resources that have developed different competencies. Given these differing resource bases and competencies, the firms may be expected to develop strategies best suited to their particular circumstances. In Figure 12.8, these strategies are represented by $\alpha$ and $\beta$. In the car industry example used above, these were market coverage and range of products, but they could be any combination of the factors identified by McGee and Thomas in Table 12.4. Firms are placed within the strategic space depending on the $\alpha$ and

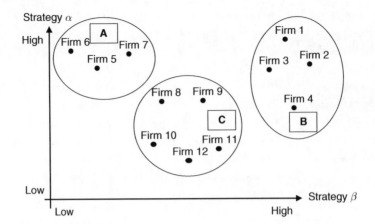

**Figure 12.9**
Strategic groups in
the widget
industry

$\beta$ strategies they are pursuing. Thus firm 1 has a high $\alpha$ strategy and a high $\beta$ strategy (in the car example this may be Ford with a global market coverage and a full range of vehicles) whereas firm 6 follows a high strategy for $\alpha$ but only low for $\beta$ (which could be Ferrari that sell cars globally, but only a very limited range of cars are available). Figure 12.9 suggests that there are clusters of firms within the industry that, as a result of similar resource and competency bases, are following similar strategies.

These clusters of firms form strategic groups of which there appear to be three:

Group A – following high $\alpha$ strategy and a low $\beta$ strategy
Group B – following high $\alpha$ and $\beta$ strategies
Group C – following mid $\alpha$ and $\beta$ strategies.

Movement between the groups is restricted by the resource and competency base of the firms, for example, those firms in group A may not have the resources and/or the competencies to move to group B; Ferrari (group A) has not got the capacity, skills and knowledge to become a full-range car producer and join group B. What the differing resources of the firms have done is create three sub-groupings of firms out of the original 12 firms in the industry. In terms of market structure, the widget industry consists of three oligopoly markets rather than a more competitive market of 12 firms. Each of the three strategic groups will try to preserve and strengthen the mobility barriers that prevent entry into the group from one of the other two groups.

Theoretically, the resulting abilities of firms within a group being able to create and sustain levels of abnormal profits match the discussion in Section 4.3 in relation to entry barriers – the stronger the mobility barriers, the higher the potential price–cost margins within the group. Whether the firms achieve the full potential abnormal profits depends on the ability of the firms within the group to co-ordinate their activities as discussed in Chapter 10. In terms of Figure 12.9, it would appear that strategic group A would have the best chance of coordinating their behaviour as there are only three firms. Similarly, you would expect group C, with five firms, to be the most competitive and hence the hardest in which to gain all the potential abnormal profits that the mobility barrier may protect.

Of the three common methods used by strategist to assess the environment, the strategic group concept for analysing a firm's immediate market environment rests on the most firm theoretical base.

## 12.4.2  Strategic groups in the UK food-retailing market

Figure 12.10 shows how the UK food-retailing market may look if divided into strategic groups.

The strategies that have been used to define the strategic space are the range of food products sold and the geographical coverage. Four strategic groups have been identified:

- Group A – wide range of goods and national coverage (the big four – Tesco, Sainsbury's, Asda/Wal Mart, Morrisons).
- Group B – wide range of goods and regional coverage (regionally focused supermarkets such as Budgens and Waitrose).
- Group C – limited range of goods and local coverage (convenience stores/corner shops).
- Group D – limited range of goods and national coverage (the 'pile them high, sell them cheap' strategy – Aldi, Lidl).

Focusing on group A, we can identify the isolating mechanisms from Table 12.4 being used to protect their market position. These are the resources and competencies required to maintain a national chain with a wide range of goods:

1. Market-related: product range, geographical coverage
2. Industry-supply characteristics: economies of scale, distribution system
3. Characteristics of the firms – diversification into non-food goods, size and power.

However, as noted previously, isolating mechanisms can be overcome. Indeed, 30 years ago Tesco actually belonged to group D – the 'pile them high, sell them cheap'

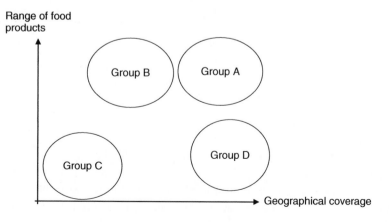

**Figure 12.10**
Strategic groups in the UK food-retailing industry

group. Over the last 30 years, Tesco has developed the resources and competencies to move from group D to group A. A much quicker route to switching groups is by merger and acquisition. Morrisons moved from group B to group A in 2004 by the purchase of a group A firm, Safeways, whilst Wal Mart entered from outside of the UK market by a similar route with the purchase of Asda.

## 12.5 | Review and further reading

In strategy textbooks, the idea of 'efficiency' tends to appear in relation to operational efficiency, a type of efficiency that is more akin to what economists call productive efficiency, or cost minimisation. This is not surprising, given that the economists' concern with the wider idea of economic efficiency is absent from the firm-specific focus of the strategists. The equivalent overriding objective for the strategists is the idea that firms should be aiming to add, and retain, as much value as is possible. This idea of adding value has been looked at in some detail in this chapter and is central to understanding the strategists' perspective on efficiency.

Throughout the chapter, we have looked at a variety of models/methods taken from the strategic management literature that relate to how value can be created, protected and divided up. Johnson, Scholes and Whittington (2005) and Lynch (2002) provide much fuller treatments of all the frameworks and methods used in this chapter. However, the frameworks and methods reviewed in this chapter are only a narrow section of the strategy literature; there are many other means of adding value through, for example, innovation in products and processes, or mergers and acquisitions, or the creation of unique resources and/or competencies, and many more. Readers interested in the wider range of strategic approaches are referred to Whittington (2002) and Mintzberg, Ahlstrand and Lampel (1998).

One of the key differences between economics and strategy identified in Chapter 1 was the diversity of strategy and the lack of any widely accepted underlying generic theoretical framework. However, if we take 'adding value' as the strategists' equivalent of the economists' 'economic efficiency', then the widely used (and abused) method of SWOT comes closest to providing an underlying unifying framework for strategy's range of methods, models and concepts. SWOT stands for

*S*trengths
*W*eaknesses
*O*pportunities
*T*hreats

The classic representation of how a firm should try to maximise its added value is by using its internal *S*trengths (whilst trying to minimise its *W*eaknesses) to take best advantage of the environmental *O*pportunities and nullify any potential *T*hreats. SWOT was one of the earliest methods developed by strategy as an

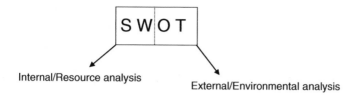

academic subject area back in the late 1950s/early 1960s (Figure 12.11). Barney has characterised the development of the subject in the following terms:

> The history of strategic management can be understood as an attempt to 'fill in the blanks' created by the SWOT framework; that is, to move beyond suggesting that strengths, weaknesses, opportunities, and threats are important for understanding competitive advantage to suggest models and frameworks that can be used to analyze and evaluate these phenomena. (Barney, 1995)

The methods we have been looking at in this chapter are all concerned with environmental analysis and, ultimately, about trying to identify possible opportunities and threats in that environment. STEP is a method of trying to make some sort of sense out of the macro-environment and to identify the key drivers in that environment for a particular firm. Some of the drivers identified may turn out to be threats. For example, a rising level of national income may be a threat if you are producing an inferior good such as cheap shoes. Alternatively, other identified environmental drives may provide opportunities. An aging population, for example, provides opportunities for furniture manufacturers to diversify into producing specialised furniture for the growing numbers of older, less mobile people. The five-forces method was originally devised to help firms identify industries that offered the best opportunities for future profit. The potential threats are embodied in the five-forces that work to shape the industry – possible new entrants, possible new substitutes, the potential power of suppliers and consumers and the possible effects of a competitive environment. The strategic group approach provides, for firms, the possibility of developing strategies that are consistent with their resource base and may lead to mobility barriers that enable to take advantage of the opportunity of rising price–cost margins.

The strengths and weaknesses part of SWOT relates to the identified internal strengths and weaknesses of the firm. This internal audit relates back to the resource-based view of the firm and the idea of a value chain as explored in Chapter 7. The resource-based view of the firm shows how a firm should identify and use its core competencies and resources as strengths from which it can create and sustain abnormal profits. One method of doing this is by using value chain analysis to dissect the firm and look for these strengths, and, at the same time, trying to identify any weaknesses.

As suggested earlier, there are many more methods of assessing external opportunities and threats, just as there are other ways of identifying internal strengths and weaknesses. However, if a firm is trying to create, sustain and protect added value then, as stated earlier, it must use its internal *S*trengths (whilst trying to minimise its *W*eaknesses) to take best advantage of the environmental *O*pportunities and nullify any potential *T*hreats. SWOT is not a concept like economic efficiency that can be supported by reference to a range of models, but it does provide a framework that gives some underpinning to the plethora of methods, models and concepts that strategists have developed over the last 40 years.

This chapter and the previous chapter have reviewed the main models of environmental analysis used by economists and strategists. There has been an attempt to show that there is a lot of common ground between the means of analysing the environment developed by the two subject areas (indeed some of the strategists' models have evolved from economics). At the core of both the economists' and strategists' models remains the idea of an industry which is comprised of firms that undertake the basic transformation process of turning inputs into outputs. Whilst the concepts of 'profit' and 'value' are not the same, the perceptions of the motivation of firms and how they behave within their environments are very similar:

- Firms try to create added value (strategists)/create and sustain abnormal profits (economists).
- Firms try to maximise their value take from a production chain (strategists)/use competitive strategic behaviour (economists).
- Firms try to protect value from extra-industry threats (strategists)/erect strategic entry barriers (economists).

However, as pointed out at the beginning of the chapter, whilst the two subject areas may share a common view on the nature and motivations of a firm in relation to its environment, they disagree fundamentally on what is meant by 'efficiency'. As was discussed in the introduction to Chapter 11, economists are interested in efficiency in relation to how an industry allocates resources, not in relation to the profitability of individual firms, which is the strategists' concern. Chapter 13 moves very defiantly back into the economists' realm by looking at what public authorities can do when they find that an industry is not operating according to the economists' idea of efficiency.

## 12.6 | Student exercises

### 12.6.1 Review exercises and points for discussion

1. Provide brief and clear definitions of the following key terms and concepts as used in this chapter.

   a. Value added
   b. Value creation
   c. Value net
   d. STEP analysis
   e. Five-forces analysis

     f.  A strategic group

     g.  Mobility barriers

     h.  SWOT.

2. Chapter 5 used the firm Sarah's Pencils to illustrate the idea of a chain of production. This simple chain of production can also be used as an example of a value net with four participants: the lumber firm supplying the wood for the pencils; Sarah's Pencils as the producer; the gift shops that are Sarah's Pencils customers; and, at the end of the chain, the customers of the gift shop. Assume the following about the added value per ten pencils produced at each stage in the value net:

- The cost of the wood to the lumber firm is £2.

- The lumber firm adds £1 of value.

- Sarah's Pencils adds £2 of value.

- The gift shops add £1 of value.

- Consumer surplus is £1.

    a.  What is the total value of this production chain?

    b.  What is the added value of this production chain?

    c.  What is the price of the pencils to the final consumer ?

3. How may the distribution of the added value change between the four participants in the value net in question 2 in the following circumstances:

    a.  Sarah's Pencils merged with two other leading suppliers of novelty pencils.

    b.  A poor summer reduces the number of tourists visiting gift shops.

    c.  An increase in the price of timber.

4. Looking at the STEP and five-forces frameworks, how do these relate to the economists' more familiar demand and supply conditions, particularly in relation to the distinction made in Chapter 4 between endogenous and exogenous factors?

## 12.6.2  Application exercise

Using the industry information gathered for the exercise at the end of Chapter 11:

a. Complete a STEP analysis, five-forces analysis and identify any strategic groups within the industry.

b. Compare your conclusions with the conclusions you drew from the SCP analysis. Comment on the differences shown between the economic efficiency of the market and the strategic efficiency of the market (it might be useful to access the DTI value added scoreboard (DTI (c))).

# 13 Competition Policy

## LEARNING OUTCOMES

On completion of this chapter, the reader should be able to

■ Explain the basis and functioning of competition policy within the UK

■ Outline the issues that arise from the existence of natural monopolies

■ Compare the policy options open to deal with the issue of natural monopolies

■ Assess the policy issues raised by market dominance

■ Discuss the policy approach adopted in the UK and EU to market dominance and its application in practice.

## KEY NEW CONCEPTS

| | | |
|---|---|---|
| Franchising | Restrictive practices | Price regulation |
| Public ownership | Anti-competitive practices | |

## KEY NEW MODELS

| | | |
|---|---|---|
| Natural monopoly | Chicago school economics | Austrian school economics |

## MODELS AND CONCEPTS DEVELOPED FURTHER

| | | |
|---|---|---|
| Mergers and collusion | Economic efficiency | Price–cost margins |
| Strategic entry barriers | Contestable markets | Monopoly |
| Structural entry barriers | Market co-ordination | Price- and quantity-fixing cartels |

As was discussed in Part III, just because decisions taken by firms can lead to them increasing their profits does not mean that consumers are also automatically better off; in some cases it can mean just the reverse. Within the UK, there are a whole range of quasi-governmental bodies that have the role of protecting consumers from the decisions and actions of firms that may work against the interests of the consumers. These include bodies such as the Competition Commission (CC), the Office of Fair Trading (OFT), Trading Standards, Ofcom, Ofwat and many more. On the wider European level, the European Commission and courts also serve to protect consumers across the EU. In terms of the five-forces method discussed in Chapter 12, all these bodies are trying to counterbalance the power relationship between firms and their consumers – particularly where those consumers are individuals rather than other firms. Without this sort of protection, the firms would take the majority of the value added from this relationship, reducing consumer surplus to a bare minimum (see Section 12.1). From an economic perspective, these quasi-governmental bodies are the outfacing institutions charged with implementing the state's competition policy.

Chapters 11 and 12 reviewed a wide range of models and methods used for analysing a firm's external environment. As was discussed in Chapter 12, the broadest method used by strategists is the STEP method which encompasses the influence of elements from the macro-environment. As was seen, the macro-environment is divided into the broad groupings of political, economic, social and technological influences, with one of the key points being that an individual firm has little influence over the elements that make up its own STEP environment. Competition policy is one of the key elements of the political environment that potentially impacts on all firms in the economy. In this chapter, we will look at the underlying theory on which the UK and the EU competition policies is based, much of which has already been covered in the preceding chapters of this book. In Chapter 14, we will look at how competition policy, and the underlying economic theory, is used in practice.

Competition policy takes the form of a body of the UK and the EU legislation that has evolved over the last 50 years or so and is enacted by a series of quasi-governmental public bodies. The attitude of these public bodies to how firms operate in trying to achieve their objectives of cost minimisation and revenue maximisation is a key factor in a firm's relationship with its macro-environment. The competition authorities have the legal powers to limit and monitor a firm's behaviour and, if deemed necessary, to intervene in the actions undertaken by firms. The underlying motivation for the competition authorities, as discussed above, is to try and counteract the imbalance in the power relationship between the firm and the consumer.

*The basis of the UK competition policy.* The first question to ask is what should be the basis of competition policy? When should the state, in the form of its competition authorities (in the case of the UK, these are the OFT, the CC and the European Commission and court), intervene in the workings of particular markets? One extreme view taken by economists who belong to the so-called Chicago school is that the state should never intervene in the workings of a free market. From the

Chicago school perspective, any inefficiencies and market failure will always be eliminated by the long-term working of the price mechanism. Any intervention by the competition authorities in markets will simply lead to a distortion of the market and prevent the market reaching its full efficient potential. At the other end of the spectrum is the old socialist planning view that the state should control certain 'strategic' markets so as to ensure that social welfare is maximised, rather than simply firms' maximising their profits (see Section 13.1.2). At the extreme of this view were the former centrally planned economies where all markets were replaced by state control.

In practice, competition policy, as it has developed in the UK and the EU, lies somewhere between the two extremes, recognising that some interference in some markets may be necessary where that market is not working as efficiently as it should, but without the need to take over these markets completely. As we shall see through examples in Chapter 14, more recent interventions tend to be aimed at making markets work more efficiently by the removal of entry barriers, not a heavy-handed forced restructuring of industries and firms.

The attitude of the UK authorities to competition policy is best summarised by the four quotes given below, all of which come from a document posted on the DTI website (DTI is the Department for Trade and Industry – the government department responsible for the UK competition policy) (DTI (a)).

1. 'Competitive markets provide the best means of ensuring that the economy's resources are put to their best use by encouraging enterprise and efficiency, and widening choice'.
2. 'Where markets work well, they provide strong incentives for good performance – encouraging firms to improve productivity, to reduce prices and to innovate; whilst rewarding consumers with lower prices, higher quality, and wider choice'.
3. 'However markets can and do fail. Competition policy is therefore used to ensure the efficient workings of markets and to avoid such market failures, most notably to prevent the abuses of market power'.
4. 'Market power arises when one or a small number of firms dominate a market and it is difficult for other firms to enter'.

Underlying the views expressed in quotes 1 and 2 are the arguments about economic efficiency presented in Sections 4.2 and 11.1. Quote 1 is an explicit statement regarding the desirability of markets as the most efficient way of organising resources to achieve the most efficient economic outcome. Quote 2 expands on this faith in markets by expanding on what is regarded as good performance and benefits that efficient markets deliver. Quote 2 relates directly back to many of the issues discussed in Chapter 4 in connection with price–cost margins, welfare loss and possible results of entry barriers being established in a market. As we discussed in Chapter 4, the quote emphasises the undesirability of price–cost margins that are responsible for pushing prices up and also reflects entry barriers to the market that keep potential entrant firms out, hence restricting choice and dampening innovation.

Quote 3 provides the justification for competition policy; the authorities need to intervene in order to try and correct markets that are not operating efficiently through 'market failure' and/or 'abuses of market power'. However, quote 3 also illustrates a long-standing feature of the UK competition policy, namely that market power in itself is not a problem, rather it is the abuse of that power that becomes a problem. The UK competition policy has always taken a pragmatic approach to market dominance, recognising that this can arise through a firm simply being more efficient than any of its rivals (reflecting the Chicago school perspective). A more efficient firm has lower costs and hence may achieve market dominance by being able to charge lower prices than its rivals. In economic terms, the firms have simply created structural entry barriers of the type discussed in Section 4.3.4, either by producing at a lower direct production cost than their competitors or by having an efficient management structure that reduces their management costs or both. Where market dominance becomes an issue for the competition authorities is when a dominant firm tries to abuse this position by creating strategic entry barriers, and hence price–cost margins that are not built on the basis of efficiency alone.

Quote 4 is also of interest as it directly links to the idea of contestability discussed in Section 4.3. The perceived problem of market power relates to the ability of the dominant firms to restrict entry to the market and not simply to the size of the dominant firms. This is very definitely taking the contestable market approach as opposed to the perfectly competitive approach. As was discussed in Section 4.3, one of the key differences between the two models is their view as to how efficiency is achieved. The perfectly competitive model relies on having many small firms in the market – efficiency increases as the number of firms in a market increases. If this view was taken by the competition authorities, then the way you would deal with inefficient markets is either by introducing new firms to the market or by breaking up the existing dominant firms into competing smaller entities. This has happened in the past (see Section 13.1); however, the sentiments of quote 4 lie very much with the contestable market view of efficiency. Efficiency relies on potential entry rather than actual entry, and this is achieved by reducing entry barriers, not by breaking up dominant firms. Current policy takes the view that the problem is entry barriers and not just the number of firms.

Section 13.2 deals with the issues surrounding market dominance in more depth, recognising that there are two aspects to this problem that competition policy needs to deal with:

- The acquisition of dominance
- The maintenance of dominance.

However, before looking at this, we need to consider another means by which a firm can acquire a dominant position: in situations where the most efficient market structure is actually a monopoly. These types of markets are usually referred to as natural monopolies.

## 13.1    The problem of natural monopoly

### 13.1.1    Definition of the problem

The formal mathematical definition of a natural monopoly is as shown below in relation to the production of a specific product.

$$C(Q) < C(q_1) + C(q_2) + \cdots + C(q_n)$$

where $C$ is the cost of production; $Q$ is the output of a single firm; and $q_1 \ldots q_n$ is the output of firms $1-n$.

What the equation says is that the costs incurred by producing the product in a single monopoly firm ($C(Q)$) will be less than the costs of splitting production among a number of non-monopoly firms ($C(q_1) + C(q_2) + \cdots C(q_n)$). Figure 13.1 shows the reason for this.

The figure shows a market where there are significant economies of scale in relation to the size of market demand. ($Q_{max}$) represents the maximum demand for the product at which a firm can cover its costs – to meet demand beyond ($Q_{max}$) the firm would be incurring a loss. As can be seen, this level of output is very close to the minimum efficient size (MES) for a firm. In other words, for a firm to take advantage of all the economies of scale present in the market (and hence produce at the lowest possible cost ($C_{min}$)), it needs to be producing at an output level which is close to the maximum output level required by the market ($Q_{max}$). If the market was equally split between two firms, then the two firms would each produce at output level ($Q_{max}/2$); the costs of these duopoly firms would be ($C_{duo}$). However, if the market was a monopoly, then this single firm could meet the market demand, ($Q_{max}$), but at a much lower cost ($C_{min}$). In essence, what Figure 13.1 demonstrates is that there may be some markets that can be most efficiently supplied by a monopoly firm; these are the markets referred to as being natural monopolies.

Figure 13.1 shows a natural monopoly that arises due to the extent of economies of scale that is present in the market in relation to the size of demand. A similar

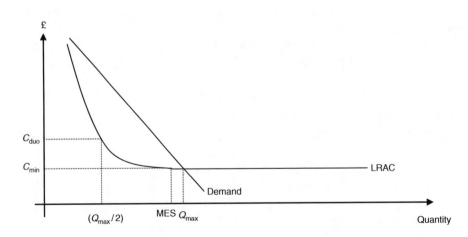

**Figure 13.1** The problem of natural monopoly

situation can arise due to economies of scope where the production of one product leads to similar cost efficiencies in the production of a related product.

$$C(Q_x, Q_y) < C(q_x) + C(q_y)$$

What this equation says is that the costs of producing product $x$ and product $y$ are less when undertaken by a single firm than when the products are produced by two separate firms. We have already seen an example of this in Chapter 7 when we looked at the increasing integration of the retail end of the utilities industries. The similarity in the resources and competencies needed to market and collect payments for gas, electric and water services leads to economies of scope – the cost of one firm undertaking this function across all three areas will be lower than the combined cost of three individual firms from each of the three areas.

Therefore, the most efficient market structure for some industries appears to be a monopoly. However, this, of course, raises a major problem for the formulators of competition policy – how do you ensure that the natural monopolists do not behave in the profit maximising manner associated with monopolists generally? Figure 13.2 illustrates the efficiency problem created by natural monopolies.

The profit maximising natural monopolist would aim to maximise profits by equating marginal cost and marginal revenue. This would lead to a price ($P_{mono}$) at an output level of ($Q_{mono}$). As can be seen from the figure, this creates a large price–cost margin equal to ($P_{mono} - P_{min}$), with the monopolist making abnormal profits equal to $\Pi = (P_{mono} - P_{min})(Q_{mono})$.

The problem for policy makers is, therefore, how to ensure that a single firm supplying a market, which is a natural monopoly, operates at a cost level that is close to ($P_{min}$), in Figure 13.2, when this is not actually the profit maximising position for the firm. Put another way, how can the potential cost benefits of production by a single firm be gained without the disadvantages of monopoly behaviour?

In the real world, natural monopolies tend to be associated with the large capital-intensive national industries such as electricity generation, gas supply, railway lines and the provision of water and sewage facilities. All these industries initially incur large sunk costs and large ongoing maintenance costs, which make for large

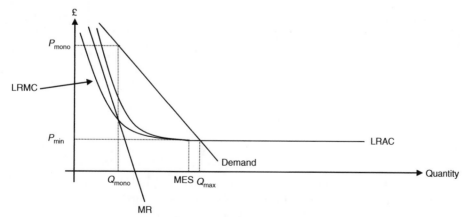

**Figure 13.2** The efficiency issue

economies of scale to be present, and hence the industries tend to be regarded as natural monopolies. However, natural monopolies can arise in more localised situations such as a mini-market supplying a small remote community in the Scottish highlands. Public policy in the last 50 years has, however, focused on the first type of natural monopoly – the large national industries that can be identified as natural monopolies.

Over this period, four distinct approaches have been adopted to deal with the problem of achieving efficient production in these markets, but with a single firm supplying the market. Vickers and Yarrow (1985) identify the four as being

- Public ownership
- Regulation
- Competitive forces
- Franchising.

Examples of all four can be found within the present UK economy. These are discussed in detail below.

## 13.1.2 Public ownership

### 13.1.2.1 The basis of the approach

The approach to the problems caused by natural monopoly is to take the monopoly out of private ownership and place it under the direct control of the public sector. In effect, instead of the firm being owned by a group of private shareholders, it becomes owned by the public sector and is run either through a government department or by a government appointed body. By taking the industry into public ownership, the objective of the firm moves from one of seeking to maximise profit to one of seeking to maximise social welfare – which will then equate with the socially efficient level of output. As was discussed in Section 11.3, the economically efficient level of output occurs when the cost of the last unit of resource used exactly matches the value placed on that unit by society. In terms of Figure 13.2, instead of the private firm trying to maximise profits at the point where $MC = MR$, the publicly owned firm aims to maximise social benefit by producing at the point where $P = MC$ (at $P_{min}$, $Q_{max}$), the economically (socially) efficient point. Thus, through public ownership and the resultant change in the firm's objective the desired efficient outcome is achieved.

### 13.1.2.2 Public ownership in practice

The approach to the problems caused by natural monopolies was the predominant approach taken by successive UK governments from the 1940s until the early 1980s. During this period, all the major national natural monopolies operated as public sector nationalised industries. These included the companies supplying the main public utilities such as gas, water and electricity (the Post Office, which included the telephone network, had always been a public sector industry) and the national airline, rail and coach networks. All these industries exhibited high sunk costs and large economies of scale in relation to demand associated with natural monopolies. In addition, they also represented industries that needed to be provided, as far as possible, to everybody, not simply to those who could pay the higher prices a profit maximising monopolist would charge. In other words, part of the maximisation of social welfare included the principle of universal coverage.

In accordance with the principles of economic efficiency (see Section 11.1) during the 1960s and early 1970s, these industries tried to price at the point where marginal cost equalled price. During the late 1970s, the requirement to price at marginal cost was replaced by a series of financial constraints within which the nationalised monopolies had to work. Other industries during this period were also taken into the public sector at various times, for example, steel, coal and the parts of car industry, but these tended to be nationalised for strategic and/or purely political reasons and not because they were natural monopolies.

This attempt to apply economic theory to real-world natural monopolies ultimately failed for a number of reasons. As discussed at various points earlier in this book, the identifying of marginal cost is, in practice, extremely difficult. The problems are even more difficult for large, complex, multi-product markets that were being supplied by the monopoly firms of the nationalised industries. Another by-product of trying to price at marginal cost to maximise social welfare was that in some cases this resulted in the firm operating at prices that were below long-run average cost, that is, they were operating at a loss.

Other problems were caused by the institutional arrangements under which the monopolies operated. As outlined above, the nationalised firms were not set up as independent bodies but usually as either part of a government department or nominally independent bodies but whose boards of directors reported directly to a minister of state (who also often appointed the directors). This led to, in many cases, a politicisation of the decision-making. Decisions were often not taken for economic reasons but for political reasons. During the 1970s, for example, the Labour government was repeatedly accused of using gas and electricity price rises as a means of increasing tax yield, whilst appearing to keep direct and indirect tax rates artificially low. Decision-making in many nationalised monopolies was, as a result of the politicisation of decision-making, inconsistent with no clear lines of authority and accountability. As a result, many of the cost savings that should have arisen from operating as a natural monopoly were lost due to organisational inefficiencies, such as overmanning and poor cost control.

The Conservative government elected in 1979 decided that the public ownership approach to solving the problem of natural monopolies had failed and set about shifting policy to the other three approaches discussed below. By the end of the Conservative rule in 1997, all of the industries identified above as being national natural monopolies, with the exception of the non-telecommunications part of the Post Office, had been taken out of public ownership (as, indeed, were all those other public sector industries that were taken into public ownership for political and strategic reasons).

### 13.1.3  Regulation

#### 13.1.3.1  The basis of the approach

Traditionally, the alternative to public ownership of natural monopolies was to impose regulations. In theory, one means of trying to control the potential abuse of monopoly power by a firm supplying a natural monopoly market could be by the imposition of constraints, either on the level of abnormal profits made or on the price the monopolist is able to charge. In terms of Figure 13.2, the approach suggests that you try to control the price–cost margin by either imposing a price that is close to $(P_{min})$ or limiting the size of the abnormal profit represented by the area $(P_{mono} - P_{min})(Q_{mono})$.

#### 13.1.3.2  The regulation method adopted in the UK

During the 1980s, the government replaced public ownership as a means of controlling many of the public sector natural monopolies with a form of regulation. Gas, telecommunications (which split away from the Post Office and became British Telecom, BT) and water were sold back into the private sector and became subjected to a system of regulation. The system adopted was a form of price control and monitoring by an independent watchdog body. The method of price control adopted was by a formula commonly known as 'RPI – $x$'. The idea was that each year price rises by the natural monopoly would be constrained by the current retail price index minus a fixed percentage figure. For example, if the RPI was 5 per cent, the value of $x$ for the privatised BT might be fixed at 2 per cent, thus limiting BT to a price increase of only 3 per cent, in effect a real price cut. BT was thus being forced to become more efficient to make the cost savings required by the falling revenue and, at the same time, moving the price to the consumer closer to $(P_{min})$ in Figure 13.2.

This method of price control was slightly adapted for the water industry where the formula used was 'RPI – $x + y$'. The '+$y$' reflected a variable figure that corresponded to each individual water company's requirement for capital investment.

The other part of the regulatory regime introduced was the establishment of a watchdog body (commonly referred to as Ofcom, Ofwat, Ofgas, etc.) that was independent of the government (thus avoiding one of the main weaknesses of the former nationalised industries) and under the control of a full-time director. The purpose of the regulatory bodies was to watch out for the interests of the consumer in trying to ensure that the industry's monopoly firm did not abuse their position in the market.

#### 13.1.3.3  Regulation in practice

As with any system based on regulations, there is always the possibility that the firms being regulated will try to find ways around the system and/or manipulate the regulations to their own advantage. The tradition of regulation of natural monopolies has a much longer history in the USA, and a number of US writers (see, for example, Demsetz (1968)) have raised the problem of 'regulatory capture'. This is a problem caused when the senior managers of the regulated company and the regulators, who, by necessity, need at times to work quite closely together, may develop personal relationships that reduce the independence of the regulators. Similarly, there is evidence from the USA that where the regulatory mechanism has been via the placing of restrictions on the rate of return on capital employed (a proxy for profits as discussed in Chapter 11) that the monopolist can earn, this has led to an inefficient over-investment in capital by the company.

There have been attempts by the privatised natural monopolies in the UK to manipulate the system in similar ways. For example, in the early days of BT, the firm was accused of routinely manipulating the 'RPI − x' limits on price rises for its own purposes. In the mid-1980s, prior to mobile phones, all calls were made via landline and the market broke down into two broad categories: domestic calls made inside the UK and international calls. BT would ensure that overall the price rise matched the Oftel limit imposed by the RPI − x formula, but they would increase the price of the more inelastic overseas calls by more than the RPI − x figure and limit the price increases for the more elastic domestic calls to a figure below the RPI − x limit.

### 13.1.4 Competitive forces

#### 13.1.4.1 The basis of the approach

The competitive forces approach to dealing with the problem of natural monopoly draws on the contestable market hypothesis discussed in detail in Section 4.3. As discussed previously, one of the outcomes of a market being perfectly contestable is that the market will be efficient, irrespective of the number of firms present in the market. Therefore, if this is applied to a natural monopoly market, then by making that market contestable the monopolist will be forced to charge a price at ($P_{min}$) in Figure 13.2, and the market will be efficient despite only having a single firm. In effect, you get the best of both worlds – a monopolist that is able to take advantage of all the economies of scale present in the market and the price that is at the economically efficient level where $P = MC$. The role for the competition authorities is, therefore, to remove any entry barriers to the market that may exist. Indeed Kay and Thompson (1986) found that whether the firm was left in the public sector or moved to the private sector was in the end irrelevant, what mattered most was whether competitive forces were introduced into the market.

#### 13.1.4.2 Competitive forces in practice

This type of solution was used in a range of markets in the 1980s. For example, local and national bus services were deregulated in this way. Previously, the entry barrier had been a statutory one, in that the only legal providers of national coach services were the nationalised firm National Coach, and similarly, the only legal providers of local bus services were the local government authorities. In the mid-1980s (1985 for local buses, 1988 for the national coach service), the legal entry barriers were removed and both national and local bus services were opened up to competition from the outside.

The electricity industry provides another example. When privatised in 1993, the electricity industry was split into three separate operations – generation, distribution and retailing. The natural monopoly element was thought to be on the distribution side of the industry, with the national gird representing a massive capital investment. Therefore, on privatisation, this aspect of the industry was retained as a single firm. With the major entry barrier of the national grid removed, the generation and retailing sides of the industry were opened up to competitive forces: generation was divided into three companies, and the market was opened up to other potential entrants. Retailing was left in the hands of the regional electricity companies, but they were free to compete outside of their old regional boundaries and other companies could enter the market.

The success of this approach has been varied but, in most cases, entirely predictable in relation to the contestable market hypothesis. National Coach, for example, still has a widespread monopoly on long-distance coach travel. The reason being that there is another major entry barrier that was not dealt with by the privatisation legislation, namely that the firm has access to coach stations in the centre of every major town and city in the UK. A new entrant would find it extremely difficult to replicate this investment, and hence a major structural entry barrier into the industry still remains. On the other hand, however, the electricity retailing market is now extremely competitive and as a result has seen major benefits to the consumer in terms of price reductions. The difference in this industry is that the entry barriers are relatively low, and there are a reasonably large number of firms in related industries (gas retailing, for example) that have the same competencies in terms of billing, metre reading and handling a large (and overlapping) customer base as those required in the electricity retailing market (as discussed in Section 7.1).

Therefore, the use of competitive forces as a means of controlling natural monopolists relies heavily on the ability of the public authorities to remove all the major entry barriers to the market. Given that one of the principle reasons for the existence of natural monopolies in the first place tends to be high sunk costs and economies of scale, which lead to structural entry barriers, this severely limits the scope for making these markets more contestable.

### 13.1.5 Franchising

#### 13.1.5.1 The basis of the approach

The final approach identified by Vickers and Yarrow (1985) to try to deal with the efficiency problems caused by natural monopolies is referred to as franchising. Franchising is a means by which there is periodic competition for the natural monopoly market. The franchise to produce the good or service is awarded to the successful firm for a limited period of time after which they must submit themselves to a competitive bid process to keep the market. The idea is that whilst they have the franchise the incumbent firm is forced to try and produce efficiently; otherwise, it may lose the contract once its period of tenure is up. In effect at the end of the contract period, the market becomes perfectly contestable, and if the incumbent firm is not to become subject to hit-and-run tactics at the end of its tenure, then it must produce somewhere near the efficient level whilst it has the contract.

### 13.1.5.2  Franchising in practice

Franchising as a means of trying to cope with natural monopoly actually has a surprisingly long history in the UK dating back to the 1950s. In 1956, commercial television (ITV) was established; previously only the non-commercial BBC had been available. From that time until the advent of satellite TV in the early 1990s, the ITV stations had a natural monopoly over television advertising. The means adopted to try and regulate this natural monopoly was by a franchising system. The country was split into regions (the North West, West Midlands, London, etc.). Interested companies were then asked to bid for the rights to provide the ITV channel for a particular region of the country. After a specified number of years (initially about seven), the contract for the provision of the commercial TV channel for each region was opened up for competitive bids. The incumbent channels had to bid with potential new entrants to keep their ITV contract. The whole franchising process was overseen by the Independent Television Authority (ITA) who, in addition, also had much the same remit as the watchdog authorities set up later in the 1980s to regulate the newly privatised public utilities companies.

More recently, the franchising approach has been used in a number cases, perhaps most notably in the case of the railway system. The railway network was taken out of public ownership in 1996. As with the electricity industry, it was broken down into separate entities. In the railways case, the running and main-taining of the actual track and stations was separated out from the running of trains. The running of train services does represent a natural monopoly as defined in Section 13.1. There are large economies of scale present due to the high sunk cost of the rolling stock, and, without the inefficient laying of thousands of miles of new track, there tends to be only one track between most destinations. The government decided to arrange the natural monopoly of running train services on the basis of a franchise system. As with commercial TV 40 years previously, the national rail network was divided into a series of regions; these were then offered for tender to companies wishing to operate train services in those regions for a specified number of years. At the end of the period, the regional service was opened up to new bids in which the current incumbent provider could take part.

As with the other possible approaches to trying to cope with the problems raised by natural monopolies, the franchising approach does have its problems. One major initial problem is the actual setting of criteria for the awarding of the contract in the first place. Economic theory may suggest that you simply go for the lowest price bidder, as they should be the firm that can provide the service at the nearest point to ($P_{min}$), Figure 13.2. However, in practice, this may not always be appropriate. Take the example of the ITV franchises. In this case, the lowest price bidder may not be the company that is going to produce the best or most appropriate TV service; thus the criteria for the awarding of the ITV contracts used to include quality of service also. The problem is, of course, that this immediately introduces a subjective element into the bid process. The rail franchises operate to a series of clearly defined performance criteria against which the incumbent operators are judged.

Another major problem is the setting of the length of the contract. If the contract is set for too short a length of time, then companies will be put off bidding for the franchise, as they need to have sufficient time to recoup their initial investment. If the contract is for too long a period of time, then the incumbent firm has an incentive to simply maximise its returns by behaving as a monopolist and taking the consequences at the end of the contract time. Finally, there is the issue of how to encourage long-term investment when the current incumbent may only have the contract for a limited period of time. In the old ITV system, when an incumbent lost a contract, often all the capital equipment (and in some cases personnel) was simply bought out lock, stock and barrel by the incoming new firm. Long-term investment has also been one of the major issues in the privatised railway system.

## 13.2 | The problem of market dominance

The second area of concern for public policy is that of market dominance. The core of the problem relates to markets where there are, or potentially may be in the future, clear price–cost margins. As discussed in Chapter 4, in a strict neo-classical world, the existence of price–cost margins indicates abnormal profits that in turn indicate efficiency loss (Figure 4.8). In essence, firms are abusing their market power to extract excessive profits from the market at the expense of the wider economic good. However, as discussed earlier in this chapter, there are other schools of thought that view abnormal profits in a different light. As we discussed, the Chicago school economists argue that the existence of abnormal profits is the reward to a firm for either being more efficient or exploiting market opportunities more effectively than its rival firms – the entry barriers are structural rather than strategic. The problem for competition policy is to devise a policy that allows the authorities to decide which interpretation of the abnormal profits should be applied in a particular market. Are they a result of the abuse of market power, or are they a temporary 'reward' for being more efficient or innovative?

The problem of market dominance breaks down into two separate issues namely

- The acquisition of dominance
- The maintenance of dominance.

The acquisition of dominance relates to how firms acquire a dominant position in a market in the first place. The issue for the competition authorities is whether the acquisition of a dominant position by a firm, or firms, in a particular market is likely to be in the 'public interest'. In other words, is it likely to lead to efficiency loss as the new dominant firm(s) abuse their newly found market power, or are there clear efficiency or other benefits that outweigh the possible efficiency loss? In practice, the most common means by which a firm achieves market dominance is through mergers with, or acquisition of, its rivals. In game theory terms, we are looking at the second stage of market co-ordination, that of reaching an optimal agreement (Section 10.2). In effect, the firms agree to co-ordinate their behaviour by means of a horizontal integration. The issue for the competition authorities is to ensure that the resulting optimal outcome for the firms does not occur to the detriment of their customers.

The second aspect of market dominance is quite different in nature: the maintenance of dominance. In game theory terms, we are now looking at the third stage of co-ordination, that of sustaining the optimal outcome. In this case, competition policy needs to address the means by which some dominant firms are sustaining their dominance of markets and, again, the issue is whether the means being used are 'in the public interest'. As with the acquisition of dominance, the competition authorities need to make a judgement as to whether the means by which dominant firms are sustaining their abnormal profits are at the expense of the wider economic good. Quote 2 from the DTI in Section 13.1 summarises the role of the competition authorities in relation to market dominance as being '... ensuring that the economy's resources are put to their best use by encouraging enterprise and efficiency, and widening choice'.

### 13.2.1  The acquisition of dominance

As discussed briefly above, the acquisition of dominance relates to how firms acquire a position of dominance in a particular market. Generally speaking, there are three means:

1. Merger
2. Collusion
3. Efficiency.

The first two of these were discussed in detail in Chapter 10 in relation to how firms may try to co-ordinate markets so as to reach their preferred outcome (merger was referred to as horizontal integration). The discussion in Chapter 10, however, was presented from a firm-specific viewpoint – the co-ordination was to enable the firms to reach their mutually beneficial preferred outcome in the game. However, when looked at from the broader viewpoint of overall economic efficiency, it may well be that this preferred outcome for the firms is not actually the preferred outcome for society as a whole, particularly the firms' customers.

In Figure 13.3, $(P_m, Q_m)$ shows the profit maximising (and hence the least efficient outcome) price and output for the market, whilst $(P_c, Q_c)$ shows the perfectly contestable (and hence the most efficient outcome) price and quantity. The majority of markets will lie at some point between these two extremes, with prices somewhere between $P_m$ and $P_c$ and output somewhere between $Q_m$ and

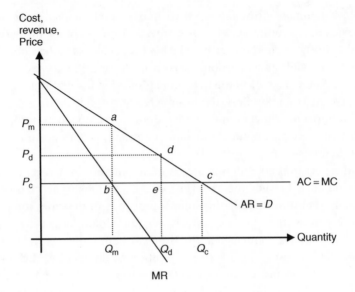

**Figure 13.3**
Mergers and
collusion

$Q_c$, exactly where depends on how contestable the market is (that is, how high the entry barriers are, see Section 4.3.3). Assume in this case that the market is a duopoly and each firm is charging the price $P_d$ and producing $Q_d$. In terms of the profit game used in the introduction to Chapter 10, the price $P_d$ represents the $(L_p, L_p)$ Nash equilibrium point of the game. The firms preferred $(H_p, H_p)$ is represented by the profit maximising price of $P_m$. However, what Figure 13.3 illustrates is that from a wider perspective of economic efficiency, the $(H_p, H_p)$ outcome, although preferable for the two firms, is not preferable for the society as a whole. The efficiency loss at $P_d$ (the Nash equilibrium $(L_p, L_p)$) is the area $(c,d,e)$, whereas the efficiency loss at $P_m$ (the $(H_p, H_p)$ outcome) is area $(a,b,c)$ as can be seen quite clearly

$$(c, d, e) < (a, b, c)$$

In other words, the firms' preferred outcome $(P_m)$ leads to a much greater efficiency loss than the Nash equilibrium outcome $(P_d)$. In these circumstances, the move from $P_d$ to $P_m$ by the duopolists would constitute, in DTI's words, 'an abuse of market power' and would need to be dealt with by the competition authorities.

How the move from $P_d$ to $P_m$ could be achieved was discussed in Chapter 10; however, it does need to be re-examined from this wider economic efficiency perspective. The most obvious way for the move from $P_d$ to $P_m$ to take place would appear to be for the duopolists to merge and become a monopolist and hence simply charge the profit maximising price of $P_m$. This is what traditional neo-classical theory would predict. Hence, from this perspective, the merger would be detrimental from the society's viewpoint, and the competition authorities should prevent the merger from taking place. However, what contestable market theory tells us is that in practice this may not happen. $P_d$ may show the maximum price that can be charged without attracting entry, irrespective of whether the market is a duopoly or a monopoly. If this is the case, then the merger of the duopolists may have no effect at all on efficiency loss, and there is no reason for the competition authorities to take action. In fact, the merger may actually lead to cost savings due to the elimination of overlapping costs (running two corporate headquarters, for example) and hence the AC in Figure 13.3 may move downwards.

In other words, the competition authorities need to decide whether the merger is going to give the newly merged firm a degree of monopoly power over the market, as reflected in its ability to raise prices (a position defined as a 'hypothetical monopolist' – to be discussed in Section 14.1) or is the new firm to achieve beneficial cost efficiencies that will be passed on to the consumer. As we shall see, the application of competition policy for dealing with mergers and acquisitions quite often revolves around the debates on how much actual market power the merger will give and whether the merged firm will be 'leaner and fitter' and hence able to be more competitive.

The other aspect to mergers, which is not captured by the traditional economists' models, relates to the power a merged firm may have over its suppliers. Porter's five-forces model demonstrates this (Figure 12.6). The discussion in relation to Figure 13.3 is essentially about the power of the newly merged firm to extract additional value from its customers by charging higher prices or, put another way, transferring some of the consumer surplus into abnormal profit for itself. However, the newly merged firm may also have the power to extract value from its suppliers by forcing down the prices it pays for its inputs (causing the AC curve in 13.3 to move downwards). Again, as we shall see when we look at some actual cases, the additional power of a newly merged firm over suppliers can also be a cause of some concern.

The other means for the acquisition of dominance most overtly dealt with by competition authorities is collusion and in particular cartels (discussed in Section 10.2). The setting up of a cartel is another means by which firms can move from the Nash equilibrium $P_d$ in Figure 13.3 to their preferred outcome of $P_m$. Figure 13.4 reproduces the figure from Chapter 10, which illustrates how a cartel works.

The duopoly firms reach an agreement that either they will fix the price at $P_m$ and supply half the market each (a price-fixing cartel) or they will both produce $(Q_m/2)$ and hence force the price up to the desired level of $P_m$ (a quantity-fixing cartel). The efficiency outcome is the same as for the merger; the cartel agreement leads to a much greater efficiency loss than the previous duopoly situation. However, this time, there are no counter-arguments about cost savings as both firms continue to exist as separate entities. For this reason, cartel agreements have been banned under the UK competition legislation since the 1960s.

The final means by which a firm can acquire market dominance is through efficiency (Figure 13.5).

Consider a market where one firm (firm 1) is more cost efficient than the other firm (firm 2). In Figure 13.4, $P_1$ represents the minimum price that the cost-efficient firm 1 could charge and $P_2$ the minimum price of firm 2. In order for firm 1 to acquire total dominance of the market, all it has to do is charge a price that is

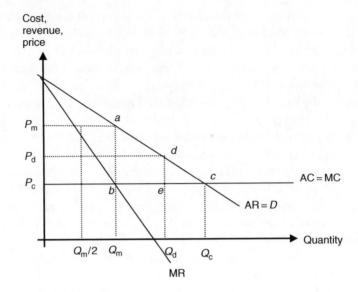

**Figure 13.4**
A cartel

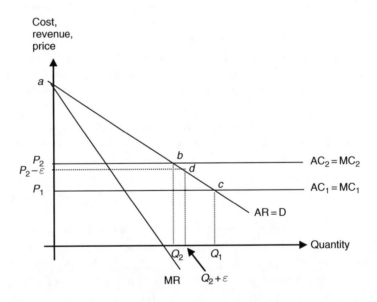

**Figure 13.5**
Market dominance
through efficiency

just under $P_2(P_2 - \varepsilon)$, in other words, a price that is below the less efficient firm's minimum costs. In efficiency terms, the most efficient outcome for firm 2 yields a maximum consumer surplus of $(a, b, P_2)$. However, even if firm 1 undercuts this with a price just below $P_2$, overall consumer welfare will increase by the area $(P_2, P_2 - \varepsilon, d, b)$. Potentially, consumer welfare could increase to a maximum of $(a, c, P_1)$ if firm 1 charged its minimum price. From a competition policy point of view, the situation where a firm has acquired market dominance by being efficient does not require any action as it is entirely in line with one of the tenets of competition policy as set out by the DTI in quote 1 in Section 13.1, which explicitly refers to '... encouraging enterprise and efficiency' (DTI, 2004). However, the competition authorities do need to ensure that a dominant market position acquired through efficiency is not then abused by the erection of strategic entry barriers that make it '... difficult for other firms to enter' (DTI, 2004) as in quote 4 in Section 13.1.

The obvious question to ask is why firm 1 in the above example was more efficient than firm 2. The answers could be due to firm 1 having a lower cost base (Chapter 4), lower management costs (Chapter 6) or access to unique resources or competencies (Chapter 7). Any of these types of entry barriers may lead to one firm acquiring a cost advantage of the type summarised in Figure 13.4.

### 13.2.2 The maintenance of dominance

The means by which firms maintain positions of dominance has already been examined in detail in Chapters 9 and 10. The problem for the competition authority lies in trying to balance potential gains to the consumer of such behaviour against the possible restrictions on competition that might arise. At one level, it can be argued that the types of strategic behaviour discussed in Chapters 9 and 10 can be seen as '... rewarding consumers with lower prices, higher quality, and wider choice' (quote 2 in Section 13.1). Take the toothpaste example from Section 9.2. The horizontal product differentiation of having different brands of toothpaste along the minty–tasteless characteristic space can be seen as increasing consumer choice and increasing consumer utility. The increased number of brands available means you are more likely to find a brand of toothpaste that matches your particular taste and hence increases your utility.

However, set against this benefit to consumers is the possibility that the horizontal differentiation of brands by one company is completely filling the characteristic space and is being used as a strategic entry barrier to reduce contestability and hence allowing the incumbent firm to increase its price–cost margin. In some cases, the 'characteristic space' may actually be physical shelf space in a shop. The dominant toothpaste manufacturer, for example, may insist that a shop stock all its range of toothpastes even though the brands at the two extremes of the minty–tasteless spectrum do not sell very well. The shop is forced to comply because if they do not then the popular mid-range brands will not be supplied and the shop will lose customers. This practice of 'full-line forcing' effectively fills the shelf space dedicated to toothpastes with the dominant firm's own brands, thus eliminating or restricting shelf space to other firms' brands of toothpaste. Other aspects of strategic behaviour discussed in Chapters 9 and 10 give rise to similar trade-offs between consumer benefits and restricting competition: limit-pricing lowers prices to consumers but can also restrict entry and hence the benefits of competition; the practice of matching competitors' prices may benefit consumers by forcing prices down to the lowest cost producer but can also be used to force the dominant firm's price across the market.

## 13.3 The UK and the EU competition policies

### 13.3.1 The acquisition of dominance

The UK competition policy dates back to the 1948 Monopolies and Restrictive Practices Act. The Act set up a semi-independent body, the Monopolies Commission (MC), which was charged with the investigation of monopoly situations. This approach of establishing independent bodies was, and still is, a feature of the UK approach to competition policy that set it apart from both the US and the EU approaches, both of which tend to rely on a more legalistic approach through the courts. The other significant feature of the 1948 Act is that it established a legal definition of monopoly as a market where one dominant firm sold at least 33 per cent of goods to the market (subsequently reduced to 25 per cent by the 1973 Fair Trading Act). The work of the MC was significantly increased by the 1965 Monopolies and Mergers Act when the MC was given the power to investigate proposed mergers that would lead to a monopoly situation. In effect, this Act gave the MC the right to pass judgements on the acquisition of dominance as discussed in Section 13.3.1.

However, the MC (or the MMC – Monopolies and Mergers Commission after the 1973 Act) was only a semi-independent body, with the ultimate power being reserved for the Secretary of State for industry (or the President of the Board of Trade as the post was until the 1960s). It was the Secretary of State that referred mergers to the MMC or asked for monopoly situations to be investigated. Likewise, it was the Secretary of State that decided whether the MMC recommendations, after an investigation, were acted upon. The obvious weakness of this system is the potential for political objectives to replace the purely economic objectives reflected in an MMC report. However, from 1948 until the 2002 Enterprise Act, this was, by and large, the system by which the problems associated with the acquisition of dominance were dealt with in the UK.

### 13.3.2 The maintenance of dominance

The approach to the problem of the maintenance of dominance followed a similar path through the use of the Restrictive Practices Court. One of the outcomes of the establishment of the MC in 1948 was that through its early investigations it became clear that the UK economy was riddled with anti-competitive practices (or restrictive trade practices as they were referred to at the time) – price- and output-fixing cartels, price rings, full-line forcing, resale price maintenance and many more. This led to the establishment in 1956 of a Registrar of Restrictive Trade Practices and the establishment of a court of restrictive trade practices. Under the terms of the Act, firms had to register with the court all agreements between themselves, which imposed restrictions on prices, the terms or conditions of sale, quantities or types to be produced, the process of manufacturing or the person or area from which the goods are to be acquired. Once registered, the court would decide whether the restrictive trade practice was justified. This process involved the firms trying to persuade the court that the trade restriction was 'in the public interest', which was achieved by passing through one of the eight so-called gateways (seven were in the original 1956 Act; the eighth was added in 1968). The gateways defined what was meant by the term 'in the public interest' and covered things such as health and safety, serious loss of jobs, loss of exports and less concrete gateways such as counteracting the power of a large supplier or to support other agreements that are in the public interest.

In practice, it proved to be very difficult to convince the court that a restrictive trade practice was in the public interest; only about 30 per cent of agreements were allowed, with approximately 90 per cent of registered agreements being either abandoned or substantially altered before they even reached the court. The 1973 Fair Trading Act replaced the Restrictive Practices Court with an OFT and a Director General of Fair Trading. However, the basic approach to making judgements about the maintenance of dominance by forcing firms to justify their actions in terms of them being in the public interest continued up until the 1998 Competition Act.

### 13.3.3 The EU competition policy

Running alongside the specific UK competition legislation is the legislation relating to competition within the EU. The EU competition legislation is applicable to cases that affect markets that go across national boundaries and thus are considered to have a 'community dimension'. As with the UK legislation, the distinction is drawn between, on the one hand, the acquisition and abuse of market dominance and, on the other, the maintenance of market dominance. The abuse of market power is dealt with under Article 82 (formerly Article 86) of the Treaty of Rome, the founding treaty of the EU back in 1956. Article 82 prohibits, with no exemptions, the abuse of a dominant market position insofar as it affects trade between Member States.

A separate related regulation (the EC merger regulation, ECMR) prohibits a merger that '... creates a dominant position as a result of which effective competition would be significantly impeded in the common market' (DTI, 2004b). The maintenance of dominance is dealt with under Article 81 (formerly Article 85). Article 81 '... prohibits anti-competitive agreements which may have an appreciable effect on trade between Member States and which prevent, restrict or distort competition in the Single Market' (DTI, 2004b). There are exceptions to this if the practice can be proved to be necessary in order to improve efficiency or the promotion of research and development.

### 13.3.4 UK competition policy since 1998

Although the basic principles and aims of the EU and the UK competition policies were essentially the same, prior to 1998, there was a major difference in the means by which they were implemented. Whereas the UK operated with a series of quasi-judicial institutions that basically acted as advisors to the Secretary of State, the EU policy was implemented through the formal legal body of the European Court of Justice. The central body of the EU, the European Commission, conducts the formal investigation into possible breaches of Articles 81 and 82, but the Court of Justice undertakes the implementation of the findings after a judicial review of the decisions taken by the Commission.

The 1998 Competition Act passed by the UK government, and enacted in 2000, was a major review of the UK competition policy, with the primary aim of bringing the UK policy more closely in line with the EU policy. The 1998 Act, together with the 2002 Enterprise Act, represents a significant shift in emphasis in the UK competition policy. The 1998 Act has two main prohibitions that are closely modelled on Articles 81 and 82 of the EU policy – one prohibiting anti-competitive practices and the other the abuse of monopoly power. However, of more significance in relation to the approach taken previously in the UK is the removal of both the idea of 'public interest' and the political dimension in the application of legislation. Under the terms of the 1998 and 2002 Acts, anti-competitive behaviour and the abuse of market power are judged, not by whether they are in the public interest but solely on their effects on competition. Judgements should therefore now be made based purely on the economics of the case. However, not only judgements but also the implementation of those judgements are now purely based on economics. The OFT and the CC now have the authority to implement their decisions in relation to anti-competitive behaviour (the OFT) and mergers (the CC) without reference back to the Secretary of State. In addition, in line with the approach taken in the EU, the OFT has powers to fine and even imprison offenders.

## 13.4 | Review and further reading

At the outset of this book, one of the themes in Chapter 1 was the differences between the two subject areas of economics and strategy. One of the key features identified was that economics had grown partly out of the need to have some underlying principles on which to guide public policy. The discussion in this chapter clearly shows how much of the economics developed throughout this book has had, and continues to have, a direct influence on public policy in relation to competition policy. As we shall see in Chapter 14, the tools of strategic analysis discussed in Chapter 12 do have some role to play in helping to clarify issues; however, it is the economics that is driving the development and outcomes of competition policy.

As can also be seen from the discussion in this chapter, the central concept to the development of competition policy is that of economic efficiency – ensuring that society is using its limited resources to the greatest benefit of all (which comes directly from the utilitarian basis on which neo-classical economics was built). The other theme to have emerged is that competition policy is primarily aimed at ensuring that the power relationship between a firm and its customers is not skewed too much in favour of the firm. This can be seen in all three areas of policy discussed in this chapter:

- Policies towards natural monopoly are about trying to ensure that the benefits of lower cost production are not lost due to the firm fixing monopoly prices.

- Policies towards the acquisition of dominance try to balance the motivation of the firms to achieve their optimal outcome against any deterioration in consumer benefits this may involve.
- Policies towards the maintenance of dominance try to ensure that the competitive practices of firms are not working against the interests of their consumers – the firms are not taking too larger slice of consumer surplus in abnormal profits for themselves.

The theory of competition policy and its application is one of the most accessible areas for students wishing to see how economic theory is of direct relevance to the real-world microeconomy. The DTI, CC and OFT websites have a wealth of information and, in the case of the CC and OFT sites, all the recent reports carried out into various aspects of the UK economy. Chapter 14 deals with three examples of these investigations to show how the competition policy outlined in this chapter is actually used.

## 13.5 | Student exercises

### 13.5.1 Review exercises and points for discussion

1. Provide brief and clear definitions of the following key terms and concepts as used in this chapter.

   a. Competition policy
   b. A natural monopoly
   c. Economies of scope
   d. Public ownership
   e. Privatisation
   f. Franchising
   g. A restrictive practice.

2. What role is played by each of the following bodies in the application of competition policy?

   a. The Competition Commission
   b. The Office of Fair Trading
   c. The European Court of Justice
   d. Articles 81 and 82 of the treaty of Rome
   e. Ofwat/Ofgas/Ofcom.

### 13.5.2 Application exercise

Please see the exercises at the end of Chapter 14.

# 14 Competition Policy in Action

On completion of this chapter, the reader should be able to

■ Outline the means of defining market boundaries

■ Use the economic models and concepts developed in this book to analyse Competition Commission and OFT cases

■ Use the strategic frameworks for environmental analysis to clarify Competition Commission and OFT cases

Standard Industrial          The hypothetical
Classification (SIC)         monopolist

No new models

Product differentiation          Strategic entry barriers

Chapter 13 outlined the economic basis of competition policy and showed how this had been used in the development of competition legislation in both the UK and the EU. The purpose of this chapter is twofold: first, to look at how competition policy is actually used in practice by looking at three recent cases from the UK; second, to show how some of the models, concepts and frameworks developed throughout this book can be used to analyse and assess these real-world cases.

The first case is that of an investigation undertaken by the Competition Commission (CC) into the UK supermarket industry. The case is used principally to illustrate one of the key aspects of any CC (or OFT or EU) investigation, the issue of clearly defining the market to be investigated. Section 14.1, therefore, begins with a discussion of the issues and problems surrounding the obtaining of a clear definition of a 'market' – something that is usually taken as a given in textbooks, but, as we shall see, is fraught with difficulties in practice. The second case considered relates to mergers in the UK cinema market and provides an interesting example of how the CC goes about trying to protect consumer interests against a firm that is seeking to achieve a dominant position in a specific market. The final case looks at an example of an Office of Fair Trading (OFT) investigation into a fairly clear-cut case of restrictive practices. The case concerns the British horse-racing industry and the degree of control exercised over the industry by one of the governing bodies, the British Horseracing Board (BHB).

# 14.1 | Case 1 – market definition in the supermarket industry

In the press and many textbooks, the terms 'industry' and 'market' are often used as being synonymous with each other. However, for our purposes in this chapter, we need to clarify exactly what we mean by the term 'industry' and also to distinguish a firm's markets into two types – input markets and output markets. A firm's 'industry' relates to the input side of a firm – it is the source of the firm's inputs. More specifically, it refers to the set of input markets from which it obtains its factors of production (Figure 14.1), whereas the goods and services produced by firms are sold into an entirely different set of output markets. The term 'industry' is used to refer to the set of input markets shared by a group of firms. In economic terms, the industry/input markets refer to a firm's supply side and relate to the structure of its production costs, whereas a firm's output markets are on the demand side and are the source of the firm's revenue. The markets on the supply side are not the same as the markets on the demand side, in fact a group of firms may draw resources from the same set of input markets (that is, belong to the same industry), but sell their output on to an entirely different set of output markets.

For example, consider the motor car producer Morgan Cars. Morgan Cars belongs to the motor industry: the firm obtains its inputs from a range of input markets such as motor car component suppliers, raw material suppliers, and its workforce

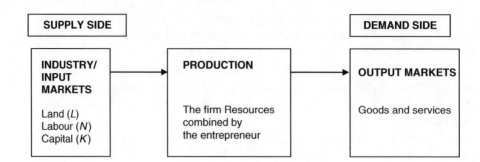

**Figure 14.1**
Industry, markets
and the firm

comes from a series of labour markets. All the other producers in the motor industry will have similar inputs drawn from a similar range of input suppliers. As outlined in Chapter 2, the inputs undergo a transformation process within Morgan Cars and what is produced are high-performance cars. These cars are then sold, in competition with similar high-performance cars, into a particular output market. However, the number of motor manufacturers that produce cars for Morgan Cars market segment is only a small subset of the entire motor industry. Thus, Morgan Cars belongs to the same motor industry as the mass market producers such as Ford, GM and Toyota, but only produces output for the specialised niche high-performance car market.

The importance of the distinction between industry/input markets and output markets becomes apparent when considering the range of approaches devised to try and classify firms into groupings. In practice, they fall into three general categories, which mirror the three elements in Figure 14.1:

1. Industry/input market/supply-side classifications
2. Output market/demand-side classifications
3. Process/firm-based classifications.

In the rest of this section, we shall examine each of these approaches in turn and, in the process, highlight some of the inherent difficulties involved in using classification methods. However, it is worth considering first why economists, statisticians and others have felt the need to try and devise such methods. Generally, three motivations can be identified:

1. For the purposes of public policy
2. Research into specific sectors of the economy
3. To assist firms in the formulation of their strategy.

First, there is the need to have clearly identified groupings of firms for the purposes of public policy, our main concern in this chapter. Later in this section, we shall discuss in detail how the CC (and OFT), when setting out to investigate a particular industry and its related output markets, needs to start the process by identifying exactly which industry and output markets are they are to investigate. However, even though this will be the focus of this chapter, there are other reasons for the government to have clear definitions of industry and output markets. In the past, for example, a government devising an aid package to help industry X needed to know first of all exactly what it meant by industry X. Another reason for having clear definitions of markets is the need of economic researchers to have classification methods to group firms, to model and test theories developed by economic theorists. Finally, the firms themselves need to have some idea, in particular, of their markets and who their main rivals may be, in order to develop and implement strategies.

### 14.1.1  Defining a firm's industry/input markets

The UK government has used industry-based definitions for the classification of economic activity since the introduction of the Standard Industrial Classification (SIC) in 1948. The SIC is a structured hierarchical classification system working down from large general areas of industrial activity to more closely defined industries. Being a classification of industry, it is supply based with firms being grouped in terms of inputs required for the production process. The SIC is revised periodically to take into account changes in the structure of the UK economy. The last major revision took place in 1992 when the SIC was brought into line with the European Union's equivalent classification of industries referred to as the NACE (Nomenclature general des activities economiques dans les Communautes europeenes). There were some minor revisions made for 2003, but the SIC (2003) remains basically the same as SIC (92).

The Department of Trade's (DTI) own introduction to the SIC (92) gives a useful summary of its purpose:

The Classification provides a framework for the collection, tabulation, presentation and analysis of data about economic activities. Its use promotes uniformity of data collected by various Government departments and agencies. In addition it can be used for administrative purposes and by many non-government bodies as a convenient way of classifying industrial activities into a common structure. (http://www.dti.gov.uk)

As stated above, the SIC is a hierarchical classification system which moves from broad industrial sections at the highest level to much more focused subclasses at the lowest. The 1992 revision established the following structure:

17 Sections
14 Subsections
60 Divisions
503 Classes
142 Subclasses

The best way to illustrate how the SIC (92) works is by way of an example. The manufacture of tents has a full SIC (92) classification of DB17.40/2. This classification is determined as follows:

Section D    Manufacturing
Subsection DB    Manufacturing of textiles and textile products
Division 17    Manufacture of textiles
Group 17.4    Manufacture of made up textile articles
Class 17.40    Manufacture of made up textile articles
Subclass 17.40/2    Manufacture of canvas goods.

The industry, or supply side, input basis to the SIC can be seen from this example. From the subsection level down, the classification is purely based on the main inputs into the production process, in this case the production of textiles. The limitations of an industry-based classification can also be readily demonstrated. The SIC number would clearly aid the 'collection tabulation, presentation and analysis of data' relating to tent production; however, it provides very little help when looking at the output side of the tent industry. The output market into which tent producers send tents has two other products that make up the main competitors: trailer tents and caravans. Thus, to examine and analyse the tent producers' output markets you would need to look at not only other tent producers but also caravan and trailer tent producers. However, to do this SIC would be of little use. The manufacture of caravans, for example, has an SIC number of DM34.20/3. Only at the highest level of D (manufacturing) is the manufacture of caravans placed with the manufacture of tents, the reason being that even though they would appear to be close substitutes in terms of the demand-side output markets, they are actually made from quite different inputs. Thus, tents are grouped with the manufacture of canvas goods (sacks, blinds, banners, pennants, etc.) and caravans with trailers and semi-trailers.

## 14.1.2  Defining a firm's output markets

Defining a firm's output markets is in many ways more important from the firm's perspective and for the purposes of competition policy – but it is also a lot more difficult. If a firm is to compete and fulfil its role of generating profits then it is important that it has a clear idea of the market it is competing in and who its main competitors are. Similarly, if the competition authorities are to look at the effects of a firm's actions on economic efficiency then they need to know exactly what output market they are dealing with. In the neo-classical world with homogenous products, this is a trivial problem as a firm's market is clearly defined simply by the product being produced. A firm producing widgets knows it is competing in the widget market and its competitors are all the other firms producing identical widgets. The boundaries of the market are clear, as are the firms producing output for the market.

However, in the real world, the situation is almost always not black and white. One of the commonest features of real-world markets is the widespread existence of product differentiation. Chapter 9 dealt with product differentiation in detail. In that chapter, we referred to product differentiation as being the means by which firms try and set their own product apart from their competitors and, in the process, create output markets that are typified by heterogeneous and not homogenous products. As discussed in Chapter 9, the means by which firms try to differentiate their products can be classified into two general types, vertical and horizontal. Some firms seek to differentiate their product by means of producing products that are of a higher quality and thus aim for vertical differentiation (or quality differentiation). To produce higher quality products almost always means the use of more expensive materials and/or more costly production processes. Thus, the firm incurs higher production costs and therefore charges prices that are correspondingly higher.

Using the example from Chapter 9, consider disposable Bic biros and gold-nibbed Mont Blanc fountain pens. Both are the same product in that they ultimately serve the same function – they are both pens used for writing. However, the higher quality, and hence higher production cost and price of the Mont Blanc pen, sets it apart from the disposable Bic biro. What we can say is that the higher quality Mont Blanc pen is vertically differentiated from the cheaper disposable Bic biro. The second type of product differentiation is horizontal (or range) differentiation. In this case, the products are of the same quality but are differentiated by their characteristics. For example, cheap disposable pens come in a range of colours (both ink and casing) and nib types (fine or medium).

Both vertical and horizontal product differentiations create markets with hetero-geneous goods and services and not the homogenous markets found in the neo-classical world – the theoretical and strategic implications of this have been discussed in Chapter 9. One other outcome of product differentiation is that it makes the definition of a market in the real world much less clear-cut than in the neo-classical world, where there would be one homogenous pen produced by all pen-making firms. But in the real world with vertical and horizontal product differentiations, drawing boundaries around markets becomes more difficult. Do expensive Mont Blanc pens belong to the same market as cheap disposable Bic biros? Do Mont Blanc pens actually belong in the 'pen' market at all, or are they in another market we might refer to as the 'expensive gift' market competing with Rolex watches and crystal whisky tumblers. Similarly, you could also ask the question, do red biros compete directly with blue biros? What is needed is a method that can be used to help define clearly what the market for product X actually is. Four possible approaches to trying to define market boundaries are considered:

1. Cross elasticity of demand
2. The hypothetical monopolist
3. The judgement of participants
4. Price bands.

### 14.1.2.1 Cross elasticity of demand

Economic theory provides one possible method that can be used to clearly define market boundaries, the concept of cross elasticity of demand. Cross elasticity measures the responsiveness of demand for one product to changes in the prices of another. The formula is

$$\text{Cross elasticity of demand } (\eta_x) = dQ_x/dP_y$$

A value $>0$ indicates $x$ and $y$ are substitutes showing that as the price of $y$ increases the demand for $x$ rises – as the price of coffee rises then the demand for the substitute product tea will also rise. A value $<0$ indicates that $x$ and $y$ are complements showing that as the price of $y$ rises then the demand for $x$ falls – the rise in the price of coffee will lead to a fall in the demand for coffee percolators. Therefore, if a high positive value of $\eta_x$ is found between two products then this demonstrates a high level of substitutability between products. This in turn indicates that they are in close competition with each other and therefore, we could conclude that they belong to the same market. We may reasonably expect this to be the case with tea and coffee, but perhaps not the case with coffee and apple juice. Coffee and apple juice are both drinks, but there is not likely to be much of a $\eta_x$ relationship between them, thus we cannot put them in the same market. In general, one outcome of product differentiation is the division of markets into a series of sub-markets, and the use of $\eta_x$ is one method of dividing a market into its various sub-markets (consider Figure 14.2).

The figure shows a matrix of cross elasticities between six related products in the imaginary widget market. In the figure, 'H' indicates a high positive $\eta_x$, 'L' a low positive $\eta_x$ and 'M' a middling $\eta_x$. From the figure there seems to be high cross elasticities existing between the following pairs of products: 2 and 4; 1 and 6; 3 and 5. Therefore, we can conclude that these pairs, in effect, are defining the existence of three clear sub-markets within the overall widget market. However, the figure also reveals the relationship among the three sub-markets. The sub-markets represented by the pairings 2–4 and 5–3 seem to have low $\eta_x$ suggesting that they are not particularly close substitutes, whereas the sub-market 1–6 appears to have some substitutability with the other sub-markets. This can be summarised in Figure 14.3 (this representation is based on Shepherd (1990)).

The figure shows the three sub-markets A, B and C. Within each market there is a high degree of $\eta_x$ between the products – product 2 is a close substitute for product 4, for example. What the diagram also shows is that market B contains

**Figure 14.2**
Cross elasticity of demand and market definition

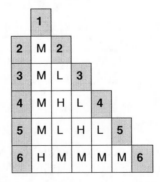

**Figure 14.3** Division of sub-markets within the Widget market

products 1 and 6 which have a close substitutability with each other, but also some substitutability with all the other products, hence its positioning between markets A and C. Both markets A and C, however, have low substitutability; hence they are positioned apart from each other. Thus, if the price of product 1 rose then we would expect to see a significant raise in the demand for product 6. However, we may also see some effect on the demand for products 2, 3, 4 and 5 – not as significant as for product 6, but still some positive relationship. If, however, the price of product 2 rose then we would see a significant raise in demand for product 4, some increase in demand for products 1 and 6, but no significant change in the demand for products 3 and 5 in sub-market C.

To illustrate, consider the pen example used to explain vertical product differentiation previously. In Figure 14.3, the three sub-markets could be low-price, mid-price and high-price pens. Products 2 and 4 in Figure 14.3 could be two of the popular makes of fairly cheap disposable pens, Bic and Staedtler for example, whereas products 5 and 3 could be expensive Mont Blanc and Waterman pens, respectively. You would expect that the $\eta_x$ between Bic and Staedtler pens would be quite a high positive figure indicating the sensitivity of one to changes in the price of the other. However, you would not expect changes in the price of Bic pens to have effects on the demand for Mont Blanc or Waterman pens. There may, however, be some weaker price sensitivity between the demand for Bic pens and the price of some mid-range pens, say Parker pens, and similarly some weak relationship between Parker pens and Waterman pens. If this was the case then Figure 14.4 summarises the three sub-markets and the relationship between them.

Thus, the use of cross elasticity of demand could be one approach to the defining of the boundaries around markets. In principle, this approach could be used in more complex markets than those considered in Figure 14.2. For example, there could be a product 7 that had some unique features that gave it a middling $\eta_x$ with all the other six products. This would add a fourth sub-market (Figure 14.5) ranging across the other three as shown in Figure 14.4.

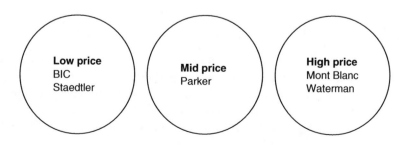

**Figure 14.4** Subdivision of the pen market

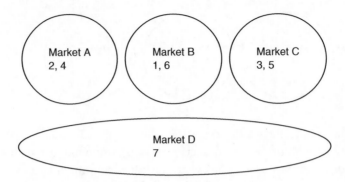

**Figure 14.5** More complex set of sub-markets

Cross elasticity, therefore, gives us a rigorous theoretical means for the defining of market boundaries. The problem, however, with using cross elasticity is that in practice estimating the co-efficient and coming up with a matrix as in Figure 14.2 is extremely difficult and not very practical from a firm's point of view.

### 14.1.2.2 The hypothetical monopolist

Another method of trying to establish market boundaries which also uses economic theory is to use the concept of a hypothetical monopolist. Economic theory defines a monopoly as being the situation when the firm is the industry, and therefore, has the ability to raise price to the profit maximising point where $MC = MR$. Therefore, the question when trying to define a market should be: if we put together the three largest firms competing in market X would that combined firm have monopoly control over the market, that is, would the combined firm have the power to raise the price to the monopolist's profit maximising level? If the answer is yes, then you have defined the market. But if the answer is no then there must be firms that have been left out that are acting as a competitive restraint on the hypothetical monopolist. Thus, for example, if Bic and Staedtler were merged would the newly merged firm have monopoly control over sub-market A in Figure 14.4, the market for low-priced pens? If yes, then Bic and Staedtler cover the entire market for low-priced pens and hence could raise prices, if no then there are other firms in sub-market A that do not appear in Figure 14.4.

### 14.1.2.3 Judgement of participants

One commonly used method, for example by the CC, to determine a market boundary is to ask the companies involved, or the consumers, their opinions on what they consider the market for a particular product to be. For example, to determine the market for low-price pens you could ask the manufacturers of Bic and Staedtler pens who they thought their main competitors were.

## 14.1.2.4 Price bands

This is a common method of breaking identifiable markets down into various sub-markets using the idea of vertical product differentiation. As discussed previously, vertical product differentiation reflects quality differences between the products concerned, and hence prices. Products of similar quality and price would be grouped together in price bands, and you would expect prices to move together within each price band. Returning to our example of the market for pens, you would expect that the closest competitors to Bic, Parker and Mont Blanc, respectively, would be those pens in the similar price band. You would, therefore, expect that when Bic changed prices then Steadtler would respond, but Mont Blanc would not. The reasons for the price movements could relate to a change in the price of some common input (for example, a rise in the price for plastic due to high oil prices) or could be evidence of price leadership within the market segment.

## 14.1.3 Process base definitions

A process-based definition is the least common method used in categorising firms and is closely linked to the resource-based view of the firm discussed in Chapter 7. This approach uses the actual production process itself to classify firms, thus firms using similar production methods would be grouped together.

Whilst less common, this approach can help explain some less than obvious diversification and merger decisions that have taken place which, when looking at supply- or demand-based definitions, appear odd. For example, in Chapter 7, we looked at the movement in the UK in recent years of the merging together of the retail end of the gas, electric, fixed line telephone and water industries – the part of these industries' production chain that constitutes the actual provision of the service to the final consumer. Using a demand- or supply-based classification method, with the possible exception in a demand-based definition of gas and electric firms, these industries/markets would not be particularly close to each other. The inputs into the four industries are quite different as, with the above exception, are the outputs. However, when the firms supplying these utilities are looked at from a process-based perspective, they are actually employing very similar processes – competencies to use the terminology developed in Chapter 7. As noted previously all of them involve the management of a large consumer base with very similar requirements in terms of billing and collection of payments. Two of the four services require visits to property to obtain the billing information (and increasingly water billing is being based on a metering system).

## 14.1.4 An illustration of market definition

To illustrate, some of the methods and issues involved in market and industry definition, it is useful to look at a particular example. As mentioned previously, competition authorities are faced with having to define markets and industries every time they are asked to investigate a case. The example used here is the CC investigation into the UK supermarket sector.

Early in 2003, the predominantly north of England-based supermarket chain Morrisons launched a takeover bid for the rival supermarket Safeways. Prompted by the fear of losing market share, the other three large national supermarket chains of Asda, Sainsbury's and Tesco immediately put in counter bids for the Safeways chain. The entry of Asda, Tesco and Sainsbury's into the bidding war led the OFT to commission a report from the CC, in the belief that merging Safeways into any of the other national supermarket chains may give the new group too large a market share and be detrimental to competition within the industry. In the terms used in Chapter 13, the CC were worried that the merger could give one of the newly combined supermarkets a position of market dominance.

The report was published in September 2003 (Competition Commission, 2003). As with all CC reports, one of the first issues tackled was to try and produce a clear definition of the market under investigation and, given that we are talking about a national market, this provides a particularly interesting example of how the CC approach this issue.

The CC report reveals the process that was gone through in order to define the output market they were looking at – industry definition was largely taken as given. They considered two aspects:

■ The identification of market segments
■ The identification of geographic markets.

### 14.1.4.1 The definition of market segments

The CC were not working from scratch on this aspect of market definition as there had been a report carried out in 2000 that required a similar definition of the markets that supermarkets were operating in. In effect, in 2003, the CC concentrated on ensuring that the 2000 definition was still valid. Of the four approaches discussed in Section 14.1.2, the method used was the judgements of participants. The supermarkets, customers (via previous supermarket and independent surveys) and a trade association (Association of Convenience Stores) were consulted. The conclusion was that there were two clear sub-markets: 'one-stop shopping' and 'convenience shopping'.

The definition of 'one-stop shopping' from 2000 was 'one-stop grocery shopping carried out in stores of 1,400 sq metres or more' (Competition Commission, 2003, p. 163), where a one-stop shop is defined as a store that provides 'the range and depth of goods in order for consumers to fulfil their main shopping needs in one visit'. The CC tested this definition by asking the supermarkets for their views as to whether this definition was still valid. The result was a difference of opinion over whether the term 'grocery' was still appropriate due to the growth of non-grocery items since 2000 offered by supermarkets. All of the firms now offer an increasing range of clothes, electrical goods, books, stationary and many other non-grocery products in their larger stores. However, evidence from customer surveys suggested that the one-stop shopping still referred predominately to grocery shopping, as Asda pointed out 'one stop shopping . . . is based on a weekly grocery shop, because consumers did not shop weekly for non-grocery items'.

The CC identified a second sub-market that was defined as convenience shopping. Again the market definition adopted was based upon the method of asking the market participants, which this time included a trade association, the Association of Convenience Stores (ACS). The definition given by the ACS was of stores that 'embraced a wide range of products, usually and increasingly, for consumption within two hours'. The market is also made up of a range of stores from a variety of backgrounds such as tobacconists, confectioners, news agents and those with a groceries background. The CC also considered whether there was a third market segment, a 'top-up' market for consumers who supplemented their groceries in between the main 'one-stop' shop. The conclusion, again based on the evidence of the supermarkets, was that this did not constitute a clear separated market segment.

Therefore, the report splits the market into two broad categories, one-stop shopping and convenience shopping. The two markets appear to be clear and distinct with the one-stop market being an oligopoly dominated by the large national chains, whereas the convenience market is more competitive due to the large numbers of stores and low entry barriers.

### 14.1.4.2   The geographic market

The CC, however, did not use these broad categories as their final definition of the market. They came to the conclusion that within both broad categories the actual competitive market place should be split down further based upon customer travel times. The definition that was arrived at not only used evidence from the supermarkets, but also makes use of the concept of the hypothetical monopolist as discussed in Section 14.1.2. However, before considering the definition arrived at it is worth dwelling on a difference of opinion that is recorded in the report, between Tesco on the one hand and Asda and Sainsbury's on the other. The debate highlights the sort of issues that can arise in any attempt to find a clear definition of a market.

Both Asda and Sainsbury's claimed that the market was a local market defined in terms of time the majority of consumers were prepared to travel to the store, roughly 10 min for urban areas and 15 for rural areas. Figure 14.6 illustrates this.

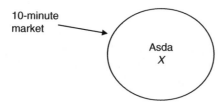

**Figure 14.6**
Geographical-based market definition

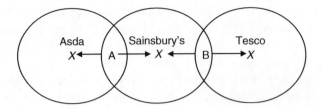

**Figure 14.7** The continuous chain of substitution

The urban Asda store is at the centre of a 10-min drive market boundary. The argument made is that if Asda was the only store within this market boundary then this would make the store a hypothetical monopolist within its local market, the store could raise prices without a significant reduction in revenue. However, Tesco tried to argue the counter case – that their output market is not a series of local markets but one large national market. They make use of the concept of a 'continuous chain of substitution'. Consider Figure 14.7.

Let us look at the case of consumer A who lives within the boundaries of two geographical sub-markets, one where Asda is the hypothetical monopolist and one where Sainsbury's is the hypothetical monopolist. In other words, he lives just within the 10-min drive time limit for Asda if he goes one way and Sainsbury's if he goes the other; however, the distance between the two supermarkets is greater than a 10-min market defining boundary. Customer A has a choice between Asda and Sainsbury's; both are within the required 10-min drive boundary. Customer B is in a similar position being within the boundary of both Sainsbury's monopoly area and Tesco's. The point made by Tesco is that this, in effect, creates a chain of overlapping local markets which means that none of the supermarkets actually have any monopoly power in their own 10-min monopoly area. The actions of Asda need to take account of Sainsbury's in the next market. If Asda were to suddenly raise prices this would lead to the loss of customer A and all those in the overlapping area. There are similar considerations for Sainsbury's and Tesco in relation to customer B. The interlinking of local markets creates in fact one chain of markets with all three supermarkets in competition with each other. Thus, none of the three supermarkets have the monopoly power to raise prices, in fact Figure 14.7 shows one combined market, not three separate local markets. Tesco supported this view by demonstrating that in the Birmingham and Wolverhampton area this idea of chains of local markets creates one market with over 1 million customers.

However, in the end, the CC did not accept Tesco's case for the one-shop market being a single national market. It is not clear in the report why this is the case, but even a brief consideration of Tesco's argument shows some serious flaws. For example, Sainbury's could raise prices in their local market and indeed lose customers A and B, but this could be more than compensated for by the additional revenue raised from the remaining customers. The CC adopted the definition of the supermarkets' output markets based upon a series of local markets defined by the distance that customers were prepared to drive. The CC also adopted a similar view in relation to the convenience store market.

In the final report, the merger between Morrisons and Safeways was allowed to take place. However, when a newly combined Morrison-Safeways was created in the same market as an existing store Morrisons were forced to sell one of the stores to one of their supermarket rivals. What this example clearly illustrates is how some of the methods of market definition may actually be used in practice, and also some of the difficulties of arriving at clearly defined markets.

## 14.2    Case 2 – Mergers in the cinema industry

The second example we shall deal with relates to the UK Cinema industry. The information used in this section comes from the CC report 'Vue Enterprise Holdings (UK) Ltd and A3 Cinemas (UK) Ltd: A Report on the complete acquisition of A3 Cinemas by Vue Entertainment Holdings (UK) Ltd' dated 24 February 2006.

### 14.2.1    The basis of the referral

In April 2005, one of the UK's leading owners of cinemas, Vue Entertainment, acquired a smaller rival group called A3 Cinemas (who operated under the name of Ster). Prior to the takeover Vue owned 42 cinemas (409 screens) whilst Ster owned 6 cinemas (97 screens). The total market share of cinemas in the newly merged group increased as a result by 2.2 to 16 per cent of the UK national market. However, what concerned the OFT was not the increase in national market share, which was still well below the 25 per cent required to trigger a possible referral under the 'share of market' test, but the effect in four of the locations. From Vue's perspective, one of the principle motivations for taking over the Ster cinemas was that they complemented their current chain being located mainly in locations which Vue felt did not overlap with their existing cinema complexes. However, the Commission did not agree.

As with the supermarket case in Section 14.1, the market for cinemas was defined in local not national terms. Also, as we saw with the supermarkets, the basis of the market definition was in terms of drive time – two cinemas within a 10/20 min drive of each other were considered to be in direct competition. On this basis the takeover by Vue of the Ster cinemas in Basingstoke, Edinburgh, Leeds and Romford failed the market share test. In each of these towns/cities, the newly merged Vue would effectively remove the only competitor within a 20 min drive of their existing cinema. This formed the basis of the referral by the OFT to the CC of the takeover of Ster by Vue.

### 14.2.2    The nature of the market

The revenue earned by the cinema operators comes from two main sources: box office admissions and 'concessions' (sales of drink and food). In 2004, the total revenue generated by box office admission was £650 m whilst concessions

**Table 14.1** Main national cinema operators in October 2004

| Operator | Screens | Market share (%) | (Market share/100)² |
|---|---|---|---|
| Terra Firma (Odeon – UCI) | 924 | 27.6 | 0.076 |
| Cineworld | 787 | 23.5 | 0.055 |
| Vue | 409 | 12.2 | 0.015 |
| National amusements (Showcase) | 237 | 7.0 | 0.005 |
| National total | 3342 | | |

*Source*: Competition Commission Report (2006) 'Vue Enterprise Holdings (UK) Ltd and A3 Cinemas (UK) Ltd: A Report on the complete acquisition of A3 Cinemas by Vue Entertainment Holdings (UK) Ltd' paragraph 4.10.

produced £204 m of revenue. In 2004, there were 171.3 million cinema admissions, the highest since 1972, although there has been a decline since. At the end of 2004, there were a total of 646 cinemas in the UK with 3342 screens. The industry is dominated by four national chains, summarised in Table 14.1.

On the basis of this data, we can see that even though Vue had a 13.8 per cent share of cinemas prior to their takeover of Ster, their share of screens was lower at only 12.2 per cent (note that this is lower than the 16 per cent share of cinemas quoted above suggesting Vue have fewer screens per cinema than the industry average). We can use the information in the table to calculate some of the concentration measures developed in Chapter 11 (see Section 11.3.1). Summing the market shares of these top four firms gives a $CR_4$ for the industry of 70.3 per cent, which points to a fairly highly concentrated industry. By summing the squared market shares as shown in the final column of the table, we can calculate the HHI for the industry (on the basis that the operators' market shares outside of these four are insignificant) as being 0.151 which translates into a numbers equivalent of 6.62. Again this suggests an oligopoly structure to the industry. However, as has been discussed above, the CC recognised that cinemas do not compete on a national level but at a much more localised town-based level. Therefore, interesting as the information in Table 14.1 might be, it does not really reflect how competitive the market actually is.

Using the five-forces framework discussed in Chapter 12, we can clarify some of the issues raised in the report, in relation to not only the competitive forces at work but also the nature of the industry's structure (Figure 14.8).

### 14.2.2.1 Sellers

Around 450 films are released a year and these are rented by the cinema firms from the film distributors. The power relationship in Figure 14.8 is shown as pointing both ways to indicate that there is probably equality in the relationship between the suppliers of films and the large national cinema chains that show the films. The cinemas rely on the film distributors for the rental of the

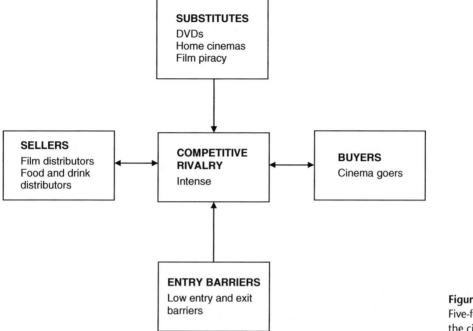

**Figure 14.8**
Five-forces analysis of
the cinema industry

films and, equally, the film distributors rely on the cinemas for showing the films across the country. Where the power relationship may change is when we are dealing with either smaller non-national chains or small niche suppliers of films. For example, recently Easycinema was set up as an off-shoot of the Easyjet brand offering the same 'no-frills' cinema experience as the airline and cut price admission compared with the national chains. However, the firm had difficulty renting the most recent and popular films as they were only located in a small number of locations and the film distributors were worried about upsetting the more powerful national chains. The power lay with the film distributors, not the brash new Easycinema group.

### 14.2.2.2 Buyers

In the relationship between the cinemas and their customers, the power balance rests on whether the customers have a choice between cinemas or not. If there is a choice then the balance of power lies with the customers as they can choose which cinema to go to. If there is no choice then the balance of power rests with the cinema, as the CC found little evidence that there was much competition to cinemas from other types of leisure activities.

### 14.2.2.3 Substitutes

The CC concluded that DVDs, home cinemas and film piracy were significant factors increasing the competitive nature of the industry.

### 14.2.2.4   Entry barriers

During the last 20 years, 11 companies have operated within the industry, most have now either left or been taken over by rivals. The CC took this as evidence that both entry and exit barriers to the market are relatively low – buying and selling cinemas is fairly easy.

### 14.2.2.5   Competitive rivalry

Taking the low entry barriers as a whole, strong pressure from substitutes and (where there was local competition) consumer choice leads to an intensely competitive industry. This was further supported by the fact that even though cinema attendance had declined since the high of 2004, the number of customers per screen has increased.

### 14.2.2.6   The nature of competition

Price was found not to be the main factor in attracting customers. The main competitive factor was location. Cinemas need to be accessible, either close to or even in shopping complexes or have easy access by car and adequate parking – the ideal location is one that combines both elements. Secondary in terms of competition is a whole range of non-price factors such as quality of service, cleanliness and audio–visual standard.

## 14.2.3   The Competition Commission findings

Before considering the effect of the merger on each of the four locations where the market share of Vue would have increased beyond the 25 per cent trigger value, the CC considered whether Ster would have remained a competitive threat to Vue if it had remained independent. In their submission to the CC, A3 (the owners of Ster) indicated that part of their strategic plan had been to give the Ster cinemas 3–5 years to prove themselves as profitable concerns. If at the end to this period, the cinemas were not thought to be profitable, then A3 would have sold the chain. The CC concluded, therefore, that Ster would have remained as a competitive rival to Vue, either as an independent chain or as part of one of Vue's rivals.

The CC looked at each of the four identified local markets which failed the initial market share test in some detail. In the case of three of the markets – Edinburgh, Leeds and Romford – they found in favour of the Vue. The CC considered that as each of these markets is part of a major urban conurbation, and there were sufficient alternatives for consumers within a reasonable distance, the merger of the Ster cinemas in these locations into the Vue group would not significantly reduce consumer choice. However, in the case of Basingstoke the conclusion was that there was potentially a significant problem.

The takeover of the Ster cinema in Basingstoke, in the judgement of the CC, would give Vue a monopoly in the local market, as defined by the 20-min drive time rule. In addition the CC suggested that there was some evidence that on acquiring the Ster cinema complex in Basingstoke that Vue would close down their older and less conveniently located current cinema complex. In summary, the Commission raised three possible adverse effects of the takeover by Vue of the Ster cinema complex in Basingstoke:

1. The monopoly position would enable Vue to raise prices.
2. Due to the lack of competition there would be no incentive for Vue to improve the quality of their cinemas.
3. The monopoly position, and the possible closure of one of the cinemas, would reduce consumer choice.

As is usual Vue were given the opportunity to respond to the issues raised by the CC. In the report, these are presented as 'behavioural remedies'. In response to the potential price issue, Vue suggested that the CC should consider imposing a price cap which would keep prices down to the norm elsewhere. This was rejected by the CC as being too complex to administer and open to wide interpretation. In response to the second issue, Vue proposed that they would commit themselves to an equivalent maintenance budget for both cinema complexes to ensure the physical environment of both locations. The CC rejected this on the basis that maintaining the physical infrastructure of the two cinema complexes was only a partial means to maintaining quality – quality went a lot further than well-maintained buildings. In response to the final issue, Vue did offer guarantees that they would keep both cinemas open and not reduce the number of screens available. This the Commission accepted.

However, overall the Commission felt that the 'behavioural remedies' offered by Vue were insufficient – they only really dealt with the third issue in full. The final recommendation of the Commission was that Vue were to sell one of the cinema complexes in Basingstoke, thus safeguarding the cinema-goers in Basingstoke from a possible increase in price, reduction in quality and reduction in choice.

## 14.3   Case 3 – Restrictive practices at BHB and the Jockey Club

For the final case, we deal with an example of a firm abusing its position so as to maintain a position of market dominance, rather than create one as in the previous two examples. The case illustrates an example of restrictive practices that was investigated by the OFT.

In April 2003, the OFT published a report that presented the conclusions of its investigation into the British horse-racing industry, 'The British Horseracing Board and the Jockey Club: a summary of the OFT's case' (OFT (a)). The report highlights what the OFT considered to be overrigorous control of the horseracing industry by the British Horseracing Board (BHB) through its 'Orders and Rules' which, in the view of the OFT, constituted a clear case of restrictive practices. In the months following the report, the BHB and OFT negotiated an agreement on changes to be made by the BHB to its Orders and Rules, summarised in a June 2004 press release (OFT (b)). The following is a summary of the OFT case and the resulting changes agreed by the BHB as a result of the OFT report.

### 14.3.1 The structure of the British horse-racing industry

The horse-racing industry in the UK is controlled by two bodies – the Jockey Club and the BHB. Figure 14.9 summarises the production process for the industry.

The inputs are the horses and their owners, the jockeys and the trainers. These inputs are brought together by the racecourse owners who then produce the output which is the actual race meetings. As can be seen from the diagram, the Jockey Club has a central role in this production process acting as a licensee for the inputs. The Jockey Club also have a role in overseeing the integrity of the output – a vital role in an industry where gambling is the principle source of income.

The BHB is a relatively new body having been set up in 1993 by the Jockey Club who had controlled racing since 1752. The BHB has four members: the Jockey Club; the Racecourse Association Ltd; the Racehorse Owners Association Ltd and Industry Committee (Horseracing) Ltd (representing the jockeys, trainers and others involved in the industry). The BHB's role is twofold. First, it is responsible for the strategic development of British horse racing and its promotion and marketing. Second, the BHB acts as the main organising body for the industry. In effect, it controlled, through its Orders and Rules, the link in Figure 14.9 between the production and output – in other words it controls the output market. On investigation, the OFT found that this control over the output market covered:

- Frequency of race meetings
- The scheduling of race meetings
- The number of races allowed at each meeting
- Ensuring that no race meetings take place at the same time within a 50-mile boundary
- Setting the minimum and maximum levels of prize money
- Determining the distribution of prize money between races.

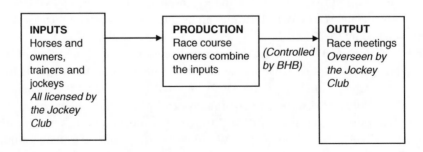

**Figure 14.9** The production process of horse racing

It was this control of the production–output link, and hence the output market, which the OFT found to be objectionable. In OFT's view, the list above represented a list of restrictive practices that were acting as a check on competition in the industry:

> in the absence of centralised BHB control of racecards, racecourses would be free to respond to consumer demand by increasing the number of races on a card, changing the mix of races; changing the way they classify races; and providing more racing opportunities for lower rated horses. (OFT (a), p. 5)

In addition, the OFT found that the BHB was also creating a strategic entry barrier by maintaining sole control over information relating to runners and riders. This is, of course, crucial information for bookmakers and racecourses, information which could only be obtained from the BHB. In effect, the BHB was acting as a monopoly supplier of the key information required by the industry in order to generate revenue. The OFT's view of this practice was:

> 'that the Orders and Rules underpin the BHB's monopoly supply of race and runners data and stop both racecourses and third parties from collating and supplying race and runners data on a commercial basis directly to book makers in competition with the BHB'. (OFT (a), p. 6)

The OFT concluded that this was, again, an illegal restrictive practice.

The OFT report on the BHB and the Jockey Club was published in April 2003 and the two industry bodies were asked to respond to the allegations made in relation to restrictive practices. By June 2004, the OFT had reached an agreement with the BHB (the Jockey Club were not seen to the culprits in the practices outlined above) under which the BHB had agreed to:

- An increase in the overall number of racing fixtures.
- The introduction of a new process by which racecourses will be able to compete for existing racing fixtures and to bid for new ones.
- An end to the '50-mile rule', which prevented racecourses within 50 miles of each other from offering racing on the same date.
- An increase in racecourses' freedom to determine the types of racing they each put on.
- The creation of a new body, British Horseracing Enterprises, which will be responsible for commercialisation of the BHB racing database.
- The introduction of a new method by which income from the commercialisation of racing data will be passed on to racecourses in direct relation to their success in attracting betting.

■ The introduction of an arbitration mechanism to provide a pricing safeguard for bookmakers in the event that BHB proposes specified increases in the price charged for access to its racing database.

In OFT's view, these measures would increase competition within the industry and increase choice for the consumers.

## 14.4 Review and further reading

The three examples show the type of investigations and methods the competition authorities in the UK undertake to try and ensure that economic markets work effectively. As can be seen in each of the three examples, the customers of the firms were of primary concern. In the first two cases, the CC considered carefully the most appropriate means of defining the output market and in both cases fixed on a geographical definition based on the ability of consumers to access the products of the firms, in one case a supermarket and in the second case a cinema complex. Therefore, in both cases the market definition used was a localised definition recognising that, even though the firms may be national firms, for most consumers their own economic market for many goods and services is defined by a 10–20-min drive time from their front doors. The focus of both the CC reports was to maintain consumer choice and prevent the firms creating localised monopolies which would allow them to transfer some of the consumer surplus to themselves as abnormal profits through the raising of prices. The cinema example also shows that not only price but other non-price factors such as quality and service are also important considerations; this echoes quote 2 from the DTI discussed at the opening to Chapter 13:

> Where markets work well, they provide strong incentives for good performance – encouraging firms to improve productivity, to reduce prices and to innovate; whilst rewarding consumers with lower prices, higher quality, and wider choice. (DTI(a))

The third example relates to the use of strategic entry barriers by the BHB to restrict both entry to the output market and severely limit competition in the market. In this case, the OFT's role was to lower the entry barriers and hence try to make the market more contestable. Again the interests of the consumers were at the forefront, and also, in this case, the racecourses who were being restricted in terms of responding to what they saw as consumer demand – more race meetings at times were determined by them, not the BHB.

As commented on at the end of Chapter 13, the DTI, OFT and CC websites contain copies, all the reports used in this chapter and many more. They also contain papers on the methodologies adopted and used by the competition authorities.

# 14.5 | Student exercises

## 14.5.1 Review exercises and points for discussion

1.  Provide brief and clear definitions of the following key terms and concepts as used in this chapter.

    a.  Supply-side market classification
    b.  Demand-side market classification
    c.  Process-based market classification
    d.  The hypothetical monopolist
    e.  Cross elasticity of demand.

2.  From the information in Section 14.2, on the UK cinema industry briefly summarise the main elements of market structure, market conduct and market performance. Would the SCP framework be an appropriate method to assess this industry?

## 14.5.2 Application exercise

Select a recent CC report.

a.  Outline the method of market definition used.
b.  Use one of the models or frameworks of environmental analysis discussed in Chapters 11 and 12 to analyse the market.
c.  Summarise the outcome of the report and discuss how this relates to the stated aims of competition policy as set out in the four quotations from the DTI website used in the introduction to Chapter 13.

# References

Alchian, Armen A. and Demsetz, H., Production, Information Costs and Economic Organisation, *American Economic Review* 62 (5), 777–795, 1972

Ansoff, H. Igor, *Corporate Strategy* (New York, McGraw-Hill, 1965)

Backhouse, Roger E., *The Penguin History of Economics* (London, Penguin Books, 2002)

Bain, J., *Barriers to New Competition* (Cambridge, MA, Harvard University Press, 1956)

Barney, J., Looking Inside for Competitive Advantage, *Academy of Management Review* 9 (4), 1995

Barney, Jay, *Gaining and Sustaining Competitive Advantage* (Reading, MA, Harlow, Addison-Wesley, 1997)

Baumol, W.J., *Business Behaviour, Value and Growth* (Harcourt, New York, Brace & World, Revised Edn, 1967)

Baumol, W.J., Panzar, J.C. and Willig R.D. *Contestable Markets and the Theory of Industrial Structure* (Harcourt, New York, Brace and Jonanvitch, 1982)

Begg, D.K.H., Fischer, S. and Dornbusch, R., *Economics* (London, McGraw-Hill, 2003)

Berle, A.A. Jr and Means, G.C., *The Modern Corporation and Private Property* (New York, Macmillan, 1932)

Brandenburger, A.M. and Nalebuff, B.J., The Right Game: Use Game Theory to Shape Strategy, *Harvard Business Review* (July–August 1995)

Chandler, A.D., *The Visible Hand: The Managerial Revolution in American Business* (Cambridge, MA, Harvard University Press, 1977)

Clarke, R. and McGuiness, T., *The Economics of the Firm* (Blackwell, 1987)

Coase, R.H., The Nature of the Firm, *Economica* 4, 1937

Cyert, R.M. and March, J.G., *A Behavioural Theory of the Firm* (London, Prentice-Hall, 1963)

Demsetz, H., Why Regulate Utilities? *Journal of Law and Economics*, pp. 55–65, 1968

Department of Trade and Industry (DTI (a)), http://www.dti.gov.uk/ccp/topics2/ukpolicy.htm 13/02/2004

Department of Trade and Industry (DTI (b)), http://www.dti.gov.uk/ccp/topics2/ecpolicy.htm 13/02/2004

Department of Trade and Industry (DTI (c)), http://www.innovation.gov.uk/value_added/home.asp?p=home 13/05/2006

Dixit, A., Recent Developments in Oligopoly Theory, *American Economic Review, Papers and Proceedings* 96, 1982

Faulkner, D. and Child, M., *Cooperative Strategy: Economic, Business and Organisational Issues* (Oxford, OUP, 2001)

Foss, N. (ed), *Resources, Firms and Strategies* (Oxford, OUP, 1997)

Fudenberg, D. and Tirole, J., *Game Theory* (Cambridge, MA, MIT Press, 1991)

Hamal, G. and Prahalad, C.K., *Competing for the Future* (Boston, MA, Harvard Business School Press, 1994)

Hannah, L. and Kay, J.A., *Concentration in Modern Industry* (London, Macmillan, 1977)

Hay, Donald A. and Morris, Derek J., *Industrial Economics and Organisation* (OUP, 1991)

Hey, D. (ed) *Current Controversies in Microeconomics* (Basingstoke, Macmillan, 1991)

Hotelling, H., Stability in Competition, *The Economic Journal,* pp. 41–57, 1929

Jensen, M.C. and Meckling, W.H., The Theory of the Firm: Managerial Behaviour, Agency Costs and Ownership Structure, *Journal of Financial Economics*, 3, 305–360, 1976

Johnson, G., Scholes, K. and Whittington, R., *Exploring Corporate Strategy* (Harlow, FT, Prentice-Hall, 7th Edn, 2005)

Johnson, P. (ed.), *The Structure of British Industry* (London, Allen & Unwin, 1988)

Kay, J.A. and Thompson, D.J., Privatisation: A Policy in Search of a Rational, *The Economic Journal,* pp. 18–32, 1986

Kay, John, *The Foundations of Corporate Success* (Oxford, Oxford University Press, 1995)

Koutsoyiannis, A., *Modern Microeconomics* (London, Macmillan, 2nd Edn, 1979)

Learned, E.P., Christensen, C.R., Andrews, K.R. and Guth, W.D., *Business Policy: Texts and Cases* (Homewood, IL, Irwin, 1965)

Lipsey, R.G., *An Introduction to Positive Economics* (London, Weidenfeld & Nicolson, 7th Edn, 1989)

Lynch, Richard L., *Corporate Strategy* (Harlow, FT, Prentice-Hall, 2002)

Marris, R., *Theory of 'Managerial' Capitalism* (New York, Macmillan, 1964)

McGee, J. and Thomas, H., Strategic Groups: Theory, Research and Taxonomy, *Strategic Management Journal* 6, 1986

Milgrom, Paul and Roberts, John, *Economics, Organisation and Management* (London, Prentice-Hall, 1992)

Mill, J.S., *The Principles of Political Economy* (London, Longmans, 1911)

Mintel (2005a) Mintel 'National Newspaper UK', October 2005 http://reports.mintel.com (accessed 16th August 2005) 03/05/2006

Mintel (2005b) Mintel 'Food Retailing UK', November 2005 http://reports.mintel.com (accessed 16th May 2006)

Mintzberg, H., *The Structuring of Organisations* (London, Prentice-Hall, 1979)

Mintzberg, H., Ahlstrand, B. and Lampel, J., *Strategy Safari* (Europe, Prentice-Hall, 1998)

Modigliani, F., New Developments on the Oligopoly Front, *Journal of Political Economy* 66, 1958

Mullins, Laurie, *Management and Organisational Behaviour* (Harlow, FT, Prentice-Hall, 2004)

Nalebuff, Adam M. and Brandenburger, Barry J., *Co-opertition* (London, Harper-Collins Business, 1996)

Nelson, R.R., Why do Firms Differ, and How Does it Matter, *Strategic Management Review* 14, 1991

Nelson, R.R. and Winter, S.G., *An Evolutionary Theory of Economic Change* (Cambridge, MA, Harvard University Press, 1982)

Neuman, John V. and Morgenstein, Oscar, *The Theory of Games and Economics* (Princeton, Princeton University Press, 1944)

Office of Fair Trading, Market Definition–Draft competition law guide, *OFT paper 403a* (2004)

Office of Fair Trading (OFT (a)), http://oft.gov.uk/report#654 29/04/2006

Office of Fair Trading (OFT (b)), http://www.oft.gov.uk/News/Press+releases/2004/94-04.htm 29/04/2006

Office of Fair Trading (OFT (c)) http://www.oft.gov.uk

Office of Fair Trading (OFT (d)) http://www.oft.gov.uk/News/Annual+report/2004 29/05/2006

Penrose, E., *The Theory of the Growth of the Firm* (Oxford, OUP, 1957)

Peteraf, M.T., The Cornerstones of Competitive Advantage: A Resource-Based View *Strategic Management Journal,* 14, 1993

Porter, M., *Competitive Strategy: Techniques for Analysing Industries and Firms* (New York, Free Press and Macmillan, 1980)

Porter, M., *Competitive Advantage: Creating and Sustaining Superior Performance* (New York, Free Press and Macmillan, 1985)

Ricardo, David, *The Principles of Political Economy and Taxation* (London, Dent, Everyman's Library, 11, 1911)

Rowlinson, M., *Organisations and Institutions* (London, Macmillan, 1997)

Scherer/Ross, *Industrial Market Structure and Economics Performance* (Boston, MA, Houghton Mifflin, 3rd Edn, 1990)

Schelling, Thomas C., *The Strategy of Conflict* (Cambridge, MA, Harvard University Press, 1960)

Shepherd, William G., *The Economics of Industrial Organization* (London, Prentice-Hall, 1990)

Simon, H.A., A Behavioural Model of Rational Choice, *Quarterly Journal of Economics,* 69, 99–118, 1955

Simon, H.A., *Administrative Behaviour* (New York, Macmillan, 2nd Edn, 1961)

Sloan, A.P., *My Years at General Motors* (London, Sedgwick & Jackson, 1963)

Sloman, J. and Sutcliffe, M., *Economics* (London, Prentice-Hall, 2003)

Smith, Adam, *The Wealth of Nations* (London, Dent, Everyman's Library, 1911)

Stacey, Ralph D., *Strategic Management and Organisational Dynamics: The Challenge of Complexity* (London, Prentice-Hall, 2003)

Stacey, Ralph D., *Strategic Management and Organisational Dynamics* (Harrow, FT, Prentice-Hall, 2003)

Stiglitz, J.E. and Matthewson, F., *New Developments in the Analysis of Market Structure* (Basingstoke, Macmillan, 1986)

Sylos-Labini, P., *Oligopoly and Technical Progress* (Cambridge, MA, Harvard University Press, 1957)

Vickers, J. and Yarrow, G., *Privatization and Natural Monopolies* (London, Public Policy Centre, 1985)

Wernerfelt, B.A., Resource-Based View of the Firm, *Strategic Management Journal* 5, 1984

Whittington, Richard, *What is Strategy–and Does it Matter* (London, Thomson Learning, 2002)

Williamson, O., Managerial Discretion and Business Behaviour, *American Economic Review* 53, 1963

Williamson, O., Credible Commitments: Using Hostages to Support Exchange, *American Economic Review,* 73 (4), pp. 519–539, 1983

Williamson, O., The Economics of Organisation: The Transaction Costs Approach *American Journal of Sociology,* 87 (3), pp. 548–577, 1981

Williamson, O.E., *Markets and Hierarchies, Analysis and Antitrust implications. A Study in the Economics of Internal Organisation* (New York, Free Press, 1975)

Williamson, O.E., *The Economic Institutions of Capitalism: Firms, Markets and Relational Contracting* (New York, Free Press, 1985)

# Index

*Page numbers in bold represents section headings.*